ACCLAIM FOR THE FIRST EDITION

"Most tells these stories in the voices of the protagonists, who give the basin's complex history an illuminating immediacy that infuses the entire book. It is a mark of his achievement that he has been able to make these historical, cultural, and environmental pieces into a comprehensive whole. *River of Renewal* is the best source available for those wishing to think clearly about this cumulative tragedy, as well as a first-rate model for regional land use anywhere in the American West."

— *Orion Magazine*

"Most's account is one of the best in recent years for its integration of Native with newcomer, past with present, and myth with reality."

— *Environmental History*

"This book should be mandatory reading for anyone who cares about environmental problems and the complex tangle of modern society and its competing economic and political interests."

— *The Journal of the West*

"*River of Renewal* offers an impressionistic, highly informative trip through the Klamath Basin's contentious past, and it does that particular job quite well."

— *Oregon Historical Quarterly*

"If a new book of regional history aspired to classic status, it would be ingeniously conceived and gracefully written. It would break new ground and offer penetrating insights. It would prove indispensable to understanding a controversial current event. Stephen Most has written such a book."

— *The Oregonian*

RIVER OF RENEWAL

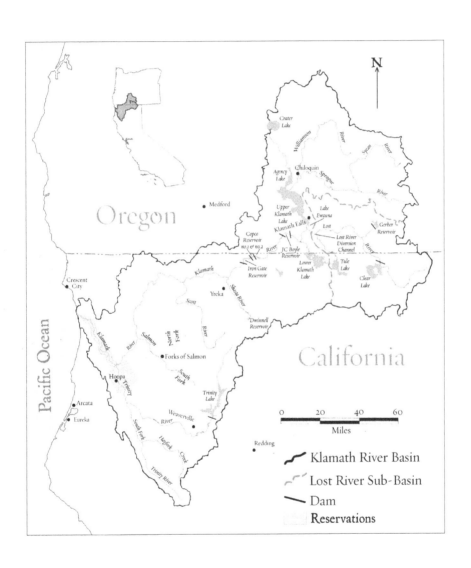

N

Crater
Lake

Williamson

River

Sycan

River

Agency
Lake

Chiloquin

Sprague

River

Medford

Upper
Klamath
Lake

Lake
Ewauna

Gerber
Reservoir

Oregon

Klamath Falls

Lost

Lost River
Diversion
Channel

Copco
Reservoir
no.1 & no.2

River

JC Boyle
Reservoir

Iron Gate
Reservoir

Lower
Klamath
Lake

Tule
Lake

River

Crescent
City

Klamath

Yreka

Shasta River

Clear
Lake

Scott

Dwinnell
Reservoir

California

Salmon

North Fork

River

Forks of Salmon

South
Fork

Pacific Ocean

Hoopa

Trinity

Trinity
Lake

Arcata

Eureka

Weaverville

River

South Fork

Hayfork

Creek

0   20   40   60

Miles

Redding

Trinity River

Klamath River Basin

Lost River Sub-Basin

Dam

Reservations

River of Renewal

Myth and History in the Klamath Basin

Second Edition

STEPHEN MOST

Oregon State University Press   Corvallis, Oregon

Cataloging-in-Publication data is available from the Library of Congress.
ISBN 978-1-962645-18-8 paperback
ISBN 978-1-962645-19-5 ebook

♾ This paper meets the requirements of ANSI/NISO Z39.48-1992
(Permanence of Paper).

Oregon State University
OSU Press

Oregon State University Press
121 The Valley Library
Corvallis OR 97331-4501
541-737-3166 • fax 541-737-3170
www.osupress.oregonstate.edu

Oregon State University Press in Corvallis, Oregon, is located within
the traditional homelands of the Mary's River or Ampinefu Band of
Kalapuya. Following the Willamette Valley Treaty of 1855, Kalapuya
people were forcibly removed to reservations in Western Oregon.
Today, living descendants of these people are a part of the Confederated
Tribes of Grand Ronde Community of Oregon (grandronde.org) and the
Confederated Tribes of the Siletz Indians (ctsi.nsn.us).

For my wife & partner in life,
Claire Schoen

Verifiable knowledge makes its way slowly, and only under cultivation, but fable has burrs and feet and claws and wings and an indestructible sheath like weed-seed, and can be carried almost anywhere and take root without benefit of soil or water.

—Wallace Stegner

Human societies live enveloped in myths and legends. Sometimes those myths and legends serve a positive function, but they become harmful when they obscure reality. History, its Spirit, does not favor those who refuse to examine reality in its nakedness.

—Czeslaw Milosz

Contents

Part IV. Fixing the World

Preface

In the Klamath Basin, geography is destiny. What nature provides shapes human lives there—and all other lives.

For geography, geology is destiny. Each place where people live may seem durable, yet its appearance is a freeze-frame in the slow-motion picture that plays out geological time.

Only in some respects does geology follow a fixed course. The planet's tectonic plates move inexorably; the Klamath Mountains continue to rise. But in other ways, geology is historical. Human beings shape what nature provides on a geological scale of magnitude, transforming the work of eons within brief spans of time.

Over the ages, various technologies—from the spear to the chainsaw, from dynamite to the hydroelectric dam, from the internal combustion engine to the Bomb—have exercised that power. In the western United States, the control of water has literally reshaped the landscape, supporting agriculture on arid lands, enabling large cities to exist far from their water supplies, providing electricity that drives a multitude of machines while allowing people to live without regard to climate or natural light.

Humanity's increasing power to alter nature coincides with an unprecedented obliviousness of natural processes. Anticipating and directing the means whereby human beings transform nature are belief systems as well as science. Where different modes of living on Earth collide, differences between forms of knowledge and belief with regard to nature can matter greatly.

Such a place is the Klamath. The gap between rural and urban ways of life is not significant here, for the Klamath Basin is predominantly a rural area. Its largest town, Klamath Falls, Oregon, has a population of fewer than 25,000 people. There are many farms and ranches, and some scattered communities remain off the electrical grid. American Indians constitute the region's largest minority, and some of them maintain their traditional ways of life. Almost nowhere does one find people living at the remove from nature that characterizes urban lifestyles.

The Klamath Basin is a bioregion, but its story is more than local. Because water, fish, and other gifts of nature are vitally important for people who live there, because different ways of living on Earth clash there, because it is a breeding ground for myths and a testing ground for conflict resolution, and because the outcomes of the bioregion's conflicts have consequences beyond its boundaries, the Basin's story needs to be told within the larger contexts of American and world history.

The Klamath Basin comprises springs, lakes, marshes, and wetlands, the waterworks of the Klamath Project, dams and reservoirs, creeks and tributary rivers, and the Klamath River, which flows 254 miles from its headwaters in Oregon through California to the Pacific Ocean. Except where it is pumped for irrigation and hydroelectric power, the Klamath does not flow uphill, but in two respects it is the reverse of the usual watercourse. Its wetlands and marshes are near the headwaters, not the mouth, and its water quality improves as it moves downstream.

While the Klamath River unites the Klamath Basin, the drainage is divided by more than the cultures, economic practices, and perceptions of people who live there. Dividing it also are lines, administrative and political—state lines, property lines, district boundaries of federal agencies—all of which correspond to power to affect the land and waters and thereby the future of the entire region.

Those who know the region are few. That is the case even though the Klamath is a major river of the American West—the fourth in volume after the Columbia, Sacramento, and Colorado. Its beauty is extraordinary. Novelist Zane Grey called the estuary "the most thrilling and fascinating place to fish I have ever seen," while near the headwaters, Mount Shasta and other volcanoes within the southern Cascade mountain range inspire awe. Wealth and goods have poured from the mines and forests and fisheries and fields of Klamath country—and from the water itself. The Klamath Basin also has treasures that cannot be extracted—biological riches, including forms of life that exist nowhere else.

The geography of Klamath country has fated it to be little known. Road maps and state maps do not distinguish the Klamath Basin, which is defined by mountains and water rather than by routes, borders, and destinations. Few California residents know that the Klamath River even exists. Many are immigrants or newcomers to the state; and almost everyone lives elsewhere, within the Central Valley or the large urban areas. The major media markets of southern and northern California cast almost no light on country that is many hours' drive north of the San Francisco Bay. The four California counties through which most of the Klamath River runs—Siskiyou, Trinity, Humboldt, and Del Norte—have but two area codes among them.

While California's terra cognita lies far to the south of the Klamath, Oregon's is north, at the other end of the state. The history of Oregon has always been top-heavy. It was the Columbia River that Lewis and Clark explored, the Columbia that challenged the emigrants on the Oregon Trail. The great wave of settlement that put Oregon on the map of the United States headed for the Willamette Valley. Naturally, Portland, the state's major city, grew at the confluence of the Willamette and Columbia rivers. Until recent years, the archives of the Oregon Historical Society, based in Portland, had few materials on the southcentral part of the state.

The Klamath Basin is a mystery even to those who live there. This is due in part to its size. The Basin extends over ten and a half million acres, or 16,400 square miles, an area equivalent to three entire states—Connecticut, Rhode Island, and New Hampshire. It is also due to the fact that the river is not navigable. The Klamath has a small opening to the sea through a shifting gap in a sandbar. Upriver, its rapids attract rafters but block commercial traffic. Only salmon traveled the river in its entirety—until dams barred their passage to the headwaters.

Consequently, the Klamath that people know is several rivers. People who know the land through which it flows tend to divide it into separate parts defined according to politics, economic activities, and their various and very different populations.

The region of the headwaters, the Upper Basin in southcentral Oregon and northeastern California, is primarily ranch, farm, and forest country. Water from springs, streams, marshes, and rivers flows into Upper Klamath Lake. Between Upper Klamath Lake and Iron Gate Dam in California, the waters of the Klamath resemble what historian Richard White, writing about the Columbia, calls an "organic machine," for the drainage of the Klamath and Tule Lake basins is channeled through a system of pumps and canals, dams and reservoirs designed to move water for irrigation and hydroelectric power. Yet within that part of the Upper

Basin, between the Boyle Reservoir and the lake above the Copco dams, a twenty-two-mile stretch of the Klamath River rushes through a deep canyon near the states' border, a reach that whitewater rafters love. Fishermen frequent the Klamath below Iron Gate Dam and its hatchery, which at some times of year is rich in pen-raised salmon.

Most of the land that the river runs through between Interstate 5 and the Klamath's confluence with the Trinity River is national forest. Near the confluence with the Salmon River, the Karuk fishery at Ishi Pishi Falls is one of the few places on the continent where Indians still practice dipnetting—fishing with a net attached to a ten-foot pole to pull salmon from the rapids.

The forty-two miles downriver from the mouth of the Trinity to the mouth of the Klamath is largely forested—or logged out. Where ancient redwoods once towered, Simpson Timber Company, a major landowner, established a "tree farm." Much of this stretch is roadless, and tourists take scenic jetboat rides along the lower river. The Yuroks have a one-mile strip on either side of the Klamath for a reservation. On the river, Yuroks catch salmon, especially fall chinook, in gillnets. When salmon are running, anglers flock there like seabirds.

Sometimes people come from the headwaters to fish near the estuary. Sometimes downriver people go upstream to Klamath Falls; and Yuroks, Hupa, and Karuks participate in each other's ceremonies. Still, generally speaking, those who are at home on one part of the river have little knowledge of the rest of it.

"History, the recorded time of the earth and of man, is in itself something like a river," wrote Marjory Stoneman Douglas. "To try to present it whole is to find oneself lost in the sense of continuing change. The source can only be the beginning in time and space, and the end is the future and unknown. What we can know lies somewhere between." Yet even to know the in-between part of Klamath Basin history is challenging. Until recent years, its residents did not perceive it as a whole entity in space, nor did they share a sense of its continuity in time. Those who live by the life cycles of anadromous fish feel time quite differently from those who live by the seasons of planting and harvest, and fishing and farming peoples have different perceptions of time from the region's many government employees, whose work is governed by each fiscal year's appropriations. For generations, people living in different parts of the Basin or doing different kinds of work there have seen little connection between their own existence and the lives of their culturally distant neighbors. Consequently, a narrative history that establishes links from one part of the Basin to another in a consecutive and chronological order cannot correspond to history as it has been perceived, and lived, in different places within the drainage.

Each place has its own stories. To weave these stories in a way that conveys a sense of the Basin's history as a whole, I have drawn from three different strands of historical storytelling. One is oral history, including interviews conducted for a documentary film and the oral history of a Yurok gillnetting family. This method is particularly valuable for a region that has a significant Indigenous population. As Skagit storyteller Vi Hilbert once said to me, "All the important information of our people was committed to memory." Another strand is narrative history, with the narratives linked to particular places within the Basin, for the sources for the stories of these places begin at different points in time. The third strand goes back to the original Greek meaning of the term *historia*. Before Herodotus and Thucydides turned their attention to human events, the pre-Socratic natural philosophers used this term to mean "inquiry," the search for knowledge. Questions about how to interpret events and critical perspectives on how others interpret them are part of *historia* in this sense. So are scientific questions concerning matters such as hydrology, forest ecology, and aquatic biology that are germane to events in the Klamath Basin. Critical inquiry—in addition to the oral history, which draws on no documents and is subject to the vulnerabilities of memory, and the narratives, which provide accounts of events that are seen differently from different vantage points—is especially valuable in a study of this kind, for in the Klamath Basin myth plays a part in the awareness people have of each other and of what has happened to their world.

A myth is an idea supported by stories, or a story conveying an idea, that is culturally transmitted. Myths illuminate the world in which people feel themselves to be living. They can be amusing, they can be terrifying, but they are always instructive. They provide role models on how to live—and how not to. They determine relationships between groups of people, yet they lack roots in real soil, drawing nourishment instead from the stuff of dreams.

To come to terms with the conflicts over resources that have occurred throughout Klamath history, it is necessary to understand the roles that myths have played in that history. Like the basin of the Columbia River, Klamath country is a homeland of the sacred salmon, that totem of the Pacific Northwest. The rising mountains of the Klamath drainage are also the home of Bigfoot, the cousin of Canada's Sasquatch and the Himalayas' Yeti. Coyote's home turf, at least in Karuk stories, lies between Katymin, the center of their world, and the confluence of the Klamath and Trinity rivers. And near the mouth of the Klamath, giant statues of Paul Bunyan and his ox, Babe, stand beside the highway. Taken together, these characters represent a range of conflicting relationships between human beings and nature: salmon as an awe-inspiring provider; Bigfoot awesome as well, but also to be feared, a strange yet familiar figure; Coyote the ultimate survivor, expressing the extraordinary ability of the tribes to maintain their way of life in spite of devastating opposition; and Paul Bunyan the epitome of the man-over-nature thrust of Western civilization.

The dam became a symbol of twentieth-century technology, which watered and provided power for the arid West. Although the dams on the Klamath are not fabled like the mighty Hoover that plugs the Colorado or the Grand Coulee on the Columbia, they loom large here. Iron Gate Dam—which blocked the passage of spring chinook, the king of the salmon—and other dams above Iron Gate generated power that Klamath Project farmers purchased at low rates. The licensing of those dams expired in 2006. The debate over what would happen next—whether the dams were to be relicensed or decommissioned and destroyed—was influenced by the mythological status of both the wild salmon and the dams.

Near the origin of the river, in Klamath Falls, a ten-foot sheet-metal bucket greets passersby. The giant bucket is a fitting symbol of the Klamath Project, which has drained lakes, diverted rivers, and channeled waters through a mountain while pumping them out of one drainage into another.

Explicitly, the bucket commemorates the Bucket Brigade, the farmers' civil disobedience campaign of 2001. Protesting the Bureau of Reclamation's decision that year to close the valves that control irrigation, the Bucket Brigade and the farmers' subsequent vigil at the headgates of the river were episodes in a national uprising against the environmental movement and federal control of land and waters. But they were also expressions of outrage from a community facing a serious threat to its way of life.

Most of the farmers and ranchers of the Klamath Basin are not ideological at all, and many love wildlife just as environmentalists do. Some have increased wildlife habitat — by restoring wetlands on their own property, for example. These good-faith efforts only increased their fury at having irrigation cut off from the fields where they grew potatoes, alfalfa, mint, sugar beets, wheat, and barley.

They are primarily family farmers. There are 1,400 farms on the 210,000 acres of the Klamath Project, their income averaging less than $15,000 per year. They are hard-pressed to compete with U.S. agribusinesses and with foreign producers given access to U.S. markets by international trade agreements. To lose a year of water or to have water supplies uncertain can ruin them and destroy their way of life. It is not a surprise many farmers and ranchers turned to civil disobedience against a government that would do that to them.

If these rural rebels had achieved mythic stature through their actions, they would have filled a vacuum. Klamath country is the home both of cowboys and of Indians, staples of western mythology, yet visitors do not encounter their archetypes here. The ranchers of the Klamath Basin are far from the roaming heroes seen in Western movies who bring justice to the anarchic land. Much of the country is overseen and regulated, if not owned and managed, by the federal government. Besides the Bureau of Reclamation's Klamath Project, there are seven wilderness areas, six national forests, six national wildlife refuges, two national monuments, and two national parks within the drainage of the Klamath River system. Given the predominance of federal management in the Basin, the heroism of rural people that the giant bucket celebrates consisted in their resistance to government authority. Instead of wresting order out of anarchy like the cowboys of old, they took on the powers-that-be in the name of freedom.

What some of the farmers and ranchers have in common with their mythic predecessors is the perception of Indians as adversary. There are three Indian reservations in the Klamath Basin, two in California and one in Oregon. One of the largest tribes, the Karuk, though federally recognized, has no reservation. Among the local tribes, only the Modocs had the makings of a national archetype. They attacked wagon trains, that classic confrontation on the frontier, killing white emigrants. In 1873, Modocs successfully fought off a six-month siege by the U.S. Army. In the Basin, as elsewhere in the West, myths shaped the relationship between the dominant population and Indigenous people. The myth that eventually prevailed in California over the image of the "savage" was that of the "vanishing Indian." If, contrary to expectations, Indians did in fact exist, their ordinary apparel suggested to some that these were not "real Indians."

American Indians are a small portion of the U.S. population, and many live in remote areas—the reservations they were removed to or that remained of their aboriginal territory. Consequently, the non-Indian public experiences them primarily through symbolic representations—photographs and other media images.

The anthropological study of American Indians, to which the Klamath River tribes contributed a great deal, reinforced the notion that Indigenous peoples are essentially of the past. Recording their ways, languages, and stories that reached back to precontact culture, anthropologists created the impression that these were people who did not change over time and who were somehow removed from American history.

Many historians have left the study of American Indians to anthropologists. This is more than academic courtesy. One cannot rely on written records alone to research the stories of Indian Country, and it is often difficult for non-Indians to gather information from American Indians. Travel is required, and most reservations are far from cities and university campuses. Because Indians have reason not to trust strangers who want something from them, repeated visits until some trust is earned may be necessary. With the exception, then, of events that capture national attention, such as the occupation of Alcatraz in 1969 or the upsurge of casinos run by gaming tribes, the public mind ignores Indians as contemporaries or participants in a shared history. The Smithsonian Institution in Washington, D.C., long kept its American Indian collections in the Natural History Museum along with stuffed wild animals rather than in the Museum of American History. Nor does the Smithsonian Museum of the American Indian, which opened in 2004, represent Indians in the context of American history.

Myths obscure reality, yet imagination is needed to understand the lives of the Indians and ranchers of the Klamath Basin. "Imagination alone," wrote Hannah Arendt, "enables us to see things in their proper perspective." It is imagination that enables us "to bridge abysses of remoteness" and also to put that which is close to us at a distance "so that we can see and understand it without bias and prejudice." By imagining the real, one can look beyond myths that shape perceptions of and within this region.

An abyss of remoteness separates contemporaries from the geohistory that formed the Klamath Basin. Although geography is shaped by geological events, it challenges the imagination to think in terms of geohistory. "The human brain evidently evolved to commit itself emotionally only to a small piece of geography, a limited band of kinsmen, and two or three generations into the future," observed biologist E. O. Wilson. "For hundreds of millennia those who worked for short-term gain within a small circle of relatives and friends lived longer and left more offspring—even when their collective striving caused their chiefdoms and empires to crumble around them. The long view that might have saved their distant descendants required a vision and extended altruism instinctively difficult to marshal." It is precisely a larger awareness of place and a longer view of processes of change that these times require, as people become increasingly able to make changes on a geological, Earth-altering scale.

Such changes have occurred and are occurring in the Klamath Basin. Today, it is clear that the farmers are not the only ones who have suffered from competing demands on water and other resources. For their descendants to maintain their way of life in one of the last places where family farms still exist on the continent, for fishing people to prosper off the coast as well as along the river, for tribes to maintain cultural practices that are inextricably bound with the wildlife of the region, a shared vision must come into focus. That vision, while requiring imagination, would incorporate multiple perspectives that have reality in common rather than myth.

The alternative is a future that almost no one within the Klamath Basin wants—a place whose rivers, lakes, mountains, and clear skies are merely scenery, no longer sustaining an abundance of life; whose soil is a paved platform for residential developments where people have lost their connection with the past and with life itself even here, a place where that connection can be readily grasped. Such a future would take from the people of the Klamath their deepest heritage. Those who know the

Klamath as a river in time understand that the links between Euramerican history and Indigenous history and between human history and geohistory are visible and relatively unbroken here.

The western mountains—known as the Klamath Mountains, the Siskiyous, and the Trinity Alps—were, according to geologists, once part of the Sierra Nevada. Probably originating as an island chain in the South Pacific, these mountains came to California on a tectonic plate that carried them into a slow-motion collision with the plate that bears North America. Naturalist David Rains Wallace describes the Klamath ranges as "an exceptionally rich storehouse of evolutionary stories, one of the rare places where past and present have not been severed as sharply as in most of North America, where glaciation, desertification, urbanization, and other ecological upheavals have been muted by a combination of rugged terrain and relatively benign climate."

East of these mountains rise the less wizened Cascades, with Lassen Peak and Mount Shasta at the southern end of a chain of magnificent snow-topped cones that continues for 600 miles into Alaska. The volcanoes are juveniles among mountains, having emerged within the last million years. The neighboring mountains in the chain are also newcomers, geologically speaking. A mix of sedimentary, igneous, and metamorphic rock, they are about 25 million years old.

The Pacific Northwest arc of the volcanic Ring of Fire surrounding the Pacific Ocean helps to explain the extraordinary biodiversity of the Klamath Mountains west of the Cascades, where exists, according to the National Geographic Society, "one of the four richest temperate conifer forests in the world." The place is a refuge. Some of its species come from lava-strewn highlands to the east and north. The sulphurous fumes that spew from Shasta's peak, the lava beds that border Tule Lake, the black-glass mountain near Medicine Lake, and Crater Lake, that emerald within a cinder cone in Oregon, are reminders of violent geological events in the region's past. These cataclysms include the explosion that blew the top off Mount Mazama about 7,000 years ago and the less spectacular eruption of Mount Lassen in 1915 that made fauna flee and flora migrate from lands riven by molten rock.

Ice as well as fire drove creatures to the Klamath. When a thousand-foot glacial sheet covered Puget Sound during the Ice Ages, many species, plants and animals alike, migrated to the forested mountains in the south.

The combination of complex mountainous terrain and temperate climate provided a multitude of niches for newcomers to inhabit.

Salmonids evolved within almost all of that region's aquatic habitats—from the ocean to the estuary and main stem of the Klamath River into the tributaries and creeks, up to the lakes and streams of the headwaters. Salmon, wrote Jim Lichatowich, are "woven deep into the fabric of the Northwest ecosystem." They are a prime source of its abundance of life. Bringing nutrients from the ocean into the river, they are not only food for people, bears, eagles, and other fish-lovers but also nitrogen for forest soils, nourishing the growth of plants.

The power of the myth of the salmon may derive from the fact that wild salmon spread out across the Pacific Northwest about the same time that human beings did, at the end of the last Ice Age. So fundamental have salmon been for the peoples of the Klamath that the Yurok word for salmon, *nepu*, means food itself, "that which is eaten," and the Karuk word *am* is both a noun and a verb—"salmon" and "to eat." Both the Yurok and Karuk creation stories speak of a divine being who gave the people salmon, along with other foods, for their survival.

Since the last Ice Age ended about 12,000 years ago, human beings have traveled along the Klamath and its tributaries; and many, finding an abundance of food, have stayed. The three major tribes of the Klamath River and its major tributary, the Trinity, have languages of three distinct linguistic subfamilies: Algonkian, Hokan, and Athapaskan. That suggests that the ancestors of the Yurok, Hupa, and Karuk made separate migrations, at different times and from different places. The language of the Shasta Tribe was native to southern Oregon and the Klamath Basin. They may have been the earliest inhabitants. Over millennia, the Shasta learned to live with people whose languages were entirely different from theirs, until, in the nineteenth century, English-speaking miners and settlers waged a "war of extermination" against them.

During many centuries of cultural diffusion, the tribes of the Klamath developed a cycle of annual and biannual ceremonies. Karuks call these events, which include the Jump Dance and White Deerskin Dance, *pikyávish*, which means "fixing the world." Anthropologist A. L. Kroeber called them "the World Renewal cult system." Conducted on sacred grounds beside the Klamath and Trinity rivers, these dances, performed over several days, ritually bring the world back into balance. The coordination of salmon fishing with these ceremonies—the building of weirs at special spots on the Klamath and Trinity, then taking them down after ten days so that large numbers of fish could continue upstream—is additional evidence of the tribes' long habitation of the area.

Non-Indigenous people have lived on the Klamath for a comparatively short time. The Yuroks of the lower river were among the last of North America's native people to encounter non-Indians. In part due to the lateness of this first contact, which did not occur until the 1840s, a Yurok village on the estuary, Rekwoi, has remained continuously inhabited from times beyond the reach of memory to the present.

Although the peoples of the Klamath Basin have a bioregion in common, they do not perceive a common history. In this situation, myths of the Other hinder a mutual recognition of reality. Yet with the sharing of oral histories, the telling of narratives linked to place, and ongoing inquiry, the past can become open to all. That is particularly the case in the Klamath Basin, whose history gives another dimension to Wallace's idea that past and present have not been severed as sharply here as elsewhere on the continent. Only two long lifetimes separate contemporaries in the early twenty-first century from the era when non-Indians arrived as explorers, gold-seekers, and settlers. The people who transformed this region by mining, canning, logging, ranching, and farming, and by building roads, bridges, and dams, not only left letters, memoirs, and other writings but also photographs, sound recordings, and films. From those sources as well as from the land itself, which bears its own signs of the changing relationship between humanity and nature, come a long view of history and a perspective on potentialities for the future.

What members of all Klamath Basin communities hope the future will bring is renewal. Some put their emphasis on habitat restoration, others on economic revival, and many consider those goals to be interdependent. Already the Klamath is a river of renewal in several respects. Every river renews itself through the annual and perpetual water cycle driven by gravity, climate, and the energy of the sun. Going to any wild river, one experiences refreshment of the senses and a renewed connectedness with life. Any salmon-producing river is a spectacle of renewal as runs come in, drawing birds, otters, bears, and other wildlife; enriching the forests with nutrients brought from the sea; attracting people who like to fish back to the water; and reviving the industries and activities that support them.

When Yurok, Hupa, and Karuk tribal members celebrate the return of the salmon with their cycle of ceremonies, they dance to renew the delicate balance between land and water, between the diversity of life and the unity of spirit that their world depends on. Were the Klamath Basin to be restored ecologically as well as economically, its renewal would deserve the admiration of the world at large, for this project would revive the crucial connection between humanity and nature.

Introduction

When experiencing Mount Shasta for the first time, John Muir wrote, "All my blood turned to wine, and I have not been weary since." When nineteenth-century writer Joaquin Miller first looked "upon the mountain in whose shadows so many tragedies were to be enacted; the most comely and perfect snow peak in America," his comparisons reached beyond Earth: it was "lonely as God, and white as a winter moon."

This is the mountain that inspired a religion. A book published by the Rosicrucian Press in 1931 tells how it came to pass that survivors of a lost civilization inhabit Mount Shasta. Their former volcanic home, Lemuria, was an Atlantis of the Pacific. After a colossal eruption destroyed and submerged their world, the Lemurians came to California. A muscular, brainy people, each more than seven feet tall, they brought with them advanced technologies and sacred ceremonies. According to the Rosicrucian text, Lemurians somehow maintain their way of life out of sight of the tourists, climbers, and spiritual seekers one encounters on the flanks of the giants' sanctuary.

The Lemurians may have mastered the art of invisibility, or, like Bigfoot—another tall and fabulous creature of the Klamath Basin—they are adept at hiding from prying human eyes. Or their secret might be that they live inside the mountain. According to Joaquin Miller, Shasta Indians believed that after the Great Spirit created the mountain, he molded it into a wigwam with a fire burning inside. Then, wishing to remain on Earth, the Creator brought his family down from the heavens, "and they have all lived in the mountain ever since." Why not Lemurians as well?

This tale has the ring of truth. Over many centuries of living among the mountains of northern California and southern Oregon, Shasta villagers observed fire bursting from the volcano and passed the memory on to their descendants. During the last three millennia, there have been at least ten eruptions of the 14,000-foot volcano, most recently in 1786.

Surely there was fire within the mountain. Surely the spirit of the place or some great power of the Earth hollowed the mountain out.

From a Western perspective, the mountain is an inanimate object, uninhabited by spirits, neither a being nor a source of power but a thing to be explored—aesthetically for art, strategically for sport, geologically for science—and placed on the map of knowledge. The first time a European became aware of Shasta was in 1786. French explorer and scientist Jean-François de Galaup, comte de La Pérouse, was sailing south from Alaska off the California coast when he saw a vivid flame a hundred miles to the east. Fog rapidly obscured the sight. For him, the eruption was information to note in his log. Four decades would pass before fur trappers working for Hudson's Bay Company entered the Klamath Basin and saw the mountain itself. Two more decades would pass before the first non-Indian immigrants came within sight of Mount Shasta.

One evening, Jack Kohler and I stood by a white van, looking at the mountain. Seen beside the rising moon in the evanescence of dusk, its glacier gleaming in the last rays of sun, Shasta seemed at once timeless and immediate, a transcendent presence in the here and now. We had driven north from San Francisco to begin production of a documentary about the wildlife and water crisis in the Klamath Basin. Once Michael Pryfogle, our coproducer, pulled onto the shoulder, we scrambled out of the van to look at the mountain looming to the east, the moon hovering beside its south flank. Carlos Bolado, our director, ran down the road looking for a spot from which to shoot. He gestured at Michael, who followed with camera and tripod. After framing the scene with his hands, his thumbs and fingers at right angles, Carlos—tall, bearded, and intensely focused—started shooting.

This country was new to Jack even though his ancestors on his father's side were Klamath River Indians, Yurok and Karuk. He had grown up in San Francisco and had studied engineering at Stanford University. Jack maintained an Indian identity nonetheless. He began a second career as an actor when he played a character based on a Yurok gillnetter in *Watershed*, a play I wrote that was first produced in 1992. That is how we met. With the classic square-jawed good looks of an American Indian hero, Jack played Tecumseh for several years, acting on an outdoor stage in Ohio in front of large summer audiences. In another summer pageant, he played Captain Jack, the Modoc leader during the Modoc War.

I had wanted a picture of the full moon rising over Mount Shasta to give the documentary an iconic image of northern California, one that would serve as a symbol for the region whose latest crisis we had come to record. After Carlos and Michael shot the sight from several angles at different points down the road, Jack and I helped put the equipment in the back of the van. Turning from Interstate 5 onto 97, which angles northeast to Klamath Falls, Oregon, we photographed the mountain's north face, the moon now poised above its peak.

The spectacle made me wonder. The sight of a moon beside a volcano is one that inhabitants of Earth would have in common with creatures on other planets. Were tourists to visit Mars, they would take pictures of the full Phobos or Deimos rising beyond the largest volcano in this solar system—thirteen-mile-high Mount Olympus.

Seeing our moon beside Mount Shasta put the present moment into a larger context in time as well as space. Earth's satellite is the remnant of an event that happened more than four billion years ago when our solar system, still forming, swarmed with errant objects. According to current theory, a Mars-sized planet crashed into the nascent Earth, shattering its crust and hurling the debris into orbit, where it eventually coalesced. Composed of ancient Earth rocks and scarred by meteors, the satellite is a reminder of cosmic violence in an unwitnessed era of geological time.

Mount Shasta is maybe a million years old, young for a mountain. We do not know for certain how long ago people were here to see it, but it was at least 11,000 years ago, according to the carbon-dated age of tools found in Fort Rock Cave in Oregon's Lake County, about a hundred miles away. Archaeologists found the tools near a pair of 9,000-year-old sagebrush sandals buried beneath a deposit of pumice, which the eruption of Mount Mazama thrust across the Pacific Northwest almost 7,000 years ago. Then there is the scale of written history. The span of three long lives bridges the time between La Pérouse's observation of the fires of Shasta in 1786 and the evening in 2001 when we videotaped Mount Shasta.

Arriving in Klamath Falls, where the Klamath River begins, the four of us checked into a motel near Veterans Park. A rally in the park was to kick off the next day's activities. The inn's parking lot was packed with pickups and other trucks and some large vans, including two mobile television units.

That day, May 7, 2001, promised to be historic. Farmers and ranchers of the Klamath Basin had planned a Bucket Brigade, an act of civil disobedience to protest the cutoff by the Bureau of Reclamation of irrigation water to the Klamath Project. For the makers of a documentary about the crisis over natural resources in the Klamath Basin, the event was not to be missed.

The dispute over water that we were about to capture on camera exemplified a global issue. Resource shortages are likely to set off many conflicts, including wars, throughout the twenty-first century. More precipitation falls in the Klamath Basin and the northern Sierra than in the rest of California, which is ranked fifth among the economies of the world. From the Klamath Mountains come sources of the Sacramento River, as well as streams and tributary rivers that flow into the Klamath. Millions of people, whether they know it or not, have a stake in what the waters of the Klamath produce—trees, crops, fish, beef—and in the water itself.

The family farmers who work the lands of the Klamath Project were the latest victims of resource scarcity in the region. They and thousands of their supporters intended to protest the federal agency's curtailment of irrigation, a direct assault on their livelihood. The Bureau had acted in response to legal actions under the Endangered Species Act of 1973. The Biological Opinions that triggered the lawsuits were based in part on scientific studies of endangered aquatic species that biologists had done for the Klamath Tribes. Two of the species at risk were suckers endemic to the region.

The Klamath, Modoc, and Yahooskin Snake maintain an aquatic research facility in Chiloquin, about thirty miles north of Klamath Falls. Tribal representatives had turned down at least one interview request, from Fox News, to talk about the conflict, preferring a low profile as farmers and ranchers converged to defy a federal decision favoring Indian interests. But they had agreed to talk to us. A documentary takes a longer view than the sensation-seeking daily news, and Jack Kohler had been able to assure a tribal official that our coverage would be fair.

Driving north to Chiloquin in bright early morning light, we looked west across the railroad tracks to Upper Klamath Lake and to the impressive Cascade Mountains beyond. Above the lake, we found the research hatchery that is run by the Tribes' Natural Resources Department.

Nothing about the warehouse-sized building exposed its position at the epicenter of the current controversy.

Larry Dunsmoor met us at the door. A slender man with short blond hair and glasses, the fishery biologist told Michael Pryfogle that he had received threatening phone calls and that he no longer felt safe driving in a truck with the Klamath Tribes' logo. This was disturbing news, but not surprising. The reports that used his data were more than opinions. They were weapons used in a lawsuit against the Bureau of Reclamation.

The tribes of the Basin had joined commercial fishermen as plaintiffs in a legal action designed to wrest water from the irrigators to meet the needs of wild fish. The initiative seemed likely to succeed. Ever since the U.S. Supreme Court's decision on *Winters v. People of the State of New York* in 1908, the federal government has recognized that its treaties with Indian tribes—which guarantee hunting, fishing, and gathering rights— implicitly, if not explicitly, include water rights within traditional Indian territories. Because treaties are superior constitutionally to legislative statutes and because Indian water rights precede the rights granted to farmers, cities, wildlife refuges, and other interests, they generally prevail in court.

Even in 1984, long after the Klamath Tribes' official status had been terminated and their reservation sold, a federal court ruled that Klamath Indians were entitled "to as much water on Reservation lands as they need to protect their hunting and fishing rights." In 1986, when the Klamath Reservation was restored, though without its former land base, the Tribes banned tribal members from catching the once-abundant *c'waam* and *koptu*. The Tribal Council also began pressuring the federal government to protect the fish, known in English as shortnose and Lost River suckers.

Fifteen years later, after a winter of drought and after the Biological Opinion concluded that lack of water threatened the suckers' survival, a U.S. district judge ruled that the Bureau of Reclamation had violated the Endangered Species Act by not conferring with other federal agencies about the water needs of listed species. On April 6, 2001, the Bureau announced that instead of delivering 550,000 acre-feet to the farmers and ranchers of the Klamath Project, the Bureau would provide no more than 70,000 acre-feet.

The news "hit like an atomic bomb," said Steve Kandra, the grandson of Czech farmers who had homesteaded in the Klamath Basin in 1916. "Lots of people are hurting in the Klamath Basin, but they only beat up on us." Jeff Boyd, a third-generation potato farmer, foresaw disaster for his community, Tulelake, thirty miles southeast of Klamath Falls in California. "No water. No farming. No fertilizer. No packing sheds. No grain silos. No town." For these farmers, the loss of water felt devastating.

Inside the research facility at Chiloquin, juvenile suckers, both Lost River and shortnose, swarmed in identical tanks. The tanks were arranged in rows, with an array of pipes coming into them and out of them and connecting across the ceiling. Dunsmoor reached into a round tub and pulled out a ten-year-old shortnose. A large dark gray fish with a snout, the sucker gasped for breath as the biologist spoke about its longevity and life cycle.

Writer William Kittredge, who was raised on a ranch in Oregon's Warner Valley a hundred miles to the east, remembers catching suckers in Upper Klamath Lake with his friends when they were in high school. "Somebody would hang a hook in the side of one of those prehistoric-looking creatures, drag it in, and we'd leave the poor gasping thing with its blowhole mouth on the bank to die," he wrote in *Balancing Water*. "Such were the glories. Who would have thought those suckers would turn up on the endangered species list?"

The sucker was once considered the most important food fish of the region. For the Klamath Tribes, *c'waam* brought relief after long, snowbound winters. The people welcomed the source of fresh food as a gift from their Creator in a Return of the *C'waam* Ceremony held by mid-March. Klamaths built stone weirs in the Sprague and Williamson rivers to trap the fish, catching them, according to Kittredge, with "dip nets, gillnet baskets, two-pronged harpoons, and multi-barbed spears." On Lost River, Modocs and Klamaths spent weeks at a fish camp, "catching and drying an estimated fifty tons of fish." Non-Indians also benefited from the abundance of suckers. During the early years of the twentieth century, commercial processors rendered great quantities of the fish into oil and sold them as dried fish and canned goods.

Shortnose, like their Lost River cousins, are omnivorous bottom-feeders. Sensitive to water-quality conditions, great numbers expire in Upper Klamath Lake whenever blooming algae crowd its nutrient-rich shallow waters. Many others are stranded in irrigation canals. As a child, Bob Anderson, a Tule Lake farmer born in 1920, filled gunnysacks with suckers that were trapped in canals and flushed onto his family's flood-irrigated fields.

They are a prolific fish. Spawning suckers release and fertilize more than 40,000 eggs. But in recent decades, few juveniles have enlarged the population. Larry Dunsmoor did not know how many suckers there were, but for him the evidence of decline was unmistakable. One of the reasons Dunsmoor raises juveniles in tanks is to understand what has happened to them; another is to ensure that there is a next generation.

Dino Herrera met the production team at the hatchery. A heavy-set man with a broad mustache, Herrera was director of the Klamath Tribes' Culture and Heritage Department. He wore a brown cap and dark glasses; white shells dangled from his ears. He told Jack, as they walked down the road together, that he is Klamath and Modoc and that his people had been here "since time immemorial."

Jack told Herrera that his father, Jack Kohler Sr., lived in Hoopa, California, on the Trinity River. He didn't mention that he was from the Bay Area. In San Francisco, childhood classmates assumed that Jack was Mexican until he brought a *National Geographic* to school for show-and-tell. A photograph in that issue showed his Yurok grandmother posing in the doorway of a redwood plank house.

As the two men headed downhill toward the Sprague River, Herrera pointed to the place around the bend, below Cave Mountain, where the Klamath Tribes hold their annual Return of the *C'waam* Ceremony. "They ran a lot of timber through here," he said. "The Euro-Americans see something they like, they move right into it and move the Indian people out." Herrera described precontact times "as a Garden of Eden, basically. You had berries, you had fisheries, you had big game, you had waterfowl, abundant waterfowl. Everything was here." His grandfather had predicted that in his time the salmon would go away. This happened in 1918 with the completion of the Copco 1 Dam, which blocked the passage of spring chinook into the Upper Klamath Basin. His grandfather had also foreseen that in Dino's father's time the *c'waam* would go away. "Now they're on the endangered species list and we can't utilize them. And then he said, 'in your time and your son's time the trout would go away,'" Herrera continued. "We understand certain trout are going on the endangered species list. My grandfather could see into the future, I guess."

"What will happen to the culture when they're gone?" Jack asked.

"We won't have a culture. We are a lake people, a water people," said Herrera. "We're the caretakers of this land and the resources like this water out here. It's the life blood our creator has given to us, and we need to protect it."

The rally at Veterans Park had already begun by the time we got back into Klamath Falls. Hundreds of people, many carrying banners, faced a podium where a procession of speakers held forth. Arranged squarely behind the podium were two American flags on tall poles rising behind a large sign: "SUPPORT THE AMERICAN FARMER/Amend the ESA." The slogan was designed for the halls of Congress. Organizers of the Bucket Brigade were looking ahead to a bill that could garner enough support to pass. This event would demonstrate grassroots opposition to the protection of endangered species in the name of farmers, veterans, and the American way of life.

Since World War I, veterans have received Klamath Basin homesteads from the federal government to reward their services to their country—a tradition that goes back to the Revolutionary War, when George Washington, unable to pay his troops, promised that the victorious United States would give them land. In Veterans Park, the rhetoric from the podium was patriotic and feelings were high. One World War II veteran made a sad declaration: "Fifty-five years ago we were welcomed home as heroes and asked to feed a hungry world. Today we are welfare recipients standing in line for cheese and food stamps. Our government has betrayed us!" A blonde woman who could have been his daughter asked the crowd: "Where is the honor in giving water and land to the veterans who stood proud to defend this country and then turning around and cruelly taking it away?"

John Crawford, a farmer recommended by the rally's organizers, the Klamath Water Users Association, as someone to interview, angrily denounced the Biological Opinions as "rampant speculation." The required "lake levels and river flows, which are destroying this community," he declared, "will not help fish."

Among the politicians who gave their blessings to the day's events were Oregon Senator Gordon Smith and Representative Greg Walden, whose district borders Klamath County to the west. State Senator Steve

Harper, a fellow Republican from Klamath Falls, excited the crowd by shouting: "We don't want your stinking welfare. We want our water!"

"We want water! We want water!" became the chant of the day. It was a need that everyone could feel. The day was hot. The flags drooped. Even in mid-morning people sought shade under the trees of Veterans Park.

Signs caught our attention: "Without Water No Future," "People Over Fish," "Basin Farmers Betrayed," "A Future of Desperation," "Feed the Feds to the Fish." Many signs portrayed suckers. One cartoon showed a pacifier in a fish's mouth. "Phuck the suckers!" "ESA—Don't Be a Sucker—Save a Farmer," and "Suckers Ain't Endangered—There's One Born Every Minute." Like the wild salmon, the sucker had become famous. Unlike wild salmon, the sucker had become a fish with a negative image, its strange face deployed to make environmentalism and the ESA look bad.

One sign, "Suckers Taste Like Spotted Owls," recalled an earlier battle. Just as environmentalists had used federal protection of the spotted owl to keep old-growth forests intact, a campaign widely blamed for the decline of the logging industry, so now the sucker was their tool to put farmers out of work. Today's slogans were "Klamath Farmers Are Endangered Species," "Farms Are Habitat Too," and "Consider Environmental Impact On People."

Shortly after the speech-making, the media gathered on the shore of Lake Ewauna below Veterans Park. The waters of Upper Klamath Lake flow into this small lake by way of the mile-long Link River. On the other side of Lake Ewauna, the Klamath River begins its journey to the Pacific. In the spring and summer, some of the water that passes through Link River Dam and heads toward the Klamath is diverted for farms, pouring into "A" Canal, the largest of the irrigation canals in the Bureau of Reclamation's Klamath Project. This day, however, protesting the closed headgate valves, the Bucket Brigade would draw water from Lake Ewauna, bring it hand-by-hand along Klamath Fall's Main Street, carry it uphill from the high school, and pour the precious liquid from a bridge directly into "A" Canal.

This well-orchestrated defiance of the federal cutoff of water was an act of civil disobedience. That was one reason for the many declarations that those who had assembled to violate federal law were patriotic. They were asserting the independent spirit of America. The color guard marched proudly in the park; a children's choir sang "The Star-Spangled Banner." "We, the people" could not obey a tyrannical federal bureaucracy, especially when "U.S. Betrayal On Water Is Destroying Our Community." Hell, no! Rather than go down the drain economically, the community was taking matters into its own hands.

A bucket brigade evokes images of good neighbors putting out a fire on their neighbor's property—a symbol of civic response to an emergency. Clustering on the north shore of Lake Ewauna, news crews from CBS, NBC, ABC, Fox News, and CNN captured the ceremonial first bucket. With the national anthem sounding from loudspeakers, Jess Prosser, an eighty-five-year-old World War II veteran, lowered a star-spangled bucket into the lake. He proudly pulled it up, brimming with water, and passed it on to members of his family. They handed the bucket to Senator Smith, who gave it to Representative Walden, who passed it to California Representative Wally Herger, who gave it to someone on his uphill side.

There were more buckets to come, white and blue buckets with stars painted around the slogan "Amend the ESA"—one bucket for each state plus the District of Columbia. Carlos aimed his camera and followed one bucket as it moved from person to person up the hill and on past the thousands of people who had lined up along Main Street. He and Michael climbed aboard a pickup truck crowded with people from the media.

I elected to stay with Jack, to talk to people along the route as he wielded his camera, to give him support in case he needed it. For about a mile I kept an eye on him, but Jack was moving rapidly along the line of hands reaching for and releasing each bucket; and although there was not another Indian in sight, no one seemed to pay attention to the copper skin and long black hair of the man behind the lens.

Near the long line of bucket-passers in the center of Main Street, a horse carrying a man and an American flag pranced on the pavement. A pickup, also flying a flag, with the logo of a radio station written on the cab, rode along Main Street, its loudspeakers playing patriotic music— "America," "The Star-Spangled Banner," "Proud to Be an American." Dressed in jeans and a western shirt, a man stood in the truck bed, his expression and bearing the picture of pride. Depending on the song, he stood at attention or, when his hand was not on his heart, he waved to onlookers or bent down to shake the hands of admirers.

After walking the length of Main Street, I followed the brigade into the Klamath Union High School's Modoc Field and uphill to the bridge over "A" Canal. On the bridge, someone called out the name of each state as the bearer of the respective bucket poured its contents into the stagnant water below. Each time, the crowd that lined the banks of the canal cheered. My production team was near the bridge taping the event, capturing the sight of police marching two brothers, who had been caught with a .38 in their backpack, across the bridge.

Looking for John Crawford, the farmer who had denounced the Biological Opinions in Veterans Park, I headed toward the high school stadium, where people were seating themselves, preparing to hear more speeches. Near the grandstand, a group of young Indians held signs— "Support Water Rights," "Respect the Land!" Jack had already interviewed one of them. They were members of a Klamath family, the Chiloquins. The young woman Jack had spoken to was a granddaughter of Edison Chiloquin, a World War II veteran who received two Purple Hearts for his courage in combat. He later became a hero among Native Americans for defying the termination of the Klamath Reservation by reinhabiting his grandfather's village site. It was for Edison's grandfather, Chief Chiloquin, that the town of Chiloquin was named. I thought his grandchildren were courageous, appearing in front of that huge gathering of people who appeared to have no sympathy for the *c'waam* or for Klamath Indians. "We're out here standing up for our rights just like these people are," a teenage girl told Jack.

I finally spotted John Crawford, whom I had spoken to by phone to arrange the interview. His strong rhetoric from the podium made me wonder how he would respond to being interviewed by a Yurok/Karuk and having a Mexican direct the shoot. So while introducing myself, I hastened to mention that my late uncle, Al Fradkin, had grown seed potatoes near Tule Lake. Crawford knew his name. Still, he seemed tense when I brought him to meet the crew. Then he surprised us by telling Jack of his "ties to the Native American people at the mouth of the Klamath. The best man at my wedding was a Yurok Indian," he said. "I cherish those friendships."

As he had at Veterans Park, Crawford challenged the Biological Opinions as "agenda-driven," a tool in what he called "the biggest taking of private property rights in the history of the ESA." He painted a picture of devastation in a Klamath Basin that in the last month had become "truly a horrible place to be. Land that would have been irrigated, that would have been planted with crops, that would have been growing and green, has eroded irreparably." He spoke of topsoil blowing from the fields and darkening the sky, of children with asthma and "old folks on oxygen," of "25,000 people that are directly impacted including the farmers and their families, the farm workers and their families, and the businesses that are completely dependent on irrigated agriculture for their survival."

A complete reversal seemed to have occurred. These white farmers who deplored the damage to their lands, the violation of their rights, and the loss of their way of life were feeling victimized by the tools of civilization, scientific studies and federal laws that the Indians were using to advance their interests. Was the story we were witnessing "how the West was lost?" Or was this merely one battle in America's longest war, the encounter between Euramerican and Indigenous people? Could there be a happy ending, a mutually acceptable accommodation between them? Or would these troubles in the Klamath Basin leave everyone the loser— people, wildlife, and the land itself?

As the production team drove south past Mount Shasta that evening, it struck me that not only was this story irreducible to the sound bites and commentary of an item on the news but also that no documentary could adequately contextualize the episode we had witnessed.

What was at stake was life. When satellites orbiting Mars and rovers probing its surface search for evidence of life, they look for a shoreline, a lake bed, the course of a stream indicating the presence, at some point in that planet's history, of water, the theory being that wherever energy, carbon-based molecules, and liquid water coexist, life may emerge as it did four billion years ago on Earth. Elemental also was the contest over water in one of the major catchments in western North America, where the use of water determines the course of life. The dispute not only involved landowners, the federal government, and the tribes, but also relationships between human beings and other species and between American ways of life and the biosphere. It would take a mountain's-eye view to understand this story.

PART ONE
Headwaters

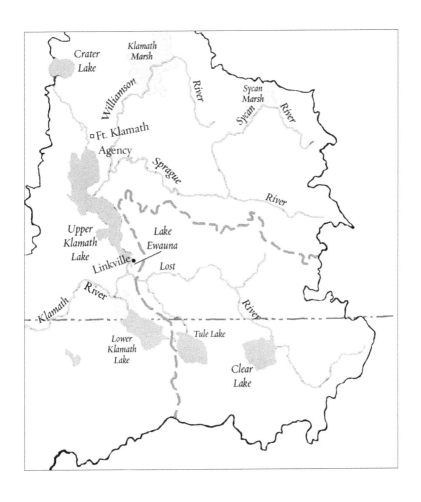

Chapter One
Land of Waters

When trapper Peter Skene Ogden first came to the Upper Basin of the Klamath drainage in 1826, he observed "the Country as far as the eye can reach being one continued Swamp and Lakes." Pioneers in the mid-nineteenth century who had traveled across the arid Great Basin and along the Applegate-Scott Trail must have marveled as they encountered Goose Lake, Tule Lake, Lower Klamath Lake, Agency Lake, and Upper Klamath Lake. The upper lake alone was and still is the largest body of fresh water—in area, though not in volume—west of the Rockies. If this land posed a problem in the settlers' eyes, it was that it had too much water, too little solid ground. Even in the late nineteenth century, when farmers and ranchers began to drain marshes and shrink lakes to make room for cattle and crops, who could have imagined the time would ever come when the Klamath's Upper Basin would lack enough water for everyone?

Mountains define the Upper Basin and the headwaters north of Upper Klamath Lake. To the northwest rises Mount Thielsen and to the west of the upper lake, Mount McLoughlin, both more than 9,000 feet above sea level. At the southcentral edge of the Klamath drainage towers the 14,000-foot Mount Shasta. All are snowcapped volcanic peaks in the Cascade Range.

Appropriately, the range is named for water—the falls and rapids of the Columbia River Gorge, where the great river passes between Mount St. Helens in Washington and Mount Hood in Oregon. Today, however, the turbulent waters that gave the Cascade Range its name have disappeared, tamed by Bonneville Dam.

The mountains of the Upper Basin that border the Klamath's headwaters created the high desert of the Great Basin, as they form a wall across Oregon that blocks moisture coming in from the Pacific. A look at the ice and snow on these mountains leads one to think that melting water running down their flanks swells the lakes and renews the rivers of the Klamath Basin every spring. But geologists, looking beneath the surface of the land, say that the headwaters are primarily springfed.

This is land where rocks float and water sinks. Porous lava rocks float on water, and water disappears through seismic cracks in volcanic country. The northern part of the Upper Basin is layered with up to forty feet of pumice, a remnant of the eruption of Mount Mazama. That volcano's most destructive explosion, which left deposits as far as Greenland, destroyed more than fifteen cubic miles of mountaintop while spewing three times that quantity of magma into the western skies.

The most beautiful legacy of that cataclysm seven thousand years ago is Crater Lake. Brilliantly blue, it sparkles two thousand feet below the rim of the topless volcano's six-mile-wide caldera, with a young volcano, called Wizard Island, rising above its surface. Crater Lake's waters extend almost two thousand feet beneath its azure surface. There is no deeper lake in the United States.

Crater Lake is one of many sources of the waters that nourish the Klamath Basin. The mountains edging the lake country are riddled with crevices, and through these fissures numerous springs emerge from the ground. From the highlands near Yamsay Mountain flow the springs that launch the Williamson River. Near Gearhart Mountain, the headwaters of the Sprague River burble to the surface. It is from there that the Sprague flows into the Williamson, whose waters join Upper Klamath Lake.

Before lands were drained for ranching and agriculture—with irrigation ditches, berms, roadways, and railroad tracks altering the normal flow of water—the Wood, Sycan, Williamson, Sprague, and other rivers of the Upper Basin meandered through extensive floodplains. These held the spillover when swollen rivers overflowed their channels. Year-round, Sycan Marsh, Klamath Marsh, and other wetlands of the region serve as giant sponges, absorbing floodwaters together with waters that stream down the mountains, seep up from the ground, and fall from the sky.

People first came to the Upper Basin while the last Ice Age was thawing. Water covered far more of the land then. Areas that today are marshlands were once part of large, shallow lakes, such as Upper Klamath Lake. In fact, during the late Pleistocene, about ten thousand years ago, Upper Klamath Lake was part of an immense shallow lake that covered a thousand square miles, of which Lower Klamath Lake and Tule Lake are also remnants. With a drier climate, the water level receded and land intruded, making portions of that great lake separate lakes.

Over millennia, reeds and grasses that grew within the lakes rotted and built up, forming peat-rich soils. Flying over Upper Klamath Lake, one can almost see this process in action. Flatlands covered with ranches and farms appear to have once been between the lake shores.

The waters of this region also generate great forests. Ponderosa is the most widespread pine in North America, ranging from Canada to Arizona. Named for its ponderous height, which can reach above a hundred feet, the ponderosa found an ideal habitat in the dry, high-altitude climate east of the southern Cascades, and its roots found fertile soil in volcanic ash and pumice. It is more abundant here than anywhere else. Also thriving in this region are lodgepole pine, white pine, juniper, and incense cedar. These trees and the soils of the forest floor absorb and store great quantities of water.

Not surprisingly, the Upper Basin is a spa for wildfowl, a prime resting and feeding place for birds that travel the Pacific Flyway. The snow geese that crease the skies above the lake country, according to writer Barry Lopez, create "one of the most imposing—and dependable—wildlife spectacles in the world." There are ducks in many varieties—mallards, canvasbacks, northern shovelers—along with bald eagles, kestrels, blackbirds, marsh hawks, barn owls, tundra swans, tree swallows, and Savannah sparrows, about 250 species in all.

The fish of the Upper Basin are also abundant, though not as numerous in kind. In addition to trout and sucker, its lakes, rivers, and streams once offered habitat and spawning grounds for spring chinook, the largest and most powerful salmon.

The people who first came to the Klamath Basin lived beside the waters, which offered an abundance and variety of food. But in winter, with the elevation of the Upper Basin at 4,000 feet, the lakes froze and snow covered the trails used by humans and animals. People had to store food for the cold season.

Most likely the earliest residents inhabited caves. Evidence for this includes the seventy-five sandals that were found in Fort Rock Cave in Lake County, Oregon. Dated at 9,000 years old, they had been buried beneath ejecta from Mount Mazama. Those who wore this sagebrush footwear were not necessarily the ancestors of modern Klamaths and Modocs. They may have been nomadic hunters drawn to the area by the wealth of wildlife. After the great eruption, those who survived may have fled.

The legend of Mount Mazama has come down to the present day over centuries and perhaps millennia of oral tradition. It preserves an awareness of the apocalyptic scale of the eruption among the peoples that have lived for countless generations near Crater Lake. Their story tells of a war between the Chief of the World Below and the Chief of the World Above. During their battles, Llao, governor of the netherworld, stood on Mount Mazama; Skell presided over the heights from Mount Shasta. Their combat ignited forests, sent boulders hurling into the air, and darkened the skies for seven days, a darkness broken by flames flashing from the chiefs' volcanic strongholds. Finally, Skell triumphed with the collapse of Mazama, which dropped Llao into the depths from which he came, leaving behind the caldera that holds Crater Lake.

According to the Klamath creation myth, K'mukamtch, "old man," created the world and its people. In a Modoc version, everything was water until the Creator scooped a handful of mud from the bottom of Tule Lake and used it to sculpt a world around himself. As Edison and Leatha Chiloquin told it, "He made the earth, prairies, mountains, lakes and the islands, and he gave each a name. K'mukamtch created the *maklaks* [the people] from the Sarvis berry bush and provided them with fish, game, and vegetal products and the means to secure them for their needs."

Another story, collected by anthropologist Theodore Stern, explains how the Creator distributed the peoples of the region. Having made a journey to the underworld, he brought two bones to Klamath Lake. Then K'mukamtch put another two bones in Modoc country.

Then said Gmukamps, "I placed these bones too close together. They might understand each other's language." Then again he went. Once again he went. Pit River country. In this direction to the north he put down another two bones and a little further away again placed two more. . . . Next day, climbing up on top of his house and sitting there, he looked around to see whether any smoke was rising. That day smoke was rising in several places. He looked around to the

north, he looked eastward, southward. He was content. He talked to
himself, "May you live well, people!"

The Klamath and Modoc spoke dialects of the same language. Not
only did they understand each other, but they also shared an identity, calling themselves *maklaks*, or people. Collectively, the *maklaks* comprised
a number of groups, some living along lakes, others by rivers or marshes.

The E'ukskni *maklaks* were the "people of the lake." The largest
E'ukskni group had a permanent village on the marshes north of the lake.
People there built houses on the water atop stone and gravel foundations,
securing them with pilings sunk six feet underground. The Mo'dokni
maklaks were from Moatak, today's Tule Lake, but they also lived on
Lower Klamath Lake, Lost River, and Clear Lake. The Plaikni *maklaks*
were uplanders, inhabiting the Sprague River Valley. Their territory also
included the area where the city of Klamath Falls is today. E'ukskni called
them "arrowhead-making people."

Anthropologist Verne Ray has argued that the Klamath and Modoc
were distinct peoples and that Modocs shared more cultural traits with the
Pit River tribe to the south than they did with their northern neighbors.
Ray considered the Modoc belief system—for example, the shamans'
reliance on guardian spirits—closer to that of California tribes, and the
belief system of the Klamath more typical of Plateau peoples like the
Yahooskin Snake. He regarded the resemblance between the northern
and southern branches of the *maklaks* as "similarities consequent upon
occupancy of the same environmental province." Yet the similarities are
profound, and the two peoples have long considered themselves to be
related.

Evidently, the *maklaks* who inhabited the Upper Basin and stayed did
not come from far away. Their language is of the Penutian family, and
tongues closely related to theirs are found among tribes of the Plateau near
the Columbia River. More distantly related Penutian languages are spoken
in central and coastal California, on the Oregon coast, and in Canada.

Penutian peoples traded with each other along a web of routes.
One prime trading place was Olompali, a Coast Miwok village on the
northwest shore of San Francisco Bay. Another was at The Dalles on the
Columbia River. Obsidian from the volcanic Upper Basin was a coveted
trade item, as it made the best arrowheads.

Within the land of waters, canoes were the primary mode of long-distance transportation. Canoes carved out of fir and rafts made of tule reeds were also used for gathering food. Women harvested *wokas*, the pond lily seed that was a staple of the Klamath diet. Men took canoes and rafts out on the lakes at night to fish by torchlight.

The creator K'mukamtch, it was said, built stone weirs to trap suckers. He instituted the Return of the *C'waam* Ceremony, a much-awaited event, for the arrival of the long-lived, prolifically breeding *c'waam* meant that the deprivations of winter were coming to an end.

When spring came, there were many sources of food besides fish: the eggs of wildfowl and the birds themselves, berries of various kinds, camas and other roots, wild celery and mosses, and game. Modocs hunted antelope and mountain sheep; Klamath shot antelope, deer, and elk. They killed other mammals as well. The Sahaptin-speaking Warm Springs Indians called the *maklaks* Aikspalu, "people of the chipmunks."

A number of animals were sacred to the Klamath. The gray fox was the guardian of the *maklak* spirits who have departed the earth, taking the path of the sun to the underworld. Raven was K'mukamtch's main ally. Kakamtch, as Raven was called, had the power to transform people into stones, perhaps preventing their spirits from making the westward journey. These animal deities, together with the theme of the journey to the underworld, reveal the importance of shamanism in *maklak* culture.

The practice of shamanism among the Klamath Tribes is one of the connections one can grasp between present-day experiences, recent history, and the distant past. Shamanism may seem a marginal and exotic activity in contemporary North America, but seen in the context of the entire span of human life, going back to the era when *Homo sapiens* first gained the capacity for symbolic expression, shamanism, or something like it, has been a large part of humanity's cultural experience.

Shamanism is usually considered a kind of religious activity combined with the art of healing, but it also encompasses the original forms of art and science. The significance of shamanism as a nexus of culture per se is evident from the roles played by Klamath shamans in their society. Prior to reservation life, which began in 1864, and clandestinely afterward, shamans provided entertainment, therapy, weather forecasting, prophecy, and spiritual inspiration.

In February, after putting on a bearclaw necklace and a buckskin cap adorned with woodpecker feathers, the shaman staged an entertainment lasting five days and five nights (or five nights only, among the Modocs). Some of the events children could see; others only invited adults could attend. The spectators witnessed magic tricks. The doctor swallowed arrowheads and burning sticks. He or she also made things suddenly appear. A basket of water would turn red with blood or have seeds suddenly floating in it. The shaman might reach into the water to catch a fish that hadn't been there before. In ceremonies staged for adults, shamans summoned spirits from the underworld. Fasting and often lying down, the shaman—or doctor, for this was a form of healing—needed help to perform this task. One assistant lit the shaman's pipe. Another led the audience in dancing or in singing sacred songs.

During these five days and nights, the shaman's lodge was a sacred space. The poles of the house were painted for the occasion, and stuffed power animals hung from the roofbeams. Sometimes, in a ceremony, the animals appeared to come to life. Participants sought power for themselves, power that brings success in hunting or in finding a mate. Through their immersion in the sacred in a time and place set aside from mundane activities, individuals received supernatural aid.

At puberty, boys fasted for five days and went to a place of power. After falling asleep near Medicine Lake, a Modoc youth awakened to a power song, one to remember throughout his life. A girl's power song might come in a dream during the five-night ceremony that celebrated her coming of age. One such song goes like this: "M'bu/shant Kaila Hamola"—in the morning the Earth resounded.

Besides leading winter ceremonies and puberty rites, a doctor conducted special healing rituals. Like the sucking doctors of many California tribes, the Modoc healer sucked "pains" out of the patient's body.

The traditional *maklak* shaman not only had the power to heal but also the power to kill. Belief in the evil that sorcerers may do was hardly confined to the Klamath Basin. In Peru, for example, one service that *curanderos* (shamanic healers) offer during their all-night ceremonies is to counteract the harm, or *daño*, that *brujos* (sorcerers) threaten to do to the shaman's clients. Peruvian *brujos* are believed to have the ability to travel through the air in spirit form to attack their victims. Apparently, Modoc shamans had this power as well. Jenny Clinton, a Modoc who was born in the mid-nineteenth century, told the story of Jakalunus, who used his shamanic prowess to wage war.

> Once when Warm Spring warriors came to Modoc country and killed a few men this great doctor sent his spirits to combat them. The invaders wondered why their men died without an observable cause.

Considerable danger accompanied the associated powers of healing and of killing. If a cure did not succeed and the patient died, the kin of the deceased might not only hold the doctor responsible, but they also had the right to avenge that death. One of the better-known instances of this practice occurred in June 1871, when Kintpuash, a Modoc subchief known by whites as Captain Jack, called in a medicine man to treat a child who had a malignant disease. After the child died, Kintpuash and four of his men followed the doctor to Clear Lake and shot him in the head.

Shamans the world over claim the power to travel Orpheus-like to the underworld and bring the dead back into the land of the living. In Siberia and many other parts of the world, one finds the belief in rebirth from bones. The scholar of comparative religions Mircea Eliade found examples in Africa, India, among ancient Germans, and in the ancient Middle East. Ezekiel, who is immortalized in the Old Testament, recalls his vision in which "I prophesied, there was a noise, and behold a shaking, and the bones came together, bone to his bone. And when I beheld, lo, the sinews and the flesh came up upon them." The story of the bones that K'mukamtch brought up from the underworld to people the Klamath Basin and its surroundings may derive from the ritual of an aboriginal Ezekiel.

Shamans were unable to counter the smallpox brought by Spanish sailors to the Pacific Northwest in 1779. The Big Sick infected Indians along the Columbia River, where Klamaths came to trade, and elsewhere; pandemics of malaria and measles were to follow. The spread of malaria alone in the lower reaches of the Columbia beginning in 1830 took the lives of three-quarters of the native population there, according to Dr. John McLoughlin, the Hudson's Bay Company chief factor at Fort Vancouver. The *maklaks* suffered from contagion as well, though not to the extent of the tribes to their north. In 1847, when settlers from the United States began to travel through their country, smallpox killed 150 Modocs.

The tragedy of the Big Sick and subsequent pandemics is palpable in the words of a Salish-speaking elder, Teequalt, who told a child (who became the author Mourning Dove) how smallpox had ravaged her people:

> It was early in the fall when some people came back from the west, where there is a big saltwater lake. They had gone to trade furs for shells and got a sickness that was very bad.
>
> We called it "breaking out." Most of those traders died on the way home, but a few made it, fearing that they had been diseased by a hostile shaman. A few days after they reached home, everyone started getting sick. All were frightened and called on the wisest shaman to doctor them, but they died anyway. Shamans also died. Some tried to use the sweat lodge, but when they jumped into the cold water after sweating they got worse and died faster. The dead were left in tepees when survivors moved away. Dogs and coyotes ate their flesh. Sometimes only a small baby survived, starving at the breast of its mother. Many of the old and weak survived, however, because they went to bed and kept warm while the strong and healthy died.

The decimation inflicted on the tribal population by disease challenged the authority of shamanism. But in the 1870s and 1880s, shamanic leadership revived when a new ceremony known as the Ghost Dance spread rapidly throughout the Pacific Northwest, the Great Basin, and the Plains. While doing the powerful dance, doctors and their followers returned in trance to the land of the dead to bring back the world of their ancestors. In 1873, the Ghost Dance would play a crucial role in the Modoc War, when Modocs, having left the Klamath Reservation and returned to their homeland, fought to restore their way of life. Its appeal demonstrates the continuing power of the shamanic worldview long after the exposure of Indigenous people to European Americans.

Still, even before the appearance of non-Indians in their country, *maklak* society was transformed by non-Indian influences. Horses changed the economic life of Klamaths and Modocs alike. Wild herds migrated to the Pacific Northwest via the Great Plains and the Southwest after the Spanish brought them to this continent. By the eighteenth century, when horses became available on the Columbia Plateau, Klamaths and Modocs began to conduct raids against other tribes to acquire slaves to trade for horses.

One Klamath warrior, Chiloquin, who in later life became a Plaikni chief, recalled those days:

> We made war without provocation on the Pitt Rivers, Shastas and Rogue Rivers, but they never made willing war on us. Those wars lasted a great many years. We found we could make money by war, for we sold the provisions and property captured for horses and other things we needed. It was like soldiers nowadays who fight for money.

In addition to trading their own captives, the Klamaths served as middlemen for the Modocs, transporting their slaves to The Dalles.

Modoc slaves who were not traded for horses and other goods became part of Modoc society. A female captured in war might become a concubine. A young male slave could win his freedom by marrying a Modoc girl. Slaves were worked hard, but they "were quite well treated," according to Verne Ray; slaves were allowed to participate in ceremonies and go wherever they pleased. They could not go home, however—their villages would not take them back—and they ran the risk that their owners might kill them in anger.

Raids to capture slaves made the Modocs, unlike most California tribes, a martial society. Modoc war parties might comprise ten men from one village or up to a hundred drawn from a number of villages. Not all of their forays were slave raids; some were retaliatory, following an attack, and some responded to encroachments into Modoc territory.

Leading a raid was a war chief; the tribe's political leaders remained at home, as did most of the people. Recognized for his skills as a warrior, the war chief could maintain this status throughout life, but he could not order others to follow him. Modoc society functioned as a participatory democracy, with men as the only participants. Asked to do battle, men would raise questions concerning the timing of the raid or the level of risk to themselves; they might propose, instead, a truce with the rival tribe. Often the tribe's political leader played a decisive role in the debate, arguing, for example, that it would be better to trade with their neighbors than to capture them for use in trade.

Helping to inspire confidence in a prospective battle was the shaman who would accompany the war party. Once a raid was decided upon, he performed magic, swallowing arrows that the spirit later drew from his body and dropped onto the ground. In encampments the night before an attack, the shaman led ceremonies designed to bring about success by keeping the men spirited and alert. During and after the battle, he applied his healing techniques to the wounded.

As the Modoc talent for slave-raiding brought them horses and laborers, the range and frequency of their forays increased. In their expeditions to the south, the Modocs met little opposition. Other northern California tribes lacked experience in war beyond the settling of scores. The killing of a Yurok, for example, might inspire a raid on the murderer's village, but the outcome was often a ritualized form of confrontation followed by a payment of some kind.

Few California tribes had any need to make war or to defend themselves against war parties. The breadth and variety of the lands in California and the abundance and diversity of wildlife separated tribes into habitats that satisfied each group's need. Various groups migrated from the mountains into the Central Valley or from the shore to the coastal hills for seasonal hunting and gathering, but they had no reason to fight other small tribes for territory or sources of food. They could trade for whatever they needed that they did not already have. The stability of some California groups is evidenced by shellmounds on the north coast and around San Francisco Bay, which reveal undisturbed habitation and slow but steady cultural evolution for thousands of years.

In such a benign environment, the Modocs might have become the kind of dominant society that political theorist Andrew Bard Schmookler considered to be a major driving force in history. Only if all tribes living within reach of one another choose peaceful ways, Schmookler wrote in *The Parable of the Tribes*, can they live in peace. If just one tribe becomes ambitious for expansion and conquest, then every other has to react by fleeing, by fighting back and trying to prevail, or by allowing itself to be conquered and assimilated. Every tribe has to adapt to the ways of war or submit to them. In this manner, the parable suggests, human beings everywhere are taken over by dominant societies that use violence to enforce their will.

The first white people in the Klamath Basin were mountain men. Working from Fort Vancouver on the Columbia River, the western headquarters of the London-based Hudson's Bay Company, their objective was to trap as many beavers as possible. The purpose of their expedition to the Basin was not only to obtain and sell beaver pelts but also to create a "fur desert" that would leave American trappers no reason to enter the Oregon Territory, then being disputed by the United States and Britain.

Finan McDonald and Thomas McKay arrived in the Klamath Basin in 1825. Like many trappers of their time, they had close relations with Indians or were part-Indian themselves. An imposing Scotsman, six-foot-four with red hair and a beard, McDonald was married to a Spokane Indian woman. McKay's father was Scottish, his mother was Cree, and his wife was the daughter of a Chinook chief. Influenced perhaps by the mountain men's ability to relate to Indigenous people, the Klamath, when encountering the party of thirty-two trappers, warned them to beware of the Indians to the south, the Modocs.

The next year, McKay returned to the Klamath Basin under the command of Peter Skene Ogden. This expedition comprised two dozen mountain men, who did the hunting and trapping, and their Indian wives, who prepared game and cured hides.

When they reached Klamath Marsh in December 1826, Ogden encountered what he called the "Clamitte Indian Village." There he obtained fourteen fish of a kind he had not seen before and nine dogs. Ogden named Upper Klamath Lake "Dog Lake" after his newly acquired food supply.

Ogden's party encountered Modocs on January 2, 1827. His men were starving, having had little success hunting deer that winter, and Ogden decided to return to a Klamath village to trade for more food before venturing farther. During this outing, Ogden passed a village that he believed the Modocs had abandoned. "We took the liberty of demolishing their Huts for fire wood, . . ." he wrote in his journal. "I should certainly regret that our side should cause a quarrel with these Indians, for so far their conduct toward us has been certainly most correct and worthy of imitation by all."

Accompanied by two Klamath guides on January 12, a stormy day, the party saw the Klamath River headwaters and looked over the lakes and marshes to the south. "The River here is a fine large Stream about ¼ of a mile in width deep and well lined with Willows," wrote Ogden, "taking as far as the eye can reach a Southern course." He was describing the widening of the river at Klamath Falls that today is called Lake Ewauna. Although Ogden's men reported that some of the Klamath tributaries were disappointingly "destitute of Beaver," his party took hundreds of beaver pelts from the Shasta and Scott rivers and from streams that flow into them. The scarcity of beaver compared to other hunting grounds within the company's reach accounts for the lack of trapping expeditions in the Klamath Basin after the mid-1820s. "It is to be regretted this country has been allowed to remain so long unexplored," wrote Ogden on January 27, "but why go far in quest of Beaver when the Willamette afforded a sufficiency."

Although the Hudson's Bay Company never followed up on Ogden's expedition, the Upper Klamath Basin remained within the Oregon Territory for many years afterward. No adventurers, explorers, or trappers came from the south either. With the collapse of the Spanish empire by 1822, California became a sparsely populated province of Mexico. The coastal areas and the rich ranchlands of the Central Valley offered all the land the Californios could use, a climate they enjoyed, and access to coastal ports for trading their hides and other goods. Even had they known about the highlands north of Mount Shasta, the Mexican ranchers would have had no desire to go there.

It was not until the 1840s that non-Indians returned to Klamath country. This time they came to settle permanently despite the Indian presence. Conquest by the newly arriving dominant society seemed inevitable, as it followed centuries of conquest of Indigenous people by Euramericans. Yet white dominance of the Upper Klamath Basin would prove difficult beyond all expectations.

Chapter Two
Manifest Destiny

Before wagon trains rolled toward the Oregon Territory, carrying more than 50,000 emigrants from their departure points along the Missouri River, Christian missionaries traveled from the United States to the Pacific Northwest. Sent on a reconnaissance party by the American Board of Commissioners for Foreign Missions, they found the massive mountains, prodigious rainforests, and mighty rivers formidable. All posed challenges to what then was an expanding agricultural nation. Americans were used to older, smaller, more rounded mountains; to flatter, more hospitable terrain whose forests fell rapidly under the ax; to readily navigable rivers that wound their way through flatlands and plains. Yet they had reason to believe the Gospel saying, "Nothing will be impossible for you." For they were a people who had benefited from a succession of inventions ranging from the iron plow to the harness, from the water mill to the steam engine, a people whose cities were witnessing the combined power of labor and machines in the Industrial Revolution, an unprecedented increase in humanity's ability to transform the world.

The outlook of these Americans could not have been more different from the philosophy of the tribes of the Klamath Basin. They, like other Indigenous peoples around the planet, assumed and still assume their existence to be inextricably woven within the web of life that they experience. Their creation stories express this view. They and other creatures were made for the world where they have always lived; the Creator gave them everything they needed to survive there. For pioneer missionary Dr. Marcus Whitman, the Indians' right to continue living in their land depended on their rejecting such beliefs and converting to Christianity. "When a people refuse or neglect to fill the designs of Providence," he argued, "they ought not to complain at the results." Not surprisingly, the Cayuse Indians to whom Dr. Whitman preached were less than receptive to his teachings. The missionary understood that only the arrival of white settlers to Oregon could make his vision of Providence a reality.

Many who traveled the Oregon Trail during the Great Migration of 1843 had caught "Oregon fever" from the speeches of Whitman and other missionaries who came East in search of followers from the United States. Whitman himself led the largest of the wagon trains that brought pioneer families into the Oregon Territory that year. Most of the immigrants stopped at his mission, and some stayed, for it was located strategically on the Oregon Trail near present-day Walla Walla, Washington.

"We are the nation of human progress, and who will, what can, set limits to our onward march?" asked columnist John L. O'Sullivan in 1839. To bring freedom and equality to the world "is our high destiny, and in nature's eternal, inevitable decree of cause and effect we must accomplish it." The political expression of faith in what for Marcus Whitman and other frontier missionaries was the design of Providence became known as Manifest Destiny. Combining the power of Old Testament prophecy with the ideas of progress, liberty, and equality that had animated the French and American Revolutions and energized by the optimism of a young and growing nation, the ideology that Americans forged in the nineteenth century was a "destiny" that could trump geography. American settlement would alter lands, waters, and mountains, even arresting salmon on their upward course.

Underlying the enthralling rhetoric of Manifest Destiny was the limited ability of the fledgling United States to support its booming population. The population of the original thirteen states had grown fourfold in the decades between 1800 and 1840. With more than twenty million Americans needing work and food, the demand for land, especially agricultural land, was increasing. Already Jefferson's Louisiana Purchase had added more than two million square miles—from the Mississippi River to the Rocky Mountains—to the land base of the United States. Meriwether Lewis and William Clark had explored some of that territory in the early nineteenth century; and once those western lands were won, there was country to conquer all the way to the Pacific, opening up the prospect, as far-seeing minds understood, of trade with Asia. The idea of Manifest Destiny, that American civilization would conquer the continent, served in the 1840s to legitimize the emigration to Oregon as well as the Mexican–American War.

Debate in Congress pitted those who sought expansion into Oregon against those who, like President John Tyler, did not want to risk war with Britain. Missouri Senator Thomas Hart Benton, a leading advocate of expanding the United States, secured an appropriation to the Corps of Topographical Engineers for a survey of lands west of the Mississippi. Benton saw the need for a scientific expedition that fixed latitudes and longitudes and reported on soils, streams, flora, fauna, and terrain with respect to the land's potential for productive settlement.

Leading the expedition was Benton's son-in-law, John Charles Frémont. An intelligent, handsome, and daring southerner, Frémont won the love of the senator's daughter in spite of his lack of social standing. Frémont mother, a Virginian, had left her first husband for a French émigré, Charles Frémont, who, when he died, left her in poverty. John Charles had grown up in Norfolk, Virginia, and Charleston, South Carolina, before gaining experience as a surveyor.

In order to explore and map western terrains expeditiously, the southern city boy needed a capable scout who knew the country between Missouri and Oregon. Kentucky-born Kit Carson, a mountain man who had covered much of the West trapping beaver for the fur trade, filled the bill. "Cool, brave, and of good judgment," Frémont said of Kit Carson in his memoirs, "a good hunter and a good shot; experienced in mountain life, he was an acquisition, and proved valuable throughout the campaign." Not only was Carson experienced and trustworthy, but he also spoke French, Spanish, and some Indian languages. He knew how to defend an expedition against Indians and, when necessary, how to fight them.

It was through his association with Frémont that Kit Carson became a legend. Frémont later described his first impression of the frontiersman "with a clear steady blue eye and frank speech" as "quiet and unassuming." Carson, in his memoirs, recalled telling John Charles "that I had been some time in the mountains and thought I could guide him to any point he wished to go."

After the explorer, the mountain man, and their party returned from their first expedition between St. Louis and the Rocky Mountains, Frémont's wife, Jessie Benton Frémont, applied her considerable literary gifts to their report in a manner that stimulated interest in westward expansion. Together, the Frémonts, Senator Benton, and his allies built support for exploring beyond the Rockies.

On his second expedition Frémont explored Oregon. Accompanied by Indian guides, his party of twenty-five men on horseback crossed the Blue Mountains to the high plateau above the Walla Walla River. Seeing man-made clearings in the distance, Frémont led his men to Dr. Whitman's mission. Whitman himself was away, visiting The Dalles downriver on the Columbia, so Frémont bought potatoes and skipped the sermons.

Then he proceeded to Fort Walla Walla, an outpost of the Hudson's Bay Company near the confluence of the Walla Walla River and the Columbia. The fort's factor, Archibald McKinlay, who was married to a daughter of Peter Skene Ogden, hospitably invited Frémont and the leaders of immigrant parties camped nearby to dinner. That night Frémont met Jesse Applegate, whose family was to play a major role in the settlement of southern Oregon.

Applegate was traveling the Oregon Trail with his brothers Lindsay and Charles and their families. He had begun his career as a surveyor before settling down to work his family's lands in Missouri. Then times got tough. The Panic of 1837, a financial crisis following a bubble of speculative investments, threw the U.S. economy into a depression that lasted for six years. With multitudes unemployed, prices of pork and other goods fell so low that there was no point in taking them to market. The Applegates had an additional motive for moving their families to new lands. They were opposed to slavery. Jesse believed slavery degraded the masters even more than the slaves, and his brother Lindsay may have voiced similar views, for he was reported to have had a confrontation with a pro-slavery mob. After Jesse received a letter from a friend who, having emigrated to Oregon, praised its virtues, the brothers decided that was where they would go.

Hard times back home did not prepare the Applegates for the hardships of the Oregon Trail. The worst calamity struck soon after they left Fort Walla Walla and sped down the Columbia in six flat-bottom boats, which were more than fifty feet long. As they rafted through the narrow channel near The Dalles, the mighty river swept three of their children away, killing two of them. Their deaths may have motivated two of the three Applegate brothers, Jesse and Lindsay, to open a new branch of the emigrant trail, one that would bring wagon trains to the Willamette Valley through southcentral Oregon.

Watching the formidable Columbia and hearing about its waterfalls and rapids downstream, Frémont decided to travel overland. After passing the treacherous Dalles, he and some of his men took a Chinook cedar canoe, paddled by Wasco Indian guides, to Fort Vancouver, headquarters of the Hudson's Bay Company. There Chief Factor John McLoughlin greeted him, and Frémont obtained the supplies, horses, and mules he needed for his return journey.

Reunited with his main party, which he had left in the hands of Kit Carson, Frémont turned south along the Cascade Range. On December 9, 1843, his expedition came upon a large meadow bordered by a pine forest. Frémont had expected to find Klamath Lake at this place, but he was thirty miles north of the lake, near Klamath Marsh. The pasture was what the animals needed, its terrain more welcoming than the snowy mountain passes the explorers had been traversing. Frémont set up camp.

On the opposite side of the marshland, smoke rose from a Klamath village. Frémont had heard that the Klamaths were tough warriors. To intimidate them, he fired off the howitzer that he had taken great trouble to bring with him across many rivers and mountains. It produced a strange and powerful sound that, Frémont reported, amazed his Indian guides and inspired them "with triumphant feelings; but on the camps at a distance the effect was different, for the smokes in the lake and on the shore immediately disappeared."

Frémont did not want to frighten the Klamaths altogether. He needed to make contact with them to obtain directions and possibly new guides for his continuing travels. So he, Carson, and several other men, including an Indian guide, rode toward the village at a gallop. Two people walked toward them. Frémont learned that "they were the village chief and his wife, who, in excitement and alarm at the unusual event and appearance, had come out to meet their fate together. The chief was a very prepossessing Indian, with very handsome features, and a singularly soft and agreeable voice—so remarkable as to attract general notice." Neither Kit Carson nor Broken Hand, the guide, had heard the chief's language before, but they knew the Chinook jargon, the trading language of the Columbia region. That is how they understood that the *tyee*, or chief, and his wife were inviting them to visit their village.

In his report on the expedition, Frémont described the earth lodges where *maklaks* lived throughout the winter. "They were large round huts,

MANIFEST DESTINY   33

perhaps 20 feet in diameter, with rounded tops, on which was the door by which they descended into the interior. Within, they were supported by posts and beams." He was impressed with their crafts—the shoes woven of grass, "which seemed well adapted for a snowy country; and the women wore on their head a closely woven basket, which made a very good cap. Among other things, were parti-colored mats about four feet square, which we purchased to lay on the snow under our blankets, and to use for table cloths." More generally, Frémont recognized how "these people seem to have adapted themselves to the soil, and to be growing on what the immediate locality afforded." But, exposing his sense of superiority, the explorer noted that the people were "almost like plants" in their adaptability. Their country, he wrote, was "a picturesque and beautiful spot; and, under the hand of cultivation, might become a paradise."

Kit Carson's first impression of the Klamath Indians, according to his memoirs, was more negative, but he wrote his account after the violent encounter he had on the next expedition in 1846, which clearly colored his memories: "We started for Klamath Lake. A guide was employed and we arrived there safe and found a large village of Indians having the same name. We had with them a talk. We pronounced them a mean, low-lived, treacherous race, which we found to be a fact when we were in their country in 1846."

The winter weather impelled Frémont to continue on his return trip with little delay. He asked the Klamaths to travel with him as guides, but no one agreed to, yet they did offer information about the lands and waters ahead. Leading his expedition toward the east out of the Klamath Basin, Frémont did not encounter the Upper Klamath Lake on this trip. Instead, he crossed a tributary of the Sycan River, whose waters flow into the lake.

In the two years between Frémont's departure from the land of the *maklaks* and the time when he prepared for his third expedition, the United States changed significantly. James K. Polk, an expansionist, was in the White House. His campaign platform had called for the annexation of Texas, the self-proclaimed Lone Star Republic that Mexico continued to claim. When President Polk sent troops to the Rio Grande, 150 miles south of the international boundary previously recognized by both countries, Frémont had reason that he would declare war on Mexico. Once that happened, the conquest of California was in the cards.

Historians debate what Frémont knew about Polk's intentions. He and Senator Benton met the president-elect not long after the explorer returned from his second expedition, and they found a new ally in George Bancroft, the historian whom Polk appointed as secretary of the Navy. The War Department, however, in its directives for the third expedition, did not order Frémont to go to California or Oregon. First Lieutenant and Captain Frémont (he received this double brevet as a promotion following the second expedition) was to direct his efforts "to the geography of localities within reasonable distance . . . of the streams which run east from the Rocky Mountains." Did Frémont have secret orders, or did he disregard the directives from the chief of the Corps of Topographical Engineers on his own initiative?

Although the War Department considered Frémont's expedition "of a scientific character, without any view whatsoever to military operations," the explorer brought with him a large and well-armed contingent. He gave twelve of his sixty men fine rifles to reward excellent marksmanship. And he led his party to California, lingering there for months as if awaiting new orders, as if anticipating the outbreak of a war in which his exploring mission could play a military role. It so happened that on the day that Frémont left Peter Lassen's ranch in the Sacramento Valley heading north, April 24, 1846, hostilities between American troops and Mexicans on the Rio Grande finally broke out.

Frémont and his men were camped beside Upper Klamath Lake when Frémont learned that a courier, Lt. A. H. Gillespie, was on his trail carrying messages from Washington, D.C. Immediately, the explorer formed a party consisting of Carson and nine others to ride with him, beginning at daybreak, to meet the officer.

After questioning Gillespie, then staying up late re-reading the letters, Frémont wrapped himself in his blankets, failing, for only the second time in his career, to post a sentry. Near dawn, the sound of an ax striking a man's head awakened Kit Carson, who sounded the alarm. Indians, possibly Modocs who had followed Gillespie north, or possibly Klamaths, rushed the camp.

As Carson recalled this incident, "The Indians had then tomahawked two men, Lajeunesse and a Delaware, and were proceeding to the fire, where four Delaware were lying." Having broken his rifle while cleaning

it, Carson had only a pistol, so after firing at the lead attacker, he withdrew. But Joseph Stepperfeldt, a gunsmith from Illinois,

> fired, struck [an Indian] in the back, ball passing near the heart, and
> he fell. The balance of his party then run. He was the bravest Indian
> I ever saw. If his men had been as brave as himself, we surely would
> all have been killed. We lost three men and one slightly wounded. If
> we had not gone to meet Gillespie, he and his party would have been
> murdered. The Indians evidently were on his trail for that purpose.

The next day, in retaliation, Frémont and Carson attacked and
burned a Klamath village and killed fourteen men. Although Frémont
recalled sending Carson ahead to reconnoiter, Carson's memoir suggests that he acted entirely on his own. "I discovered a large village of
about 50 lodges," he wrote, "and, at the same time, by the commotion
in their camp I knew that they had seen us and, considering it useless to
send for reinforcements, I determined to attack them, charged on them,
fought for some time, killed a number, and the balance fled."

Frémont's report of a subsequent encounter in which he saved
Carson's life by attacking an Indian who was about to shoot an arrow at
him reads like a novel. The explorer's description of how he fired at the
man, missed, and then jumped his fearless horse directly onto the Indian,
hurling him to the ground and making his arrow go wild blurs the line
between myth and history. "I had now kept the promise I made to myself,"
recalled Frémont, "and had punished these people well for their treachery; and now I turned my thoughts to the work which they had delayed."

Frémont saw himself as an instrument of fate, or at least he wanted
the world to see him in that light. "How fate pursues a man!" he declared,
regarding Gillespie's mission to bring him letters from Washington concerning California. The implication was that it was Frémont's personal
destiny to fulfill the Manifest Destiny of his nation by extending the
United States to the Pacific Ocean.

His account of the violence near Klamath Lake that preceded the part
he played in the conquest of California helped build up Frémont's reputation as a hero. Clearly the Pathfinder had posterity in mind. Frémont
imagined how this phase of his expedition would be remembered in future
times—by his readers, of course, but also by his victims' descendants via

oral tradition. "When the Klamaths tell the story of the night attack where they were killed," wrote Frémont, "there will be no boasting. They will have to tell also of the death of their chief and of our swift retaliation; and how the people at the fishery had to mourn for the loss of their men and the destruction of their village. It will be a story for them to hand down while there are any Klamaths on their lake."

If justice is blind, then injustice is one-eyed. What it sees, it sees intensely; but lacking perspective, it has no understanding. The lesson that *maklaks* learned from the destruction of their village is that non-Indians would avenge themselves against a tribe that did not attack them. Scholars disagree about who exactly raided the Frémont-Gillespie camp that night in April. Robert Ruby and John Brown claim it was a Modoc party. Theodore Stern says the attackers were from a group located near present-day Klamath Falls, some thirty miles south of the village on Upper Klamath Lake that Carson burned to the ground. Keith Murray's story is that Modocs tried unsuccessfully to raid the horses of Gillespie's party as he headed toward his rendezvous with Frémont but that a Klamath war party attacked the Frémont camp near the southern end of the lake. No one believes, as Frémont and Carson evidently did, that it was the chief of the village they burned who led the attack on them. Not long after the Pathfinder headed south to advance American interests in California, his misdirected act of revenge against the Klamaths brought another turn in the spiral of violence.

Within months of Frémont's misadventure near Klamath Lake, a party of Willamette settlers led by Lindsay and Jesse Applegate was exploring a southern route that immigrants could take to their new homeland. In search of an alternative to the difficult and dangerous stretch of the Oregon Trail across the Blue Mountains and along the Columbia River, the Applegates traveled through the Rogue River Valley, crossed the Siskiyou Mountains, and headed east near today's California-Oregon state line toward Lower Klamath Lake. There they were greeted by Modoc smoke signals, warnings to other *maklaks* that the *Boston*—"white men" in Chinook jargon—were coming. When one member of the surveying party went hunting in the lava beds near Tule Lake, Modocs reacted with alarm. They packed their canoes and paddled rapidly across the lake to a safer place, lest they be hunted themselves.

The Applegate party continued east to Goose Lake and on to Nevada and the Humboldt River, then northward to Fort Hall, a stop on the Oregon Trail near present-day Pocatello, Idaho. There the trailblazers persuaded a wagon train of about 150 Missourians heading toward the Willamette Valley to follow them along the new South Emigrant Road. That first contingent passed safely through Modoc country; subsequent ones did not.

A geographical feature of the region helped Modoc warriors prevail with bows and arrows against rifle-toting wagoneers. A long, high ridge comes to a point like the tip of a peninsula near what was then the shore of Tule Lake. The immigrants reached the lake after a long day's travel down from the Clear Lake highlands. It was a natural resting spot, a place where animals could drink and browse. Hiding behind the ridge, Indians had success ambushing wagon trains, especially in the early years before that spot won fame as Bloody Point.

Estimates of the number of would-be settlers who died at Bloody Point are unreliable. After several attacks had occurred, the immigrants considered the Modocs the generic "hostile Indian," and they were blamed for incidents in which warriors from other tribes confronted whites, especially along the Applegate Trail. Yet although eighty wagons took the South Road to Oregon in 1847, there may have been no Modoc attacks that year or the next. Modocs had reason to avoid non-Indians during that year, when a devastating smallpox epidemic struck them. In 1849, a government report noted that Modocs killed eighteen whites and concluded that they were back in business.

At the same time, the fear of Indian warfare in the Pacific Northwest reached a fever pitch. Cayuse Indians living near the Whitman Mission on the Oregon Trail lost many lives from an epidemic of measles, which they blamed on the immigrants. A grief-stricken band of Cayuse stormed the mission, killing Marcus and Narcissa Whitman and eleven other whites. Many non-Indians feared that the attack would spread into a large-scale war of resistance.

By 1849, the Gold Rush greatly increased traffic along the South Emigrant Road. The stretch between northern California and the Willamette Valley filled with people heading south, not north as the Applegate party had expected. Although most of the gold-seekers from the East took cross-country trails into California that passed far to the south of Bloody Point, the rush to the gold fields rutted the route between Fort Hall and Tule Lake as well. Those who pursued their fortunes regarded Indians whose territory the southern road crossed, especially the Modocs in California and the Rogue River Indians in southern Oregon, as intolerable and dangerous obstacles.

In 1851, a major gold strike occurred on a tributary of the Shasta River on the southwestern edge of Modoc country. Thousands of miners swarmed into the region and staked claims, and the town of Yreka sprang into existence to meet their needs. That summer a group of Indians raided a pack train and stole forty-six mules and horses. The raiders might have been Pit Rivers, even Paiutes, but the horses ended up in Modoc country. Men who had been sitting on bar stools and around card tables in Yreka found some excitement when the owner of the stolen animals assembled a vigilante party.

One man riding with the posse was an Indian fighter who had won his spurs in the Cayuse War avenging the massacre at the Whitman Mission. Ben Wright had been born into a religious family in Indiana twenty-three years earlier (according to one source, his father was a Presbyterian minister). He combined a hatred of Indians with a pseudo-Indian lifestyle, wearing buckskin and growing his curly black hair shoulder length. Wright cohabited with Indian women and cut off scalps and other trophies from the bodies of Indians he killed. He was flamboyant and fearless.

The Yreka vigilantes crossed a natural lava bridge on Lost River, rode past a Modoc village on Tule Lake, and made camp several miles beyond it. After pretending to sleep, the men doubled back to the Tule Lake village. At dawn they attacked, capturing women and children, killing several of the men, and driving others into the tule marsh that fringed the lake. The Modocs surrendered and gave the posse enough horses and mules to send them away triumphant.

The following year, 1852, Bloody Point more than earned its name. Hearing that wagon trains and pack trains of miners were heading down the South Emigrant Road, a band from Yreka rode east to warn them of the dangers in Modoc country. The first train ignored the warnings. All but one of that group, a man named Coffin who cut the pack off his horse and galloped away, were killed.

Another wagon train, whose leaders heeded the warnings of the Yreka men, defended itself at Bloody Point, circling the wagons before the

Indians could attack. The Modocs set a grass fire around the wagons and prepared for a siege, confident that the immigrants' ammunition would run out. When the men from Yreka, returning home, encountered this confrontation, they had to seek shelter within the corral of wagons. Then they heard the hoofbeat of horses coming from the west. More Modocs, they feared. But it was Ben Wright leading a rescue party. Those men managed to drive the Indians off, killing some of them, before escorting the wagon train to safety in Yreka. Ben Wright became a hero.

No one knows how many people the Modocs killed near Bloody Point in the summer of 1852. Bodies and burned wagons lay beside the emigrant road, and there were lurid stories of a massacre. One corpse, the mutilated remains of a young woman, especially infuriated the white men in Yreka.

Ben Wright formed a posse of fifteen men who camped near Bloody Point for several months. His objectives were to protect traffic on the road, to recover property that the Modocs had taken from wagons before they burned them, and to avenge the deaths of the whites who had been killed. Attacks on travelers ceased, but the Modocs returned nothing to Wright, and one Indian reportedly boasted that a band in Willow Creek held two teenage white girls captive.

By late October, some of Wright's men went back to Yreka. Meanwhile, an increasing number of Modocs moved into winter villages near his encampment. By November, Wright was running short of supplies, yet the men he sent to Yreka to replenish them went on an election-day drinking spree that lasted the better part of a week.

After the supplies finally arrived, Ben Wright made his move. The legend has it that Wright bought strychnine to season a Thanksgiving feast that he would serve the Modocs. It is possible that he did invite Modocs to a meal with the intent of killing them, but only two came. They were given presents as well as food, and they left, evidently unharmed. Knowing Wright was their enemy, the Modocs knew better than to go to his camp in numbers, and they must have known that vigilantes used poison to kill hundreds, if not thousands, of Scott Valley Shasta a year earlier. That event, though never reported in the press, lives on in oral history to this day.

In late November, with his men stationed out of sight on a bluff overlooking the Modoc camp, Wright walked into their village. He wore a poncho with a pistol—or two, in some accounts—concealed beneath the blanket. Old Schonchin, the village *tyee*, or headman, was absent, so

Wright demanded of the next in charge that the *Boston* captives and property be returned. He was refused. Wright shot the man dead, then quickly
zigzagged out of the camp, avoiding bullets as his vigilantes came out of
hiding and fired on the village. Forty-one Modocs were killed, among them
the father of Captain Jack, who, a generation later, would lead his people
in war against the whites. Among the five who escaped was Schonchin
John, Old Schonchin's brother, who would also lead Modocs in that war.

Wright and his men paraded in triumph through Yreka, waving
scalps. He and his rangers were rewarded with more than glory. It was
California's policy to pay vigilantes for every Indian they could prove they
killed. In 1853, the state legislature appropriated $23,000 to remunerate
them for their services.

In spite of the massacre, the Indian wars spread. When gold was
discovered in southern Oregon, the influx of miners triggered a series
of assaults and counter-assaults between them and the Rogue River and
Umpqua tribes. The U.S. Army came to the Siskiyou region with orders to
protect the Indians from the miners. The Interior Department had other
priorities. During this Rogue River War, it hired Wright as the Indian
agent overseeing the tribes in Oregon south of Coos Bay.

A heavy drinker, Wright went too far when he forced his interpreter,
an Indian woman, to strip naked and then whipped her up and down the
streets of Port Orford. Chetcoe Jennie turned to Enos, a former guide of
Frémont's who was now working for Wright, and together they plotted
revenge.

Their opportunity came later that year of 1856 at Gold Beach in Oregon. As partying white men danced with Native women, an angry group
of Indians assembled on the opposite bank of the Rogue River. Told that
Enos was with them and making trouble, the Indian agent and another
man crossed the river. The story goes that Enos murdered Wright with an
ax and cut his heart out of his body and that Jennie ate a piece of it.

Whatever actually occurred, Wright's demise stoked continuing outrage at the Indians. Stories of Ben Wright's deeds provided entertainment
for some while provoking others. The legend of Ben Wright long outlived
him, and Jennie was not the last of his victims to avenge themselves.

Chapter Three
Theater of War

The world rushed into California in search of gold, riding horses and horse-drawn wagons across the continent, taking steamships from the Atlantic ports of the United States and Europe and from the Pacific ports of China and Australia. Wealth-seekers converged on what were then among the most remote areas on Earth, places they called Murder's Bar, Whiskeytown, Yreka, places whose inhabitants prior to 1850 had rarely or never seen anyone from outside their own region. Within fifteen years, the miners had gone, leaving in their wake towns and tailings. Yet the Klamath Basin once again drew the attention of the world when the Modoc War became international news in 1873. In this era of the penny newspaper, the first of the mass media, the war became a spectacle, with news correspondents racing to Yreka on horseback to file stories that, after traveling as dots and dashes over telegraph wires, appeared in papers as far away as London. This rapid diffusion of information made possible a form of storytelling in which villains and heroes aroused emotions among people of great cultural difference as well as geographical distance from their lives.

The domestic consumers of news were also a constituency, and their cheers and jeers had the power to influence policymakers. With armchair spectators receiving a sensationalized version of events of the war, accented with bold headlines and dramatic illustrations, politicians felt pressure to play to the crowd. Political leaders learned how to master media and control the impressions the public received. Just as the beginning of the Modoc War ushered in the international news spectacle, its last act opened the curtain on a news event staged for the media—the show trial and four-man hanging that ended the war.

The story of that war as presented by the newspapers did not offer the understanding of situations or of character that one finds in historical narrative or a play. To follow the action in the context in which it occurred, one needs to know the setting—the Upper Klamath Basin—and the way that it changed between the heyday of Ben Wright and the death of Captain Jack. During those years, the town of Linkville (later renamed Klamath Falls), the army base at Fort Klamath, and the Klamath Reservation all sprang into existence; and settlers, primarily ranchers, inhabited choice lands throughout the region.

In 1852, at the height of vigilante activity and bloodshed at Bloody Point, nineteen-year-old Wallace Baldwin became the first non-Indian to settle in Klamath country. Baldwin drove fifty head of horses from the Rogue River Valley along the Applegate Trail into the Upper Basin. He had packed only enough food for his trip, and he had no gun. Klamath tribal members helped him survive. They brought him game and taught him how to eat *epaw*, the tuber that was their potato. Baldwin found fertile ground for pasturing his horses and a sunny climate. Other settlers followed. They put up fences, planted crops, and turned cattle out to graze. Soon it was the Indians who lacked food, having lost access to country where they had hunted game and gathered edible plants.

When the United States became embroiled in the Civil War, the Oregon legislature asked Congress for a military post that would keep the Indians of the Upper Basin under control. In March 1863, Maj. C. S. Drew selected a site in the Wood River Valley, north of Upper Klamath Lake. In addition to having abundant water, ample grass to feed horses and mules, and an extensive pine forest to provide fuel and building materials, this was where the Oregon Central Military Road met the trail between the Rogue River Valley and the land east of the Cascades.

Trout and suckers crowded the lakes and streams; elk, antelope, ducks, geese, and other game offered hunters countless targets from the spring through the fall. Yet food became a problem once the fort was garrisoned. Long, snowladen winters isolated Fort Klamath, blocking the supply routes from the California coast and the Rogue River. Indians taught soldiers how to spearfish through ice, but winter fare was rarely fresh. The men dined on dry bread and potato meal, boiled chunks of formerly frozen beefsteak, two-inch-thick squares of "mixed vegetables," and coffee.

George Nurse, a civilian who supplied Fort Klamath with goods, built a small store near the Link River and stocked it with a wagonload of trinkets and necessities. In May 1867, he established a ferry service across the river on the trail between the fort and Yreka. Buildings soon clustered from the hillside on the north to the swamps on the south and east. A saloon, a harness shop, and a U.S. Land Office were among Linkville's early attractions. A pack train brought supplies from Yreka, and a stage service provided weekly mail delivery from Ashland. Travelers tied their horses to the hitching post in front of Nurse's Hotel.

Jeff Mitchell, a former chairman of the Klamath Tribes, described this situation as it appeared to his ancestors:

> People who were at first open and friendly now had to look at things in a whole different light. Now we had folks that weren't just passing through, but were staying, and here we had a fort come up right in the homeland of the Klamath people—the upper end of Agency Lake. To the south the Modoc people saw the changes that were going on with the other tribes further south during the California Gold Rush and how that drove tribes in Northern California to the brink of extinction with the hostilities and the massacres that occurred. Those stories made their way up into our country and created a lot of concern for our people.

Klamath leaders decided, Mitchell said, that the wisest course of action was to find a way to live with the newcomers.

Kintpuash, the Modoc leader whites knew as Captain Jack, came to the same conclusion. In Yreka he asked the Indian agent, appointed by President Lincoln, to draw up a treaty. Judge Elijah Steele lacked the authority to do this. He may have known that Congress had rejected treaties made with many California tribes in 1851–1852, allowing their lands to be taken without compensation or legal claim. Nonetheless, Judge Steele made an agreement with Captain Jack to try to establish a reservation in the Tule Lake area. In return, Modocs were to stop stealing livestock.

Back in Washington, D.C., the Office of Indian Affairs decided to negotiate a different treaty that would contain all of the Indians of the Upper Klamath Basin on one reservation in Oregon. Indian Superintendent J. W. P. Huntington convened more than a thousand Indians at a place they called Council Grove, north of Upper Klamath Lake. In return for ceding their traditional territories—more than 20 million acres of southcentral Oregon and northeastern California, including an expanse of high desert country to the east of the Klamath Basin—Modocs,

Klamath, and the Yahooskin Band of Northern Paiutes were to inhabit fewer than two million acres on Klamath lands.

No whites except for Indian Agency employees and U.S. Army personnel were supposed to live there. In addition, the Indians were to receive thousands of dollars' worth of supplies over the next decade and a half, after which they were expected to become self-supporting. Supplies did not arrive for several years, however, until the Senate ratified the treaty. Even after the goods came, the Indian agent failed to distribute them fairly or fully.

As soon as local Indians were removed to the Klamath Agency, white settlers extended their holdings, digging ditches to drain wetlands and bringing cattle onto lands that had supported tribal members. N. B. Ball, a Kentuckian, kept 500 head on a 3,000-acre ranch in Butte Valley. John Fairchild grazed 3,000 head of stock on 2,700 acres nearby.

The soldiers at Fort Klamath had two major problems on their hands. One was coping with boredom. Some ran off, attracted by dreams of gold. If captured, a deserter was court-martialed; those found guilty were tattooed with a "D" on the left hip. The other problem was keeping Indians on the reservation. Members of the Yahooskin Tribe left the year the treaty was signed. Captain Jack's band of Modocs returned to their homeland south of Linkville in 1870. That gave the soldiers a new problem: they were poorly positioned to protect settlers from Indians and Indians from settlers.

Some of the new residents of Modoc country feared the Indians' return. Ranchers complained of broken fences and stolen cattle and claimed they scared women and children. Other settlers, such as John Fairchild and Henry Miller, befriended Modocs. Contradicting those who claimed that Indians extorted white settlers for "rent" in the form of hay for their horses, Miller maintained that he never paid them a nickel for his land. Instead, he hired them as herders. Miller also rejected the notion that the Modocs were "hostiles," saying that they "are not more insolent to whites than whites are to whites."

At a meeting convened by Maj. Elmer Otis, Captain Jack expressed his concerns. "We are willing to have whites live in our country, but we do not want them to locate . . . where we have our winter camps. The settlers are continually lying about my people and trying to make trouble." Captain Jack knew that some ranchers were demanding that the army round up his people and march them back to the reservation. But the trouble came from both sides. Shortly before the outbreak of the Modoc War, Indians stampeded the herd of George Miller, a Langell Valley rancher who was driving more than 300 steers to Arizona. Miller retrieved fewer than 40.

Adding to the tensions was the emergence of the Ghost Dance religion, the inspiration of Smohalla, a medicine man from Priest Rapids on the Columbia River. Smohalla taught his people how to enter a trance in which they would receive teachings from the spirits of their ancestors. He prophesied that an earthquake would expose the ancestors' bones and bring them back to life. Then, together, the living and dead generations would rid the land of white people.

A Nevada Paiute shaman, Tavibo, preached a variant of this faith. He believed that an earthquake would kill everyone, Indian and white, and that on that day those who held firmly to the ways of their ancestors would rise, reclaim the land, and renew the world as it was before the whites came to the West. A Walker River Paiute brought this teaching to the Klamath and Modoc people. Modocs who performed the trance-inducing circular Ghost Dance learned that when dancers fainted, their spirits met the spirits of the dead. These reunions in dreamtime would inspire their ancestors in the other world to join the living to fight against the white man. The Ghost Dance faith restored the power of shamans in the Pacific Northwest and encouraged intransigence among those who believed in it. One prominent Ghost Dance leader was Curly Headed Doctor, who led Modocs around a circle for five nights of visionary dancing at their winter village beside Lost River.

The settlers were restless. There were numerous attempts to talk Captain Jack into bringing his people back to the Klamath Reservation, and sixty-five settlers petitioned the Oregon governor to call out a militia of volunteers to round up the renegades. Governor Grover's response was to write an urgent letter to Gen. E. R. S. Canby, who commanded the Department of the Columbia. General Canby, however, awaited a decision from Washington, D.C., regarding the Lost River reservation that former Indian Superintendent A. B. Meacham had recommended for the Modocs. In the meantime, Canby instructed the officers at Fort Klamath to protect the settlers.

Canby had considerable experience with war and its aftermath. After fighting in the third Seminole War, he had helped remove members of the Cherokee and Seminole tribes to Indian Territory. He had come to believe that the Indians trusted him; by his report, they gave him a name that means "Friend of the Indian." Canby took part in the Mormon War of 1857 and helped quell the draft riots in New York City in 1863. He captured Mobile in 1865; and, having risen to brigadier general, he managed the military occupation of several southern states after the Civil War. He seemed the right man to handle the situation with the Modocs; and as President Ulysses S. Grant had just been reelected on a platform calling for peaceful resolution of conflicts with the Indians, the establishment of a reservation on Modoc land seemed a viable solution.

Yet the very month that Grant was reelected, in November 1872, Maj. John Green sent troops from Fort Klamath to Lost River to bring Captain Jack's band back to the Klamath Agency. One of the mysteries of the Modoc War is why he did so. He had received no order to take action, either from General Canby or from Col. Frank Wheaton, who headed the District of the Lakes under Canby's command. The commissioner of Indian Affairs had directed T. B. Odeneal, Meacham's replacement as Indian superintendent in Oregon, to remove the Modocs to the Klamath Reservation, "peaceably if you possibly can, but forcibly if you must." But that order did not bind the officers at Fort Klamath, certainly not without authorization from their superiors.

Major Green made this dangerous move after a visit from the reservation sub-agent, Ivan Applegate. Applegate's authority in this dramatic meeting came from his family, his life history, and the force of his character. He had immigrated to Oregon as a child along the Oregon Trail in the company of his father Lindsay Applegate and his Uncle Jesse, who had explored the southern route that became known as the Applegate Trail. His father had been the first agent for the Klamath Reservation. Jesse had established a large ranch on Clear Lake, which Lost River flows into, and Ivan's younger brother Oliver was in charge of the Modocs who had remained on the Klamath Agency. Ivan's family had not only opened up the Klamath Basin for white settlement but also had accepted responsibility concerning the Indians they and their followers had displaced. Moreover, as a member of a rescue party at age sixteen, Ivan had witnessed the death and destruction of a massacre at Bloody Point. It was his conviction that Modocs had to be brought under military control without waiting for the government to set aside a reservation for them. "The white settlers are very opposed to establishing a new reservation for this band of desperadoes," he explained in a letter to Odeneal, "and their determined opposition would keep up a continual conflict." Applegate may have warned Major Green that settlers were on the verge of attacking the renegade Modocs on their own unless the army acted immediately.

What happened was the worst of both worlds: an unplanned, undermanned military operation combined with an undisciplined and uncoordinated civilian foray. With Ivan Applegate serving as his guide, Capt. James Jackson led thirty-eight soldiers and a small pack train carrying supplies on an overnight march. Their destination: the Modoc winter village that was on both sides of Lost River. Their plan: to enter Captain Jack's camp at daybreak and surprise the Indians. They arrived before daybreak, while a group of settlers gathered in a gully on the other side of the river to offer support.

But those who were surprised that dawn were the soldiers and settlers. Scarfaced Charley, a member of Captain Jack's camp, had been gambling across the river in the camp of Hooker Jim and Curly Headed Doctor. Having returned in a canoe, Charley tripped climbing up the bank and accidentally shot off his gun. From the top of the bank, he saw the line of soldiers. His warning gave the Modocs time to rise from their beds and reach for their rifles before the troops entered the village.

Captain Jack remained out of sight, but some of the men left their lodges with weapons in hand. Ivan Applegate translated for Captain Jackson, who attempted to assure the Modocs of his peaceful intent. For the better part of an hour he asked them to disarm and return with him to the reservation. Then the settlers, believing everything was under control, came out of hiding and rode into Hooker Jim's camp. Seventeen armed Modocs, who had been watching the standoff across the river, turned toward the intruders. Oliver Applegate, who was among them, tried to defuse the situation by shaking Curly Headed Doctor's hand. "I have come to save you and befriend you," he announced. But Hooker Jim jumped into a canoe, trying to flee, and was brought back at gunpoint. Shortly thereafter, firing broke out on both sides of the river.

A failure of dialogue during an attempt to force compliance sparked the hostilities. The Modocs in Jack's camp were stacking their rifles on the ground when Captain Jackson ordered Lt. Frazier Boutelle to take Scarfaced Charley's pistol from him. Scarfaced refused, according to Jeff Riddle's published account, saying, "You got my gun. The pistol all right. Me no shoot you." Boutelle then walked toward him. "Here, Injun," he

said. "Give that pistol here, damn you, quick!" "Me no dog," was Scarfaced's response. "Me man. Talk to me like man. Me no 'fraid you. You
talk to me just like dog. Me no dog." That did it. A few more words flew
back and forth; then the two men shot at each other simultaneously,
both missing. As Hannah Arendt once observed, "Violence begins where
speech ends."

Across the river, the whites opened fire and the Indians scattered.
Several children, two men, and at least one woman were killed, among
them members of Hooker Jim's family. The rest of the Modocs fled, their
destination a natural lava-bed fortress south of Tule Lake. On the way,
Hooker Jim and his men killed a number of whites, including Henry
Miller, who had befriended and defended Modocs. No one had warned
them of the operation to round up the Indians. Now that they were dead,
war was inevitable.

Within the lava walls, about sixty people—men, women, and children—endured six cold weeks of winter before the curtain opened on
the second act. Against these families, the U.S. Army assembled a force of
330 men. The odds seemed overwhelming against the Indians, yet Curly
Headed Doctor insisted that they would prevail if they believed in the
Ghost Dance religion. He had hundreds of feet of red-dyed tule rope
made and laid around the lava-bed stronghold. No bullet could penetrate
that magical perimeter, he promised, no one within it would be harmed,
so powerful were the spirits. He erected a medicine pole from which hung
a mink skin and feathers and formed a circle lined with rock. It was there
that the people danced as they awaited battle.

Curly Headed Doctor drew from age-old shamanic knowledge in
strengthening the spirits of his people. Central to an Indigenous worldview is the idea that the Great Spirit is manifest in the natural world. An
example is the Karuk creation story in which the Klamath River origi-
nates through the tears of the Creator. He cries, fearing there will not be
enough food for the creatures he has made. Those tears, appearing as
rain and snow, are the source of the river and the life it sustains. So when
Curly Headed Doctor told his people on the eve of battle that a heavy fog
would blind the *Boston* invaders and prevent them from killing even one
of the *maklaks*, he was invoking not only the spirits of their ancestors but
also the Great Spirit itself.

On January 17, 1873, heavy fog over the Tule Lake Basin was a factor in frustrating the first federal assault. The terrain was another unexpected difficulty. From a distance, one does not see the waves of lava-rock walls that impede motion and provide cover to opposing forces. A carefully planned military operation became a rout, with Modocs shooting at will. That battle left thirty-seven soldiers and civilian volunteers dead or wounded. Not a single Modoc was harmed.

Concluding that the army could not dislodge the Indians from their stronghold without a great cost in lives, General Canby decided to negotiate an end to the war. Although Canby favored a Modoc reservation on Lost River, he was not authorized to offer one. Instead, he tried to pressure the Indians to surrender by bringing more troops and weapons into the lava beds. Surrender was not an option for Curly Headed Doctor and his followers. The prophecy had come true. They had reason to hope not only that their ancestors would continue to fight beside them but also that members of other tribes, together with their spirit people, would join them. White people had reason to fear a general Indian uprising if the war were not soon brought to a conclusion.

Hooker Jim and other members of his band—including Boston Charley, One-Eyed Mose, Long Jim, Rock Dave, and Humpy—had a personal reason for refusing surrender. They had killed settlers during their flight from the Lost River camp to the lava beds. Were their tribe to give up the fight and return to the Klamath Reservation, they would almost certainly be hanged.

Captain Jack was the political leader of the Modocs in the lava beds, while Scarfaced Charley was the military leader and Doctor the spiritual leader. Leadership among the Modocs, as among other California Indians, did not entail the power to command and compel obedience. Jack was able to represent the tribe in dealings with Judge Steele and others. He had the capacity many leaders have that the philosopher Immanuel Kant called an "enlarged mentality"—the ability to understand the perspectives of others, even people from another culture. This made him an effective negotiator. But in making fateful decisions, the tribe practiced a kind of face-to-face democracy, and Kintpuash was bound to act accordingly. One of his sentences, preserved in the Modoc language, expresses this commitment. The literal translation reads, "Where the heart of my people goes, there with it will I go."

Despite opposition from Doctor, Hooker Jim, and their followers, Captain Jack persuaded the besieged Modocs to enter into negotiations with the Peace Commission led by General Canby. He may have thought that he could reach an agreement with General Canby, or he may have been stalling for time, holding off another army assault until spring when the people could go into the mountains and live off the land while hiding from the military.

Captain Jack's dialogue with Commissioner A. B. Meacham between official sessions of the peace talks shows the Modoc leader's brilliance. In the exchange he recorded, Meacham rejected the notion of a Modoc reservation unless the tribe gave up the men who had killed settlers along Lost River.

"Who will try them," Jack asked, "white men or Indians?"

Meacham: "White men, of course."

"Then will you give up the men who killed the Indian men and women on Lost River, to be tried by the Modocs?"

"No, because Indian law is dead; the white man's law rules the country now; only one law lives at a time."

"Will you try the men who fired on my people, on the east side of Lost River, by your own law?"

"The white man's law rules the country,—the Indian law is dead."

"Oh yes, I see; the white man's laws are good for the white man, but they are made so as to leave the Indian out. . . . No, I cannot give up my young men; take away the soldiers, and all the trouble will stop."

This exchange may have made Hooker Jim's faction feel that he had considered negotiating away their lives. At a subsequent meeting in the stronghold, Hooker Jim insisted that Captain Jack kill General Canby at the next negotiation session. Hooker and his followers did more than speak; they humiliated Kintpuash. They pushed him to the ground, put a shawl over his shoulders and a woman's basket cap on his head, called him a coward and a white-faced woman, and told him to kill the general or be killed himself. When Jack arose, he agreed to "do a coward's act." The heart of his people had spoken. His only hope lay in changing the general's mind.

The arrangement for the next meeting included guarantees that both parties arrive unarmed. The Modoc woman who had translated for the Peace Commission, Toby Riddle, passed on a warning from a member of the Modoc band of their intent to kill the commissioners. Yet Canby refused to believe that they had treachery in mind. "I have had more or less connection with the Indian service for thirty years," he told Meacham, "and I have never made a promise that could not be carried out."

On April 11, 1873, Good Friday, Captain Jack shot General Canby dead. Boston Charley killed a second peace commissioner, the Reverend Eleasar Thomas. John Schonchin wounded Meacham, who saved his life by drawing a concealed derringer from his clothes. Schonchin, who had survived the Ben Wright massacre—in which forty-one Modocs were killed during what purported to be a peace talk—got his revenge, but at a heavy price.

After these killings, Gen. William Sherman ordered the "utter extermination" of the Modocs, and the U.S. Army launched a new assault on the Indian stronghold. Troops cut off the trail between the lava beds and Tule Lake, their water supply. That night, the Modocs fled their natural fortress.

One party of twenty-two warriors led by Scarfaced Charley did not go far. They ambushed Company E of the 12th Infantry, killing twenty-five and wounding sixteen men. Fears of an Indian uprising intensified. Then four Modoc warriors surrendered; and, in exchange for amnesty, Hooker Jim and three others offered to lead the army to Captain Jack. They finally caught up with him in a canyon near Willow Creek.

The captured Modocs were kept in a stockade at Fort Klamath awaiting the tribunal. The six leaders who went on trial had no defense counsel. Testimony included an account by the injured A. B. Meacham of the attack on the peace commissioners. Hooker Jim, turning state's evidence, said: "I have been a friend of Captain Jack, but I don't know what he got mad at me for." Captain Jack, speaking in his own defense, recalled going to the lava beds after the raid on his Lost River camp. "I had never told Hooker Jim and his party to murder any settlers," he said. Jack added that the four turncoats "all wanted to kill the peace commissioners; they all advised me to do it."

Predictably, the tribunal sentenced Captain Jack and five other men to death by hanging. President Grant commuted two of the sentences. After the executions of Schonchin, Black Jim, Boston Charley, and Captain

Jack, the men whose lives Grant had spared were imprisoned in Alcatraz. The other prisoners of war were marched in chains to Yreka and put on a train to Oklahoma, the territory that the nation had set aside for Indians. Some Modocs still live there. Others are members of the Klamath Tribes in Oregon.

The Modoc War was a tragedy—a double tragedy, one might say. The tragic flaw of both of its principal victims, ironically, was their humanity. Each understood the other's needs; both wanted a peaceful resolution of the conflict between their peoples. Yet both were under pressure to prevail—peaceably if they could, by force if necessary. "The essence of tragedy," I. F. Stone once wrote, "is a struggle of right against right. Its catharsis is the cleansing pity of seeing how good men do evil despite themselves out of unavoidable circumstances and irresistible compulsion."

No catharsis of cleansing pity came in the wake of the Modoc War. Instead, the event became the occasion for a medicine show celebrating the exploits of Daring Donald McKay, leader of the Warm Springs Indian scouts who helped the army fight and, in the last stages of the war, track down the Modocs. A. B. Meacham exploited his role in the war with a Wild West lecture tour, parading Modoc warriors before large audiences in San Francisco, Boston, and New York City. The star of the show was Toby Riddle, the translator for the Peace Commission, whom he renamed Winema, "little woman chief." Meacham credited her with saving his life during the Modoc assault on the commissioners. As Winema, Riddle perpetuated the Pocahontas myth of the Indian woman who loved a white man and chose civilization.

Like the wire news reports that made the war an international sensation, these pageants presented a struggle of right against wrong in which civilization prevailed against savagery, decency against treachery, good against evil. From the perspective of history, however, this conflict can be seen as an episode in a multi-century struggle of right against right. Its antagonists represented different relationships human beings have with the land—that of the hunter-gatherer and that of the farmer-rancher. A way of life in which the Modoc Plateau remained open to wildlife of the land, waters, and air, as it had been for millennia, gave way to one in which its waters would be channeled and its lands divided for cultivation to provide food to people living at great distances from the region.

Chapter Four
Reclaiming the Land

On the eastern ridge of the Tule Lake Basin, a father and son whose family has farmed and ranched this land for almost a century looked out over farmland that once was lake bed. Early in the twentieth century, Bob Anderson's father caught a boat from Sweden, lived for a while in Minnesota, and then continued west to Klamath Falls, where he raised potatoes and alfalfa on a forty-acre farm. Bob, who was born in 1920, recalls "handling hay and stacking hay and shocking it" as a boy. After returning from military service in World War II, he became eligible for federal Klamath Project land. A hundred parcels were distributed to veterans in a lottery. His number, 87, drawn from a pickle jar in a public ceremony, gave him his own farm.

That is where Bob's son John grew up. John Anderson described himself to Jack Kohler as a "born hunter, my first love. I was quite aware of the wildlife." During his childhood, "It was just unbelievable, the number of birds." Pointing toward Bloody Point, John told Jack about the old wagon tracks he saw when he was a kid. Old-timers, he said, spoke to him about pulling harnesses and pieces of charred wagons out of the ground back when the Bureau of Reclamation was digging ditches for the Klamath Project. John himself collected arrowheads and stone tools. "We'd get irrigators out there, they wouldn't irrigate," he said, they were so busy picking arrowheads up.

Two ways of life had collided in the Upper Basin as farming and ranching displaced the hunting, fishing, and gathering economy of the Native people. Farming and ranching entailed clearing the earth's surface so it could be plowed and grazed. That meant draining thousands of acres of shallow lakes as well as cutting down trees and other unwanted vegetation. "Irrigation came about," explained historian Rachel Applegate Good, "because of the necessity of utilizing more area than the swamp lands afforded, or to make valuable the desert portions upon which some of the newcomers had been forced to settle."

Indians also shaped the land to serve their needs. The sticks they used to dig up roots (an activity that inspired the Forty-Niners' pejorative "digger" for California Indians) stimulated soil, aiding the growth of favored plants like *epaw*. Their primary technology in the Upper Basin was fire. Ponderosa pines have thick bark, and their seeds survive intense heat. Frequent light burns hastened the growth of plants. Fire cleared out undergrowth in the forest that competed with seedlings while cycling nutrients, such as nitrogen from ceanothus leaves, into the forest soil. Open forests drew large game animals. Deer and elk hooves turned the soil over, while their browsing pruned the grasses they fed on.

The domestication of plants and animals that non-Indians brought across the continent marked a radical departure from hunting, fishing, and gathering. Not only were rivers and lakes, landforms, and soils transformed, but unwanted species were removed. Farmers eradicated what they called weeds in a never-ending struggle as shoots popped up and winds blew in new seeds. Undesired wildlife, from bears and wolves to geese and ducks, were hunted down or chased away. Gophers and moles, crop-loving insects, and crop-destroying fungi became the enemy.

By creating artificial landscapes and substituting domesticated species for wild ones, human beings drove a wedge between "man" and "nature." Technologies that used steam, electricity, and gas to replace human power with "horsepower,"—moving things faster and at greater distances than they had gone before, making things larger and more durable than people had built before—only widened the separation.

The experiential ties between human life and the natural world lost complexity and richness as a result. Knowing nature beyond what people needed to know to remake it for human purposes seemed to matter little. Most of the federally supported scientific research in the nineteenth century was in agronomy funded through the Department of Agriculture. Even in naturally bountiful regions such as the Upper Klamath Basin, for non-Indians the benefits of food production trumped the value of what the lands and waters provided without their intervention.

The settlers' way of life was new to the Klamath Basin, but it had proven itself over thousands of years, farther south in the Americas as well as in the Near East, Asia, Africa, and Europe. What large-scale domestication does, of course, is intensify food production so that animals and crops raised in one region can feed populations elsewhere. In its earliest stages, agriculture supported fifty to a hundred times more people than foraging, fishing, and hunting ever did. That proportion increased by orders of magnitude as technologies of farming developed, from the invention of the iron plow to the harnessing of draft animals, the mechanization of farm vehicles, and the green revolution of chemical fertilizers and pesticides.

There was a downside, however. The new intimacy between humans and domesticated animals—especially cattle, chickens, and pigs—generated new forms of disease: smallpox, flu, plague, measles, cholera, and tuberculosis. These became, as Jared Diamond wrote, "the major killers of humanity" due to the concentration of populations in cities that the growing of crops and livestock eventually made possible. By the time Europeans came in contact with Indigenous Americans, they had antibodies to counteract the viruses and bacteria that had devastated their ancestors. Indians had no such immunity. In this way, indirectly, domesticated food production undermined Indigenous populations.

Acquiring lands and giving them away for its citizens to settle was the major achievement of the United States during the first century of its history. The Louisiana Purchase, the Mexican–American War, the Oregon Treaty, and many wars and treaties with Indian nations put approximately two billion acres under the flag. The General Land Office did a "land-office business" disposing of public lands, mainly in 160-acre lots, from 1812 on. By mid-century, there were a million and a half farms. After the Civil War, railroads received land grants of nearly 200 million acres. Railroad companies sold most of those parcels to farmers, ranchers, and timber barons, including Frederick Weyerhaeuser, who bought up giant forests in the Pacific Northwest. The products of the buyers' industries were to ride the rails and build prosperity.

Those rails consumed more than the lands they crossed. Millions of ties held the Iron Road in place, all made of wood; and in those days before preservatives, every crosstie had to be replaced within seven years before it rotted. This demand felled 20 million acres of forest, arousing fears of a "timber famine." The forests of the Northeast were the first to be stripped bare. Then Midwestern woodlands turned into timber. The great forests of the Pacific Northwest, particularly the stands of tall, straight, even-grained ponderosa pine in southcentral Oregon, which extended across much of the Klamath Reservation, grew in importance as America moved West.

Congress after Congress passed law after law that turned public land into private enterprise. By the end of the nineteenth century, a billion acres had passed into private hands. Even lands that remained public were being stripped of minerals, trees, and other resources without penalty. Across vast tracts of untitled land, sheep and cattle populations exploded, increasing from the thousands to the millions during the 1880s. Competition over access to forage sparked range wars. A "deadline" was a ridgetop or other boundary that, when crossed, might trigger the killing of the transgressor's cattle or sheep. Barbed wire resolved some disputes but created a new problem. With foraging confined between fenceposts, overgrazing stripped away vegetation and eroded soil.

Indian reservations became part of the great giveaway with the Allotment Act of 1887. That legislation divided reservation lands into parcels owned by individuals. Swindles ensued. Non-Indians "adopted" Indian children without their knowledge, thereby acquiring their property. Indians living on timbered land were paid by settlers for trees taken off of it only to find that the deed of sale they signed gave away their entire allotment.

Klamath tribal lands, however, unlike reservations elsewhere in the country, were not sectioned off into allotments. That was the result of a lawsuit over the boundaries of the Klamath Reservation. According to Rachel Good, "A survey made in 1871 excluded about 600,000 acres of land in the Bly section that the Indians understood to be part of their reservation by the treaty of 1864." The Klamaths' litigation, asserting that the survey had cheated them of treaty lands, prevented the Allotment Act from taking effect on the reservation. Parcels within it could not be allotted to tribal members as long as the extent of their lands remained at issue.

Non-Indians had good reason to covet the Klamaths' forested lands. Before the farming economy took root, timber drove the prosperity of the Upper Klamath Basin. In 1877, William Moore built a mill on Link River whose capacity was 10,000 board feet per day. Thirty years later, his sons opened a mill on the shore of Lake Ewauna, between the Link and the Klamath Rivers, that turned out 50,000 board feet daily. But the harvest of logs had hardly begun. The timber industry in Klamath County took off after 1909 when the Southern Pacific Railroad line came to Klamath Falls.

As the fruit industry in California expanded, ponderosa pine was increasingly in demand to make boxes. The Ewauna Box Company, which started work in 1912, became the second largest box factory in the United States.

After the railroads arrived, the preservation of the ponderosa forest on the unallotted Klamath Reservation, which had remained intact due to the unresolved litigation over its boundaries, became an economic boon for the region. As the president of Pelican Bay Lumber Company observed in 1923, "The great forest resources of the Klamath Basin, quite conservatively estimated at thirty billion [board] feet, are sufficient to ensure the Klamath district of becoming the great white pine producing center of the entire United States." For tribal members, that meant per capita timber payments ranging from fifty dollars to several hundred, some years amounting to a million dollars for the entire tribe.

In 1929, the Weyerhaeuser Timber Company built a huge modern timber mill near Klamath Falls. To start the day's work, the boss shouted "Pull the plug." A worker did so, water flowed in, and the machinery began to operate. The mill's location by the tracks enabled it to run year-round. Other mills, such as the Collier outfit on Swan Lake, had to shut down each winter. Its horses were unable to haul lumber through the snow to the railroad to get the product to market.

A migratory workforce of about thirty bindle stiffs—so named for the blanket rolls, or "bindles," they carried from job to job—found seasonal employment at the Collier mill. Mornings before going to the forest, the lumberjacks warmed themselves at the fire in the cookhouse and ate great quantities of food. Once in the woods, men chopped down each tree with an ax, used crosscut saws to cut it into logs, and tied the logs to horses or oxen that dragged them to the mill.

In other western regions, such as the wheatfields of the Palouse in eastern Washington, bindle stiffs played an important part in agriculture as farmers relied on migrant labor when planting and harvesting their lands. But agricultural settlement of the Klamath Basin developed gradually, and most of the farms remained relatively small, constrained in many cases either by overabundance or scarcity of water.

During the early years of white settlement in the Klamath Basin, land speculators claimed but did not yet drain much of the wetlands. The federal government had given the states title to swamplands in 1860, so "swamp grabbers" could buy up lowlands and wait for land values to rise. Their purchases forced settlers to work upland areas that required irrigation. In the three decades between the Modoc War and the initiation of the Klamath Basin Project in 1906 by the Bureau of Reclamation, entrepreneurs dug ditches to move water from one place to another. The Linkville Water Ditch Company was incorporated in 1878 to divert water from Upper Klamath Lake. Knowing that Lower Klamath Lake had a higher elevation than Tule Lake, J. Frank Adams and the Van Brimmer brothers filed claims on land whose value others did not yet recognize.

Little of Lower Klamath Lake exists today, but until the early twentieth century it offered a form of wealth besides the water itself. Known as "the most profitable field in the West," the lake was the seasonal home to thousands of birds, many of which were killed for their plumes, to use on women's hats. The shooting of grebes, terns, and gulls produced bales of feathered birdskins for the milliners of New York City. Also popular were "game birds," ducks and geese that hunters shot for San Francisco restaurants. According to William Finley, who photographed birds of the Lower Klamath for national magazines, "when the birds are flying, each hunter will bag from 100 to 150 birds a day." The profusion of wildfowl in the Klamath Basin was a planetary phenomenon. Among the migratory birds that came and still come there from the Arctic Circle are plovers that travel as far south as the Argentine pampas. Rachel Carson described the mountainous Upper Basin as "the narrow neck of a funnel, into which all the migratory paths composing what is known as the Pacific Flyway converge."

Concern about wildlife in the eastern United States engendered a conservation movement that would have a major impact on the lands, waters, and skies of the Klamath Basin. In New York, Theodore Roosevelt and other aristocratic hunters founded a national sportsman's organization, the Boone and Crockett Club. Named for two legendary frontiersmen, the club concerned itself with the extinction of species and the destruction of their habitat. Roosevelt lamented the degradation of places such as the cutover Adirondacks, where he had gone hunting and fishing since boyhood. He had also gone on long horseback rides across a continent barren of bison, whose skies were no longer darkened by flocks of passenger pigeons, a once ubiquitous bird that would become extinct in 1914, and he foresaw the same fate for many species of game animals throughout the country. Not only were wildlife at stake as forests fell in the wake of cut-and-run speculators, producers of railroad ties, farmers, and other interests, but deforested lands were rapidly eroding. The stripping away of moisture-absorbing vegetation, especially on mountainsides, facilitated flooding, while the loss of topsoil threatened agriculture.

The long-term consequences of the degradation of places such as the Adirondacks had been widely recognized since the publication in 1864 of *Man and Nature,* by George Perkins Marsh. A former U.S. senator from Vermont and U.S. counsel in Italy and Turkey, Marsh warned that the abundant wildlands in the United States could become barren wastelands if America did not protect them. Lacking wild places, the country, like the once fertile lands in the Middle East and along the Mediterranean (whose sterility Marsh decried), would suffer irreparable economic as well as esthetic losses.

Meanwhile, John Wesley Powell, the charismatic one-armed explorer of the Grand Canyon, sounded another warning: the West, whose population was booming, was arid country. He took on the challenge of mapping the waterways of western lands. Recognizing that those who controlled headwaters could control the economic well-being of large territories, dominating and exploiting their neighbors, Powell recommended the formation of democratically run water districts, each in a watershed. Rather than divide the West into two-dimensional entities drawn with straight lines at ninety-degree angles, territorial boundaries would correspond to the terrain, from ridgetop to ridgetop, that governed the flow of water.

Powell's vision of terrain-based political boundaries went nowhere, yet his concerns about protecting forested mountains and other headwater regions did strike a chord. In 1891, congressmen influenced by Roosevelt and other Boone and Crockett Club members made a momentous yet almost unnoticed change in the nation's relationship with its land. They managed to insert into a bill designed to reform the Land Office—a notorious haven for corruption and fraud—an amendment permitting the president to establish forest reserves. For the first time, instead of getting rid of public lands, the United States was setting lands aside.

But what to do with them? That was the question a National Forest Commission set out to answer. In 1896, for three months, the commissioners traveled across the country, some on horseback, others by train. They divided into two camps, philosophically and politically. The head of the commission, Harvard's Charles Sprague Sargent, believed that the military should patrol the reserves to keep cattlemen and woodsmen out of them. John Muir, the great preservationist who accompanied the commission, agreed. The other approach was conservation. Commissioner Gifford Pinchot, a forester who belonged to the Boone and Crockett Club, had been inspired by Marsh's *Man and Nature*. Wealthy, young, and politically well-connected, Pinchot believed that the nation's natural resources must be used wisely so they could be conserved while also benefiting local communities. A forest, he argued, can be harvested sustainably in ways that produce a crop of trees without impairing its recreational, wildlife, and water conservation benefits. Were the reserves not to be used as an economic resource, in Pinchot's opinion, the federal government would be unable to maintain over the long run the political support it needed to preserve wild places.

The conflict between conservationism and preservationism would become intense after the San Francisco earthquake and fire of 1906, when controversy raged over turning the Hetch Hetchy Valley in Yosemite National Park into a reservoir for San Francisco's water supply. But during the commission's travels, the wizened Muir and the green Pinchot got along famously. Muir was a great talker, and Pinchot loved to hear stories of his wilderness adventures. Often they stayed outdoors at night when the other commissioners sought shelter. In the Klamath Basin, a thunderstorm surprised them one day as they and two fellow commissioners rowed across Crater Lake. After rowing hurriedly to the shore, Muir and Pinchot built a fire and stayed the night under heavy rain.

Conservationism became a guiding philosophy for Theodore Roosevelt's presidency, which took the nation by surprise with the assassination of William McKinley in 1901. The expansion of the forest reserves and the promotion of Pinchot as chief of a new national Forest Service in 1905 were manifestations of the idea that federal lands should be managed by experts for maximum public benefit. Conservationism was the natural counterpart of Progressivism, which sought to bridle the large corporations that were rapidly gaining control of the nation's resources. Roosevelt established the right of the federal government both to exercise regulatory control over corporations and to establish and manage public lands. During his presidency, Roosevelt added 20 million acres of national "forest" to the public lands, much of it mountain and open range, and he created five national parks, eighteen national monuments, and fifty-one wildlife refuges. Among the nation's earliest protected habitat for waterfowl was the Lower Klamath National Wildlife Refuge. By protecting a 187,000-acre area of marshlands and shallow lakes on the Pacific Flyway, Roosevelt responded to William Finley's writings and photographs, which had exposed the wholesale killing of migratory birds there.

The agencies Roosevelt established had a decisive impact on the uses of land throughout the Klamath region. More than 60 percent of the 10-million-acre basin is federal land, including eleven wilderness areas, six national forests, and the Klamath Project. Sixty-five percent of the land in the watersheds along the Klamath River, excluding the Upper Basin, is national forest.

Animating the federal government during Roosevelt's presidency and beyond was the belief that science would bring progress with limitless benefits for society. Projects run by scientific experts—whether foresters, engineers, or physicists—were sure to succeed. Early in the twentieth century, before relativity theory and quantum mechanics undermined the certainties of classical physics, Newton's laws plus Maxwell's equations inspired confidence not only that nature was a known quantity but also that its power could be controlled by those who understood it. Already people could communicate across great distances. Voices and images from the past were now preserved on film and wax cylinders. Electromagnetic energy promised to revolutionize industry and bring great advances in transportation while lighting the world. There seemed to be no limit to what science could do.

One place where scientific progress was sorely needed was the arid West, which was rapidly being populated as immigrants poured into the United States and crossed the continent by train. Water in the West had to be stored and channeled to meet the needs of cities and farms. Places such as the San Joaquin Valley of central California had too little water; the Klamath Basin to the north had too much. These "wasted lands" had to be reclaimed so that people could benefit from nature's bounty. With the headwaters of western rivers secured within the National Forest, science would distribute the water wherever it could best be used.

Underlying the faith in science were strong economic motives. What paved the way for the National Reclamation Act in 1902 were decades of failed attempts by entrepreneurs and corporations, irrigation districts, and states to fund and carry out irrigation projects in a responsible and fiscally sound manner. Despite their rugged individualism, westerners finally turned to the federal government to build the infrastructure that would irrigate their fields. Eastern interests saw that providing water to farms in the arid West would open up new markets while providing an outlet for workers whose agitation for improved labor conditions was leading, they feared, to a revolution.

Although the major goal of the new Bureau of Reclamation was to irrigate dry farmlands, one of its first projects helped settlers farm lands where water interfered with cultivation—the marshy, lake-rich terrain of the Upper Klamath Basin and the Lost River drainage. In order to do so, the Bureau required the states of Oregon and California to cede to the federal government its rights and title to Tule Lake, Lower Klamath Lake, and the land surrounding them.

Originally, the reclaimed lands were to be sold in eighty-acre home-steads. Payments would then subsidize reclamation of other lands. Yet the Bureau of Reclamation neither pressed farmers for their payments nor penalized those who farmed more lands than were allowed. New congressional appropriations provided what the Bureau needed to gener-ate new projects and, in the Upper Klamath Basin, to build headgates, irrigation canals, ditches, sumps, dams, reservoirs, hydroelectric turbines, and pumps to move the water.

The results seemed promising. In 1909, three members of the Czech Colonization Club in Omaha, Nebraska, investigated western lands in search of a region suitable for farming. After their journey, Land Com-mittee member Vaclav Vostrcil recommended "the project in Klamath Falls, Oregon, for our Czech settlement." Vostrcil had found that "the government project near Klamath Falls has the largest supply of water which we have seen along our tour." He considered the climate "mild and favorable" and the land adaptable for irrigation, "having a mild slope over the whole grade." Vostrcil admired the pine forests and fruit orchards of the vicinity, and, he noted, "here we saw the best alfalfa and the tallest rye." Because of the "abundance of fish" and "numberless flocks of ducks, geese, and pelicans," Vostrcil concluded, "for lovers of sports, the locality is perfect paradise." "This country has before it a big future," he predicted. "Lumber for building is cheaper here than in other western countries and water power guarantees the industry of small business." Another sign of the region's "big future" was the railroad, which had come to Klamath Falls only three months earlier.

Frank Zumpfe, who had traveled with Vostrcil on the selection tour, returned to Nebraska and immediately brought his family to the Klamath region. He bought sixty-eight acres near Tule Lake, with a large house and a broken-down barn on his land. Before the year was out, fifty members of the Czech Colonization Club had bought Klamath Project land. Meeting in the Zumpfe house, the Czechs established a settlement, the town of Malin, which they named for a kind of horseradish that grew in Czechoslovakia.

After World War I, Klamath Project plots were given to veterans who applied for them. In 1929, a West Virginia stockbroker came to the dry climate of the Basin for his health. As a veteran of the Great War, James Staunton applied for a Klamath Project homestead. When the market crashed, wiping Staunton out, he became a full-time farmer. The Stauntons had been a prominent family in the East, and they became so again in the Upper Klamath Basin. A Staunton ancestor had come to North America in 1635 on a mission from King Charles to solve the "Indian problem." Two and a half centuries later, James's father Edward was the mayor of Charleston, West Virginia. James built his fortune using the million-dollar estate that Edward left him and married a classical musician from Boston. Farming did not appeal to her at all, but James came to love it. His son John recalls his father taking up a clump of soil in his hand and saying to the five-year-old boy, "Isn't this great?"

On the Anderson farm, the major crops were potatoes, wheat, and alfalfa. Bob Anderson remembers digging potatoes, which he put into sixty-pound sacks that his father threw onto a wagon, and bundling wheat into stacks that were tossed into a threshing machine. One day, when Bob was seven or eight, his father was stacking hay when a horse kicked him in the nose, splitting his head open. The boy ran three miles to the neighbors, who took his father to the hospital. Not long afterward, the Andersons bought their first tractor, switching from horses to horsepower.

Life was Spartan for the early homesteaders on Klamath Project lands. They lacked electricity, running water, and telephones. Their farms were spread out, without roads between them. Some drivers used the railroad tracks to avoid being mired in mud. The homesteaders lacked political representation, police, and a fire department, and they had to create their own schools. They found the Reclamation Service unresponsive, and local officials could do little for them. A Tule Lake Community Club formed in 1928 to speak for the homesteaders and attempt to meet their needs. Through a series of losing battles, what it did succeed in creating were two schools and a sense of community.

For National Park Service historian Ann Huston, the story of the wildlife refuge on Lower Klamath Lake is "an outstanding illustration of the twentieth-century conflict between utilitarian (or reclamation) interests and conservation interests in the use of public lands." It is also an example of conflicting and apparently unreconcilable points of view. According to John Staunton, "Agriculture and wildlife go hand in hand because not only are we providing habitat, but we're also providing a food source." But some Klamath Project farmers did not want the government to establish bird refuges on agriculturally valuable land, even if most of those acres were on periodically flooded bottomlands. By 1915, their organization, the Klamath Water Users Association, had persuaded President Woodrow Wilson to reduce the Lower Klamath Lake Refuge from 80,000 acres to 53,600. Meanwhile, the Bureau of Reclamation used the Southern Pacific railbed as a dike to block overflow from the Klamath River that refilled the shallow lower lake. Its waters quickly evaporated under the abundant sunlight of the Upper Basin. By 1922, all that remained of the lake were fewer than 400 acres.

Nesting colonies of migratory wildfowl disappeared. Lands east of the lake became infested with grasshoppers, whose leaping population birds no longer restrained. Peat soils, which normally hold water, become a fire hazard when drained. When the peat soils formerly within the Lower Klamath Lake began to burn, rising clouds of ash obscured the skies of Klamath Falls. On October 26, 1922, the *Klamath Evening Herald* proclaimed: "DUST CLOSES SCHOOLS. Storm Held Worst in History of City: Housewives Aroused!"

William Finley described what was once Lower Klamath Lake as "a great desert waste of dry peat and alkali." President Calvin Coolidge responded in 1928 by establishing the Tule Lake National Wildlife Refuge. Six years later, President Franklin Roosevelt's Fish and Wildlife Coordination Act required agencies that managed water, including the Bureau of Reclamation, to consider the needs of wildlife as they planned their projects. A Federal Aid in Wildlife Restoration program provided funds to train professional wildlife managers.

The science of wildlife management made major advances during the 1930s in large part through the work of Aldo Leopold, a former Forest Service supervisor. Early in his career, Leopold had believed that wildlife could be protected by eradicating predators, but his advocacy of killing wolves to safeguard deer for hunters contributed to the eruption of deer populations that severely damaged wildlife habitat in the Kaibab Plateau above the Grand Canyon and elsewhere. Leopold came to understand that predator and prey depend on each other. In order to protect wildlife, one needs to manage not on a species-by-species basis but with a view to the entire ecosystem. Because the species of any given place are interdependent, their common habitat needs to be preserved both quantitatively and qualitatively. The challenge for human beings, as Leopold put it, is "to live on a piece of land without spoiling it."

Waterfowl require more than one kind of habitat for breeding, resting, and feeding. Not only wetlands are needed; so are shelter and food. Having crops such as alfalfa grow within the refuges, providing cover as well as nutrients, was not necessarily incompatible with the needs of wildfowl. The question was who would manage the refuges and whose interests — the birds' or the farmers' — would receive priority. Unquestioned was the assumption that scientifically trained managers would solve the problems created by having wildlife refuges within a region reclaimed for farming.

The experts appeared to redeem themselves in the 1940s when the Bureau of Reclamation built a 6,000-foot tunnel through Sheepy Ridge and pumped runoff water from the Tule Lake Basin up sixty feet into the Lower Klamath drainage. This feat of engineering refilled the wetlands, and birds began to return. By the fall of 1956 an estimated 7 million birds visited the Lower Klamath and Tule Lake refuges, offering innumerable opportunities for wildlife photographers in the William Finley tradition. John Staunton recalled that in the 1950s, when he was in high school, "I'd have to sleep out in the grain fields in the fall and shoot shotguns just to scare the birds off. There were so many ducks they would come and eat the grain before it was harvested." Some farmers went to great lengths to protect wildfowl. "I've had ducks that would nest out in the alfalfa field, where we had cut alfalfa," Bob Anderson recalled, "and there's a number of times when I uncovered a nest with a swather." At times he took the eggs and put them in incubators and raised the ducks in his backyard before setting them loose.

The question of whose interests came first was resolved in favor of agriculture by the 1957 Klamath River Basin Compact between California and Oregon. Farmers received prior water rights; the water needs of the refuges came last. Yet the Compact did not end the lobbying for preservation by wildlife advocates or the pressure that farmers put on the Interior Department to allow additional homesteading of refuge lands—if not to do away with the refuges altogether.

The Kuchel Act of 1964 seemed to resolve the debate by dedicating refuge lands for wildfowl conservation. This victory for wildfowl was also a victory for farmers in California's Central Valley, who feared that the loss of habitat for migratory birds in the Upper Klamath Basin would make their fields a prime breeding and feeding ground for denizens of the Pacific Flyway. The farmers of the Upper Basin also did well, winning the right to "optimum agricultural use that is consistent" with waterfowl management. Judging what was consistent was the Department of the Interior, which administers both the refuge and, through its Bureau of Reclamation, the Klamath Project.

Some of the crops grown in the refuges are cereal grains that wildfowl consume. John Staunton claimed that farming on the refuges "is the best thing that has ever happened in the Pacific Flyway for ducks and geese." Not only are portions of crops left in the wetlands for wildlife, but the refuge also grows a buffer of barley to draw wildfowl away from the farmers' lands. Gerda Hyde, whose ranch uses hundreds of tons of hay grown in the Klamath Marsh National Wildlife Refuge each year, maintained that the harvest stimulates the growth of plants within the marsh. "The hayed areas," according to Hyde, "produce more ducks and geese." But agricultural practices on and near the refuges do not protect wildfowl from pesticide pollution. The remains of Tule Lake in particular have served as a sump for the surrounding fields, concentrating pesticide runoff. In 1960, Rachel Carson reported that "the refuge staff picked up hundreds of dead and dying birds at Tule Lake and Lower Klamath."

In the decades since the Kuchel Act, the numbers of migratory wildfowl have dropped below a million a year. Even though the region remains, as Barry Lopez wrote, "one of the richest habitats for migratory wildfowl in North America," in times of water scarcity fish and farms have priority over visiting birds in their claims for water. Of the hundreds of thousands of acres of wetlands once found in the Klamath Basin—an area that varies seasonally and annually, according to climate and precipitation—less than a third remain; three-quarters of those wetlands, even within the national wildlife refuges, are farmed.

The concerns of Rachel Carson, noted in her epochal book *Silent Spring*, and the land ethic of Aldo Leopold, as explained in his posthumous publication *A Sand County Almanac*, would influence a new generation of conservationists, some of whom, at the beginning of the twenty-first century, took sides in the conflict over water use in the Klamath Basin. They called themselves environmentalists to distinguish their movement from the Roosevelt/Pinchot philosophy of conservationism. Pinchot, who founded the U.S. Forest Service with the aim of managing natural resources "for the greatest good for the greatest number over the long run," had been on the cutting edge of conservationism. But observers inside as well as outside that agency believed that it had betrayed these principles after World War II with its use of clear-cutting, herbicides, extensive road-building, and other high-impact forestry practices.

The environmentalists were more than latter-day conservationists. A formative experience for their generation was seeing the entire Earth from space, as photographed from an Apollo moonshot. Paradoxically, the extreme expression of world alienation—putting men on the moon—gave rise to the mythic symbol of the "whole Earth." Humans could now gaze on the precious home of life, itself even more of a divine and vital being than the gods for whom other planets are named. With the planet captured in one iconic blue image, it became obvious that, despite our experience of its vastness, it is finite. Some understood that humanity's impacts on Earth's life-support systems would have irreversible consequences.

The curtains opened on a new era of confrontation. In the Pacific Northwest, wild birds, in particular the spotted owl, once again played a symbolic role. But in the Klamath Basin it was wild fish, especially salmon, that took center stage.

Upper Klamath Lake and Mount Pitt (*OHS neg., CN 000393*)

Bloody Point, 1998 (*by permission of the Bureau of Reclamation*)

Indians harvest *c'waam*, or suckerfish, at the end of winter, 1905 (*courtesy of the Klamath County Historical Museum*)

Ben Wright, Indian fighter
(*OHS neg., OrHi 1711*)

George Nurse, founder of Linkville
(*OHS neg., CN 012867*)

Captain Jack and Schonchin John, imprisoned at Fort Klamath in 1873, were sentenced to death by hanging for their participation in the Modoc War (*OHS neg., OrHi 45974*)

Memoirs of My Life, John Charles Frémont, contained this lithograph titled "Tlamath River Attack by Tlamaths" (*OHS neg., OrHi 81088*)

Spool donkey, Klamath County, 1880s (*OHS neg., OrHi 45974*)

Klamath Falls (formerly Linkville) in 1905 (*by permission of the Bureau of Reclamation*)

William Finley and Herman Bohlman make camp at the Narrows on Lower Klamath Lake, California, in 1905 (*OHS neg., no. A-1603*)

Klamath Project canal under construction, which began in 1906 (*by permission of the Bureau of Reclamation*)

Requa cannery at the mouth of the Klamath River (*Schoenrock Photograph Collection, Humboldt State University Library*)

74

Robert Spott, who coauthored *Yurok Narratives* with A. L. Kroeber (*courtesy of the Phoebe Apperson Hearst Museum of Anthropology and Regents of the University of California, 15-16765*)

Sportsmen displaying hunted Klamath waterfowl in about 1920 (*courtesy of the Klamath County Historical Museum*)

Tule Lake Civilian Conservation Corps, 1935–1942, site of Japanese internment during World War II (*by permission of the Bureau of Reclamation*)

PART TWO
The Mouth of the Klamath

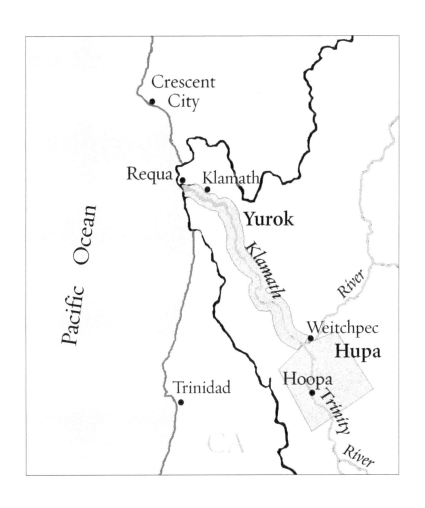

Chapter Five
Rekwoi

Where the Klamath River meets the Pacific, a sandspit narrows its channel. Like a tongue, the peninsula of sand reaches almost entirely across the mouth of the river. From year to year, even from month to month, that tongue moves, opening to the ocean in a different place. At times the river flows into the waves near the south bank; at times the waves surge into the river near the north bank; at times the channel where freshwater and saltwater mingle crosses the center of the sandbar. And there are months, during drought years or when too little water passes through Iron Gate Dam, when the river lacks enough force to reach the ocean at all. With the mouth closed, the estuary becomes a widening lake. Smolts, the juvenile salmon that prepare physiologically for their plunge into saltwater, have to wait for high tides to breach the barrier of sand before they can make their way into the ocean. Mature salmon returning from the ocean to spawn need tidal surges to carry them into the river.

As salmon pause in the estuary before beginning their ocean journey or wait among ocean waves before reentering the river, sea lions gather, barking expectantly. Pelicans and other seabirds fly in great flocks across the estuary, wheeling from shore to shore.

The mouth of the Klamath has stories to tell. Its riches of fish and birdlife, mollusks and lampreys, otters and other mammals that feed on the wealth of the river have sustained human life for thousands of years. Little more than a century ago, those who lived beside its banks prayed in sweathouses and occupied family homes made of redwood planks with sunken chambers and distinctive oval doorways. Today, on the north bank above the estuary, a scattering of houses, a network of trails, a large hotel beside Requa Road, and boat landings below it are the latest incarnation of Rekwoi, a village that has been continuously inhabited by Yuroks since ancient times.

In one of the old plank houses, whose wood was carbon-dated late in the twentieth century as being 600 years old, a Yurok elder, Geneva Mattz, used to spread out the family wealth of jewelry made of dentalium shells, buckskin dresses, and tightly woven baskets with geometric designs. Then she told stories—traditional stories and tales of her childhood when she lived in this house with her grandparents, before the two-story building where she lived when I met her was built just down the hill.

"We are the family that had a home by the road," Geneva told oral historian Helene Oppenheimer. "*Las awa*—that means a trail by the house. As those people there, back then, were intelligent men. They had Indian costumes; they could put on an Indian ceremony, things of their own, because other people helped. They could have Jump Dance and different things in their lives. As far back as is known, they were the Big People. We were called the Big People."

The plank house beside the trail was remarkable in a part of the world that lacks ancient structures. In modern-day California, an old building is a late eighteenth-century mission or an 1840s adobe fort. Native California was a country of villages made of perishable materials, such as reeds and grasses, planks and branches, bark and mud. Today, covering Indigenous village sites are the fields of farms, the water of reservoirs, and city pavement. In some cities, the paving of the original streets was mixed with fill from shellmounds.

By the twenty-first century, Geneva's "home by the road" lay in ruins. Yet, no less valuable than the house itself is the continuity of culture and of memory that it represents. In California, this land of gold, the destruction and displacement of Indigenous peoples was brutal and far-ranging. Massacre, enslavement, and the theft of Indian children were widespread. Still, the remoteness and relative geographic inaccessibility of tribal lands in the northwestern California portion of the Klamath region helped preserve continuity of culture in a few places.

Geneva Mattz used to tell her version of the Yurok creation story in the old plank house. It went like this: In the beginning of time, the Creator came to the mouth of the Klamath. He stood on the beach and thought: "This is a great river. I want to leave my children here. But there's nothing for them to eat." So the Creator called to the spirit of the river, Pulekukwerek, and said: "I want to leave my children here, but you will have to help me. They will need food. What can you do to help?" Pulekukwerek answered, "I can feed them. I can send fish." "That is good," said the Worldmaker. "But don't send the fish all at one time. My children need to have different kinds come in at different months. That way they will have something to look forward to and they won't get tired of it." And so Pulekukwerek made eels for the winter run, candlefish for the spring, and sturgeon for the summer. Greatest of all, Nepewo entered the river each fall, leading the salmon people. Then the river spirit made human people. He showed them the great guardian rocks he had put on either side of the river's mouth to protect them. He showed the people how to catch the food of the river and how to prepare the food of the land. When he had finished, Pulekukwerek walked to the top of the hill. He said: "My people, I am leaving you. I have created you in this place. I have left the fish, the acorns and all the things you need to eat. You will never want for anything as long as you remember me."

Geneva gathered clams as a girl and picked seaweed as she and her grandmother walked along the beach. "There would be a fish thrown on the shore for her and she put it in her basket and then sometimes there would be a little sturgeon thrown on the shore," recalled Geneva. Or Grandma Brooks would find "a puddle of crabs just full in there — or eels." They would stay on the beach "maybe a couple of days and we just had anything we wanted to eat, [cooking] them there in camp, right on the beach."

The life of the estuary and along the ocean shore nearby remains abundant and various. In 2000, when Carlos Bolado, preparing to direct a documentary about the water crisis in the Klamath Basin, made his first trip to Requa, he saw an otter in the river, seals in the breakers, and a parade of pelicans above them. He met two teenagers armed with eeling hooks to catch lampreys. As one built a fire on the beach with a single piece of paper and a mound of driftwood kindling, the other told Carlos that they would be eeling until late at night.

Lamprey eels, clams, and seaweed continue to serve as food sources near the mouth of the river, but it is salmon that feeds the imagination as well as the stomach. During that initial visit, Carlos observed many tributes to salmon: the large redwood salmon sculpture that hangs over the entrance to Klamath, the reservation town on Highway 101 just south of the turnoff to Requa; a salmon in neon in a store window; signs advertising "authentic Indian-style salmon jerky."

More than a tourist attraction, salmon is the totemic spirit of the region and the key to its history. It was the recurring superabundance of food that must have drawn human habitation here millennia ago and that permitted permanent residence along the river, quite in contrast to the semi-nomadic lifestyle of most California Indians. It was the canning industry that gave non-Indians incentive more than a century ago to allow the continuing residence of Yurok tribal members along the river, for who could better catch salmon for canning than they? And after the State of California outlawed the Indian fishery in 1933, it was the insistence of members of Geneva's family and others on continuing to fish regardless of the law that eventually led to federal recognition of Yurok fishing rights and the reinstatement of their riparian reservation.

Geneva's ancestors enjoyed a location of extraordinary beauty and natural abundance: the mouth of one of North America's great salmon-producing rivers. Salmon entering the river here are at their peak of weight and oily flavor, having completed feeding in the ocean and not yet having spent themselves in the upriver struggle to spawn.

No one knows how long Yuroks have lived along the forty-two miles on the Klamath between the estuary and the confluence with the Trinity. Most of the tribe's fifty-four known villages were along the river, but this was not the full geographical extent of the tribe. Yuroks also inhabited ninety miles of the coast, living in scattered villages mainly to the south of the Klamath, all the way to Tsurai, now the town of Trinidad.

The Klamath Basin marks the southern boundary of the Pacific Northwest. Accordingly, the Yurok and Karuk, the Klamath River tribes, the Hupa who live along the Trinity, and the Klamath Tribes of the Upper Basin represent the southernmost extent of Pacific Northwest Indian culture. The Yurok language is Algonkian, a language family represented nowhere else in this part of the world except among the Yuroks' southern neighbor, the Wiyot. Algonkian tongues are spoken by tribes of midwestern, north-eastern, and southeastern North America. Among American place-names derived from Algonkian words are Massachusetts, Connecticut, Chicago, Wyoming, Wisconsin, and Mississippi. In contrast, the Hupa, speaking an Athapaskan language, are linguistically related to salmon-fishing tribes of Alaska and northern Canada. They are also related to the Tolowa who net salmon in the Smith River along the California-Oregon state line to the north of the Klamath. The Karuk speak a Hokan tongue linked to languages widespread across California.

Did the Yuroks arrive later than these other tribes that, as their linguistic family ties suggest, have a wide network connecting them with other cultures of the West? It is possible that the ancestors of the Yuroks displaced the Tolowa or their predecessors, or perhaps a Hokan-speaking tribe, from the lower portion of the Klamath River. It is also possible that a party of Algonkian warriors, having traveled across the country and "discovering" the Klamath, married into the downriver culture, maintaining their language while adopting a new way of life. Linguistic evidence, which has tracked one Algonkian migration from the northeast to what today is the southeastern United States, may one day put these theories to the test.

Yet, as far as traditional Yuroks are concerned, they have always lived in their homeland, having been created there, like the food they depend on, by the spirit of the river. One version of the creation story, told to A. L. Kroeber in Requa in 1906 by Petsuslo of Pekwon, describes the making of the river, the ocean, all species of fish, animals of all kinds, and trees to make fire and build boats so that human beings might live in this world. The Yuroks lived at the center of an ocean-girdled cosmos bisected by the Klamath River. The cardinal directions were upstream and downstream. Salmon were perceived as preeminent among the many resources that humans could rely on.

More than other foods that are hunted and killed, salmon come as a gift from the gods. An anadromous fish, salmon enter the ocean early in their life cycle, range thousands of miles through salt waters, then, migrating homeward, find their way to their birth river and spawning grounds. Following their schedule of happy returns, they swim in large numbers toward the human settlements that await them. As salmon make their way through narrow channels, as they crowd streams, enter rock-lined pools, and flop by the banks of rivers and creeks, they can be caught by hand, speared, or netted.

The salmon's predictable runs enabled the people of the river to build elaborate weirs to catch them in large numbers—fish dams that were among Indians' major engineering achievements. The catching of this food was highly regulated in ways that make ecological sense today, for no salmon were caught until enough had passed upstream to ensure the spawning of abundant fish for future years.

The first run of the year, spring chinook were once the most abundant of the runs. Their powerful bodies ran the entire length of the Klamath River into the Upper Klamath Lake and up the Sprague and Williamson Rivers to spawn. The spring salmon of the Klamath, like the now-extinct royal chinook of the Columbia River, were the largest salmon, their oily red flesh regarded by both Indians and the canning industry as the best to eat.

What governed the Indigenous salmon fishery was a ritualized relationship between salmon and human beings. The name of the ancient town Rekwoi comes from the singing and speaking to Nepewo during the First Salmon ritual that once occurred at the mouth of the river. Before this ceremony took place, the eating of salmon caught in the estuary was forbidden to all except the elderly.

Robert Spott, who coauthored *Yurok Narratives* with A. L. Kroeber, described the last First Salmon ceremony. It occurred sometime between the spring of 1865 and the spring of 1870, and Spott's uncle and adoptive father, Captain Spott, took part. Haaganors, to use Captain Spott's Yurok name, was assistant to the formulist, the old man who set the day for the First Salmon ritual forty days in advance. The formulist took charge of preparations for the event and conducted the ritual itself. The ceremony included encounters with two salmon: the "first salmon," Nepewo, who after a dialogue with the formulist was allowed to proceed upriver, and another fish who, following the leader, became the first salmon to be speared in the estuary that year.

Both encounters dramatize humanity's relationship with this all-important fish. Nepewo's arrival was greeted by shouts from men who, upon seeing him, stood back from the shore. Holding a harpoon, the formulist walked to the water's edge. When the salmon neared, he shouted, "Stop running," and Nepewo, according to Spott, "seemed to stop moving." Then the old man stepped back and said, "Now run again!" The fish did so until ordered to stop once again. After the fifth time, the formulist told the salmon to leave his scales at every fishing place he would pass all the way to the head of the river. "Now run on!" he ordered, at which point, "just as if he understood everything," the fin of Nepewo disappeared. The five-stage formula was repeated when the second salmon arrived, only this time, at the end, the formulist ordered the fish to stop. Once it was speared, "across the river at Rekwoi all the women wailed and cried as at a death."

The ritual continued when the fish, still struggling for life, was lifted onshore. Recounted Spott: "The old man said, 'I am glad I caught you. You will bring many salmon into the river. Rich people and poor people will be happy. And you will bring it about that on the land there will be everything growing that there is to eat.' At the end of each sentence the salmon answered by flapping its tail."

Catching the first salmon of the season had significance beyond the return of a major source of food. Traditional Yuroks understood that salmon are somehow responsible for the renewal of life on land as well as in the river. This is a biological fact. Salmon bring nitrogen from the ocean to the forest floor via the intestines of mammals that eat them. But for Yuroks, it was and remains a spiritual reality that their ceremonies are part of the annual cycle of life within their world.

Contemporary knowledge of traditional Yurok culture and of the tribe's precontact history is due in part to the contributions of the Spott family. In 1900, when Kroeber first came to the Klamath River to do research, Captain Spott, then an old man, and his brother-in-law became his cultural interpreters. Kroeber may not have noticed Robert, who was twelve that year, but Captain Spott had already recognized the boy's "excellent memory" and his "extraordinary sensitivity to the value of his native culture," qualities that Kroeber described many years later. Spott, who had been born six years before non-Indians first came into Yurok country, taught the boy everything that he could, including his own recollections, during long sessions in the family sweathouse. Robert also learned from his grandmother and others, including his father's contemporary Requa Fanny, and a mother and daughter who were known as Mrs. Tipsy and Fanny Flounder. Both women were prominent shamanic healers, or sucking doctors.

Captain Spott had sent him to school to learn English until he was nine, then removed him, most likely to ensure that the boy not be unduly influenced by whites. Other Yurok children were by that time forced to attend boarding schools far from home, where they were mixed with children of different tribal and linguistic backgrounds and were punished for speaking their language. When Captain Spott died in 1911, Robert, then twenty-three, carried a unique heritage. He knew "as much, on the whole, of old Yurok ways and beliefs as the men of his father's and grandfather's generation," wrote Kroeber. As Florence Shaughnessy, a traditional Yurok matriarch, recalled a half-century later, "he realized that in his family, he was the last." Yet Spott, like many Indians of his generation, enlisted to serve his country in World War I. After fighting in the trenches in France and being awarded the Croix de Guerre for valor in combat, he returned home to the Klamath River.

In 1923, Kroeber, who had concluded his previous research on the Klamath in 1909, sought out his old informants. He was dismayed to learn that they had died. When encouraged to look up the young veteran on a subsequent visit, Kroeber was delighted to discover a man who both knew his culture thoroughly and spoke English well. It was a difficult decision for Spott to entrust his knowledge to Kroeber. He told one friend "how it felt to be looked at like you were a bug. That is what the anthropologist did."

The decisive moment for Spott came in 1926 when he was asked to join Kroeber in an address to the Commonwealth Club on the "Conditions of California Indians." Driving in his Model T on Requa Road, Spott visited Fanny and George Flounder, his aunt and uncle. He explained that he had been asked to speak before a San Francisco audience wearing ceremonial regalia for what Kroeber called a world renewal ceremony, the Jump Dance. Fanny Flounder advised him to get on the train and go to the city. Spott could not have anticipated becoming a family friend of Alfred and Theodora Kroeber. But he did. He spent summer vacations with them for a number of years until his death in 1953. The collaboration between Kroeber and Spott, whose fruit is *Yurok Narratives*, offers a rare contribution to history: unusually detailed accounts of precontact events involving Native peoples and an eyewitness account of a first encounter between Yuroks and European Americans from an Indigenous point of view.

Requa Fanny told Spott "that she saw the first white people come to Welkwäu," a village on the south bank of the estuary, across from Rekwoi. They arrived in "a large boat . . . with trees on it. She meant the masts of course. They landed in small boats." The mariners camped by Oregos, a monumental rock on the north bank. The trail from Rekwoi to the sandspit passes by it. Oregos, whose shape resembles a woman carrying a burden basket, faces those who walk along the trail. She is considered a guardian spirit. "The people of Rekwoi went into hiding," according to Requa Fanny, but their curiosity was irresistible. "In the morning the people began to peep over the edge of the slope, and some of the children ventured down." Fanny, who was "a good-sized girl then," was among them, wearing a basket cap.

> A white man who was cooking took a potato from the ashes and gave her half of it. She did not know what it was and put it in her cap. Then he gave her something with holes in it and gestured that she should eat it. It was hardtack. She tried it and it tasted like wood, she said. The other children called to her, "You will die if you eat it."

This episode came more than three centuries after the conquest of Peru that gave Europeans the potato. It was not the first Yurok exposure to non-Indians. In 1775, when a Spanish expedition commanded by Don Bruno de Hezeta landed in Trinidad Bay on today's northern California coast, four canoes carrying twenty-four members from the Yuroks' southernmost village, Tsurai, met his ships. In 1827, fur traders with the Hudson's Bay Company entered Yurok country and reported seeing "various trading articles from American ships." The following year, explorer Jedediah Smith met Yuroks after traveling to the confluence of the Trinity and Klamath Rivers. The Yuroks had iron arrow points and wanted to purchase knives.

Requa Fanny's encounter was the first known incursion of non-Indians into the estuary of the Klamath River. This took place in the 1840s, not long before the Gold Rush changed California and the lives of its Indigenous peoples forever.

Thanks to Robert Spott, memories from the years preceding the Gold Rush on the Klamath River have been preserved. Between 1830 and 1840, Requa Fanny's family was involved in a war between Yurok and Hupa villages. Various people were Spott's sources for the story, probably including Fanny, although this event took place either before she was born or when she was an infant.

What makes his account of intertribal conflict significant in light of subsequent events is that, like every other war in the region's history, it was a fight over resources. In the belief that downriver people had used a poison to stop the salmon run from reaching their territory, a crowd of angry Hupa men gathered in front of a sweathouse in Weitchpec at the confluence of the Trinity River, which flows through Hoopa Valley, and the Klamath. A Rekwoi woman who had married into the family who owned that house had gone up the hill for firewood. Returning, she encountered these men. When the Hupas accused her, "Why do you make starvation? People are dying all about," the woman from Rekwoi made a highly insulting ten-finger gesture and said, "Tsäuh!" a curse that Spott did not translate. Then the woman turned her back. As she knelt to crawl through the small oval doorway of her house, a Hupa arrow shot her in the rectum, killing her. At this point other Yuroks joined the fray, and one of the Hupa men was killed.

Although the fight had occurred in Weitchpec, the Hupa held the village of Rekwoi responsible for their man's death. Coming down the Trinity and the Klamath in boats, a Hupa war party surrounded Rekwoi when most of the villagers were surf fishing on the coast to the north and only old people and some women and children remained. The Hupas burned the sweathouses, killing a number of elderly men. They burned all the family houses but one, that of a family a Hupa woman had married into.

Requa Fanny's aunt was hiding in a manzanita bush when a Hupa warrior pierced her thigh with an arrow. She managed to stay quiet and hidden. The invaders then took a girl from Rekwoi captive and went upriver to Weitchpec, where they did a war dance, prodding the girl with arrows to make her dance with them. This infuriated a man who was related to the "by-the-trail" family of Rekwoi, the ancestors of Geneva Mattz. After trying and failing to stop the war dance, he gathered his own war party, which included members of the Tolowa people from the Smith River and Yuroks from Rekwoi and other villages. Boating up the Trinity, these men attacked Takimildiñ, a Hupa village and ceremonial center, killed people, and burned everything, "including the sacred house and the cemeteries." Then they war danced in celebration beside a creek in Hoopa Valley.

The Hupa struck back six months later. Takimildiñ villagers hired warriors from the Whilkut, Chilula, and South Fork Hupa tribes to augment their forces. Traveling downriver along the Klamath, they captured weapons and canoes. According to the Hupa account, "They reached Requa at dawn, surrounded the village, and killed almost all of its residents, including a Yurok leader who tried to hide in a grave. Then the Hupa loaded their canoes with valuables and returned to Takimildiñ."

The story of the war illuminates a system of alliances between various villages within the region, including the Tolowa on the Smith River, and the Hupas' use of mercenary soldiers from their Athapaskan-speaking neighbors. Participation in a conflict was not automatic. The Rekwoi man who sought Tolowa help was told that only if the farthest village was willing to take part would men from other Tolowa towns join him. The consent of that village, Hinä'ig, depended on what "the old man there" agreed to.

The river tribes, each speaking a different language, had a system of international law that was used to settle crimes and acts of war once and for all. Robert Spott knew that a settlement was made following these Hupa-Yurok hostilities, but he did not know the details except that the captive girl was returned to Rekwoi and that a sister of the woman who was killed in Weitchpec was given in marriage to a Hupa household.

Robert Spott gave Kroeber an account of a different dispute that includes the ritual that sealed the deal. His story told how the "by-the-trail" family of Susie Brooks, Geneva Mattz's grandmother, acquired sea lion flipper rights. To understand the settlement, one must know that families had property rights that depended on their geographical location. If a whale came ashore between specified points on the coast near the Brookses' family house in Rekwoi, the carcass with all of its flesh, oil, bones, and skin belonged to them. Similarly, no one could fish from the base of Oregos without that family's permission; and if one caught fish there, then the family claimed the right to a share of the catch. These rights were a form of wealth. The right to take sea lion flippers, for example, could be sold, traded, or relinquished in the settlement of a dispute.

Given the wealth and power that accrued to a lineage of Big People who had a good position in the world, such as the Brookses, it is not surprising that men wanted to marry their women. But that was costly. One had to acquire a treasure, typically including strings of money, the tusk-shaped dentalium shells used in dance regalia, in order to qualify as a suitor. Women also brought dowries into a marriage. When a woman from the Rekwoi house of *higwo* married into a family in Omen, the Yurok village beside a lagoon on the coast to the north, "her father as part of her dowry gave her the flipper rights so that her children would have higher standing in the world."

Unfortunately, one of the Brookses' relatives in Rekwoi had killed a member of the Omen family that the woman from *higwo* married into. When a man who was kin of the killer passed Omen as he walked north on a visit to the Tolowa, the husband of the *higwo* bride attacked him, killed him, and left him lying on the beach. A Rekwoi widow, returning home after gathering seaweed, informed the villagers of this death. As the people of Rekwoi prepared to attack the people of Omen, Captain Spott, "who was then a big boy," rushed toward Omen unarmed to sound a warning.

As Robert Spott described it, the Rekwoi men arrived "like a swarm of bees, with bows and in full fighting equipment, and the Rekwoi women behind, wearing maple-bark dresses. The dead man's mother threw herself right on his body." It was Captain Spott's uncle who lifted her up, turned her away from the corpse, and insisted on a settlement. The brother of the dead man "wanted first to kill the killer," but he agreed to settle "because so many people of Rekwoi and Omen were kinsmen."

The deal was made a week after the funeral of the man from Rekwoi. A negotiator from Tolowa came to speak with both sides. Captain Spott's uncle served as translator, since the Tolowa man did not speak Yurok. Also involved in the settlement were a repeater, who made sure that all parties understood what was being said, and a judge who explained the implications of the agreement. In this case, the settlement required the killer's wife to renounce the right to sea lion flippers that she had brought into her marriage. The judge explained that even were she to divorce, she could not claim that right ever again. It would belong to the family of the murdered man from Rekwoi.

Then came a reconciliation ceremony. "This is when the two lines of enemies approach and shake hands and each side eats the other's food," Robert Spott explained. There was a crowd watching, people from Smith River and from several Yurok villages as well as the people of Omen. The ritual began as a dance. "A dancer was first sent out from the Rekwoi side because they had done the first killing." This man, dancing between the lines, was a "person who has supernaturally acquired bravery and strength." Next a dancer came from the Omen side, a hundred yards away or more, and did the same. Then the Rekwoi dancer returned, and behind the two men the lines of enemies moved closer to each other.

Behind the lines stood women in maple-bark dresses holding clubs in their hands. When the lines "were about ten yards apart, the women stepped out in front of the lines to prevent any sudden shooting at the killer. That is why they carried the clubs—to knock down any bow that might be raised." Soon each man in each line shook hands with his coun-terpart on the other side. Then "the two double lines passed through each other and shook hands with the women and children."

There followed visits from each side to the campfire to eat each other's food. "Now it was all settled, and they were friends again," concluded Spott. According to Kroeber, though, "such efforts were not always successful." He attributed this in part to the people's individualism and intensity of feeling and also to the fact that there was no political power to enforce a reconciliation. Bonds between villagers were strong but "did not transcend those of kinship." Although the tribes of the region recognized and jointly participated in the system of laws and rituals, no political power had the right to use force or the ability to keep the peace.

Before a new kind of law, and of lawlessness, came to their country, Yuroks were a people in a very different sense than they are today—a federally recognized tribal nation with a governing tribal council and an official roll that defines who can be counted as a member. At the time of the Gold Rush, their primary authority existed within families. What 2,600 people (as estimated by anthropologists) then living in the Yurok villages had in common was language and culture.

They did not have a shared identity. "Yurok" is a Karuk word meaning "downriver." The people downriver of the confluence of the Trinity and Klamath Rivers and along the coast seven miles north and thirty-five miles south of the estuary did not refer to themselves collectively. Their identity encompassed their family, including kin who lived elsewhere, their village, and their place in the world. They did have a larger identity as expressed in a term that meant "the human world," but that world embraced all of the tribes they came in contact with, not only those known today as Yurok.

What made the Yuroks "Yuroks" was the U.S. government. In 1851, federal agents signed treaties with Indians throughout California, papering over the invasion of their lands by gold-seekers and pioneers. Headmen of five of the villages known today as Yurok put marks on a document written in a language that they did not understand. In this manner, they represented, without authorization, a group of people who did not recognize their shared membership in a "tribe" or any common entity besides the human world.

Yet there were ties of language, culture, and family among these people, and some of these ties have persisted in spite of the radical changes of the last century and a half. A number of precontact Yurok village sites located on or near the Klamath River are Yurok villages today. At least one, Rekwoi, later known as Requa, has been continuously inhabited by members of families that lived there before the days of gold. Stephen Powers published a description of "the village of Rikwa" in 1877, which, he said, "tinkles with the happy cackle of brown babies tumbling on their heads with the puppies: and the fires within the cabins gleam through the round door holes like so many full-orbed moons heaving out of the breast of the mountains." Theodora Kroeber was referring to Yuroks of Rekwoi and other villages in 1900 when she wrote that "some, unlike most western Indians, were still living on their own ancestral land when Kroeber first reached them, their life physically much as it had been before the Gold Rush."

As gold-seekers, coming from around the world in the mid-nineteenth century, rushed into the hills, mountains, and valleys of northern California, how is it possible that any of the Yurok villages could have survived?

Geography was destiny. The Yurok portion of the Klamath River lies west of the major gold-mining areas in the Klamath Basin. To get to the goldfields along the Trinity River and along the Klamath River upstream from its confluence with the Trinity, miners sailed to Humboldt Bay, then set off cross-country from the optimistically named city of Eureka, or they traveled farther north to Trinidad Bay, where the southernmost Yurok village then existed. Carl Meyer, a German who wrote an account of the Indians of Trinidad Bay in 1851, explained that his ship's original destination was "the mouth of the Klamath River. Our captain, however, decided that he would land us thirty-five miles away, at Trinidad Bay, for he believed that at this time of the year the mouth of the Klamath would be sanded up like that of the Humboldt [Bay]."

The captain was probably right. Even when there is a channel through the sandspit, the passage is usually too narrow for a ship to traverse. The tongue at the mouth of the Klamath helped the people of Rekwoi remain in their north bank village as others along the Klamath were driven from their homes. Even so, their location did not forestall an influx of would-be settlers and their exposure to a new kind of warfare, never to be settled by reconciliation rituals, during the dangerous Gold Rush years.

Chapter Six
Between Two Worlds

The notion that gold has value when extracted from the land and the waters it enhances would not have been difficult for Yurok Indians to grasp even before the Gold Rush. They, too, had money—dentalium shells taken from the sea near Vancouver Island. It was also rare and beautiful. They might have understood Columbus's statement that those who possess gold have "all the needs of the world." Yuroks prayed for money, fasted for it, gambled for it; for them, as for the newcomers to California, money was the best way to rise in status.

Still, they did not need money to survive. Their lands, waters, and skies gave them everything they needed. It must have been difficult for Native Californians to comprehend a way of life in which the acquisition of wealth entailed destruction of the bounty nature provides. Yet from the Gold Rush on, that is what they witnessed. The economic system for which gold was a medium of exchange generated wealth by extracting goods from the natural world in ways that destroyed the productivity of life-sustaining lands and waters.

Even though Yuroks were less directly affected by the miners' incursions than the other Klamath River tribes, the effects of the Gold Rush were devastating. As Joaquin Miller observed,

> The Klamat [sic], which had poured from the mountain lakes to the sea as clear as glass, was now made muddy and turbid from the miners washing for gold on its banks and its tributaries. The trout turned on their sides and died; the salmon from the sea came in but rarely on account of this; and what few did come were pretty safe from the spears of the Indians, because of the coloured water; so that supply, which was more than all others their bread and their meat, was entirely cut off.

These effects persisted for more than a decade and a half after the mining began. In 1865, a surgeon reported to the federal government:

> Those who saw the Klamath and Trinity rivers in early days say that during the summer months they ran as clear as crystal, and thronged with salmon from the sea; now they are muddy streams and almost deserted by the fish. [Indians] gaze sadly into the muddy waters, despoiled almost of their finny prey by the impurities from the sluice-boxes of the miners at the head of the stream. . . . Their salmon fishing is destroyed to a very great extent, and with it one of their chief means of subsistence.

Land along the Klamath River was of value, salmon or no salmon, and would-be settlers lost no time in trying to reap its rewards. On March 16, 1850, the *Cameo*, a brig from San Francisco, dropped men off north of the river. Climbing a coastal hill overlooking the north bank of the Klamath, the settlers' party saw Yuroks for the first time. The Yurok men, who had been fishing, armed themselves with long knives while the women hid in the brush. As their leader made a lengthy speech to the newcomers, the women emerged and began inspecting the men from the *Cameo*. A quick-thinking member of the party, Herman Ehrenberg, offered the women beads and trinkets. Eventually, his group persuaded the Indians to ferry them across the river to the south bank. There they claimed 160 acres, naming their settlement Klamath City.

In October, the *Pacific Daily News* of San Francisco extolled the potential of the new city.

> The river abounds with the finest salmon, the valleys with deer and elk, the forest with a noble growth of pine and redwood, fit for piles, spars or lumber. The mines of the Klamath and its tributaries, among which are the Salmon, Shasta, Trinity and Ross [later named the Scott] Rivers, are paying better than many other mining sections of California, [and] during the past months have averaged from one to three ounces of gold per day to a man.

Thirty houses and stores went up in Klamath City, including a fort made of iron. The settlement did not last a year. Its inhabitants had hoped that large boats could anchor on the river bar or sail into the estuary and bring goods in from the sea. But that fall, the *Tarquin* was wrecked attempting to cross into the river. In addition, twenty-nine settlers died, killed according to one account, either "by Indians or the river. The mushrooming camp became a ghost town overnight."

In 1854, a Crescent City newspaper reported on a "war of extermination" against the Indians. Acts of genocide raged statewide but were particularly virulent in northern California. That year, thirty Indians were killed during a battle beside a north coast lagoon. In the Smith River Valley, settlers who feared an Indian uprising struck first, massacring two to three hundred Indians, many of them Tolowa.

In 1855, a Sacramento paper noted that Indians on the Klamath had killed six white men and some livestock. The editor asked,

> Who can determine their provocation or the amount of destitution suffered before the hostile blow was struck. The intrusion of the white man upon the Indians' hunting grounds has driven off the game and destroyed their fisheries. The consequence is, the Indians suffer every winter for sustenance. Hunger and starvation follow them wherever they go. Is it, then, a matter of wonder that they become desperate and resort to stealing and killing?

This remarkably sympathetic editorial was written during Ben Wright's heyday when the State of California rewarded vigilantes with payments for each Indian killed. It concluded on a tragic note: "The fate of the Indian is fixed. He must be annihilated by the advance of the white man." Appended to the editorial, an article from the Crescent City *Herald* made it clear that the Indians did not accept their fate. A writer in Trinidad, formerly the Yuroks' southernmost village, had "no doubt there will be warm times on the Klamath for some weeks, as the Indians are numerous, well armed and determined to fight."

Most of the fighting took place upriver of Yurok country and along the coast. Nonetheless, Yuroks had reason to feel threatened, despite the failure of Klamath City. Many had married into families of Tolowas who died by the coastal lagoon, along the Smith River, and of Karuks farther up the Klamath. Although they were spared a massacre, some Yuroks were shot

on suspicion of colluding with other "hostiles," and two were hanged in
retribution for the murder of a Mr. French.

Federal authorities attempted to bring order to this chaotic situation.
In November 1855, the government established a reservation on a twenty-
mile strip along the Klamath River, one mile wide on either side upriver
from the estuary. The intent was for the Indians to learn to grow crops and
otherwise adapt to the civilization that now engulfed them. They were also
allowed to sustain themselves through fishing. The first Indian agent hired
a Crescent City man to bring twine to the reservation to make fishnets. He
would bring agricultural implements, seeds, and construction tools as well.

The government established Fort Ter-Waw or Terwer six miles from
the mouth of the river. Its purposes were to keep the Indians under observation and to serve as a buffer between them and whites. Not all of the
Indians on the Klamath River reservation were Yuroks. Soldiers marched
Wiyot, Whilkut, Sinkyone, and Chilula Indians there from the coastal
mountains, valleys, and flatlands to the south and prevented them from
escaping to their homelands. During April 1860, two months after a massacre of an entire village of Wiyots on Indian Island in Humboldt Bay, the
reservation received 450 natives from that region. They were told—con-
vincingly, under the circumstances—that "if they did not go willingly,
force would be used, and any who attempted to evade the agent would
be treated as enemies." But even with all those lands freed for non-Indian
uses, settlers complained that fine timber and good agricultural land was
going to waste on the reservation along the Klamath River.

As non-Indians continued to invade the region, pressure to get rid of
the reservation altogether increased. A Mr. Bledsoe decried "the idiotic
measures of the Indian Department" that left thousands of acres and
immense resources "useless and idle." He acknowledged that the reservation was a necessity when 3,000 or 4,000 Indians overran the country. But
"as most of their warriors and braves sleep in the embrace of death there
no longer remains any reason to fear them."

Nature intervened. During the winter of 1860–1861, severe flooding
wiped away most of the arable land near the river and made Fort Ter-Waw
uninhabitable, even by soldiers. Efforts to rebuild the fort were stopped by
an order to build a new one north of Crescent City.

The status of the Klamath River reservation came into question in
1864 when Congress enacted a law limiting the number of reservations

in California to four, including one in Hoopa Valley. The act required abandoned reservations to be surveyed and the land to be sold at auction. In 1866, the Indian commissioner described the Yurok reservation as "unsettled and wild, peopled almost exclusively by Indians, to whose wants and habits it is well adapted, supplying wild food and fish in abundance. Very little of it is tillable land, and whites will never care to settle upon it." Twenty years later, an Indian agent reported: "Nature seems to have done her best here to fashion a perfect paradise for these Indians, and to repel the approach of the white man."

Some whites chose to settle there nonetheless. According to one description of Requa—the name that settlers gave the land where the Yurok village of Rekwoi was located—"There was plenty of room in the neighborhood; so the Indian houses were not too close together. This enabled the settlers when they came in to build the homes not to disturb the first inhabitants."

With their claims to the land uncertain, settlers petitioned the federal government to grant them title. This dispute bounced between Congress and the Interior Department for many years. Finally, in 1891, an executive order resolved the discrepancy between the 1864 four-reservations-in-California act and the de facto federal status of Indian country along the Klamath River. President Benjamin Harrison reestablished the Yurok reservation as an "extension" of the square-shaped reservation in Hoopa Valley, which the Trinity River runs through. His order linked the river-straddling Yurok strip to the Hoopa Square by extending it upriver all the way to the confluence with the Trinity. The extension made the Yurok portion of the reservation look on the map like the tail of a kite. The status of the non-Indian settlers there remained unresolved.

Even though the size of their reservation expanded under the executive order, it made little difference to Yurok families who had lived for many generations in Weitchpec and other towns beyond the boundaries of the original reservation. At the same time, however, the Yurok population, which was recorded as 2,000 as late as 1856, had diminished by 1891, as did that of California Indians generally, especially in the northern counties.

In the eighty years between the founding of the first mission in California in 1769 by the Spanish and the Gold Rush in 1849, the population of Indigenous Californians declined from approximately a quarter million to about 100,000 people. The colonization of California by the Spanish, Mexicans, and Russians, however, had no impact on the peoples of the Klamath. Then, between 1850 and 1880, the number of California Indians was cut in half, according to some estimates, and literally decimated, according to others, with only 10 percent remaining. Historian Jack Forbes estimates "a loss of some 80,000 during the entire thirty-year period (an 80% decline)."

It will never be known how many California Indians died and how many disappeared, for a large number were uncounted and unaccounted for. Some went into the cities, merging into the general population and often marrying non-Indians to secure their future. Numerous Indian women and children were captured and sold to Californians as slaves. According to a news article published in *Alta California* in 1854, "Abducting Indian children has become quite a common practice. Nearly all the children belonging to some of the Indian tribes in the northern part of the state have been stolen. They are taken to the southern part of the state and then sold." Among the owners of Indian children was Austin Wiley, the California superintendent of Indian Affairs, who took custody of an eight-year-old boy and kept him as an indentured servant for seventeen years.

Ironically, although California was designated by Congress as a free state, the act permitting indentured servitude was among the first passed by the California legislature. Its name was Orwellian: the 1850 Act for the Government and Protection of Indians. That same year, the California Civil Practice Act barred Indians from giving testimony for or against whites in state courts.

From the perspective of many in those times, there was no need to grant Indians rights; they would soon be eliminated from the population anyway. In the meantime, Indians were needed as a workforce. Cheap labor was in demand, from the mines in the mountains to the farms and ranches in the valleys of the Golden State. In many places, observed Forbes, "The natives labored only for room and board and protection, since to be expelled from the farm might mean death either at the hands of white terrorists or by starvation."

The hostility toward Indians in California and the absence of legal protections intimidated many to the point that they denied their Indigenous identity to all outsiders. Among themselves, however, they knew who their family members were. Away from their homelands, weddings and funerals replaced traditional ceremonies as occasions for tribal gatherings.

Meanwhile, on the Yurok reservation, non-Indians built the village of Requa and developed an economy based on dairy cattle and salmon canning. Safford's Island, eighty-three fertile acres just east of the village (an island that the floods of 1955 and 1964 washed away entirely), became a pasture. It had a baseball diamond and a field for the native stick game, evidence of coexistence quite different from the California norm.

In the mid-1850s, shortly after the reservation was established, a man named Snyder built a trading post on a sandbar near a White Deerskin Dance site. Converging there on the north bank were trails that brought Tolowas from their river, the Smith; Yuroks from coastal villages and elsewhere along the Klamath; Hupa from their Trinity River valley; and Karuks from upriver beyond the Trinity confluence. Over the years the store served soldiers, travelers, miners, settlers, and Indians.

After the military abandoned the reservation, Bill McGarvey bought Snyder's store. He kept it well stocked with whiskey, which sold for a dollar a bottle. Whether from a sense of ethics or an aversion to mayhem, the Irishman sold only one bottle at a time to his Indian customers.

Needing winter supplies, McGarvey hired five Yuroks from a nearby village to travel to Crescent City by canoe, purchase goods for him, and bring them back to the river. Unfortunately, the ocean was so rough that the canoes capsized, and all five men drowned. Indian law requires an exact settlement for such a loss. But when the dead men's relatives demanded payment from McGarvey, he refused, saying that he was not responsible for their deaths. A few nights later, a Yurok woman who was friendly to the whites warned him that he would be attacked by the relatives of the deceased.

The merchant and his friends prepared to defend the store. They brought in water and other supplies, loaded rifles, and bolted the door. As expected, a war party arrived, twenty-five or thirty armed men, their faces blackened for battle. For hours the whites held them off. Finally, one Indian who had been McGarvey's friend for many years offered to come in and negotiate a settlement. His name, fittingly, was Solomon.

McGarvey offered to pay the amount that the Indians demanded, but he claimed not to have enough money in his store to make amends. The store owner would have to send out letters to his friends in Crescent City. He asked that an Indian deliver these letters for him so that he could obtain the necessary funds. Meanwhile, a truce would be observed between the people inside the store and the warriors outside.

What McGarvey penned was a call for military assistance. Five days later, after a fifty-hour march, soldiers rushed onto the sandbar and entered the besieged store. The warriors retreated, and the soldiers remained for eight months, happy to be quartered in a place so well supplied with alcohol.

The saga did not end there. Three Yuroks and a white man would die before it ended, and the trading post would come under attack yet again. But Bill McGarvey outlived this dispute and died of an illness in 1876.

That was the year the salmon business came to the Klamath River. Shortly after the state legalized the sale of salmon caught in its northwestern counties, Martin Van Buren Jones established a fishery at the mouth of the Klamath. Because he was not an Indian, the army evicted him. So Jones moved his operation just beyond the boundaries of the reservation, up Hunter Creek. Yuroks accepted his presence there, and he employed Indians to catch fish for him.

Jones's method of preserving fish was to salt them. That was also the practice of John Baumhoff, who set up his saltery a decade later on Hunter Creek. Baumhoff made an agreement with twenty-six Yurok fishermen, who fishery biologist Ronnie Pierce described as "the founders of the first Indian fisherman's union." Pierce explained that Baumhoff "agreed to provide nets and boats and to pay Indian workers ten cents for every salmon weighing over ten pounds. The participating Yurok fishermen agreed to fish for no other non-Indian operation." The salters and the Indians who fished for them soon faced competition from a man whose family introduced salmon canning to California—Robert Deniston Hume.

Canning was a technology invented for Napoleon's army. Knowing that "an army marches on its stomach," in 1795 Napoleon offered a prize of 12,000 francs to whoever could invent a means of preserving food for the military. This inspired Nicolas Appert, a French chef, to experiment with a hermetically sealed glass container in which food was heated, killing bacteria. It was the predecessor of the steel-and-tin can.

Hume's father and grandfather had been pioneers in the salmon industry in Maine; but as that fishery was declining, Robert's brothers sought their fortune in the West. They brought with them a tinsmith,

Andrew Hapgood, who had canned lobster meat. By the time that R. D. Hume initiated his Klamath River fishery, his brothers were operating more than half of the canneries on the Columbia River. Selling thousands of cases of canned royal chinook every season, the brothers built a business second only in importance to wheat farming in the Columbia Basin. The Klamath River, which produced more salmon than any American river besides the Columbia and the Sacramento, was an obvious venture for the Hume family.

There was one problem. In 1883, the Department of the Interior turned down Hume's application to fish in the Klamath. Although the status of the Yurok reservation was uncertain, Interior considered that part of the river an Indian fishery. Four years later, undaunted by the federal prohibition, Hume brought a steam-powered fishing boat into the estuary, claiming that the reservation did not include the river itself. His rationale was that the waters of the Klamath were navigable and open to the public. "Brandishing a large-bore Henry Express rifle," as Pierce described it, "he quickly won the first argument with the local military sergeant."

Hume then brought into the Klamath a barge that was large enough to sustain a fish-salting operation, though not a cannery, and to house its non-Indian workforce. Yurok fishermen who were working for the off-reservation salteries asked the government to intervene. It did so; but instead of taking up the issue of public-versus-reservation waters, Indian agents filed criminal charges against Hume for trading with reservation Indians without a license. Because receipts showed that he had traded tea with the Indians, the court case was called *United States vs. 48 Lbs. of Rising Star Tea.*

Hume's attorneys won (the lawyer representing the United States failed to appear in court). The judge ruled that because the U.S. Army had abandoned the reservation in 1862, the federal government no longer had jurisdiction there. President Harrison's executive order reestablishing the Yurok reservation as an extension of the Hoopa Valley Indian Reservation would resolve that issue. But was the river, including the riverbed, part of the reservation? This was contested in another court case. Since a purpose of the reservation had been to provide the Indians a place to subsist by exercising their fishing rights, the idea that the reservation would exclude the river seemed absurd. The judge did not address that issue, however.

Meanwhile, Hume continued his operation. The Indian Allotment Act allowed him to purchase reservation land; and this he did, building a cannery and a store in Requa. Before long, canneries and other enterprises in the flourishing town were providing employment to the Indians.

Canning was a labor-intensive operation. Not only did workers butcher every salmon, they also hand-pasted labels on the cans. And until 1907, every can packed with salmon was made by hand. Jimmy Gensaw, a Yurok from Pecwan Creek, worked as a tinsmith, making cans from a sheet of tin, which he cut with shears. Once machine-made cans became available, the canneries greatly increased their production.

Geneva Mattz, who was raised by her grandparents after her father died, recalled that Indians worked in two of the three canneries. Her grandparents

> worked in a cannery, both of them. . . . They called it packing cans, you know, canning fish. So much a tray for each group that they finished. Each can they packed was put on a tray. . . . And Grandmother says every day long about maybe 10:30 or 11 o'clock, the cook from the cookhouse would bring them candy and put it in their mouths as she went by.

The canneries were built out over the river "because they cleaned the fish there. There were just piles and piles of fish."

An impression of the scale of the fishery comes from a report in the *Del Norte Triplicate* that so many fish were netted one evening that the gillnetters had to stop working to give the cannery time to process them all. "Your correspondent visited the cannery and viewed the wonderful sight—more than ten thousand beautiful chinook salmon, many of them weighing as much as 40 to 50 pounds. . . . As the fishermen receive 6½ cents per pound, some of the boats made as high as $200 for the evening's catch." The record for a single day's catch was set in 1912—17,000 salmon.

When the cannery wasn't running, Geneva Mattz's grandfather, William Brooks, worked on a ferry that transported people traveling the wagon road between Eureka and Crescent City. Her grandmother Susie "made and sold baskets and she always used to plant big gardens up here on the hill." The Brookses also raised cows and horses. They secured their claim to reservation land by obtaining property under the Allotment Act of 1887. This was the act that divided Indian reservations into properties owned by individual members of the tribes. In addition to the twenty acres that her grandfather had and the "forty acres on the flat with timber on it," Geneva's father received an allotment of eighty acres.

The redwood-forested hills above the banks of the Klamath made these allotments extremely desirable for those who wanted to harvest timber. An act of Congress in 1909 allowed the Indians only one year in which to secure allotments, opening more of the reservation for white settlement. Land claimed by non-Indians was denied to Indian applicants. Accordingly, non-Indians purchased more than 90 percent of the Yurok reservation, with Simpson Timber Company the largest landholder. One of the ways that timber interests obtained lands allotted to the Yuroks was by having them sign a paper they did not understand. Sometimes the pretext was the purchase of trees from an Indian's property when in fact the deed of sale transferred the land itself to the non-Indian.

Geneva Mattz told the story of one such incident. It occurred in 1912, after she and her grandparents had moved into a frame house near their redwood plank house. She was eight or nine years old when two men came down the road. One was the justice of the peace, a man named Bowie, and the other was a man carrying a satchel. Both visitors wore suits.

> "William Brooks," the judge says, "This man is here to see you today," he says, "he come to talk to you." And Granpa shook hands with him. . . . Granpa worked a lot with non-Indians and he could understand English good. He never had English schooling but he knew how to talk. So he said, "Go ahead and tell me what you're here for and I'll listen.". . .
>
> "William Brooks, known as Billy, I came to tell you that you can't set your net over there in the corner anymore on this property here, where you always set your little net," he says. "You can't set your net there any more, because you're a white man now," he says. "You sold your timber." And I could see Granpa's cheeks right here moving back and forth. He just listened to him. . . .
>
> Then he got up to talk. "All right, Mr. White Man," he says, "you came to tell me what you wanted to tell me. Now you let *me* talk to *you* now. . . . I was taught to fish and learned what to get so that I

could survive if something happened to my folks or learn to provide for my family when I grew up. Every kind of a fish I was taught how to fish and to hunt and what to kill and what not to kill. . . . And *you* come here and tell *me* that I can't fish any more for my family. I have children to raise," he says, "that we have to have fish for," he says. "I've got four children; my son died and I have to raise them."

Then Brooks turned to the Judge. "You got anything else to say, Judge Bowie?" he says like that. "Don't you bring another white man in my house," he says, "who's gonna tell me how to live. I was trained to live the way I live," he says, "and you're not going to tell me how to live." With that, Brooks ordered the two men out of his house.

Brooks's ability to stand up to the men so impressed his granddaughter that she would tell the story more than seventy years later. A point to note is the claim that Brooks "was a white man now" because he had sold his timber and, therefore, had lost his reservation lands.

A popular myth in early twentieth-century California was that the Indians had vanished. Either they died off or they turned into non-Indians—people who had changed their culture with their clothes, blending in to the dominant society. This suggested that their demise was not the consequence of specific actions and events for which people were responsible but was rather due to fate or some overarching law of nature. Social Darwinism, an ideology that turned Darwin's theory of natural selection into the thesis that "the survival of the fittest" governed the social order, combined the illusion of progress with faith in science. Its proponents maintained that the destruction of Indigenous peoples was not only inevitable, but all to the good. This ideology preserved the complacent conscience of colonists around the world.

The idea that Indians ceased being "real Indians" when they no longer practiced a precontact way of life was the contribution of a new science, anthropology, as practiced by its foremost exponent in California, A. L. Kroeber. Kroeber's mentor, Franz Boas, had made the preservation of American Indian cultures his mission. Boas's stunning displays of Northwest Coast art in New York's American Museum of Natural History supported his contention that human beings of every culture had the same capacities and potential for greatness as humans everywhere else. The cultures that were called "primitive" were in no way inherently inferior to those of "civilized" peoples. As precontact Indigenous cultures were falling prey to the pressures of colonization and national expansion around the world, it was incumbent on anthropology to preserve the remnants.

In California, Kroeber pursued the mission of what he called "salvage anthropology" with dedication and skill. He gave greatest attention to the Yuroks. They were near the coast and accessible, and their connection to the precontact way of life seemed comparatively intact. His emphasis on the remnants of precontact culture led him to disregard the evolution of Klamath River cultures in their effort to adapt to the advent of non-Indians. As he collected artifacts, observed data, transcribed myths, and took field notes depicting a culture fixed in the past, Kroeber ignored everything that appeared to be innovative and individually expressive. Although many aspects of Yurok culture survived among families whose members did not eat from elkhorn spoons and who worked for whites, their way of life fell beyond the bounds of Kroeber's anthropology. He concluded that those who did not appear to be maintaining their traditions were Indians no longer.

Kroeber's most powerful contribution to the confusion between California Indians as a people and those who practiced an aboriginal way of life resulted from his use of Ishi as a living museum display. The last surviving member of the Yahi tribe, Ishi was starving when slaughterhouse workers in the northern Sierra found him in 1911. Ishi became the only California Indian to appear as an individual in the public eye in the early twentieth century. His image as "The Wild Man of California" and "The Last Aborigine" became the image of California Indians. The light of publicity that Ishi received obscured the reality of their existence.

The myth of the vanishing race received photographic confirmation from Edward Curtis. His series of books, *The North American Indian*, containing photographic plates of Indians throughout the West, was funded by J. P. Morgan, a man whose enterprises—including the financing of railroads across the continent—benefited greatly from the belief that the Indians had somehow disappeared. Curtis had many of his Indian subjects remove their street clothes and wear traditional garments that he provided for them. He often had them pose for him in front of featureless backdrops. By removing his subjects from the physical environment in which they lived, Curtis turned real people into abstract images. Just as Kroeber had abstracted their cultural life from its contemporary context, Curtis created the impression of a people who were remnants of a vanished past.

Anthropologists also took photographs of this kind, although their subjects wore their own traditional clothes. Kroeber's photographs of Alice Frank Spott, Robert Spott's sister, taken in 1907, show her wearing a basket cap and dance regalia, with dentalium necklaces cascading over her shoulders. She is outdoors somewhere; the background is out of focus. Kroeber's photograph of Robert Spott taken twenty-five years later shows his collaborator with his face painted, wearing a ceremonial headband and dentalium necklaces, and standing in front of a blank screen. Kroeber knew them both as individuals but photographed them as symbols, representatives of "the undisturbed, pre-1850 native culture [that] seems to have been largely in static balance." In the "golden age of anthropology," the olden days were the golden days.

Chapter Seven
The Inland Whale

During the prosperity that followed World War I, American consumers began their love affair with the automobile. For those who could afford one, a car offered relief from the confines of the city and freedom to explore the vast countryside. Families drove into the woods to picnic. Sportsmen packed rods and rifles in search of game. Tourists explored scenic landscapes in the national forests and parks.

A speech delivered at the dedication of the Douglas Memorial Bridge, built to extend California's Highway 101 across the Klamath River, expressed the enthusiasm of the era: "The bridging of the Klamath . . . will open to the motorist a vacation land of virgin woods and mighty streams the like of which is to be found nowhere else. The bridge will stand for all time."

In 1923, the year before construction of the bridge began, novelist Zane Grey became one of the first sportsmen to land a salmon in the Klamath with rod and reel. Other non-Indian fishermen used hand lines, while Indians fished from "long net boats, sharp fore and aft." Indians and whites alike laughed at Grey's light tackle. Grey's account of his visit to the Klamath and his landing of a fifty-seven-pound chinook was published in *Outdoor America* and read by anglers across the country. He wrote that he had not intended to fish the Klamath; he had come to Requa only to ferry across it. But when he encountered three young men who had each caught a large salmon within an hour, Grey told his driver that they were staying.

In the light of the next morning came a revelation.

> Requa and the mouth of the Klamath did not seem the same place as yesterday. All the way down the bay, I marveled at the difference. Could it have been one wholly of spirit?
>
> Fish were breaking everywhere. Pelicans were soaring and swooping and smashing the water. Myriads of seagulls were flying

and screaming over the long sand bar. Low and clear came the sound of the surf. . . . I was struck with the singular beauty of the place.

Having caught his magnificent salmon, which Grey proudly exhibited to spectators, "I told my companions to take a last look at the most thrilling and fascinating place to fish I had ever seen."

The completion of the bridge across the estuary marked the end of the horse-and-buggy era and made the ferry obsolete. Sportfishermen, some no doubt inspired by Grey's story, motored hundreds of miles to an angler's paradise. Lodges and restaurants catering to tourists opened their doors. The Requa Inn, a three-story hotel, rose beside Requa Road. Harry Williams, a white man, and his wife Ethel, a Yurok of the Jones family, opened Dad's Camp. For a small fee, "Dad" gave anglers access to the estuary from the south bank. Postcards from the 1920s show fishermen lined up shoulder-to-shoulder along the sandspit.

But there was trouble in paradise. Cannery statistics exposed a decline in the spring salmon runs, a decline so severe that during the early 1920s Requa's canneries closed in the spring, opening only for fall chinook that ran from July to September. Salmon runs diminished even further during the last years of the decade. Sportfishermen, many of whom were affluent and well-connected, formed the Klamath River Anglers Association and lobbied the state legislature to investigate the causes of the decline.

The verdict of two committees in Sacramento was that the Indians on the Klamath had overfished the resource. The legislature ignored the impact of commercial trollers in which non-Indians harvested salmon in the ocean near the mouth of the Klamath. It also failed to consider the impact of the dams on the Klamath, which would have explained why the decline of spring chinook was much greater than that of the fall runs. Beginning with the construction of Copco 1 in 1918, dams had prevented the large and powerful spring fish from reaching their spawning habitat in the Upper Basin.

The legislators assumed that the State of California had jurisdiction over a river that ran through a federal Indian reservation, an assumption that the Interior Department did not challenge. As a result, in 1933 California closed the canneries and the Indian fishery. That August, *The National Waltonian* proudly announced that "the Klamath, famed for its piscatorial delights . . . has been saved for the public."

For the Indians of the river, salmon was the major source of their subsistence and the mainstay of their ceremonies, which had always been timed to coincide with salmon runs. One by one, the world renewal ceremonies ceased to be performed. The Jump Dance at Pecwan had occurred every two years for as long as anyone could remember. The hundreds of people who attended it ate salmon caught, if not in the weir at Kepel then by gillnetters. In 1939, this event took place for what appeared to be the last time.

Robert Spott, who had learned sacred traditions from his father and who had no children of his own, despaired of finding a youth he could teach these to. Eventually, he educated a white boy, Harry Roberts, who had grown up in Requa speaking Yurok. Geneva Mattz did not teach her children to "speak Indian." She became a Christian and advised her daughter Lavina to marry a white man. Believing that her traditional way of life had no future, she was resigned to letting her culture, which had been shaped by language and the land itself, recede into obscurity.

Meanwhile, people had to survive. Merky Oliver, who was born in Requa, recalled growing up during the Depression. "The old people up here that I stayed with most of the time were pretty poor, sometimes wondering what they were going to eat tomorrow. So we had to go out there and down an animal or put out a net and kill a fish, or kill an eel or kill a bird or something to eat." Merky's uncles were skilled hunters and fishermen who managed to evade the State Fish and Game wardens in providing food for their community. "Whenever they brought something home," Oliver remembered, "they would skin them up and that stuff would just disappear all around the neighborhood, taking care of our neighbors. And I think that stuck with me more better than anything, just cause I still believe in that, you know, giving and sharing. That's the way the Indians were years ago."

Not everyone was poor. Some Yuroks moved off the river during the Depression years to work and raise their children in Eureka, San Francisco, and other cities. Jack Kohler's grandmother, who posed for the *National Geographic* as a beautiful Indian maiden, was among them. Working in Eureka, she met a non-Indian, moved with him to San Francisco, and raised her family.

Notable among the few Indians who had some income while they continued to live by the river were Harry and Ethel Williams, who ran Dad's

Camp, and Fanny Flounder, a cousin of Geneva's Granma Brooks. "She was an Indian doctor," Geneva Mattz told oral historian Helene Oppenheimer. "She had a buggy and if she had a load to bring us, she'd bring the spring wagon that could carry more things than the buggy." Flounder brought her relatives potatoes and strips of smoked elk meat, and she bought the children clothes. "I'd get new shoes and maybe a coat or a sweater when she came to see us," recalled Mattz. "She'd buy the boys maybe socks and something, you know, every time she came, something special."

Wearing fashionable clothes and driving a buggy, Flounder did not look like a traditional Indian. Yet she earned her money as a doctor, a profession for which she trained in the traditional way. Flounder lived in Requa with her husband George Melden, who was the last medicine man to preside over the fish dam at Kepel.

In 1939, A. L. Kroeber brought Erik H. Erikson to Requa. An émigré from Europe who had trained with Anna Freud, Erikson was among the first practitioners of psychoanalysis in the United States. Kroeber must have wondered what an analyst would make of a sucking doctor, whose techniques included the sucking of "pains" from the body of a patient and eliciting confessions of misbehavior from relatives to account for the illness.

According to Theodora Kroeber, Fanny Flounder was "the last of the great Yurok Indian doctors." She considered Flounder's outstanding qualities to be "strength, humor, vividness, and an amiable directness." Erikson experienced these as soon as Alfred Kroeber left him alone with her. When he asked her where the anthropologist had gone, "The old woman laughed merrily and said, 'He give you a chance to ask alone. You big man now.'"

The psychoanalyst recognized Flounder as a fellow healer. "I could not claim to be her professional equal," Erikson wrote, referring to the treatment of physical disorders. "However, she also did psychotherapy with children, and in this field it was possible to exchange notes."

A sensitive observer, Erikson saw that Flounder had been "in an acute state of gloom when we arrived." He attributed that to her shock at having recently seen a whale enter the Klamath—a sign that the world was dangerously out of balance. As he got to know her better, he noticed "a dramatic melancholy, a positive withdrawal" that contrasted sharply with her "radiant friendliness and warmth."

It must have been Kroeber who interpreted Flounder's gloom for Erikson. He knew that the presence of a whale in the river had an ominous meaning for traditional Yuroks. He also knew that the healer had had a dream that expressed dread of a world tipping out of balance: "she saw the sky rising and blood dripping off its edge." Flounder had shared the memory of this power dream, which had called her to become a doctor, with Robert Spott, who told it to Kroeber.

The world of the Yuroks could tip off balance because, according to Kroeber's colleague, T. T. Waterman, it was a disk. The world disk, bisected by the Klamath River, was surrounded by an ocean combining the Pacific and an upriver sea, and it floated on these waters. An island world that can tilt is inherently vulnerable. As Erikson described it, the breaking of the barrier that kept whales out of the river "could only mean that the world disk was slowly losing its horizontal position . . . and that a flood was approaching comparable to the one which once before had destroyed mankind."

Flounder may have felt a dread of this circumscribed Yurok cosmos tilting at the brink of disaster at the time that Kroeber and Erikson visited her. But her sorrow had other sources as well—sources that the anthropologist and the psychoanalyst would have considered had they interpreted the Yurok doctor's dream in its historical as well as its cultural and personal contexts. Flounder must have been aware, as were Ishi and other California Indians born in the nineteenth century, of the decimation of native populations that followed the Gold Rush. Its effects continued to be felt. The doctor, whose healing practice required her to take the "pains" of her patients into her own body and spit them out in a display of blood and slime, may well have been grieving the eradication of Native people and the destruction of their world within an area much larger than the Yurok cosmos.

Later, when Erikson visited a Yurok village

In order to collect and check my data concerning Yurok childhood, I met immediately with the "resistive and suspicious temperament" which the Yuroks as a group are supposed to have. Luckily I had met and had worked with some Yurok individuals living near the estuary of the Klamath; and Kroeber had prepared me for folkways of stinginess, suspicion, and anger. I could therefore refrain from holding their behavior against them—or, indeed, from being discouraged by it.

Kroeber's generalizations about the Yurok temperament led Erikson to interpret the Indians' behavior without taking into account their feelings about non-Indians. A specialist in the analysis of children, Erikson did not understand why Yuroks refused to let him see their children except on one ceremonial occasion when all the adults were present. Regardless of any "folkways," the people he encountered had good reason to be wary of the tall, blond, blue-eyed stranger. The capture and sale of Indian children for servitude remained in living memory, and the removal of Indian children from their homes by child welfare professionals was a common practice. Ironically, Erikson met Yuroks at the very time that members of his own family and of his profession were fleeing Hitler's Germany. Had he viewed the people by the river in terms of California Indian history rather than through the ahistorical lens of Kroeber's anthropology, he might have understood them as human beings whose feelings, far from being fixed along the lines of their tribal character, responded to historical experiences no less than did Erikson and his non-Indian contemporaries.

To be fair to Erikson, the psychoanalyst in his later work drew from his insights as a clinician in writing perceptive studies of individuals in relation to the history they lived through. Erikson's analysis, beginning in World War II, of an "identity crisis" among young adults led to his recognition of a human identity crisis—the failure of human beings to understand their shared humanity with people of different nations and cultures. Erikson postulated that this failure is a necessary condition for genocide, terrorism, and the use of weapons of mass destruction. Even though his thinking on these matters was deeply influenced by the Holocaust, world war, and the nuclear threat, the psychoanalyst's encounter with Klamath River Indians played an important role, for it helped to enlarge his understanding of identity beyond personal, cultural, and historical contexts toward what he would call an "all-human identity." Speakers of the Yurok language had their own term for this—"the human world."

In the 1950s, during the last years of Fanny Flounder's life, a man-made flood threatened her world. The government's disregard of federally guaranteed fishing, hunting, and gathering rights on the Klamath River had encouraged agencies to make designs on the resources of the river. The greatest of those resources was and remains the water itself. Within a hundred miles of the estuary a hundred inches of rain falls in an average year. Annually, twelve million acre-feet of water rush through the Klamath Basin to the sea—almost the equivalent of the output of the Colorado River. In a state that has major cities and extensive farms in arid regions, this abundance of water promised deliverance from drought, desiccation, and the need for conservation.

The Bureau of Reclamation developed a plan to dam the Klamath twelve miles inland from the ocean, at Ah-Pah. More than 800 feet high, the Ah-Pah Dam would back water seventy miles up the Klamath and flood forty miles of the Trinity, turning Hoopa Valley into a lake that would be part of a fifteen-million-acre-foot reservoir. A sixty-mile-long Trinity Tunnel would route this water as needed to California's Central Valley; a peripheral canal would move it around the delta waters that flow into San Francisco Bay; and a forty-mile Tehachapi Tunnel would bring the water through the Transverse Ranges into Los Angeles.

A member of the Bureau's Planning Division, Stan McCasland, wrote that "the Northern California Diversion would not by any means constitute a complete water supply for the Southwest. It would meet the most immediate demands." His article on the project, published in 1952, galvanized opposition. Reporters from Oregon and Washington suspected that the master plan included the diversion of water from the Columbia River. Los Angeles officials suspected that the Klamath Diversion could interfere with their city's designs on the much closer waters of the Colorado. The unexpected public relations disaster forced the Bureau of Reclamation to trash its plan for the Ah-Pah Dam.

Throughout this brouhaha, Klamath River water continued to flow through dams from the Link River to Copco 1. In 1962, the dam farthest downriver on the Klamath, Iron Gate, was completed. Blocking passage of spring chinook beyond its 188-foot wall, the dam provided a hatchery at its base to replace the loss of wild fish. One purpose of the new dam was to regulate water flow for hydroelectric generation. Another was flood control.

Downstream of Iron Gate, the roadside riverbank sports a lineup of fishermen's trailers. During certain times of year, the river teems with salmon heading toward the hatchery tanks to spawn. Those fish are tough and mealy after the long upstream journey—fun to catch, but not so good for eating. The best fish are hooked or netted in the estuary. Salmon enter the river as firm and as fat and oily as they will ever be.

That is why sportfishermen returned year after year to Dad's Camp at the mouth of the Klamath for the "World's Finest Salmon Fishing," as a series of signs advertised. In *Sandspit: A Redwood Northcoast Notebook*, Francesca Fryer noted some of the things she overheard on the sandspit below the toll road: "We caught over 500 pounds last year; gave 'em all away." "You go fishing with a knife. Lines get in your way, you cut them off." "We caught four out there right in the middle of that mess two days ago. Couldn't hook but two. There were just too many boats."

By 1962, Dad's son, Timm Williams, was greeting and collecting money from the sportfishermen who came through the family allotment to fish the estuary. Fryer recorded this dialogue with Williams when she first came to Dad's Camp in 1964, the year Dad died. "Does your family own this?" she asked. "Yes, we do. It was a tidelands lease . . . a presidential grant." Fryer remarked that it sounded like he had studied land law. "Yes, I've had to," said Williams. "You see, they're always trying to take this away from us."

Indeed, "they" were. In 1964, the boundaries of Redwood National Park, which lies entirely within aboriginal Yurok and Tolowa lands, had been proposed, though not yet established. One plan would have extended the park all the way across the estuary, including the sandspit that provided the Williamses' livelihood. Timm, who lived much of the year in Marin County, and other family members, including "Dad," went to numerous public hearings to defend their right to control access to the peninsula of sand.

By that time, Timm Williams had become a symbol of the American Indian, but not as a California Indian. A Stanford graduate, Williams danced in Stanford Stadium during the halftime of football games. In his persona as Prince Lightfoot, the Stanford mascot, he wore the skins and feathers of a Plains warrior—the iconic, nationally recognizable red man. Had he worn Yurok regalia with a headdress of red woodpecker instead of eagle feathers, he might have confused fans in the stands. Public opinion held that Ishi had been the last "wild Indian" in California and thus the last "real Indian."

Fanny Flounder did not live to see the greatest floods of the twentieth century in northern California. Both occurred in 1964. The first came from
the sea. On March 28, following a 9.4 magnitude earthquake in Anchor-
age, Alaska, a tsunami struck Crescent City in several great tidal waves.
Huge logs that the rivers had carried down onto the beaches suddenly
rushed inland, battering buildings and cars. The tide of towering water
drowned ten people celebrating a birthday in the Long Branch Tavern
and damaged or destroyed 300 homes and businesses. One wave pushed
the three-story Odd Fellows Hall thirty feet from its foundation.

Then, in December, a series of torrential rainstorms made the rivers of
California's northwest swell and rise above their banks. People evacuated
towns along the Eel River, the Mad River, and Redwood Creek. As the
Klamath approached floodstage, fishermen who had driven their trucks
and campers onto the sandspit at Dad's Camp hurried to higher ground,
and Indians abandoned their riverside homes.

In a cabin in Weitchpec at the confluence of the Trinity and the Klamath Rivers, Audrey and Sam Jones were playing cards with friends when
a man rushed in. He shouted, "The river's almost up to the outhouse!"
The players laughed. This was not an emergency necessarily. Cold gale-
force rains turn to snow in the mountains, they knew, and, eventually, the
rivers subside. Still, Audrey and Sam hurried home. They noticed that
the winds had turned unseasonably warm. A tropical storm from Hawaii
was sweeping across the Pacific toward the rainsoaked California coast.
As temperatures rose, the snowpack melted. Water flooded Scott Valley.

Swelling and rising, the river washed away hundreds of houses, dam-
aging 200 buildings in the town of Happy Camp alone. Raging toward the
ocean, floodwaters destroyed bridges on the Klamath and its tributaries
and inundated the towns of Klamath Glen and Klamath. Trees that the
winds had uprooted were tossed downhill. Logs, flushed from streams by
the rising waters and forced into the river, pounded like battering rams
against the Douglas Memorial Bridge. Within minutes, a bridge dedicated "to stand for all time" disappeared into torrential waters. Logs and
trees amounting to millions of boardfeet of timber rushed from the flooding north coast rivers into the sea, jeopardizing navigation.

Unlike the flood of 1862, which drove the military away from the reservation, this flood brought the U.S. Sixth Army and an aircraft carrier, the
U.S.S. Bennington, to the Klamath. The carrier provided a base for rescue

operations. On Christmas Eve, helicopters lifted fishermen whose vehicles could not carry them across flooded roads and fallen bridges; storekeepers whose shops, bars, and lodges went dark in power outages; people marooned in isolated cabins; and those who had lost their homes, Indians and whites. A Simpson's Timber Company mill became a refugee center.

Floods are a natural disturbance of watershed ecosystems. The Klamath has a long history of flooding, but this deluge had a power that astonished even the Indians. "Everybody lost everything," recalled Geneva Mattz. "The flood took all the cattle, just wiped out the town here." Her forty-acre allotment upriver where her family had hogs, chickens, cattle, and fruit trees became a gravel bar: "The dirt was eaten by the flood."

Simpson's role as a haven for refugees was fitting. The old-growth redwood forests that had towered along the Klamath watershed near the coast captured and stored rainfall and held soil that, in turn, absorbed water. Now they were gone, turned to lumber. On clearcut slopes, nothing delayed the rush of water into streams. And in the remaining forested areas, roads built to bring logs out of the woods further eroded steep slopes of the rising Klamath Mountains. The land could no longer hold water as it once did.

But for the Indians of the river, especially after the state barred them from fishing, logging was one of very few ways to make a living. All told, the forest industry accounted for more than 90 percent of the products extracted from or made in Del Norte County during the prosperous postwar years, when housing developments were rising across the country. Trees on wheels—logs going to the mills, lumber to the stores, boards to construction sites—traveled the spreading maze of roads that linked the country with the cities and the cities with new suburbs.

"They was raftin' logs down the river then," recalled Geneva's son Raymond Mattz. "There'd be three or four hundred feet of logs all tied together like big rafts." Geneva's husband, Emery Mattz, worked for Simpson Timber, and so did their oldest son, Emery Junior. Logging was dangerous work. "He was setting chokers for a man in the woods," Geneva recalled, "when he jumped up on the cat and he missed it—fell right on his head and got hurt."

This happened in the summer. Emery Junior worried about paying his electric bills and getting clothes for his children who would soon be going back to school. He told his mother about salmon he saw going up

Blue Creek. If he caught some and took them secretly to a place where he could sell them, then Emery could buy what his children needed.

Geneva objected: "My boy, how can you take a load out? There's a game warden sitting right across the river watching, and there's another game warden right below on the sandbar. Why, they're just laying for some young fellow that's bootlegging fish."

When Emery insisted that he was going to catch some salmon for sale, Geneva decided to go with him and her daughter Janet to the praying rock across the river. "So we went across," she told Helene Oppenheimer.

> You have to move your boat a certain way because the opening is like this; that's where you have to pray that way . . . and your boat has to face that way too. So I did and I says, "We'll try, and if you get picked up with that fish, don't you ever believe Indian word anymore," I says. "That will be gone forever. If we don't do this right, you're going to go to jail because they're going to catch you with this load of fish."

Emery went fishing that night with a net and pulled more than sixty salmon into his boat. The next morning, he and Geneva drove with fish in back of their truck past the game wardens, waving to them. "And Emery took his load to Brookings. There was a cannery there, see. . . . He got over two hundred and something dollars. So he turned his lights on and he bought his children groceries and he bought his children clothes. So it worked. And that's the only time I ever did it."

Chapter Eight
Salmon War Stories

During the summer of 1957, when he was thirteen, Raymond Mattz went fishing at night with his older brother Emery. Their favorite place to gillnet was Brooks Riffle, twenty miles upriver from the mouth of the Klamath.

Wardens knew they were fishing near there and tried to catch them. "They chased us around, up and down—the Fish and Game—one whole summer," Raymond Mattz recalled. "There were no roads around here. This was all trees, all virgin timber, so they had to come down in a boat." That gave the brothers an advantage. "We'd see the light comin': we'd pick the net up and just head down the river. We never did use flashlights because we knew where we was; we was used to the dark."

The brothers talked about getting their fishing rights back. Then one night Emery told Raymond "he was tired of being chased all the time. He's the one who said, 'I guess we go to jail.' So we just laid there on the beach, and they pulled up, yeah. They put us under arrest. They hand-cuffed us up and hauled us to jail." Only Emery ended up behind bars. The wardens let Raymond go, aware, no doubt, that he was underage.

Emery intended to use his arrest to challenge California's jurisdiction in court and restore Indian fishing rights. According to Raymond Mattz, this course of action had their tribe's support. "We had a general meetin' here in Klamath and one up in Weitchpec, and everybody said, 'Go for it.'" The trial was underway when Emery Jr. was killed in a car accident.

Emery's death added emotional devastation to economic hardship. Of Geneva and Emery Mattz's nine children, Emery Jr. was one of four who died young. Betty died of tuberculosis; Jack, a paratrooper, was killed in combat during World War II; and Tony was killed by a "widowmaker"—a branch flying off a felled tree—while working in the woods.

Raymond continued fishing. Four times when he was eighteen, game wardens arrested him, booked him, then let him go. "They just kept harrassin' us—that's all it was," he said. His sister Lavina, who often went out gillnetting with Raymond, remembered that they brought a dark blanket along. When they heard the warden coming, they would pull the net into the boat, row to shore, and lie down covered by the blanket, trying not to breathe.

One of the wardens treated them with respect. According to Lavina, he "was a very nice guy. And he used to say, you know, 'as long as you're not in that boat, I won't stop.'" As he went by, the warden would flash his light over the boat where they were hidden. "He never ever stopped."

On September 24, 1969, Raymond and seven other young men were fishing and having a party near Brooks Riffle. "We had our nets piled up on the beach there," Raymond recalled.

> It was before dark and we were sitting around the fire. We went up to look for our nets and it [sic] was gone. And I said, "Well, I thought I saw the game wardens go up earlier. I'm going to ride up the river and see if they're up there." And they were up around the corner from where we were at, ya know? I went and asked everybody, "Who wants to claim their nets?" Cause you could go to jail, and we didn't want to go to jail. Someone said, "You go ahead because you already have the case goin.'" So Raymond claimed all five nets. This time he went to jail and to the courthouse.

As Lavina recalled,

> The judge told him, "If you pay a dollar fine, we'll just let it go." And he said, "No, I'm not going to, because we need to get our fishing rights back." And he [the judge] said, "well, you're not going to get that." So they appealed it, and they went to a higher court then.
>
> They just fought it and fought it for years and years. It went to one court, then to another court. It was really hard for everybody because in those times they really didn't have a lot of money. Walt McCovey Sr. and his wife used to go with Mom and Daddy and they would help pay for gas.
>
> We talked a lot about it, because when Raymond fished, he used to tell me, "You know, we need to do this." And I used to say, "Why do you keep doing it, because you know, it's so hard on everybody." And he said, "Well, we need to be able to go down and fish."

One of the people this legal struggle was especially hard on was Raymond's wife. To support their family and pay legal fees, Raymond fished and Diane Whipple Mattz, who was part Yurok and part Tolowa, "bootlegged" the salmon, driving it off the reservation for sale. Risking arrest repeatedly, Diane went to jail in Washington, where she had driven to sell a load of fish, as well as in California. Once television news showed her being led from a county jail to the courthouse in Eureka, California. A commercial fisherman, who believed that she should be in jail, contributed the sound bite: "This is worse than drug dealing." Diane's off-camera retort was, "I never heard of anybody o.d.ing on fish."

The Mattz case went from the Del Norte County Superior Court, which ordered the five gill nets confiscated, to the Court of Appeals, which affirmed the decision. The next stop was the California Supreme Court, which denied Mattz's petition for a hearing. In 1973, at the United States Supreme Court, the gillnetter's fortunes turned. That tribunal focused on the issue of whether the federal act that opened the land to homesteading had terminated the Yurok reservation on the Klamath River. Writing for the majority, Justice Harry Blackmun concluded that "efforts to terminate the reservation by denying allotments to the Indians failed completely. . . . the land within the boundaries of the reservation is still Indian country." This being the case, Raymond Mattz, as a member of the Yurok Tribe, had the right to catch fish.

But who were the Yuroks? The reservation had no tribal roll. And who was in charge of this newly recognized reservation?

There was no Yurok government. Thinking that Yurok culture was doomed by the Gold Rush and that their family-centered way of life was "the extreme of political anarchy," A. L. Kroeber had assumed that their tribal existence had no future. Because the State of California exercised jurisdiction over this strip of Indian country for most of the twentieth century, the Bureau of Indian Affairs had not established a Yurok tribal government, as occurred on many reservations under the Indian Reorganization Act of 1935.

Complicating the question of governance was the contradiction between the establishment of the Klamath Reservation in 1855 and the act of Congress that limited California to four Indian reservations, which did not include the Klamath. Benjamin Harrison's 1891 executive order achieved this by extending the Yurok strip beyond its original twenty miles upriver to the confluence of the Klamath and Trinity Rivers. That connected the Klamath Reservation to the sixteen-mile-square Hoopa Valley Indian Reservation, which the 1864 act had established as one of the four allowed within the state. If Yuroks had been living on an addition to that reservation since 1891, didn't the Hoopa Tribal Business Council govern them?

Another complication was the Jesse Short case, a long-running lawsuit on behalf of 3,800 Yuroks. Short and her fellow tribal members demanded a share of more than ten million dollars in timber revenues from the Hoopa Square. The Supreme Court decision on Raymond Mattz's case answered the central question of the case, which had been in the courts since 1960. Yuroks were entitled to timber revenues from Hoopa Valley. But again, lacking a tribal roll, who were the officially eligible Yuroks? Would the 3,800 litigants in the Jesse Short case receive their share of the funds the BIA held in escrow? Or would these timber funds be awarded to and used by a new Yurok tribal government?

This last question created a bitter split among Yuroks. The fault lines lay between those who lived on the reservation and expected to benefit from the activities of a tribal government and those who had moved off the reservation and wanted the money for themselves.

Now that the Supreme Court had affirmed Yurok fishing rights, many recognized the need for regulations governing their fishery. These would determine who could fish, where they could fish, when they could fish, and what kinds and lengths of net they could use.

Following the Mattz decision, Indians who had fished secretly at night started gillnetting openly in the light of day. Others who had never lived along the Klamath arrived during fishing season and started gillnetting. "A lot of Indians came and fished," said Lavina Bowers. "And I think that's really when people realized they had that right. And people started canning and smoking fish and just being Indians again."

The sight of Indians pulling fish out of gill nets and into their boats enraged sportfishermen. Sportfishing on the Klamath had become a large tourist industry by the mid-1970s. Thousands of fishermen parked their trucks, campers, and mobile homes in twenty-nine vehicle camps. Motels like Trees of Mystery, bars like Butch's Club, and guides who offered boat rides and fishing advice catered to them. On the river, anglers' boats ran over Indians' nets, adding to the anger on both sides.

A third constituency involved in this struggle was the offshore commercial fishery. Many who hooked Klamath River salmon from trollers in
the Pacific objected to competition from Indian gillnetters. Their problem
differed from that of the sportfishers, who competed with the Yuroks for
the same fish in the river. Commercial fishing boats catch salmon from
various runs; the fish mix and linger in the ocean before entering their
home rivers to spawn. Offshore fishers feared that gillnetting would catch
so many Klamath River salmon that not enough would spawn, reducing
the numbers that reached the ocean.

In those years, West Coast states did not limit the number of licenses
they issued for trollers. In 1965, there had been fewer than 3,000 ocean
trollers. By 1980, there were more than 10,000. Non-Indians who caught
salmon off the coast for income and those who caught them in the river
for sport joined forces, demanding restraints on the Indian fishery.

State agencies were also concerned about the salmon, whose populations were plummeting. Adding to effects of the rising offshore catch and
the impact of dams, logging, and mining on salmon habitat was a severe
drought in the mid-1970s. Some of the streams that flowed into the Klamath and its tributaries failed to reach the rivers at all, trickling instead into
sandbars and banks of gravel. Salmon that had traveled thousands of miles
for several years to return to their birthplaces lacked the strength to leap the
widening gap between river and stream. This reduction in spawning habitat
ensured that the drought would cut the numbers of fish in future years.

Yuroks were among those who took this problem seriously. A group
of gillnetters and others who lived on the river met to decide on fishing
regulations and also to discuss potential aspects of a Yurok government.
Instead of using the Karuk word Yurok, they called themselves Puliklah, a
word meaning river people as distinguished from those who had inhabited
villages along the coast. Yuroks who lived away from the river opposed the
work of this group, fearing that it comprised the nucleus of a tribal government that might receive timber revenues.

Into this turbulent situation stepped the Bureau of Indian Affairs. In
1975, the Interior Department sent Susan Kay Hvalsoe as its representative on the Klamath. Hvalsoe took part in "extensive consultation" on the
drafting of fishing regulations. From the BIA's perspective, the absence
of a Yurok government meant that tribal members had no authority to
regulate the fishery without federal authorization.

One of the regulatory disputes centered on the distinction between "commercial" and "subsistence" fishing. Would tribal members be allowed to catch salmon for sale, or would they be limited to a smaller number of fish that they could consume only among themselves? The first set of BIA regulations, published in 1977, allowed a restricted amount of fishing for commercial as well as subsistence purposes, without specifying the numbers that could be harvested.

Yurok gillnetters developed a set of guidelines for their fishery based on the salmon spawning cycle; on tides, which govern the movement of fish between river and ocean; and on crucial in-stream locations, for example, the mouth of a creek, where heavy fishing can affect the reproduction of salmon. They set a goal for escapement—that is, of salmon allowed to "escape" upriver to spawn without being caught—that was near the upper limit of what the available spawning habitat could accommodate. They also agreed to a tax on Indian commercial fishing. Those revenues would fund habitat restoration and hatcheries designed to supplement the stocks of wild salmon.

In 1978, the Interior Department issued new regulations. Bureaucrats in Washington set times permissible for fishing regardless of the tides, and they required various procedures, including the placing of identification markers on nets, to legitimize Indian fishing.

That summer federal agents made their presence known in the vicinity of the river. Many stayed in the Trees of Mystery, a tourist motel on Highway 101 that features a sixty-six-foot-tall statue of Paul Bunyan with ax in hand. A thirty-five-foot-tall blue ox, Babe, stands beneath the legendary logger. Beside the highway in the shadow of these icons of progress is a smaller wooden sculpture, a version of "The End of the Trail"—a slumping, obviously defeated Indian on horseback holding a downward-pointing spear. In 1894, when James Earle Fraser designed this popular statue, the massacre at Wounded Knee symbolized the end of Indian resistance. But eighty-four years later, the Trees of Mystery were witnessing another chapter of America's longest war.

"A long time before they really got tough, they sent guys out," recalled Richard McCovey, a gillnetter. "Now these are the feds, the fish cops. They sent guys out to infiltrate the camps, to see what we're doing." One man, who said he was vacationing, offered to buy beers for Richard and his brother Frank and started asking them questions.

The "fish cops" were agents from the Fish and Wildlife Service Enforcement Division. Fishery biologists, also from the Fish and Wildlife Service, were on the river as well. They needed to work with the Indians to weigh, measure, and record each salmon they caught. The lead biologist, Gary Rankle, used the data in his study of the causes of the decline in salmon populations. Major factors, he found, were habitat degradation, especially due to logging on the steep slopes of the watershed, and offshore commercial fishing, which took 88 percent of the salmon harvest. Fishing in the river, whether gillnetting or sportsfishing, took a small percentage of the total catch and had a negligible effect on the reproduction of salmon. In a public meeting, Rankle estimated that 200,000 fall chinook would enter the Klamath that year and that 35,000 of them could be safely harvested by Indians and sportfishermen.

Rankle's findings did not deter the State of California from imposing a total ban on sports and Indian fishing in the Klamath estuary. The Associated Press reported that this move was "prompted by a dwindling number of salmon in recent years." Ironically, sportfishers who had complained about the Indian fishery's impact on salmon were caught in the same political net as the Yuroks. The moratorium, which began on Sunday, August 27, 1978, and covered the period that was typically the height of the fall run, was a federal and state operation. Approximately seventy-five federal agents in coordination with state and local authorities were to enforce it.

On Monday morning, a squad of heavily armed federal Fish and Wildlife agents, backed by sheriff's deputies and the Coast Guard, raided Indians gillnetting in the estuary. The Coast Guard operated out of their base in Requa, located on the hill west of the ancient village site, facing the ocean. The initial theater of operations covered the three miles between the mouth of the Klamath and the rebuilt bridge, flanked by golden bears, that carries Highway 101 across the river.

"After a short chase that ended with the Indians' boat being rammed," reported Ivan Sharpe in the *San Francisco Examiner*, federal agents seized two Indians on charges of resisting arrest and confiscated their catch as well as their nets. The next day, "about 20 agents with billy clubs grabbed five Indians who were spotted boldly cleaning their fish across the river from the Chinook Resort. A crowd clapped as 59 salmon and two steelhead trout, ranging in size from 10 to nearly 30 pounds, were thrown into a van."

The Interior Department set up a Court of Indian Offenses to prosecute these cases. Presiding over this court, which was hastily convened in a truck shed, Judge John Corbett ordered the fish returned to the gillnetters. That disappointed C. R. Bavin, the chief of the Law Enforcement Division of Fish and Wildlife. "The two early decisions," he complained, "have tended to make a mockery of the time and effort expended by Special Agents. . . . LE [law enforcement] has little confidence that the court will change the pattern so far established and feels the chance of any real penalties is remote." Bavin's unhappiness with the justice system did not stop at the ad hoc fish court. "Support received to date from the U.S. Attorney in San Francisco is unsatisfactory," he wrote.

The lack of legal support did not deter the enforcement teams from their efforts at intimidation, but the Yuroks refused to be intimidated. In one meeting, about two hundred Indians told Interior officials that they would continue fishing in defiance of the ban and the federal regulations.

In the town of Klamath, sportfishermen and the merchants who served them staged a mock funeral dramatizing the death of the town of Klamath. Ivan Sharpe counted "about 100 vehicles carrying more than 300 fishermen" who participated in the demonstration. "As the six pallbearers lowered a casket into a makeshift grave," he wrote, "camp owner Bill David read a eulogy: 'Dearly Beloved, we are gathered here today for the burial of Klamath town—shot down by the Bureau of Indian Affairs. We hope and pray for Resurrection Day so all can fish in peace. Amen.' The mock funeral was disturbed by several dozen jeering Indians."

These were early salvoes in what the newspapers would call the Salmon War. On the night of Wednesday, August 30, there occurred what Del Norte County's District Attorney Robert Weir called "a miniature naval battle . . . on the estuary of the Klamath River." The *Examiner* reporter described the scene: "Under leaden skies, five boatloads of armed federal agents wearing bulletproof vests sped down river to the cheers of sports fishermen lining the north bank of the Klamath River. Waiting for them near the river mouth were the Yurok Indians—20 boatloads of them with dozens more native Americans on the beach and the south bank."

"The Feds are all out there," Richard McCovey recalled. "They were all geared up, flak jackets and machine guns and shit. None of us were armed."

"In the ensuing clash," wrote Ivan Sharpe, "boats of both sides were rammed and their crews battered with oars and riot sticks."

"I know that some of the men fought with oars," said Lavina Bowers. She described Punky Whipple "swinging at one of those guys." When Robley Schwenk, vice president of the Klamath River Indian Wildlife Conservation Association, tried to unhook the gas line from the motor of one of the federal jetboats, "this guy brings out a gun and puts it to Robley's head and says, 'Don't do that.'"

Lavina saw "the two McCovey boys in one of the boats, Richard McCovey and his brother. These were big men in this boat and Richard and his brother are no small guys. They're heavy-set. They grabbed those two guys out of that boat, like Richard's brother went flying in the boat. And they held him under the water. Cause the boats, their boats had water in them. They held them. Cause we were close enough, we watched. He [an agent] held [Frank McCovey's] face in the water until he'd come back up. And he [Frank] was saying, 'No more violence, folks.' Then he [the agent] started to put his head under there again. And each time he came up he said less and less."

"They took us into shore," recalled Richard McCovey, "and they tried to put the guns to our head. They shot my brother with the mace a couple of times, shit, he was ugly from that mace. And I told him, you guys have to take us to federal court, you can't take us to county jail. Of course that's where they took us. They kept us there four days, me and my cousin Paul Tow and Joe Hendrix and my brother. Never told us what we were charged with." (According to Sharpe, the "four Indians were arrested for bashing agents with oars and other weapons.")

On Thursday night, the combatants agreed to a truce pending the visit of Interior Secretary Cecil Andrus to the Klamath. Merky Oliver prepared a salmon bake for the secretary. Raymond Mattz was less hospitable. He had called a contact at the BIA who told him, "'They're shipping people out there to shut you down.' So I went up to the cookout to see Cecil Andrus, big sucker."

Andrus refused to lift the ban on gillnetting. "You cannot do as you please without some organizational structure," Andrus told the crowd at the salmon bake, "but we can help you if you tell us what you want."

Sharpe reported what happened next: "The secretary had a tense moment as he was enjoying an Indian salmon barbecue. Ironically, several Indians said the fish had been caught illegally. A young Indian in a red shirt detached himself from a group of taunting Indians and began forcefully jabbing Andrus in the chest to press home his arguments."

Mattz told it this way:

> I walked up to him, you know. And I said, "Hey, I just called Washington and they say you're going to put the moratorium on us." And he said, "It's not decided yet." I said, "It's decided in Washington D.C.; it's settin' on your desk; the moratorium's in effect already." And about that time, you know, he started explainin' something. So I stuck my finger right in his chest—hard—I still remember how good it felt. He had this little tiny hippie guy with him as a bodyguard. He grabs ahold of me and he spins me around. And he has a big .45. He opens his jacket. I said, "OK, OK, I'm gone." And Cecil Andrus, he was yelling, "Arrest him! Arrest him!"

Mattz was not arrested for confronting Andrus that night. Instead, he said, the next day a Coast Guard boat with seventy-five agents on board "came down to show us their power they had." Sharpe reported a clash that morning in which agents clubbed several young Indians and jailed them for resisting arrest. "During the river battle, the Indians said the agents deliberately rammed their boats and nearly capsized several of them."

The agents took Mattz to Eureka and put him in jail. At three in the morning, he said, he went to court. "And the judge, because he didn't have his clerk and everything there, he put us in his chambers. He said, 'Well, there's something to drink, if you guys want to have something to drink.' Shit, we got drunk. I said 'I can't keep drinking. My mom's going to bail me out. She'll get mad.'"

Andrus had agreed during his visit that the Indians had the right to fish for ceremonial purposes. A few days afterward, federal agents allowed Charlie Thom, a fifty-year-old Karuk medicine man, to catch salmon to feed participants in a White Deerskin Dance that was about to occur upriver in Karuk country. Two agents, John Sayre and Tom Smiley, rode with Thom in a small aluminum boat.

"Thom took two round pebbles, one much larger than the other, out of a beige purse," Sharpe reported, "and prayed for one large salmon and one small one." The pebbles, Thom explained later, "had been blessed at a sacred Indian altar on Chimney Rock, 65 miles up river." But after two hours, the gill net remained empty. "Sayre finally asked Thom if it would go better if he and Smiley left the boat. Thom agreed that it probably would. Less than a minute after the two federal officials left the Indian boat, there was a shout of glee from the Indians. Caught in a net they were hauling aboard were an 18-pound salmon and another weighing about six pounds."

The federal operation did not confine itself to the Yurok fishing areas on the lower Klamath. Even though the Hupa Tribe had what Secretary Andrus called an "organizational structure"—namely, a government—his department's enforcement effort came to Hoopa Valley. On September 11, when Fish and Wildlife agents entered the valley, Hupa Indians stopped them with a roadblock. Humboldt County sheriff's deputies helped the agents make their way to the Trinity River, where they confiscated three gill nets.

The following week, federal agents returned to the Trinity, arrested four Indians, and confiscated more nets. The Hoopa Valley Tribal Business Council responded by declaring an emergency closure of their reservation to law enforcement agents. "We have the legal right to regulate our own fishing," explained Peter Masten, the chair of the Business Council. "Nowhere in the fishing regulations does it say they should handcuff people or wave automatic weapons in their faces." Law enforcement chief C. R. Bavin had a different perspective. "The Hoopa Square remained a problem," he reported to his superior, the Fish and Wildlife service director. "An armed camp immediately behind the Hoopa Airport and the possibility of armed violence at Tishtang caused most violations on the Square to be bypassed."

Meanwhile, in a series of meetings around campfires and at people's homes, Yuroks discussed how they should respond to the federal invasion. Rather than allow more of their valuable gill nets to be confiscated, "everybody got the idea," said Richard McCovey, "to use all the old rotten nets. And when they would come, they'd just slice them all up and then take the ruined nets. So what we decided to do is just use lead lines and sometimes no nets at all." This use of unusable nets in defiance of the federal regulations was a novel form of civil disobedience. Raymond Mattz called it "protest fishing."

A number of uncivil confrontations followed. C. R. Bavin's report complained of constant attempts to harass, provoke, and intimidate officers. These include: Invective, cursing, derision, and foul language. Spitting. Death threats. Threats of damage suits. Occult threats of death, disease, impotence, etc. Thrown rocks and other objects. Slingshots. Clubs, oars and gaff hooks. Biting. Sand in the face. Passive resistance and refusal to identify. . . . The Indians used old women, pregnant women, and juveniles as arrest targets on numerous occasions.

The use by Fish and Wildlife agents of infrared scopes at night offered Indians a special opportunity for harassment. "They had night vision," Richard McCovey remarked. "I can remember showing my ass to them a few times." McCovey was not the only Yurok to turn the other cheek. On at least one occasion, when a boatload of women gave the goggle-toting agents a visual serenade, the Klamath became Moon River.

Diane Whipple Mattz and other family members were on a sandbar with a net when a Fish and Wildlife Service SWAT team of ten men swooped down on them. The women sat on the net, refusing to let the agents confiscate it. "They started shoving everybody," Mattz told Helene Oppenheimer, whose oral history of her family is a primary source for this chapter.

I reached behind me and picked up a handful of sand, and I threw it. . . . They all grabbed hold of me every which way and started dragging me. And they were macing me. . . . Tony, my boy, he was standing there, and the women hollered at him, "Don't let them take the net; don't let them have it." Tony had a can of gas—gasoline for his car—and Tony poured gasoline on that net.

"I threw a lighter on it and foom! It just freaked them out," said Raymond Mattz. "They were going for the guns. They thought it was firebombs. They ran back and they got in their boats." All that Diane Mattz could see was a flash of light. Her sister-in-law, Lavina, took her to the water's edge where she began washing mace out of her eyes. That is where the agents captured her again. After handcuffing Raymond's wife, they threw her and her son into their boat.

The boat ride gave the agents an opportunity to practice their style of intimate enmity. "They felt me all up," Mattz remembered. "They would say, 'Oh, you're cute when you're mad.' . . . And I was screaming and hollering."

When the boat landed, the agents took Diane Mattz to a patrol car, which drove her to jail in Crescent City. "She was in jail overnight," Lavina Bowers recalled. "But she had a very high blood pressure, so the doctor told them to let her go."

"Something happened every single night," said Lavina's daughter Diane Bowers. "Someone was always getting hurt; someone was always getting clubbed or thrown in a boat." On one occasion, when a group of Yuroks had a gill net on the beach, federal forces riding jetboats ran onto the shore, caught the Indians in their own net, and made arrests.

On the night of September 19, Geneva Mattz "was just getting ready to go to bed, because I had my nightgown on and my robe and my grandson came running in and he says, 'Gram,' he says, 'your whole side is just plumb full of sheriffs and the Park men, the Sheriff patrol and who all—they're all down there.'" She and Emery hurried outside, where they confronted a carful of agents. "I asked them, 'Who gave you permission to come running down here like that and scaring us people like that with all your guns and everything?'" The response was, "We can do anything we want to." Geneva retorted, "Oh, no you can't." But the deputies proved their point by arresting Emery Mattz Sr., a World War II veteran who was then seventy-eight-years old.

At about that time, members of the Mattz family were having a party on the beach when, as Diane Bowers described it, up from the hill "there came this great big flash. Like, it lit up the whole sky. It scared us all. Corresponding with that flash were lots of little flashlights." As agents holding the flashlights headed down the hill from several directions, other federal agents in jetboats started their engines in the water nearby. The deputies coming downhill onto the beach reconnoitered with the agents who rushed from their boats onto the sand. Lavina Bowers estimated there were a hundred men.

"They had these little black billy clubs," her daughter Diane Bowers recalled. "All they did was hit their hands with the billy clubs. Everybody was frightened. And right when they got within two or three feet of us, someone started singing Indian songs and drumming." The armed men backed off, according to Diane Bowers. "But after they left, people cried. My mom threw up. You thought you were going to die."

Eddie Edwards, the Bureau of Indian Affairs official "in charge of the federal forces on the river," told reporter Ivan Sharpe a different story. "He said the Indians ashore lit up the scene with headlights and spotlights, blinding the agents, while other Indians headed for the agents in boats loaded with rocks. Some of the agents said they were struck by oars as well as rocks. The Indian boat swamped and sank during a struggle to arrest an Indian."

With the arrest of her husband and the attack of her family's beach party, Geneva Mattz was determined to act. "So I told my daughter, 'We have to protest this.'" As Lavina Bowers recalled, "I said, 'Well, Momma, I'll go with you.' So we got her little burden basket and her hat and off we went down there."

"It was on a Sunday," Geneva continued. "So people, different ones, they even came in from Hoopa, from different places to come see what they were going to do with us."

The mother and daughter went out in a rowboat. Lavina Bowers described what happened next:

Her and I, we went, took a net and went out into the water, put the net in the river and we sat there. . . . And they [the agents] came down in their boats . . . the men was trying to make us, me let go of the net. Well, I wasn't going to let go of the net. And Momma was trying to tell me, "Let it go, let it go," you know. And I said, "No, I'm not letting them take it." And he said, "you're gonna let it go, or you're gonna go to jail with us." But they didn't take it. . . . At the last minute my mother got very scared and she stood up and she started praying.

As Susan Bowers Masten, Lavina's daughter, recalled this episode, her grandmother Geneva

stood up in the boat and held her arms up and sang. And the unique thing about when she sang her prayer song is there were a lot of birds that came around and were flying very close around as she was singing her song. And the agents who were there, who were at my uncle's boat, pulled up, and one of them said, "Let's get the hell out of here."

Lavina also remembered "this big mass of birds that was right over us. It was really weird. . . . And the people on shore, everybody got very excited at that moment." At this point, according to Geneva, the agents "just shriveled back like and pretty soon they all started pulling out. And that's the last time we had any trouble with them on the river."

Were the story of the Salmon War myth and not history, it would end at this moment when, facing transcendence in the form of birds spiraling above an old woman's prayer song, the federal agents left the river for good. Susan Masten, who was to become chair of the Yurok Tribe and president of the National Congress of American Indians, offered a more matter-of-fact explanation for the agents' departure: "Actually, I think what happened is that the salmon run tails off in mid-September, and it just so ended itself by the mere fact that the run was over."

One difference between myth and history is that historians attempt to understand why events occur, and explanations can ruin a good story. As Walter Benjamin wrote, "Half of the art of storytelling is to keep a story free from explanation as one reproduces it." This enables the reader to "interpret things the way he understands them, and thus the narration achieves an amplitude that information lacks." But the interpretation of an event depends in part on where the narrator ends the story.

Geneva's mythic ending achieves a classic triumph-of-the-underdog conclusion. Her granddaughter's more prosaic explanation carries another interpretation of what took place. If the objective of the enforcement division was to protect the fish from the gillnetters, as federal spokesmen claimed, or to gain political credit for doing so in response to pressure from sports and commercial fishermen, it made sense for the operation to end when the run did.

But there was more at stake than fish and politics. The 1973 Supreme Court decision created a power vacuum. Who would exercise political control, directly or indirectly, over these newly recognized reservation lands and the never-defeated Indians who lived there? Who had the authority to dispose of the reservation's resources—Indians or the federal government?

The fish war had given the Interior Department reason to be concerned about more than the Yurok Extension. By defying the federal enforcement effort in Hoopa Valley, the Hoopa Tribal Business Council, together with militant tribal members, had challenged federal authority.

On November 20, Assistant Secretary of Indian Affairs Forrest J. Gerard informed "the Hoopa and Yurok people of the Hoopa Valley Indian Reservation" that Secretary Andrus would meet his obligation "to remove all doubt about who is entitled to use and benefit from the Reservation and to formally designate the Indian beneficiaries." In the absence of "a mutually agreeable arrangement" between the two tribes for managing the reservation's assets, "it is necessary for the Department of the Interior through my office to assume complete management of the Reservation assets on behalf of both tribes." As leverage, Gerard placed a moratorium on all per capita payments until a "reservation-wide management and coordination body" was established. These payments were the sole income for many Hupa. They included the timber revenues at issue in the Jesse Short case that had long pitted Yuroks against Hupas and split Yuroks into two opposing camps.

Not surprisingly, many members of the Hupa Tribe saw this announcement as a threat to their sovereignty. Many expected that federal agents would attempt once again to invade Hoopa Valley. As for the Yuroks, Gerard's decree appeared to mean that the Interior Department would unilaterally decide who was a Yurok and who was not and that it would appoint a committee that could be the nucleus of a Yurok tribal government.

Militant Hupas assembled in Joyce Little's house in Hoopa Valley, where Pit River leader Raymond Lego recounted the history of his tribe's long-running resistance against California authorities and vigilantes. That was one way to put recent events into perspective. Another view was apparently being produced by a television news team from the Soviet Union, whose surprising presence in Hoopa Valley was noted by several tribal members.

Why were the Russians interested in this story? That fall, Polish and Russian canning factory boats were observed off the north coast of California. The Soviets had an economic interest in Klamath River salmon, but that was hardly grist for the evening news. One line of speculation was that the Russians hoped to capture on videotape the Indians' heroic resistance to federal assault. Such a drama would be a sequel to the occupation and siege of Wounded Knee, South Dakota, which had occurred five years earlier. What made colonial aggression against Indigenous people especially appealing to the Russians was the fact that it was being waged by the administration of President Jimmy Carter. His violence against Indians could counteract, in the Cold War court of world public opinion, Carter's attacks on human rights violations in the Soviet Union.

If the story of the Soviet news team, and the story within the story, were true, the Russians went back to Moscow disappointed. There was no invasion in the ensuing weeks, no Wounded Knee–style siege or violent confrontation. The drama was far from over, but, unlike dramas on stage and screen, there was no happy or tragic ending. Nor was there a definitive last act. In the absence of additional dramatic events, the conflict left the public eye. Yet tensions would remain high without any resolution for a long time to come.

Chapter Nine
Water, Fish, and Politics

The Salmon War was an act within a larger drama. On the Columbia River, as on the Klamath, dams have severely depleted populations of anadromous fish. More than anything else, the monumental Grand Coulee Dam—whose hydroelectric power ran aluminum plants that built aircraft that helped win World War II—caused the extinction of the royal chinook.

Dams cut salmon off from thousands of miles of spawning habitat. Urbanization also limits their migration. The expansion of cities and the large-scale construction of homes in new suburbs following World War II drained wetlands, leveled forests, polluted rivers and drew down their waterlines. Yet commercial and sportfishers in Washington, Oregon, and California put the blame on Indians for the declining numbers of fish and pressured their states' Fish and Game departments to stop native fishing.

In the early 1960s, Indians in Washington defended their treaty-guaranteed fishing rights by staging "fish-ins." These demonstrations and the arrest of protesters brought the native fishing people support from celebrities, including Jane Fonda and Marlon Brando, and media attention. More important, this wave of Indian militance generated court cases that eventually made their way to the United States District Court in Tacoma.

In 1974, the year after the Supreme Court's ruling in favor of Raymond Mattz, Judge George Boldt issued his decision regarding the fishing rights of Washington Indians. Boldt did more than affirm the Indians' right to catch salmon on reservations and beyond tribal boundaries; he recognized their right to harvest 50 percent of the total catch. Tribes also had the right to participate in fishery management decision-making.

Although the Boldt decision settled cases from Puget Sound, the Olympic Peninsula, and the Columbia River, its relevance to the Klamath River controversy was evident to all concerned. In the wake of the 1978 enforcement operation, Yuroks understood that the fate of their fishery and the political future of their tribe were interdependent. Only if they could continue to live off the source of their traditional livelihood and culture could they achieve self-determination. Yet their economic and political concerns had to be tackled in different ways and at different times. Management of Pacific salmon was a regional matter, and Yuroks had the potential, thanks to Judge Boldt, to take part in this process without delay. The road to self-governance as a tribe had to pass through Washington, D.C., and that would happen at a time and in a context tribal members could not choose.

The Salmon War politicized a number of Yuroks. Susan Maria Bowers was among them. She had grown up in Oregon, visiting her grandparents on the Klamath River during summers and holidays. At the time of the gillnetters' struggle, she had been living in San Francisco, building a career in public relations. Energetic and attractive with a confident smile, Bowers had worked for the United Indian Development Association, moderated television talk shows, served as an officer for California Press Women, hosted the American Indian Film Festival, and involved herself in political campaigns. "I made sure I was always at the right place at the right time," she told Helene Oppenheimer.

For this ambitious young woman, the calls she received from Requa in September 1978 posed a dilemma. After every confrontation with the "feds," her grandmother and her mother asked her to come to the river and bring the media with her. "I'd start feeling guilty," she said, "like it was my responsibility because I had that expertise."

Finally, Bowers did come with a friend who worked at a Bay Area television station. "I was amazed," she recalled, "because the tension between the Indians and the federal troops was real intense. And when I got here, it totally demolished my ideals of what's justice and what's law."

Having witnessed violence on the river, Bowers decided to stay with her family on the reservation. "I was thinking 'Now what can I do?'" It was far from clear what Bowers could do on behalf of her people. Few Yuroks wanted this assertive young female newcomer to speak for them. Nonetheless, she talked to visiting politicians and began to attend meetings about the fishery.

"When we first started out," Bowers recalled, "the commercial fishery couldn't even stand to sit at the same room with Yurok fishermen.

Emotions were so high and so intense that we tried to do a meeting in 1979 and it lasted maybe five minutes and people left the room."

That was a critical year. The returns of salmon that had spawned during the drought years were predictably low. For the first time the commercial salmon industry faced a closure of the offshore fishing season. Even if Yuroks had not been blamed for the salmon's decline, it was an upstream struggle for an advocate of Indian fishing to claim their right to a share of the run.

One representative of commercial fishing saw that, in spite of the politics, the gillnetters' case made sense. Paula Yoon had been involved with the offshore fishery for a quarter century. For eighteen of those years, she and her husband had a salmon boat. At a meeting, she said, "Now I'm going to speak for myself, Paula Yoon. And I just said, I see no reason why both the ocean and the river fishermen can't have commercial fisheries. Well, I had an application in for a job with the fishing industry. I did *not* get that job!"

Susan Bowers testified before the Pacific Fishery Management Council, which the federal Fishery Conservation and Management Act had created in 1976. It is one of eight regional management councils whose original and primary goal was to conserve fish whose numbers were falling due, in part, to the growth in numbers and technical efficiency of the international ocean fishery. The Pacific Council covers the entire West Coast. It held meetings in Idaho, Washington, Oregon, and southern California that Bowers attended at her own expense. Applying for an opening as a representative of Klamath River Indians, she became a member of the commission's Salmon Advisory Panel. But after a year, the dressed-for-success young Yurok dropped out. "I was getting all this guff from the community. They were saying, 'You don't represent us; don't be talking to this or that.' I just said, 'Enough's enough.'"

About this time Susan Bowers met Leonard Masten, a Hupa who worked for the BIA as a fishing enforcement officer. Although he was a fishcop Capulet to the gillnetting Montagues, they married. Given the enmity between Yuroks and Hupas over the Jesse Short litigation, this love match did not help Susan Bowers Masten's standing with her tribe.

Even though the Mattz decision had determined the outcome of the Jesse Short case, establishing that Yuroks were entitled to a share of Hoopa Valley timber revenue, the dispute over payment of the Yurok share remained unresolved. The BIA maintained that there could be no distribution to the 3,800 plaintiffs without official designation of who was on the Yurok tribal roll. That issue was tied up with the organization of a reservation government, which many Jesse Short plaintiffs continued to oppose for fear that it would take money they were entitled to as individuals.

The BIA's response to this double bind was to ignore the court's ruling. Instead, the agency allowed the Hoopa Valley Business Council to continue to manage the timber in the Hoopa Square and to distribute its profits among the 1,540 people listed on its tribal roll. They were not all Hupa. The Indians in Hoopa Valley come from a number of tribes — Yurok and Karuk as well as Hupa. Some of the land allotted to Yuroks is in Hoopa Valley, where hundreds of Yuroks live. Most of those who live in the Square are of mixed tribal background, including descendants of the Shasta.

The BIA's course of action not only determined people's economic well-being, it also affected their sense of identity. The timber revenue went only to Yuroks who were listed on the Hoopa Valley Business Council's tribal roll; those living outside the Square got nothing. Some families split into antagonistic camps over allocations of money from timber sales.

Meanwhile, the decline in salmon stocks continued. The drought of the 1970s along with continuing loss of habitat and overfishing in the ocean meant low returns of spawners in subsequent years. The Bureau of Indian Affairs responded to this concern in 1982 by commissioning a resource plan for the Klamath River fisheries. The plan would address the need for coordinated management of salmon harvests, both in ocean and river fisheries, and of salmon habitat throughout the Klamath Basin. In view of the number of fisheries and the array of state and federal agencies, tribal and county governments in charge of different places within the Basin, the plan prepared for an act of Congress that could create a unifying authority to bring the responsible parties together.

But salmon could not wait for effective federal action. The start of an El Niño in 1983 made matters worse. The change in ocean temperatures and currents presaged further declines.

The Pacific Fishery Management Council halted commercial trolling in the Pacific near the mouth of the Klamath, within an area it called the Klamath Management Zone. When Congress, following recommendations presented in the BIA's plan, passed the Klamath Act in 1986, it created a Klamath River Management Council that took responsibility for the harvest of Klamath Basin salmon. The Council had a seat set aside for a representative of the Yurok Tribe.

"I wasn't too sure at that time that I wanted to get involved," Susan Masten recalled in a 1987 interview. "I work full-time and I have other things that I volunteer to do, and the fisheries is such a political issue that it's a constant battle with my own people and with the other user groups."

Masten convened a community meeting to discuss the fishery and form a committee to decide what share of the catch Yuroks would try to get. That committee in turn would select a chairperson and a spokesperson. The upshot was that Masten became both chair and spokesperson.

Accompanied by fishery biologist Ronnie Pierce, Masten argued before the Management Council that Yuroks were entitled to a 50 percent share of the total catch of Klamath River stocks. With the Boldt decision giving her leverage and the El Niño commercial fishing closure no longer in force, Masten was able to obtain a share of salmon that the ocean fishery had been awarded. Yurok gillnetters, at least in principle, would be able to catch fish in sufficient quantities for sale to non-Indian buyers. Masten also insisted that in the event of another closure of commercial fisheries, Yuroks would at least retain their right to catch salmon for subsistence and ceremonial purposes.

Establishing a Yurok commercial fishery required the consent of the Interior Department. Masten and Pierce met with Fish and Wildlife Service biologists at the Requa Inn. "I'm the politician and she's just the thorn in the side," Masten remarked. At that meeting, Pierce insisted, "You'd better give it [a commercial fishery] to them, and you'd better give it to them now." Masten took the biologists off the hook by reminding them that the BIA, not Fish and Wildlife, had to approve an Indian commercial fishery. She asked them to pressure the Bureau of Indian Affairs to act.

This good cop/bad cop approach worked wonders. Soon the BIA requested that the Yuroks come up with a management plan. After another series of community meetings, Masten negotiated the details of the plan with the Bureau.

The Yurok commercial fishery was designed to generate valid information and to permit rapid responses to changing assessments of the run. Gillnetters would take their fish for sale to one place where one buyer might purchase them. Having the fish in one location made it possible to keep an accurate count of how the run was going. Then, if the run was smaller than expected, as monitored by Fish and Wildlife biologists, the commercial fishery could be shut down quickly. Fortunately, the fishing season in the fall of 1987 exceeded expectations. Yurok gillnetters received money legally for salmon for the first time since the cannery era.

Ironically, the appearance of potential prosperity that the commercial fishery created worked to the Yuroks' disadvantage in the drive toward a political settlement with the Hupas. The settlement issue reached Washington, D.C., six months after a U.S. District Court decision. District Judge Thelton Henderson ruled against the BIA for not distributing timber revenues to more than 4,000 Yuroks who were not listed on the Hoopa Valley Business Council's tribal roll.

For the Hoopa Council, more than money was at stake. The Interior Department was now under court order to manage the extended reservation, combining the Square and the downriver Extension, on behalf of both tribes. The federal takeover that Hupas had feared during the Salmon War seemed imminent. Then Congressman Doug Bosco introduced Hoopa/Yurok settlement legislation that restored to the Business Council its control of Hoopa Valley timber.

Brought before Congress at one in the morning on October 1, 1988, Bosco's bill deprived Yuroks of the timber revenue and of their rights to other resources of the Square. It also excluded all Indian residents of Hoopa Valley who were not on the tribal roll. They either had to be eligible for a new Yurok tribal roll or lose federal recognition as American Indians.

Signed into law by President Ronald Reagan on Hallowe'en, the Hoopa/Yurok Settlement Act determined who could be a member of the Yurok tribe. In addition to a "quantum of 'Indian blood'" — a measure to be decided by the secretary of the Interior — anyone born after the enactment of the legislation was ineligible. The consequence was slow-motion termination of Yurok tribal rights. Over time, intermarriage would reduce the number of those who were one-quarter Indian — the quantum of "blood" that Interior deemed sufficient. In time, no one born before 1988 would remain alive. But for those born soon enough to make the cut, there were rewards. Although the downriver Yuroks would not receive shares of timber revenue from the 89,000-acre Square, they could reap the resources of the 3,600 acres that remained in tribal hands from the 58,000 acres of

Extension lands along the forty miles of the lower Klamath. All they had to do was form their own government. People who chose to join the new tribe would collect $5,000 each, or, if fifty and older, $7,500. Those who decided to give up their rights as tribal members would receive a buyout check of $15,000. The money would come from Hoopa Valley timber revenues that the BIA had set aside for non–Hoopa Valley Indians.

The act called for the organization of the Yurok Tribe and provided a mechanism to form the first federally recognized Yurok government. The secretary of the Interior would appoint members of a five-person transition team. Those individuals would create an economic self-sufficiency plan for the tribe and take applications from individuals who were qualified, according to the act, to be on the tribal roll. The next step was for qualified Yuroks who were eighteen years and older to elect an interim tribal council. That five-member body was to draft a constitution that the Interior secretary could approve, then conduct elections for the first tribal council to hold office under that constitution.

This plan posed a dilemma for Yuroks who had long wanted to form a government. Should they comply with an act that was alien to their traditions and detrimental to their long-term interests as a tribe? The tribal membership under the act would have to waive all rights to sue the U.S. government for any harm it did them. Yet not complying with the act could also prove harmful. Individuals who did not have the tribe's interests at heart could establish the new government and spend the settlement money on themselves. One also had to consider that a tribal government, however limited its resources and land base, could do beneficial things, such as restoring salmon habitat and creating health, housing, education, and economic development programs.

What tribal leaders did was form a government without waiving their right to challenge the law's provisions. As one of the leaders, Walt Lara Sr., put it, "We can now begin to build ourselves up." Among those who agreed to work on the transition team was Susan Masten, and she became the only member of that body to serve on the first elected council. From the beginning, Masten focused on the fishery. Troy Fletcher, the tribe's executive director, recalled, "The people that were in place at that time with the council and the transition team made a point of trying to develop the strongest, most credible fishery department that we could, because we knew that we would be subject to criticism, that our science would be questioned." A Yurok fishery biologist, Fletcher was among the tribe's early hires.

Initially, the council allowed Fish and Wildlife Service scientists to continue their work on the reservation. A continuous flow of valid data was essential for a number of reasons. One was that most commercial fishing people felt that gillnetters were their adversaries.

During the early 1990s, salmon runs declined precipitously; and as the fish went, so did the offshore commercial fishing industry. In 1979, the fleet of trollers off California's north coast had numbered about 4,000. In addition to the 7,000 people who fished from those boats, many others were employed processing and distributing the salmon. Six years later, there were 3,000 boats; they caught almost half a million fall chinook and 59,000 coho. By 1992, only 1,000 vessels were seeking salmon. Their chinook catch was 163,400, and that was the last year they hooked enough coho worth counting—about 2,500.

There was no Indian commercial fishery that year. Nineteen-eighty-seven, it turned out, had been exceptional. But that did not stop commercial fishing people from blaming Indians for their lost livelihood. According to Tammy Quigley, who bought a troller with her husband in 1991, "The one disturbing issue surrounding the salmon fisheries is that we are limited on our seasons; and in the rivers, especially with the Native Americans, they're allowed to catch enormous amounts of salmon."

To judge what was fair, the number of fish actually caught by gill-netters was needed. "We could begin to collect data," said Masten, "that would show how many fish we were actually catching and that we were managing our fishery." To manage the salmon habitat and to anticipate future runs, the tribe needed to know not only the numbers of fish at every stage of the life cycle but such factors as the temperature and oxygen content of the water, the condition of spawning streams and gravel beds, and quantities of toxic runoffs, especially from herbicides sprayed for forestry. Good information made effective action possible. Concerned especially about sedimentation that damaged spawning gravels and smothered fish eggs, the tribe formed the Lower Klamath Restoration Partnership in concert with the California State Coastal Conservancy and representatives of Simpson Timber Company.

Another reason scientific research was vital for the success of the newly established tribe was that although the Mattz case confirmed the Yuroks' right to catch salmon, it never quantified the amount Yuroks were entitled to—the issue that Masten had argued before the management council. In 1993, the tribe asked for a formal legal opinion from the solicitor of the Department of the Interior. After reviewing the history of the reservation, the solicitor reaffirmed "a purpose by the United States to reserve for the Indians what was necessary to preserve and protect their right to obtain a livelihood by fishing on the reservation." Recognizing that fishing was essential to the life of the Indian people for whom the reservation was created and acknowledging the applicability of the Boldt decision to the Yuroks, the solicitor concluded that their in-river fishery was entitled to "at least a 50 percent share of the harvestable surplus of Klamath River stocks."

With Yurok fishing rights so clearly confirmed, fishing industry representatives recognized that it was more in their interest to work with the Indians than against them. They knew that the best way to increase the numbers of salmon in the ocean was to restore their habitat in the river. They understood that the river tribes not only had incentive to do this, they embraced the responsibility. A turning point came when Nat Bingham, president of the Pacific Coast Federation of Fishermen's Associations, doubted the numbers Yuroks reported for their catch of salmon and steelhead. "I challenged him," recalled Troy Fletcher, "to come out and look at our fishery. I'd take him on the river. We'd open our books. We'd talk to him about the way we managed our harvest, we'd count our fish. And after a summer of meetings with the commercial fishermen, to their credit and ours, they made commitments and said, 'You know what, Troy, we're not going to ever question the Yurok Tribe's numbers again.'"

A set of numbers that concerned the tribe and ocean fishers alike was the diminishing count of coho. In 1997, the National Marine Fisheries Service listed the coho of northern California and southern Oregon as a threatened species under the Endangered Species Act. By this time the Yurok Tribe had the largest fishery department on the West Coast, employing as many as sixty scientists. Hydrologists monitored water flows, and biologists studied the impact of water quantity and quality on salmon and steelhead stocks. When drought returned at the turn of the millennium, "our biologists were concerned," said Masten, "that if we had back-to-back critical low years, that would have serious impacts on not only the fish returning in fall to spawn but on the juveniles, the fry, in the spring."

With extinction of coho on the horizon, tribal scientists contributed to a Biological Opinion, or BiOp, that called for increased flows of water into the Klamath River. Commercial fishing organizations joined them, demanding that the secretary of the Interior allow water normally used to irrigate farms in the Bureau of Reclamation's Klamath Project to flow directly into the river instead. The BiOp concerning coho in combination with another BiOp based on scientists' studies of suckers for the Klamath Tribes successfully pressured the Bureau to comply. Otherwise, it faced lawsuits from tribal governments based on their fishing rights plus lawsuits from fishing organizations based on the Endangered Species Act.

Problematically, the two BiOps asked for contradictory allocations. Water needed for Upper Basin suckers was also needed downriver. What flowed from Upper Klamath Lake to help coho would not remain there for suckers. And water was not all that the wild fish needed. Habitat restoration was and remains key to their survival. Yet all the Bureau could do was deny water to irrigators in the Klamath Project of the Upper Basin.

Like the Yuroks in 1978, members of the farm community responded with civil disobedience. Instead of "protest fishing," they poured Klamath River water by the bucket into an irrigation canal. But the resemblance ended there. The Indians' protest was met with acts of intimidation, violence, and arrests. The federal response to the farmers was to give them what they demanded. On July 24, 2001, Interior Secretary Gale Norton announced "that about 70,000 to 75,000 acre-feet of water will be released from Upper Klamath Lake to assist farmers in the Klamath Basin Project in desperate need." Later that year, Secretary Norton appointed a National Research Council committee to review the scientific studies on which the Biological Opinions were based. The committee issued an interim report arguing that the science was incomplete and that "there is no convincing scientific justification at present for deviating from flows" that irrigators had received during the previous decade.

The next year, Yurok biologists were concerned that low flows could result in a fish kill. The biologists presented their data to Interior and asked to see the science the secretary was using to decide how much water to release into the river. She did not provide that information.

In April 2002, Gale Norton and Secretary of Agriculture Ann Veneman went to Klamath Falls to open the valves of the headgates. "This is an important step," said Veneman, "in ensuring farmers and ranchers in the region have adequate water supplies." Farm families crowded the banks of the irrigation canal, applauding the officials and chanting, "Let the water flow!" A contingent of Indians and environmental activists protested, chanting "Fish need water!" and "Fish! Fish! Fish!" Some wore large cloth salmon masks on their heads. Arguments broke out between Indians and irrigators beside "A" Canal. At that time, Susan Masten was both the chair of the Yurok Tribal Council and the president of the National Congress of American Indians. Amid the throng of supporters and protesters at the headgates, Masten made one more attempt to convince Gale Norton that fish as well as farmers needed more water. But to no avail.

Masten recounted what happened later that year: "Fall comes, and we have a good size run that's coming in. And we have extremely low water conditions and very high water temperatures. We are very concerned because we have been monitoring the temperatures up and down the river on the Trinity and the Klamath. The numbers of fish coming in are not moving upriver like they should be."

After receiving phone calls from people who saw dead fish floating in the river, Masten took a boat ride with a tribal biologist.

You can't even begin to imagine what thirty to forty thousand dead fish look like in a twenty-mile radius. There were three, four fish deep on each side of the banks of the river. There were fish floating down the river. There were hundreds of fish in every eddy. So as the flow comes down they just kind of accumulate. They are starting to smell because they are rotting. In my wildest dreams as I was warning the federal government that there would be fish kills, I could have not have imagined such a horrific scene. It made your heart sicken. Like my Uncle said, "It hurt the very soul of our people" because it is who we are. Because of who we are as a people, spiritually and culturally, that's a huge sign. You know that things are totally out of balance. And what was so disturbing to me is this wasn't an act of nature. This kind of destruction happened to this endangered species of fish because of a government policy decision. And a policy decision that wasn't based on science; and wasn't based on legal responsibilities or on their trust responsibilities; but was strictly based on politics.

As a Yurok who had experienced the Salmon War, as a fishery council representative, tribal council chair, and president of the national organization of tribal governments, Susan Masten spoke from a frame of reference encompassing the ocean and river fisheries and the complex net of laws and agencies through which the federal government affects the Klamath River. Yet the majority of the salmon that died in the lower river in September 2002 were fall chinook from the Trinity River. They were heading toward the hatchery below Lewiston Dam where they were born. While more water released through Iron Gate Dam from the upper Klamath would have helped them, far more water would have been available to lower river temperatures, flush out toxins, and raise oxygen levels had flows through the Trinity been increased.

To understand the causes of a crisis like the fishkill of 2002, the elementary approach is to follow the water, to look at the sources of the entire watershed—its headlands, tributaries, and main stem—and to track the vital liquid that is diverted, used, and sold beyond its boundaries. A visit to Hoopa Valley, which the Trinity, flowing toward the Klamath, runs through, brings this perspective into view.

PART THREE
Upriver

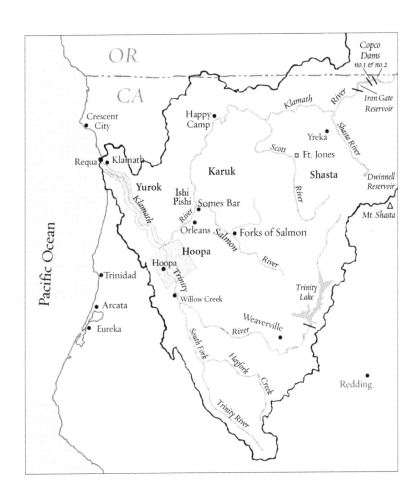

Chapter Ten
The Dam and the Weir

Rugged mountains with icy peaks and forested slopes, alpine lakes, abundant wildlife, secluded valleys, streams winding through meadows, rivers plunging through canyons. A treasure for those who love the outdoors, the Trinity Alps enrich millions of people who never go there. Here are headwaters of California's major river, the Sacramento, as well as of the Trinity and other midriver tributaries of the Klamath.

Much of the water that once ran down the Trinity is diverted. Through a network of dams, reservoirs, tunnels, pumps, and canals, the watershed contributes to the Central Valley Project, which sends water through the Sacramento River toward the San Joaquin Valley. Begun in 1937 by the Bureau of Reclamation, the Central Valley Project addresses California's major natural-resource problem. The sparsely populated mountain regions in the northern third of the state receive most of its precipitation, yet the majority of its population and most of its arable acreage are located in the arid southlands. The Central Valley Project irrigates three million acres of farmland and provides water to about thirty million people while generating 5.6 billion kilowatt hours of electricity through nine hydroelectric plants.

At a meeting in Weaverville in 1952, when Congressman Clair Engle informed locals about the proposed Trinity River Division of the Central Valley Project, he promised that not "one bucketful" of water needed within their watershed would go south. The requirement that the Secretary of the Interior take measures necessary to protect fish and other wildlife in the Trinity River Basin became part of the Trinity River Act in 1955.

For ten years after the dams were completed in 1964, however, the Division siphoned off an average of 88 percent of the runoff from the Trinity Mountains. During the first thirty years, the average diversion of Trinity River water was nearly 70 percent. The taking of all these bucketfuls

149

was planned from the start. Clair Engle Lake, later renamed Trinity Lake, is the second largest reservoir in the Central Valley Project with a capacity of two and a half million acre-feet.

With the dams on the Trinity cutting off more than a hundred miles of upstream habitat for wild fish, salmon populations fell precipitously. After thirty years, there were 90 percent fewer wild salmon within the Trinity drainage than before the dams were built. A hatchery near the dams was supposed to compensate for their loss. But during the drought years of 1976–1977, only thirteen steelhead managed to return to the hatchery. Salmonids passing through the Klamath River to other tributaries also died off, due in part to the inadequacy of Trinity River flows into the Klamath.

Among the principal beneficiaries of the diversion of Trinity River water is the Westlands Water District in the San Joaquin Valley. The politically well-connected farm owners of the largest irrigation district in the nation opposed restoration of adequate Trinity River flows in accordance with the Trinity River Act. The competing interests fought for this water via legislation, litigation, and executive branch proposals. After a twenty-year study, the Clinton Administration called for an up-to-tenfold restoration of flows into the river system, from as little as 600 cubic feet per second to as much as 6,000. Westlands greeted this plan with a lawsuit.

Eventually, in 2004, the Hoopa Valley Indian Tribe won a judgment in the Ninth Circuit Court of Appeals that the combination of habitat loss and water diversions caused by the dams had devastated runs of salmon and steelhead in the Trinity and that restoration of the river's flows must occur. The following year, Tom Stienstra, the *San Francisco Chronicle*'s outdoors reporter, announced: "The Trinity River will be transformed into one of the West's top rafting rivers this spring." In July, Stienstra reported, "The river canyon is filled with life, with ospreys and eagles the most evident. . . . The best flyfishing in California could be on the Trinity right now." Yet the best of times for the Trinity were among the worst for the Klamath. The river, "diverted and dewatered by the government, farmers, and environmental law alike, had another fish kill this past week," Stienstra told his readers. "This time 100,000 young chubs and minnows dying and washing up as floaters." The increased amount of water released from the Trinity through the Klamath main stem could not help juvenile fish coming from tributaries upriver of the Klamath-Trinity confluence.

In the conflict over the scarce waters of the Klamath Basin, those who farm and those who catch fish took sides against each other. But when looking at this issue from a larger frame of reference, one that encompasses all of the uses of the water, a deeper polarity reveals itself: the rural versus urban divide in which the farmers, ranchers, and fishers, including tribal members, are on the same side. Popular prejudice regards urban civilization as the haven of science and technology, while country people are stereotyped as "bumpkins" and American Indians as "primitives." In America, however, urbanites comprise a highly complex, mobile mass of millions of people, a large proportion of whom do not know where their water comes from. At the other end of the scale are locally based societies whose ways of life require a far more complex awareness of humanity's relationship with the natural world.

In the Klamath Basin, with the exception of the federal government, the major supporters of scientific research are the Yurok, Hupa, Karuk, and Klamath tribes. With regard to technology, the Central Valley Project—with its dams, reservoirs, and turbines that produce food and provide energy—invites comparison with the major technological accomplishment of California tribes, the fish dam or weir, which is also productive of food and, thus, the energy to live.

In September 2001, after several days of video production on the Klamath and Salmon rivers, Jack Kohler spent a weekend in Hoopa Valley where his father, Jack Sr., lives. There he witnessed the building of the first fish dam on the Trinity since 1948. "Last time they built a dam down here," one of the young men working on the weir told Jack, "people from Willow Creek and upriver, non-Indians, wanted to blow it up. They were mad, saying the Indians were up here blocking the river up, but it's not like a dam that they build—we just stop the fish."

Until the arrival of non-Indians, the weir was an important method of catching salmon on the Klamath as well as the Trinity. Its construction was timed with salmon runs in coordination with ceremonial dances, when thousands of people from the Yurok, Hupa, Karuk, and Shasta tribes assembled. These gatherings needed a lot of food, and the weirs provided it.

"The important thing about it is to stop the fish," explained Jimmy Jackson Jr., a ninety-two-year-old Hupa elder. "And the big chief, in those days, he'd call all the people, all the Indian people. Then at that time, we used to get equal amount. Everybody got one fish, two fish, three, whatever they catch. And the old man said, 'They need salmon up the river too, up that way. . . . So they opened [the gate].'"

After ten days, the weirs were dismantled so that fish could migrate upriver and into their spawning grounds. In this manner, the weirs and the ceremonies together combined ecological management with religious observance, connecting the river tribes with each other as well as with the environment they shared.

Weirs on the Klamath River were early casualties of the Gold Rush. In 1849, white men prevented Yuroks from building their fish dam at Kepel. Indians retaliated by attacking the ferry that miners used to cross the Klamath. Whites then burned four villages, including Weitchpec and Kepel. Mining on the upper Klamath in Karuk country also disrupted weir-building and ceremonial dancing. But in Hoopa Valley, the making of weirs continued without significant interruption well into the twentieth century. Jimmy Jackson Jr. was able to instruct teenagers in building one for the first time in fifty-three years.

The Hoopa Valley Indian Reservation was established in 1864. It has remained intact ever since. Here the Hupa have managed to maintain their traditional culture.

Until the 1930s, when the Indian Reorganization Act reformed tribal governance, most tribes were ruled by Indian agents who did not allow Indigenous ceremonies or other traditional activities to occur. The federal response to the Lakota Ghost Dance was the infamous massacre at Wounded Knee in 1890. How was it possible for the Hupa to keep alive their technical expertise as well as their religious observances in the face of the assimilationist demands of the dominant society?

Geography had something to do with it—and with the creation of the Hoopa Valley Indian Reservation. Hoopa Valley extends for about six miles. The Trinity River arches broadly across the valley floor, with three streams flowing into it on each side as the river rushes north toward the trinity-shaped delta of sand at its confluence with the Klamath.

As recently as 1978, during the Salmon War, federal agents had difficulty imposing their will in Hoopa Valley. The valley is highly defensible. The mountains to the west and the Trinity Summit to the east rise thousands of feet above the valley floor, and both the northern and southern approaches to the valley require a mountainous descent of about 2,000 feet. People can enter only along easily guarded or blockaded routes. With only fifty acres of flatlands, the valley never could support large agricultural or ranching enterprises, and settlers were never numerous enough to overwhelm the Indigenous population. Nor did federal plans to move the Indians elsewhere succeed.

Lyle Marshall, chair of the Hoopa Valley Tribal Council, told the story of one nineteenth-century attempt to make the Indians leave the valley.

> They'd given some of the best ag land in the county to the Indians and so they decided to move them to Round Valley, one of the other four reservations in California. . . . And when the tribe was researching its history book [Our Home Forever], they found this telegram from Austin Wiley to Washington D.C., and it said, "I've met with the Indians. Stop. They are still armed. Stop. They have advised me that they prefer death and starvation in the mountains to removal. Stop. I advise that we leave them here." And so we never got removed.

Originally, it was only the Yuroks who called the Hupa "Hupa." In their Athapaskan tongue, the Hupa called themselves Natinook-wa and their valley Natinook, "where the trails return." Their ceremonial center, Takimildiñ, "the place of the acorn feast," was a tree-shaded village near a spring on the east side of the valley.

Before hunting deer and elk, men spent days and nights in the sweat lodge, eliminating their human scent, and then disguised themselves in animal skins. They fooled mountain lions as well as browsing herds. To protect their necks from the fangs of big cats, hunters fixed sharp pins under the skins they wore.

In the river there were lamprey eels, sturgeon, and trout to catch as well as salmon. In addition to the weirs, which fed the crowds at the Jump Dance and White Deerskin ceremonies, fishermen used harpoons, bows and arrows, hand nets, set nets, and basket traps. Some netted fish from platforms built with branches and perched on rocks; some caught fish by hand.

"They used to be a lot of eels," Jimmy Jackson told Jack Kohler on camera. "We could catch half a boatful." This was such an important food source that in the canyon north of their valley the Hupa greeted the annual arrival of the lamprey with a First Eel Ceremony. "But now," said Jackson, "I didn't even get a taste of one this year." He attributed the demise of the eels to the hydroelectric plant at Trinity Dam. "I guess they got it into those big turbos, the eels," he said. "So what they did, I understand, they poisoned them up there . . . and they killed them off, so there's no more. There's no more in this river."

The destructive impacts of non-Indian technology began with the Gold Rush, but the initial contact between whites and Indians in Hoopa Valley was mutually beneficial. McCann, an elderly Hupa who lived to the turn of the twentieth century, told the story of the arrival of Jedediah Smith's expedition in 1828:

> It was winter when they heard they were coming from the south. "Let's make a dance or do something else," they said. Then they heard that they had reached Southfork. Southfork men ran down to Medildiñ and told them that the strangers did no harm. They came down to Medildiñ and camped for the night on the other side above the village. There they bought bear, fox, and coon hides, giving hatchets and knives for them.

In 1849, Maj. Pierson B. Reading struck gold on the upper Trinity River. He and his men claimed to be making forty dollars a day. Later that year, Josiah Gregg led an eight-man party to open a supply route between the upper Trinity and the coast. These men walked into a Hupa village at the junction between the south fork of the Trinity and the main stem. After its frightened residents ran away, the forty-niners helped themselves to their supply of smoked salmon, leaving some venison as payment. This did not placate the eighty armed Indians who confronted the miners in their camp that night. Gregg and his men offered gifts and attempted to intimidate the warriors with talk of their firearms. But when the Hupa insisted that he demonstrate these weapons, Gregg had to beg for time. The guns were still wet from crossing the river.

Before Gregg's party left the next day, the Indians warned him not to continue down the Trinity: "Large tribes of nations scattered all along the river to its mouth would surely oppose passage through their country." Instead, the expedition made its way across the mountains to the coast.

By the spring of 1850, towns were mushrooming along the coast, with hastily built wood frames among rows of tents on newly platted grounds. Trinidad (the site of the Yuroks' southernmost village), Union City (later called Arcata), and Eureka aspired to be prosperous port cities. Trails linking the port to the inland mines would enable local businesses to supply gold-seekers just off the boat with mules, blankets, rifles, whiskey, and other necessities.

Besides the vagaries of fortune and the mountainous terrain to the east, the threat of Indian attacks clouded the miners' and merchants' hopes for wealth. It is a common and sometimes tragic irony that anticipation of hostilities brings about the result feared. When Ernest de Massey fell behind his mining party as they traveled along a trail in the direction of Hoopa Valley, he noticed thirty young Indians following them. Their purpose, he feared, was to massacre the white men. Once the miners entered Hupa country, Indians offered their hospitality, but the whites abruptly made them leave camp. One Hupa, on his way out, took a knife from the miners' supplies. De Massey chased him; his companions shot at other Indians. That night, arrows retaliated, striking the ground near the whites' bedrolls. The situation did not escalate further, fortunately, and the next morning several Hupas made a peace offering of salmon and acorns.

De Massey and two of his partners accepted the Indians' offer to visit the tribe's spiritual center, Takimildiñ. They left Hoopa Valley quickly thereafter, heading toward Big Bar along the upper Trinity. By this time, several thousand miners were within the Trinity watershed, including some prospectors along the south fork in Hupa country. Also by this time, numerous incidents of violence had occurred. After the theft of some horses and mules, for example, French Canadian miners burned down a village and shot fourteen Indian men in a place called Burnt Ranch. Near the fork of the Salmon River, which flows into the Klamath upstream from the Trinity, miners killed more than fifty Indians and burned three villages.

No event of this magnitude occurred in Hoopa Valley. It was the Hupas' good fortune that little gold was found in a gravel bar that white and Chinese miners panned there. Even so, they must have noted the effects of a dam built upstream of their valley in the summer of 1850. A mining company used the dam to divert the Trinity into an old channel. By doing so, the miners bared three-quarters of a mile of the riverbed, which they then pored over in search of gold. Yet, according to Stephen

Powers, the reporter who visited the Hupa in 1871, "the salmon-fishing
of the Hupa was not so much interrupted by muddy water—a fruitful
source of trouble in early days—nor did they themselves come so much in
contact with the miners as did those tribes further up the river."

Among the miners who stayed to plant farms and orchards and the settlers who followed the miners to the Trinity Alps were men who intended
to eliminate the Indian population altogether. In May 1852, residents
of Weaverville blamed Indians for killing a man named Anderson and
avenged his death by attacking a village on the south fork of the Trinity.
Surprising the Indians at dawn, vigilantes managed to kill all but three of
the villagers—147 people.

The first white settler in Hoopa Valley, Capt. David Snyder, arrived in
1853. "Through his exertions," reported the *Humboldt Times* in 1855, "the
valley has been changed from a wilderness to one of the handsomest in the
state. Every foot of land has been taken up by farms, a larger flouring mill
is going up, and everything presages a permanent settlement." Additional
settlers came to Hupa country that year. The Hupa chose not to fight them.

Like the Yuroks downriver on the Klamath, the Hupas' experience in
the 1850s bore little resemblance to what befell the majority of California
Indians. In the few years since the Gold Rush, almost half of the new
state's Indigenous population, estimated at 100,000, died of disease and
violence. Thousands more were enslaved or sold. For many of the survivors, warfare against the whites seemed the only alternative to ongoing
destruction at their hands.

Recognizing the danger of a large-scale Indian war, Edward F. Beale,
a superintendent of Indian affairs for California, recommended the
establishment of reservations containing military posts. His replacement,
Thomas J. Henley, sent an agent to the Klamath River to choose a reservation site. Although the agent selected Hoopa Valley, Henley decided that
because settlers claimed land there, the government could not afford to
buy them out. Instead, President Franklin Pierce established the reservation on a strip of land along the Klamath in Yurok country.

All the Indians of the region were expected to move into the reservation. The Hupas refused, warning of consequences if they were removed
from their villages by force.

In 1858, Captain Snyder brought Captain John, a Hupa leader, to San
Francisco to convince him that there was nothing to gain by joining the

Indians in northern California who were fighting white people. Captain John was astonished by the city of 50,000 people. In the Hupa Tribe's official history, *Our Home Forever*, Byron Nelson wrote that upon returning to his homeland, Captain John "scooped up dry sand from the Trinity's bank and let it trickle through his fingers to show how numerous they [the San Franciscans] were."

Shortly after John's return, the federal government, responding to a request from Hoopa Valley settlers, established Fort Gaston there. The forces were not authorized to grant the settlers' other request, however—removal of the Hupa to the reservation downriver on the Klamath. Not only were they armed, but the Hupa also had been careful not to give the whites a pretext for their removal. According to the agent at the reservation, there was "not a tribe of Indians in California more friendly and better disposed towards the whites."

Soldiers soon alienated some of the Hupa. Hupa Tribal Chairman Lyle Marshall tells the story, which has passed down through his family. During the holiday season in December 1859, two soldiers attempted to rape a pregnant woman of the Tseweñaldiñ village. Fighting them off, she stabbed one of the men with an awl made of deerbone used in basket weaving. "The soldier later died," Marshall said, "so Tseweñaldiñ village, expecting retaliation, packed up and left." But not before Lyle's great-great-great-grandmother went into labor and gave birth to his great-great-grandfather. "They waited for three days for her to feel better and then they left. And when the soldiers crossed the river, Tseweñaldiñ village was abandoned. But the soldiers went to the next village, Takimildiñ, and attacked that and killed a lot of people."

For the next four years, Marshall's ancestors waged guerrilla warfare, hiding in the mountains while raiding ranches and attacking soldiers whenever they could. The baby was kept in a cradleboard long after he would normally have outgrown it, for the Hupa had to be ready to run at a moment's notice. Even when he was walking, the child had the basket strapped on his back, which forced him to hunch over, giving him the name Turtle.

Troubles in the valley did not end with the Tseweñaldiñs' departure. According to Byron Nelson, some people remained in that village or returned to it. One consequence was an ongoing dispute between its leaders and the leaders of Takimildiñ, Charley and Bill Hostler. Bill Hostler thought it wisest "to maintain peace with the whites," according to the Hupa historian, "while Tseweñaldiñ John and Big Jim were determined to resist them."

The feud between the two villages started in September 1860 after two white men, a soldier and a settler, killed a Hupa man in an argument over a Hupa woman. The settler fled Hoopa Valley, and the soldier escaped retaliation within the walls of the fort. Unable to punish either of the white men, the victim's village of Takimildiñ demanded that the village of Tseweñaldiñ compensate for his death. This claim followed the logic of the law of the land. Because one of their people, the pregnant woman, was the first to kill a white man in the valley, Tseweñaldiñ was responsible for the deaths that Takimildiñ suffered.

At Fort Gaston, Major Taylor concluded that bad blood between Hupa factions served his interests. With only a few hundred soldiers, Taylor preferred to let the Hupa defeat themselves. The fear of raids from "hostiles" led Hoopa Valley settlers to abandon their homesteads and seek security within the walls of the fort. Soldiers were needed to guard settlers in the valley as well as to prevent or respond to violence over a broad geographical area.

The five years of intermittent warfare on this frontier overlapped with the Civil War, which kept military forts in the West undermanned. Violent incidents occurred almost always outside of Hoopa Valley, involving many tribes. Meanwhile, the Hupa peace faction, led by Captain John of Takimildiñ, helped keep trouble away from the valley. The peacekeepers signed an agreement to aid the military by punishing any Hupa caught fighting against them.

Tseweñaldiñ John's ally, Big Jim, came from the largest Hupa village, Medildiñ. Suspecting that Medildiñ harbored three warriors who had raided a settlement on New River, a Trinity tributary, the military surrounded that village, demanded that the people surrender, marched them to a place beside Fort Gaston, and ordered them to rebuild their houses there.

The relocation of the village, which occurred in September 1863, intensified Hupa resistance. The three warrior suspects fled the valley in the company of Big Jim and thirty other men. Joining members of other tribes, they ranged across the Trinity Mountains, attacking settlements between Hoopa Valley and Big Flat. They also successfully attacked a group of soldiers on the south fork of the Trinity. By late December, when the military discovered and surrounded their log stronghold near Redwood Creek, Tseweñaldiñ John and Big Jim had more than a hundred men with them. Marshall told the story this way:

> There was a place called Bloody Camp. And Fort Gaston was always complaining about not having enough supplies and stuff, and they actually ran out of bullets and surrounded these people and shot over 2,000 rounds and went back and got more bullets. But when the sun came up, the Indians had crawled out, literally had crawled out of that, even though they were surrounded, and escaped.

Lt. Col. Stephen G. Whipple, who moved his headquarters to Fort Gaston, asked the state to send 250 volunteers to his Humboldt Military District. He feared that the Hupa fighters would join forces with Yurok and Karuk warriors. The additional men did discourage the alliance, but it did not bring the unconditional surrender Whipple had hoped for.

Then in April 1864, Hupa warriors came to Weitchpec, the Yurok village, and sent word to Whipple that they wanted to negotiate for peace. Marshall recounted what happened next: "The captain of the fort then brought the entire militia to Weitchpec to try to capture these guys, and they made so much racket that they just left and they went up the ridge behind the Weitchpec village."

According to Byron Nelson, Tseweñaldiñ John finally agreed to meet with Captain Greene if the captain came unarmed and unescorted. When Greene did so, the Hupa warrior told him that "he wanted peace; that he was tired of the mountains and wanted to come in." But John would not return to Hoopa Valley unless Big Jim and the other fighters ended their armed struggle as well.

Later that month, the major war factions met and agreed to make peace on the provision that the militants not be punished for resisting the occupation of their valley. By May, almost all of the Hupa had returned, but they retained their weapons. In August, Austin Wiley signed the Treaty of Peace and Friendship of 1864. The reservation that it delineated included, according to Marshall, "almost all of what Hupa claimed as their territory." Under Article I, Section 2, the treaty reserved "a sufficient area of the mountains on each side of the Trinity river as shall be necessary for hunting grounds, gathering berries, seeds, &c."

There are few parallels to this victory in the history of Native America. In contrast to the treaties made with California Indians in 1851 and then ignored by the Senate, this time the United States fulfilled most of its promises. Many, if not all, of the settlers left in 1865, and an Indian agent arrived to run the reservation. But it was not until 1876 that President Grant signed the executive order that confirmed the reservation's existence and withdrew Hoopa Valley lands from public sale. In 1877, the settlers received payment for their homesteads, a total of $60,000.

Two very different descriptions of the Hupa during this period exist. Reporter and pioneer ethnologist Stephen Powers, who visited the valley in the summer of 1871, praised them as "the Romans of Northern California in their valor and their wide-reaching dominions." That same year, H. L. Knight, a Eureka attorney, "found them poor, miserable, vicious, degraded, dirty, naked, diseased, and ill-fed. The oldest men, or stout middle-aged fathers of families, were spoken to just as children or slaves. They know no law but the will of the Agent." Knight also observed that the Hupa "follow the old forms of life." The lawyer abhorred such customs as the purchase of wives and the settlement of disputes with payments. "Old forms" that he did not disparage included fishing with weirs and ceremonial dances.

Ethnologist Pliny Goddard, who lived in Hoopa Valley between 1897 and 1900, wrote that the White Deerskin Dance had occurred every two years through 1897. He had observed the Boat Dance on the fourth day of the White Deerskin ceremony, finding it "spectacular in the extreme. Three large canoes are placed abreast. . . . Eight or ten men stand behind one another in each canoe. One man sits in the stern to steer. While the boats are floating down, the men flex the knees and hips in unison imparting considerable motion to the boat. The leaders make peculiar motions with their heads while they lead the boat-dance song." Noting as well the Hupa practice of praying at sacred spots on the trails they walked, Goddard remarked: "It is largely this undercurrent of deep religious feeling that makes the life and deeds of the Indian seem so strange to the white man."

Their cultural continuity enabled the Hupa to be both noble Romans within their own society and ignoble savages from the perspective of the Indian agent. The agent exerted much power over them, which had a demeaning effect. Indians could not leave the reservation without his permission, nor could they work for anyone without his consent. All of the supplies that the Hupa received—tools, blankets, food, and medicine—the agent provided. He controlled their educational system as well as their government.

Still, the agent's ability to dominate his charges was limited. He had only a few employees, and there were more than 600 Hupas. The Indians retained their firearms, which they used in hunting but which also served as reminders of their prowess as warriors. Giving additional leverage to the Hupa was the presence of a second center of authority in Hoopa Valley, Fort Gaston. The Indian agent needed soldiers to enforce his commands, but the fort's commander did not have to provide them. His job was to contend with "hostiles," not reservation Indians. The Hupa learned to report abuses of power by the agent to the commander. This gave them, Nelson observed, "the ability to send a message to Washington D.C., since the man they spoke with might report their complaints to his superiors."

Further undermining the agency's influence was President Grant's policy of turning reservation governance over to Christian missionaries, even though the conversion efforts of the Methodists who came to Hoopa Valley fell short of success. Superintendent James L. Broaddus complained that "the majority of Indians were . . . addicted to gambling, and their native dances had a demoralizing effect."

Broaddus made his own contributions to their demoralization. He refused to repair their homes and fences, sold the hay they produced at a fraction of its worth, hired his relatives instead of Hupas to harvest wheat, and disposed of the reservation's tools, equipment, and supplies. Claiming falsely that the government planned to sell the Hupas' land and that the whites would kill them all if they remained in the valley, Broaddus attempted to pressure them into moving to the reservation in Round Valley.

James Halloran, the commander at Fort Gaston, however, sided with the Indians, attributing the agency's failures to "the expressed prejudice of the Agent against this people." His attempt at ethnic cleansing thwarted, Broaddus closed the agency in 1877 and left Hoopa Valley. Halloran's successor, Capt. Richard Parker, took over governance. It was another victory for the Hupa.

Capt. John Dougherty, who assumed command in 1886, did not attempt to make the Hupa give up weir-building or other aspects of their culture. After the Allotment Act passed Congress in 1887, the commander reported to Washington, D.C., that Hoopa Valley did not have enough arable land to enable the Hupa to live off agriculture. Besides, lacking roads out of the valley, Indians were unable to send products to market. He assigned temporary plots to the Hupa nonetheless, but they were never adequately surveyed. As a result, the dismemberment and disposal of reservation lands that the legislation effected elsewhere did not succeed in Hoopa Valley. Litigation over allotments persisted for decades.

In 1890, civilian control returned to the Indian agency. The new agent, Isaac A. Beers, was displeased to find that the Hupa "cling to their old customs and laws as being far better than any others, and seem to look upon many of them as sacred." In late December of that year, the massacre at Wounded Knee signaled to the nation the destruction of the Indian way of life, and the photograph of the corpse of a Lakota named Big Foot, contorted in South Dakota snow, lent credibility to the myth of the vanishing redman. Outside Hoopa Valley and other remote places in the Klamath Basin, few realized that in California, at least, government efforts to destroy Indigenous culture and the initiatives of citizen vigilantes to eliminate Indians had failed.

On September 22, 2001, the documentary film crew checked in at the Tsewenaldin Inn on the old village site in Hoopa Valley. On the phone, Susan Masten informed me that the Jump Dance was underway not far away. Jack Kohler and Gerrid Joy, who did sound and camera work for the production, drove there with me.

The Jump Dance took place in front of a backdrop—a rough-hewn cedar fence held together with one horizontal board. Eleven men and four women took part. The men danced in a line, facing outward. Two of the women were in the line with them but facing each other; the two other women stood next to each other to one side.

The women wore white dresses with full regalia. Three black vertical lines ran down their chins. The men were bare chested and wore abalone necklaces. Long rectangular bands on their heads were decorated with red woodpecker feathers and a large white feather. On the ground in front of them lay cylindrical prayer baskets, resting on pelts. Sitting in chairs in front of the dancers were five elders, including Jimmy Jackson, who appeared to be the ceremonial leader.

Each dance began with the dancers singing the same tone. Then, holding hands, they leapt lightly and landed firmly. As they continued to move in unison, one singer lofted a soft, plaintive melody that had the feeling of a solitary seeker. As he sang, the others maintained a guttural chorus of rising and falling sounds.

The dancing occurred in an area where there were two traditional plank houses and a communal place for cooking and eating. After the Jump Dance was over and the dancers were taking off their regalia beside one of the traditional houses, Jack, Gerrid, and I followed Jimmy Jackson to the kitchen area. Jack reminded the elder that he had been filming the weir and that he had asked to interview him next time we were in Hoopa Valley. Jackson consented to the interview, which we scheduled for the following Tuesday, when Carlos Bolado, Mike Pryfogle, and cinematographer George Spies would be with us.

We lined up interviews with Leonard Masten and Billy Colgrove. Masten, who worked for the BIA as a "fish cop" for more than twenty years, includes among his ancestors a blacksmith who worked for the military at Fort Gaston. Colgrove, a forestry management professional, was then vice chair of the Hoopa Valley Tribal Council.

The ground was wet on Tuesday morning. Rain had been falling for the first time in months. Jimmy Jackson was home for his interview, but Masten and Colgrove did not show up. A message waited for us at the Inn: they had gone deer hunting. On a wet day after a long dry spell, the prospects for bagging game and bringing home venison were too good to be passed up.

The rest of the day's video shoot had to be improvised. Luckily, Stuart Lauden, who works at the center for Hupa Language, Culture, and Education, was available to speak on camera. The building of the weir was a program for teens initiated by his center. Lauden displayed the model of a weir that Jimmy Jackson had built to guide the construction. The model has stabilizing structures jutting from the backbone of the weir that the fish dam in the river did not include. "These aren't present," Lauden explained, "'cause the river used to be a lot deeper back then."

Lauden also spoke about the Boat Dance, which still occurs in conjunction with the White Deerskin Dance. The Hupa have to inform the Bureau of Reclamation several days before the Boat Dance is to take place so that enough water will be released through Trinity Dam to prevent the dancers' redwood canoes from scraping the river bottom.

During the interview, a wiry, middle-aged man with unsteady legs walked in and out of the picture. After being waved away, he stood closely behind George Spies and the camera. He was Virgil Blake, a Yurok. His brother, George Blake, is an internationally known artist whose work ranges from traditionally carved elkhorn spoons to lifesize wooden sculptures of "cigarstore white men." When the shoot was over, Blake persuaded Bolado to give him a ride home, saying that he had "the best salmon jerky in Hoopa Valley."

We drove north across the valley and up the mountain to a forested area high above the Trinity River near Weitchpec. Turning off the road, we drove past a gate into a littered homestead where a trailer house was parked. After throwing slabs of salmon jerky at his yapping dogs, Blake took the crew on a tour of his twenty acres. He showed us, hidden among trees, an extraordinary exhibition: dozens of bicycles piled up beside wheels and other bike parts; towers of stoves, washing machines, and other appliances; meadows covered with wrecked cars. Up the trail, even more cars, and down the hill, still more. It went on and on, like a combination used auto row and shopping mall.

Blake talked proudly as he rushed the documentary crew to one outdoor room of used-up and broken goods after another. We looked around in amazement, getting everything we could on camera. Our host seemed to know the history of every car—how this one got its bullet holes, where this one wrecked, how that car's collision shattered its windshield. He spoke of the work he did as a junk collector in Hoopa Valley, trucking all this stuff up to his land. Toward the end of the tour, as he showed off a suggestively shaped young tree, Blake declared that he is a "nature artist."

His exhibit seemed the opposite: a parody of the consumer society, his piles of junk as neatly arranged by category as products at a Walmart, all looking completely strange in the setting of his forested land. On the other hand, by removing all this stuff from Hoopa Valley, Blake has helped the artwork of nature remain beautiful. No less than his brother George, it seemed, he was satirizing the wooden white man, possessed by possessions that spoil the land.

During a subsequent interview, Lyle Marshall spoke about the philosophy of the Klamath River tribes in a way that threw Blake's collection of found art, or acres of junk, into perspective. Marshall drew our attention to a painting of the White Deerskin Dance by his grandmother. "What my grandmother said she was trying to represent here was that the spirits are, the deerskins are, alive. And everything that you make for the ceremony, as you make it you talk to it, you pray to it, you sing with it. And it has its own spirit, and you then have to take care of it." This dance, he said, "is a reflection of what we talk about when we talk about the river; this is our responsibility, to pray for the world: to set it in place, to put it back the way it's supposed to be. And you gather up all the bad in the world, and you send it away." Does this ethos of renewing the world underlie Blake's gathering up of junk from the valley to be hidden among trees above the river canyon? By spoiling his land is he renewing the world?

There is a tension between polarities here—the sacred and the profane, the art of nature and the work of civilization—that does not require the elimination of one in favor of the other. Speaking of the conflict "with the commercial fishermen, the sports fishermen back in the '70s when all the fingers pointed at the Indians," Marshall remarked that

> we've all come to the same realization that we have the same interests and we have the same goal, and it's not in our interest to be adversaries. And I think we have to say that same message now to the farmers: "We have to be allies here. We have to understand your needs. We have to find out what this river really needs. We have to provide as best we can to meet the needs of everybody." One can't die as opposed to the other.

Through the lens of the camera, Marshall invited farmers and the public to come to Hoopa Valley and see

> how beautiful it is. Is there a place where you can take your kids to a wild river and actually swim in it and not be afraid that it's going to poison you and irritate your skin? Is there a place where you can take your kids and you can raft and play and fish and commune and feel that you're a part of all that is? Because that's what we should be, a part of everything, a part of this Earth. We're not above it. If you can appreciate it, if you can love it as much as we do, then you'll understand why we fight so hard to protect it.

Hoopa Valley is beautiful, but it is not a pristine Shangri-la. Although the Hupa managed to build weirs and preserve many aspects of their precontact culture well into the twentieth century, Jimmy Jackson's generation was the last to grow up speaking Hupa. Service in the military, especially during the world wars, gave some tribal members an American identity. Mass media replaced local culture in providing models of how to live. Income from the timber industry after World War II made the people consumers. It was they who bought many of the cars, bicycles, dishwashers, water heaters, and other goods that now rust among the trees on Virgil Blake's land.

But during the decades of cultural renewal among American Indians that began with the fish wars of the Pacific Northwest and included such landmark events as the occupation of Alcatraz and the siege of Wounded Knee, some Indians in Hoopa Valley rediscovered their culture. The teenagers who built the first weir of the twenty-first century did so as a project for their Hupa language class, and ceremonies that were not done for many years, including the Flower Dance for a girl's coming of age, have been revived. The life of the valley is shaped by the dam and by the weir, and the balance between these two poles of influence continues to change.

Chapter Eleven
Coyote's Journey

On the grassy edge of the cliff behind the Weitchpec general store, the production team shot the influx of the Trinity River into the Klamath. The delta of sand that divides the tributary from the darker main-stem waters appeared clearly in the afternoon light. On foot, we crossed the bridge spanning the Klamath in search of a better vantage point, then drove upriver into Orleans.

At the Orleans Mining Company—a combination restaurant, general store, gas station, museum, and motel—a sign proclaimed:

> Last of the Mom and Pop Cafes
> Home of the World's Largest
> Cast Iron Collection
> It Is Everywhere!

On the grounds and in a series of small windows, the museum's artifacts were on display: an old washtub, nineteenth-century tools and bottles, and a mannequin dressed in cowboy clothes. Inside, scores of skillets and Dutch ovens hung from the ceiling. Inscribed on the skillets were names of people who have visited Orleans over the years.

Orleans was established in 1852. There are reports of miners on the upper Klamath as early as 1850, but a guide to California goldfields, published in 1851, mentions diggings only on the Trinity River, not the Klamath. Gold was bound to be found on the larger river. From a geological perspective, not only did the wealth of Trinity ore indicate good prospects along the Klamath as well; the original discovery of gold in foothills of the Sierra Nevada, along the American River, also pointed toward gold in the Klamath Mountains. As naturalist David Rains Wallace described it, "The Klamaths were just one part of a larger range that ran along the whole Pacific coast, including what are now the Sierra Nevada and the Blue Mountains of Oregon. Klamath rocks are very similar to Sierra rocks, as the forty-niners quickly discovered, finding the same gold-bearing gravels in both."

Placer gravels accounted for three-quarters of the gold found in the Klamath Mountains. Sandbars along the Klamath and two of its tributaries, the Salmon and the Scott, yielded two or three dollars per pan, up to forty dollars a day. Wage-earning Chinese did much of the labor, which included transporting goods and cutting wood as well as mining, but they earned no more than $1.50 daily. Shopkeepers, providing goods and supplies, might bring in $1,000 a day. Whoever ran the Orleans Mining Company or its equivalent in 1852 did a booming business.

Initially, about 300 men came to the upper Klamath and Salmon River watersheds in search of paydirt. Karuks welcomed them, offering to guide them and ferry them across the rivers. Stephen Powers reported that the appearance of the miners excited speculation among the Indians. One theory was "that they were of a fugitive tribe driven away from their native seats, and their women taken away from them; and this opinion was confirmed by the fact that they had no women with them and possessed long beards—a badge of widowhood among the Indians."

In addition to Orleans, the miners in Karuk country established the town of Somes Bar, where the Salmon River flows into the Klamath; Murder's Bar, whose name, after a night of drunken celebration, changed to Happy Camp; and Hamburg (originally Hamburgh), where the Scott River enters the Klamath. Most of the population of Hamburg consisted of Chinese men who worked in teams at the mines (almost all of them eventually returned to China). According to a history of Siskiyou County, Hamburg "boasted three stores, several saloons, a hotel and rooming house, livery stable, freight and passenger stage line stop, and other businesses."

Additional mines and towns sprang up in Shasta Indian country upriver of Hamburg on the Klamath, in the Scott and Shasta River valleys, and along the Salmon. Pack trains, with fifty mules or more, were the major source of supply. One popular stop was the Forks of Salmon Hotel, which "boasted a butcher shop, bar, kitchen, dining room, and eight rooms upstairs with an additional room with ten beds."

Black Bear, originally a gold mine on the Salmon River near Forks of Salmon, became a trading center with mills, a school, and housing for men and their families. One of its owners, John Daggett, was a mining engineer who in 1883 served as lieutenant governor of California and was later head of the U.S. Mint in San Francisco. Daggett employed 300 Chinese to build a nine-mile road from Forks of Salmon to his eighty-acre establishment.

Between 1850 and 1856, when the easy-to-find gold petered out, more than 2,000 miners panned the gravels of the upper Klamath and its tributaries. In subsequent years, men who had geological savvy or who, like Daggett, had engineering skills led high-tech mining operations. Lode mining took place in the mountains, as miners looked for veins of gold in quartz formations. Dredging occurred extensively on the Scott River, and hydraulic mining roiled the Klamath, affecting salmon runs.

A form of mining developed near Hamburg was the wing dam, a wooden rectangle built about seventy-five feet into the river. From this enclosure water-powered "Chinese pumps" drained the water. Then derricks pulled out the gravel, which was washed down sluices. In some locations, waterwheels lifted gravel-bearing water onto the sluices, from which it flowed into a processing area. Innovations like the wing dam set a long-lasting precedent. Gold miners were the first to turn the waters of the Klamath into an "organic machine," as historian Richard White has described the Columbia, extracting its wealth without regard to the life of the river.

There is a direct line of descent between the Gold Rush and the hydroelectric projects that generate power throughout California and the Pacific Northwest. The water cannon that a miner invented in 1852 for hydraulic mining served as the prototype of the nozzles that direct water at high pressures onto the turbines of hydroelectric dams. Moreover, the Gold Rush brought an influx of engineering talent into California that paid dividends for decades to come.

The Department of Engineering at Stanford University, founded by railroad tycoon Leland Stanford in 1891, became an engine of innovation. Rudolph Van Norden, who graduated in 1896, designed thirty hydroelectric plants and dams. Professor Harris J. Ryan, a prominent member of Stanford's electrical engineering department for a quarter century, specialized in high voltage power transmission. His students developed the technology that moves electricity long distances from hydroelectric dams to urban areas.

In the shadow of the wealth and technical success that the Gold Rush brought to the mid-Klamath region came devastation for the tribes. Near Orleans, where Camp Creek pours into the Klamath River, Karuks had a village named Panamnik. This site is one of four places where Karuks hold *pikyávish* "fixing the world" ceremonies. Karuks know it also as Coyote's hometown. Having survival skills worthy of Coyote, they managed to stay in their homeland despite diseases that killed half their population within a few years and despite violent confrontations with miners and the military.

One of California's early laws made it illegal to sell firearms or ammunition to Indians. Some miners did so nonetheless, in trade for food and sex. In 1853, the citizens of Orleans voted to kill any armed Indian on sight. That year, when Capt. H. M. Judah brought soldiers to Orleans, Karuks assembled to talk with them. Judah reported that miners gathered, threatening to shoot point-blank into the group of Indians; his forces had to restrain them.

In 1855, the people of Orleans resolved to confiscate the Indians' weapons and to whip and run out of town anyone who helped them obtain arms. A group of vigilantes raided a Karuk village that they called the Red Caps after the leader's name. The Indians were ready for the invaders; surprising them, they killed two white men.

This episode triggered raids on all of the Karuk villages, from Bluff Creek (Ishpúutach) to Happy Camp (Inaam, another *pikyávish* site). Redick McKee complained in a letter to the California governor that a group of miners from Happy Camp killed thirty to forty people, "almost in cold blood." Among the Indians who fled into the mountains were two signatories of one of McKee's treaties, which had promised federal protection for the Indians in return for land.

Red Cap became a leader of the refugees, hiding people while waging guerrilla warfare against the whites. Eventually, the U.S. Army offered Red Cap a truce, and he came down from the mountains to sign a treaty. Instead, he and a number of his men were captured and hanged. Some of the Karuks were moved to Hoopa Valley, where soldiers at Fort Gaston could watch them.

Few Karuks stayed for long, their homeland being close by, yet intermarriages between Yuroks, Hupas, and Karuks increased during the reservation period. Twenty years after the Gold Rush, when Stephen Powers visited the area, most of the miners were gone and there were ninety Karuk villages, including Panamnik. The white men who remained found that their security depended on coexisting with the Indians as best they could.

Many avoided the Karuks, living in separate settlements, but a number of men found Indian wives and fathered "half-breeds."

In 1908, two white women, a lesbian couple, came to Karuk country as field matrons for the United States Indian Service, having been assigned there by the Interior Department's special agent for California Indians. They were paid $30 a month plus travel expenses to work in what the special agent called "the roughest field in the United States." The government expected the women to bring civilization to the Indians living along the Rivers, as the area was then called. The only other representatives of government authority in the region were a sheriff and a forester for the newly established Klamath National Forest.

When they arrived, Mary Ellicott Arnold and Mabel Reed found only superficial effects of the dominant society's influence: "Karok Indians wore the clothes of the white man, built their cabins with tools, rejoiced in the rather questionable advantages of tea, coffee, and sugar, and gladly used white flour instead of acorn meal." The Indians had adopted names that miners gave them, like Little Joe and Penny Tom. Yet, "in the sixty miles between Happy Camp and Orleans, the social life of the Indian — what he believed and the way he felt about things — was very little affected by white influence."

Identifying themselves as "schoolmarms," Arnold and Reed offered instruction in literacy, mathematics, and geography, and they initiated Sunday school classes. What surprised them, "and something for which we were quite unprepared, was the intellectual capacity of the average Indian. . . . The average squaw, well beyond school age, displayed a capacity to learn and an application and mental discipline not only far beyond the pioneer women we know, but beyond our own friends and acquaintances of the same age back east."

Treating the Karuks with an attitude of respect that was hardly typical of U.S. Indian agents, the two women observed Karuk law in action. The law required that people or their families be paid in compensation for harm done to them. Now that Indians had alcohol and guns, harm was frequently done and often paid for. "From what they tell us," wrote Arnold, "killing people in this country is very expensive. You have to pay twenty-five dollars just for shooting at someone. If you hit him, it costs you fifty dollars. And if you are unfortunate enough to kill him, his relatives demand one hundred dollars."

In spite of Sheriff Offield's best efforts, there was no alternative to Indian law. "White law in Yreka, four days away over trails and mountain roads, doesn't mean much to the Indians on the Rivers, or to the white men either, for that matter." Ceremonial law was in effect on the Rivers at the appropriate times of year. No one was permitted to fish in either the Klamath or Salmon rivers before the First Salmon ceremony.

In 1909, the women witnessed a White Deerskin Dance near Orleans. They anticipated trouble, since there had been violence at the previous dance two years earlier. A friend of theirs, Big Steve, had knifed Johnny Allen after being accosted by Allen and two of his drunk friends, who were Yuroks from Weitchpec. The ethos of this *pikyávish* ceremony, which Arnold and Reed considered the Indians' New Year, calls for repairing damaged relationships and freeing oneself of bad feelings as part of fixing the world. That was too much to expect in this case, especially given the impact of alcohol. As the crowd arrived in Orleans and awaited the festivities, people stood around drinking, much to the dismay of older Indians who felt they were not respecting the sacred event. "The talk is now," wrote Arnold, "that Johnny Allen is out to get Steve, and everyone is warning Steve to keep away from the deerskin dance."

With some foreboding, the field matrons watched "the waving white deerskins and the beautiful feathered headdresses as the Indians danced and gestured in the flickering light." The movement of "naked, gleaming bodies . . . and the deep gutteral chant made our breath come quick. There was an excitement in it that we had never felt before." As the ceremony continued, "we lost all sense of time."

The final dance occurred the next night. Ignoring the warnings, Big Steve had come downriver to take part. And as the women feared, "seated in the front row, just at the end where Steve must dance and turn, we saw Johnny Allen." The women "squeezed down beside him," wrote Arnold. "Johnny's right arm was pressed tight against my side. I jammed myself as close to it as I could." Big Steve's dancing "had a power and a dramatic quality that we have never seen in any one else." Every time he danced to the end of the line in front of her, Mary Arnold felt Allen's arm tense up. But the Yurok did not strike. Then "the great deerskin dance was over. A new year was ahead of us. The world was made."

Making or fixing the world is more than a myth of which the dances are ritual enactments. Anyone who knows the rivers well has witnessed the transformation winter brings, especially after heavy snow and rainfall. Creeks and rivers rise above their banks; landslides alter the landscape; boulders and fallen trees block streams, obstructing fish passage. A crucial aspect of fixing the world is the practical work of removing physical impediments to life on the Rivers.

Arnold's memoir reveals the power of the Rivers during the times called *ti postheree* — high waters. Her description of Ishi Pishi Falls, which lie below Katimin and the pyramidal mountain A'uich at the sacred center of the Karuk world, contrasts strikingly with Kroeber's account of it. After visits in 1901 or 1902 during the dry months, the anthropologist wrote of "a shallow rapids in which the river ceaselessly roars among its rocks." Arnold not only heard but saw a formidable force of nature: "The water plunged down in a series of great waterfalls. It dashed itself against the rocks and through whirlpools and, gathering itself together, plunged down again and again. Everywhere was tumbling water."

"If the Klamath dries up, it will be the end of the world," said Nancy Richardson-Steele, a Karuk from Crescent City. She was telling a Coyote story at a California Indian storytelling festival. Karuk medicine man Charlie "Red Hawk" Thom told his version of the same story on camera for the documentary. Thom, who was seventy-five, transformed himself into "Pineifich, Coyote, mischief person," with wry facial expressions and pawlike hand movements as he spoke, sang, and beat rhythms on his square drum.

Coyote myths are popular among many tribes in the Pacific Northwest. For the Karuks, who regard their village near the center of the world as Coyote's hometown, the trickster is a comic hero. Stories in which he stars are a window onto their sense of geography, their feelings about crime and punishment, and their ethos of fixing the world.

Coyote's Journey, an epic cycle of Coyote stories, begins with boredom. "Why am I bored? Why? When everyone around me is happy?" Coyote decides to travel upriver to the Inland Ocean, dive into it, and get himself some Indian money. Also on Coyote's mind is finding himself a wife — maybe two wives.

Starting at Orleans, he heads up the Klamath. "Gosh, this river is like a snake," Coyote observes, through the voice of Charlie Thom. "It'll take me months and months to get to the ocean." So at Somes Bar he takes a shortcut across the mountains. Upslope, "Lizard is gathering his winter supply of food; getting a lot of goose berries." Lizard makes the mistake of leaving his basket of berries on the trail. Coyote comes by, hungry from hiking. "I don't think this guy would mind if I take a bite." One bite leads to another, and Coyote eats all the gooseberries. Then he finds another basketful and devours it as well, basket and all.

The animals, like the river people, have their laws of payback. Lizard and Blue Jay strike a deal: in exchange for nuts, acorns, and berries, the bird will make Coyote regret his crime. Blue Jay prepares some medicine, and "soon Coyote was beginning to feel thirsty. 'Oh my tongue, my tongue is getting dry,' he says. 'Oh well, there's a spring up here.' And he gets to the spring, he's going to take a drink, and the spring dries up." Farther up the hill, Coyote sees a creek. He runs down to it, saying, "'Oh ho ho,'" but when "he goes to take a drink, nothing, the creek dries up. 'Oh,' he says, 'I must have done something wrong.'"

Climbing over Marble Mountain, Coyote spies the Klamath River below. He runs down the slope, saying, "'That's my river, it belongs to me, that river.'" To "make sure the water is wet," Coyote puts his toe in. He wades in to his knees, then to his chest, determined not "'to drink until it gets to my lip!'" When it does, "he drank and he drank and he drank, and he got drownded."

Coyote never stays dead for long. Ants find his body on a sandbar and eat him until only the skeleton is left. But a yellow jacket, stinging what was left of his private parts, revives him, and Coyote is somehow able to reassemble his body. The saga continues from there, taking Coyote to the Scott River Valley, where he steals an egg from a goose nest. Then, with Lizard still after him, Coyote goes to Studying Rock to make medicine.

From there he sees Mount Shasta. "'Hey, if I get on top of this mountain, I can see the ocean on the other side.'" He climbs to the top, enjoys the beautiful stars, and falls asleep. It snows, and when Coyote awakens he sees the "ocean" all around him, below the peak. "He took a big run out to that ocean and he jumped in, not knowing that he jumped in the fog. He go 'Ahhhhh!' He hit the fog, hit down to rocks and sticks and everything and landed down on the ground. He started to holler, 'Help, help, I am dying, I am dying, somebody help me.'" Squirrel comes to his aid, summoning Eagle, who flies Coyote down to the Shasta River.

There, Doctor Red Hawk makes medicine to heal the banged-up Coyote. As in doctoring among the river peoples, the cure requires

Coyote to confess his crimes. At first, when accused of the thefts, Coyote says, "'Nope, I didn't do that.'" Finally, after Coyote admits, "'Yeah, I done it,'" Red Hawk puts him on a boat home to Orleans.

Coyote's adventures continue. Seeing two sisters on the bank gathering driftwood, the trickster turns himself into a piece of wood floating on the water, a "pretty stick" that they pick up and fight over. Eventually, with the help of his love song, which Charlie Thom sang for us, Coyote gets back into the boat, heading for home, with his two wives. But even then, Coyote isn't done. He has to fix the world.

> So after he got down to Orleans, he jumped out of the boat, run up the hill and says "I am going to fix this place like Scott Valley, like Shasta Valley. I am going to fix this place like that." He rolled around, rolled around, rolled around. "I shall get all the rocky bluffs out of here, make this Orleans flat." So Coyote done that. Coyote brought back the religion they call the Deerskin Dance. Then he brought back the Brush Dance, then he brought back the Flower Dance, Coyote done that. Creation time. So that's the reason why today, Orleans has a flat ground, Coyote came home and flattened it. And we have Deerskin Dance there today and Brush Dance there today because Coyote done that. Hey! That's the story of the Coyote.

After telling this story, Charlie Thom brought out his medicine. Among the numerous objects he showed us were a beautifully preserved redtail hawk, a glaring bald eagle, a medicine woman's pipe, and a round rock from Ishi Pishi Falls, at the center of the world. The rock brings to its carrier the energy of the Earth; with it "you are experiencing something worldwide." Then the shaman prepared some ochre, which he applied with his fingers to Jack Kohler's cheeks. "You got that war paint on you, we call it spiritual paint. We don't talk about war here; we're talkin' about how you get close to the eagle, how you can get out into this world and really know who you are."

Many Karuks of Thom's generation lost their language and much of the memory of their culture in boarding schools. More effective than the work of Reed and Arnold in bringing civilization to Karuk country was the building of roads and bridges in the 1920s and 1930s. With year-round access to the Rivers, white man's law took hold.

Yet the region remained a frontier. Almost everyone lived off the land to one degree or another—maintaining a garden, hunting deer, catching fish. Residents earned money from small logging and milling operations and by working for the Forest Service as firefighters and fire lookouts. During the Great Depression, hundreds of single men came to mine for gold. According to John Salter, who wrote the history of a Salmon River community, "A man willing and able to handle a shovel was assured of bringing in five to six dollars a day." Many of the non-Indians kept to themselves, preferring self-sufficiency to contact with any kind of society.

Through it all, some of the Karuks maintained their traditional culture. Charlie Thom was an orphan raised by his grandparents in Karuk country. "I really went by my grandfather's law on both sides of the family," he said. "When I was young I didn't want to go to school because of conflict with non-Indians." Rather than fight to defend himself, Thom told us, young Charlie walked away; to survive, he hung on for "dear life with my culture."

Grover Sanderson was a Karuk who performed as an extra in Hollywood films and who, in the 1930s, toured the United States as Chief Eagle Wing wearing Plains Indian regalia. Back home he filmed *pikyávish* ceremonies, Indian gambling, and stick games. In those years, women continued to make baskets of hazel and willow, men used dip nets to catch salmon, and parents ferried children across the river in canoes to and from school.

"When we went to school," Grant Hillman told documentary filmmaker James Culp in the 1980s, "we were discouraged to speaking our language." Lew Wilder told Culp the same, adding that he hadn't adequately learned what became important to him as an adult—the traditional Karuk crafts. As a boy, he said, "I seen it all done, but the fine points missed me. I didn't realize I always could go to an old-timer and get what I wanted to know. Pretty soon I was the old-timer."

Many Karuk men joined the military during World War II. "In a time of war you'd never have to draft Indians," said Grant's son Leaf Hillman. "Indians are always the first ones in line. So there's been times when there hasn't been enough male participants to carry on the ceremonies."

Despite the lack of men and "the outlawing of our religion," Hillman said, "world renewal still went on," though sometimes underground with a small group taking part.

Some of the Karuks who returned from World War II assimilated culturally to the dominant society. As the U.S. Forest Service "got out the cut" to help industry meet the postwar demand for wood products, forestry jobs became available to Karuk tribesmen. Grant Hillman, for one, worked as a road-builder for a logging company.

During this era, the termination of Indian reservations became federal policy. Two large forested reservations, that of the Menominee in Wisconsin and the Klamath in Oregon, were liquidated. A termination act aimed specifically at California Indians eliminated the state's thirty-six rancherias, small settlements in which Indians had been allowed to maintain their communities without moving to reservations.

Relocation legislation brought Indians from reservations across the country into cities, including Oakland and Los Angeles. There, living in poverty and relying on one another, some Native people forged a new identity as American Indians, understanding what they had in common as well as the differences that distinguished their particular tribes. Exposed to mass media as never before and inspired by the Civil Rights movement, many Indians rejected pressures to assimilate.

Such events as the fish-ins in Puget Sound and the occupation of Alcatraz by "Indians of All Tribes" captured media attention, but much occurred outside the glare of the public eye. David Risling Jr., a Karuk/Yurok related to Jack Kohler, helped found a number of organizations serving Native people, among them the Native American Rights Fund, California Indian Legal Services, and the Native American Heritage Commission. In Karuk country, Lew Wilder worked on cultural revival. He rediscovered his elders' techniques for carving elkhorn pipes, making square drums, shaping arrowheads from chunks of obsidian, creating jewelry for regalia, and many other things.

By the mid-1980s, Leaf Hillman was learning all that he could from Wilder. "I want to learn so I can pass it on to my kids," he told James Culp for the documentary *People of the Klamath*. Hillman also studied the Karuk language, benefiting from an Indian language program at Humboldt State University. In turn, he taught Karuk to children in the school at Orleans.

When we first interviewed Leaf Hillman in 2001, he was director of the Karuk Department of Natural Resources. Taking us out in a boat, Hillman showed us how low the river was. "You see that piece of real estate sticking out of the water over there?" he asked, pointing to a rock formation just above the waterline. It had "never seen the light of day in my lifetime." Nor had it appeared in his father's lifetime. "Now, that's science," Hillman said. "For thousands of years we've applied science. Science is repeated observation and application of that knowledge. And nowadays we have to have a scientist to go into court to say that this water is lower than it's ever been before in history."

Hillman kept his promise to pass traditional knowledge on to his children. His sons Ike at fifteen and Leaf Jr. at sixteen served as priests for *pikyávish* ceremonies just as Hillman himself had done as a boy. Leaf Hillman led the production team to a small priest house, where Ike had lived for ten days as fix-the-world priest. Most of it was underground; we looked down on its peaked wooden roof. "I trained my son here last year," Leaf Senior said. "You come and get him early in the morning, bring him out of the sweathouse, stand him up on that rock there, paint him." Then he taught Ike a prayer to use that day. Neither his father nor anyone else was allowed to call the priest by his name. "You say his name, you have to pay him money so he'll forgive you."

Once the priest is painted and dressed in deer hide and ready with his prayer, he walks the sacred trails into the mountains. On a day when he eats and drinks little or nothing, he may go ten miles before returning to the little house. During these journeys the priest is not allowed to talk with people or even see them. "He keeps his eyes on the mountain—on the prize—where he's going. So if a car comes, he doesn't notice it." This could be dangerous, but there is a sign on Highway 96: "Priest Crossing." According to Hillman, during the ten-day period at the times a priest is likely to cross the highway, tribal members stop traffic.

Ike Hillman described what he did upon arriving at the day's destination. After lighting a small fire and putting on it a tobacco offering, he prayed for "all the deer to come back to feed all the people, and for all the birds; all the salmon to come back to fill the rivers up." After saying his prayer he sat for a while before moving on. "When you're out in the mountains and when you're fasting, that's your sacrifice, so you did your part."

"From the time of the transformation, it's been happening, ever since then," Leaf Hillman explained.

> Coyote was the first priest, back when time began, when humans were transformed. He was the one who set the standard for us. Told us where to go, how to do it, all those things. The Karuk way of belief is that everything is our relation because at the time of transformation, we were all just spirit people. And then some spirit people were transformed to humans, some to animals, birds, fishes, all those things. So *pikyávish* , when we do a world renewal ceremony we're reaffirming that we're related to all those things. We're giving thanks to them. It's a reciprocal relationship between us and the trees and the water and the fish.

By maintaining silence for ten days, keeping his eyes on the mountain, the priest removes himself from the human world. This distance, in conjunction with the fasting, must have an effect similar to that of the vision quest of other tribes in which a youth remains in solitude in a natural place, fasting, praying, and dreaming, often to be visited by a spirit being. The Karuk priest's experience likewise opens up a sense of relatedness to animals, birds, fish, water, trees, an experience which, to a lesser degree, people of non-Indian cultures have when fishing, hiking, or simply being far from the customary haunts of their society. It is a feeling of renewal, awakening that within us that is more than human, a sense of being there that draws from a stratum of awareness people have in common with other forms of life.

Chapter Twelve
The State of Jefferson

Driving Interstate 5 near the California-Oregon state line, one can tune into Jefferson Public Radio, spot a bumper sticker that says "Jefferson: A State of Mind," or notice a T-shirt bearing the Great Seal of the State of Jefferson. Its logo of two ×'s symbolizes a feeling common to citizens of this mythical state that their region has repeatedly been double-crossed by the governments in Sacramento and Salem.

Never have these citizens agreed on the borders of Jefferson. Like every state of mind, it is variable. One map has it extending from the Pacific Ocean to the Nevada state line, from Douglas County to Mendocino County on the West Coast, and from Lake County to Lassen County to the east. Other maps fail to include California's Mendocino and Humboldt Counties and Oregon's Klamath County. The political visions underlying the drive to create—or the fantasy of being in—this new state have also ranged widely over the years. The spectrum runs from miners and loggers who insist on more road-building and extraction of natural resources to those who, like the characters in Ernest Callenbach's novel *Ecotopia*, seek an environmentally sensible, sustainable way of life. However divergent, these visions of a world apart have common roots—the region's biogeographical distinctiveness, its remoteness from population centers in Oregon and California, and its lack of influence over its governance.

At one time, a third state between California and Oregon seemed a real prospect. As the United States expanded to the West Coast, it acquired the State of California and Oregon Territory, today's Oregon and Washington. In 1852, a bill in the California legislature called for a State of Jefferson. It died in committee. The next year an editorial in a San Francisco newspaper advocated the creation of a State of Klamath in northern California and southern Oregon. That year, the Yreka *Mountain Herald* sought the formation of a Jackson Territory, and on January 7, 1854, citizens met in Jacksonville, Oregon, to move this vision toward fruition.

The man who called the meeting to order, Lafayette F. Mosher, was married to the daughter of Gen. Joseph Lane, Oregon's representative in Congress and later its first territorial governor. He was said to have other ties as well—with the Knights of the Golden Circle, a pro-slavery prototype of the Ku Klux Klan. Although many at the Jacksonville meeting did not share Mosher's proclivities, the majority agreed to have a convention to consider organizing a new territory. Held the following month, the convention sent a resolution to the U.S. Congress calling for the formation of the Territory of Jackson. But Mosher's background doomed this initiative, as northern legislators feared the territory would become a new slave state.

Other attempts to carve out a separate state in the region came from the California legislature. During the 1854–1855 session, the Assembly voted to trisect California. There would be a State of Shasta in the north, ranging from the Mendocino coast eastward and north to the Oregon state line. The other parts were to be called Colorado, a swath extending from Monterey Bay to the east, and California, comprising what remained. In 1859, a number of Yreka citizens, including Elijah Steele, persuaded a state assemblyman to introduce a bill that would permit Californians north of the fortieth parallel to form a separate state government. Fifty years later, a group of southern Oregonians launched a movement to create a State of Jefferson. Those efforts failed.

Decade after decade, the lack of modern means of transportation—railroads and paved roads—made residents of the elusive State of Jefferson feel an anger much like that of colonized people whose needs are neglected while wealth from their land enriches distant others. In 1880, their region had the ignominious distinction of being the last place where a president of the United States took a long stagecoach trip. Accompanied by his wife "Lemonade Lucy," a champion of temperance, and Civil War hero Gen. William T. Sherman, Rutherford B. Hayes traveled up the West Coast by train until reaching Siskiyou County. From there horse teams pulled his party from Yreka, California, to Roseburg, Oregon, where the luminaries caught a train to Portland.

In 1935, when the Civilian Conservation Corps was building public works all around the country, a Crescent City judge, John C. Childs, proclaimed himself governor of the State of Jefferson to draw attention to the inadequacy of roads on the redwood coast. Nothing succeeds like secession. The State of California responded with road-improvement projects.

This stunt paled in comparison to the achievement of Gilbert E. Gable, a retired public relations man from Pennsylvania who moved to Port Orford, Oregon, during the year of Judge Childs's bogus governorship. Gable led the drive to make Port Orford the first incorporated town in its area, and he became its first mayor. In addition, according to James T. Rock, who wrote a history of the State of Jefferson, Gable "was the organizing force and head of the Oregon Engineering Company, the Port Orford Dock and Terminal Company, the Last Frontier Realty Corporation, the Trans-Pacific Lumber Company, and the Gold Coast Railroad Company. But these projects were not enough for him."

When Gable arrived, Port Orford had neither telegraph nor railroad line. Having put the town on the map, Mayor Gable's next goal was to put the entire region on the map. In October 1941, Gable and several of his friends rushed into the county courthouse demanding that a judge support the annexation of Curry and three other Oregon counties—Josephine, Jackson, and Klamath—into California. The judge appointed a commission consisting of Gable and two of his friends to study procedures to legalize the annexation.

Gable's next move was to write California Governor Culbert Olson to request an appointment to discuss moving Oregon's border with California northward. Olson's response was, "We are glad to know they think enough of California to want to join it." The *Oregonian* weighed in with an editorial warning Curry County that "if your ambition be realized, Curry would of course immediately acquire the glorious climate of California and become a haven of retired Midwest farmers."

A club in Grants Pass, The Oregon Cavemen, raised the stakes. The leaders of this boosters' club sported Indian names: Chief Big Horn, Rising Buck, Wing Feather, and Keeper of the Wampum. Their board of directors was called the Council of Eagle Eyes. The Cavemen set up a meeting with Governor Olson for the day when Gable had an appointment with him. Their proposal was to wed Curry and Josephine Counties, forming a new state to be called Cavemania.

Olson heard both delegations on October 30. Sensibly, he recommended that Gable obtain Oregon's assent to the secession before seeking California's support. Instead, Gable's party met in Yreka to discuss a six-county alliance to promote mineral and timber development. But the Yrekans, like the Cavemen, had visions of statehood. On November 18, the Yreka Chamber of Commerce voted to begin the process of forming the State of Mittelwestcoastia. It would contain California's Siskiyou, Del Norte, and Modoc Counties and Oregon's Curry, Josephine, and Jackson Counties. The Yreka newspaper liked the idea but not the name. The winning submission to its contest to find a better one had a familiar ring, the State of Jefferson. Around this time, Yreka designated itself the new state's capital, and someone created the official seal, a mining pan etched with a double cross.

Unable to beat the Yrekans, Gable joined them, declaring himself the governor of Jefferson. The governor announced that his state would be free of taxes, strikes, and slot machines—"not in moral reproach," observed historian Richard Reinhardt, "but because they constituted unfair competition to the local stud poker industry."

This colorful controversy appealed to the *San Francisco Chronicle*, which sent its crackerjack feature reporter Stanton Delaplane to the capital of the would-be forty-ninth state. (Alaska and Hawaii did not add stars to the flag until 1959.) He arrived in time to witness its Proclamation of Independence on Thursday, November 27. A Citizens Committee declared that "Patriotic Jeffersonians intend to secede every Thursday until further notice." Complaining that "gross neglect by California and Oregon deprives us of necessary roads to bring out the copper ore," the secessionists stopped vehicles on Highway 99 and handed out fliers urging motorists to "drive down the Klamath River highway and see for yourself. Take your chains, shovel, and dynamite." Delaplane concluded that the Jeffersonians were "partly mad, partly in fun, partly earnest about the new state."

The second Secession Thursday was a national spectacle witnessed by cameramen from four newsreel companies and photographers from two national magazines. As Reinhardt described it, "Ranchers and lumbermen were out on the highway again, warming their hands around bonfires, waving shotguns, and passing out leaflets. Mounted patrols pranced around the outskirts of Yreka. Schools were let out early." An eyewitness called it "a staged production; from the loudspeaker at the rear, the crowd and the officers receive their instructions. . . . 'Don't look at the camera. . . . Show a little enthusiasm! Wave your arms!'" At twilight during a torchlit parade, marchers carried signs proclaiming:

OUR ROADS ARE NOT PASSABLE, HARDLY JACKASSABLE.
IF OUR ROADS YOU WOULD TRAVEL, BRING YOUR OWN GRAVEL.
THE PROMISED LAND — OUR ROADS ARE PAVED WITH PROMISES.

Delaplane did not observe that Thursday's demonstration. Instead, he followed "a brown sand ribbon through the tall, piney mountains alongside the Klamath River, rushing in white water toward the sea." He intended to take a road from a mining camp to the Grants Pass Highway and on to the coast, where he would meet with Governor Gable. But Delaplane halted in Happy Camp on the advice of "a miner and humanist" who warned him against "the 32-mile trip over the snowy tops of the mountains. He said cheerfully they would probably find my bones by spring all right and give them a decent burial. That is if I didn't wander from the car during my final agonies and run afoul of a hungry mountain lion."

Instead, the reporter went the long way around, traveling to Medford and Crescent City and then north to Gable's redwood cabin near Port Orford. There he and the governor drank 150-proof rum "while the Oregon skies poured dark rain into the pine-covered hills."

Delaplane was to win the Pulitzer Prize for reportage as a consequence of his Jefferson stories. The last of them was an obituary. Gilbert Gable died unexpectedly on December 2 at age fifty-five. "I think he was a man whose historical importance was yet to come," wrote Delaplane. But Gable never became, even posthumously, a twentieth-century John Charles Frémont. On December 7, the Japanese attack on Pearl Harbor brought the United States into World War II. Judge Childs, who had been inaugurated as the governor of Jefferson only days before, declared that all secession activities would cease "in view of the national emergency."

Today, the mythic State of Jefferson gives form to a feeling that persists in the Klamath Basin of living in a world apart. This is a sense shared by non-Indians and Indians alike. But unlike the agitators for statehood who had centrifugal dreams, now realized, of roads passing into and away from Jefferson, and connecting it to larger economic and political concerns, the native vision is centripetal. For Karuks, Katymin is the *axis mundi* — the center of the world. The story Charlie Thom tells of Coyote's epic journey has the trickster traveling in the Klamath Basin toward the inland ocean at the world's outer reaches.

When Thom's son, Patrick "Hooty" Croy created a poster for my play *Watershed*, which is set in the Klamath Basin, he portrayed this cosmos as woven like a basket. Its pattern turns Escher-like into salmon, some leaping up the widening river that flows through its center, some caught in a net that falls from the shoulder of a watchful woman. Across from her is another spirit being, a man flanked by white deer. Between them are a bear, an eagle carrying a fish in its claws, and a dip netter pulling salmon from the river. This world is self-contained and self-sufficient.

For the Karuk and Shasta tribes living within this world woven by nature, the trails that pack trains traveled from north-coast harbors to the mines and the emigrant trails that crossed the continent were vectors of danger, disease, and death. This was an invasion far more devastating for them than was Pearl Harbor for Americans nearly a century later. They had no effective way to fight back. To cut their losses, members of the mid-Klamath tribes agreed to abandon a portion of their country in return for secure reservations guaranteed by the United States.

On October 21, 1851, Col. Redick McKee, a federal Indian agent, rode into Scott's Valley. Cartographer George Gibbs and thirty-five riflemen were among those traveling with him from Katymin where, nine days earlier, McKee had signed the second-to-last of the eighteen treaties he made with representatives of California tribes. Turning up the Scott River, his party had gone on to Scott Bar, a prosperous mining camp. Along the way, the agent saw large mounds of dirt and gravel from the surface diggings.

"Scott's River," McKee wrote in his journal, "is the most thoroughly explored of all the gold-producing streams of Northern California, and the extent of the works upon it is astonishing, even to those acquainted with the energy with which mining operations have been carried on." He observed that the valley was the only one on the Klamath or its tributaries "in which any considerable quantity of good soil is to be found. Its extreme length is, however, not more than twenty-five or thirty miles, and its width, at the northern end, from eight to ten, diminishing toward its head to a narrow strip." In addition to lands near the river covered with bunchgrass that "becomes a natural hay without cutting," McKee found abundant high-quality pine growing in the hills and great quantities of salmon ascending the river. After the gold was gone, it was clear that the land would remain highly productive.

McKee pitched camp where Shackleford Creek flows into the Scott and sent a Mr. Kelsey ahead to Shasta Valley to invite Indians there to a treaty gathering. "He found great difficulty in persuading them of the peaceful intentions of the expedition," wrote McKee. The colonel's armed escort made them fear that he led a war party. "A few were finally collected, and the object of the Agent in visiting their country was explained to them through the Oregon Indian named 'Swill,' who lived with the tribe, and spoke their language."

Meanwhile "several gentlemen from the neighborhood" visited McKee's camp. The agent asked them to stay to provide information and advice regarding the local Indians. "In view of the importance of rendering the treaty satisfactory to the miners and settlers," McKee sent out invitations to people living elsewhere in the valley to participate in the talks, "either in person or by delegation."

McKee proceeded to Yreka, which was then called Shasta Butte City. "We found in the town a plentiful supply of provisions, and in considerable variety; game being abundant, and beef, butter, and vegetables regularly supplied from Oregon. The price of board was three dollars a day, without bed, and a dollar for horses or mules standing at hay in a yard. The restaurants were fitted up in approach to San Francisco style, and in the evenings music invited the lovers of liquor and of monte."

When McKee returned to his camp, few Indians were there, but he "found delegations from other citizens from different parts of the valley, amounting to forty or fifty." He learned that among the Indians "apprehensions existed that the object of assembling them was to kill the whole together." Still, one tribal leader sent his teenage son to observe the gathering.

A council occurred in which the few Indians in attendance "professed a willingness to divide their country with the whites, and . . . promised to desist from all hostilities, provided they were not molested in the first place." The council was adjourned without reaching any agreement so that the young man could consult with his father, Ishack. The boundaries of the proposed reserve were an unresolved issue. "No conclusion could be arrived at, on consultation with the citizens present; and it was seen that private interests would interfere with any selection."

During the interim, Major Wessels led the thirty-five riflemen who had accompanied McKee on to the Sacramento Valley. The reason given was that winter storms in the Klamath Mountains might trap them there until spring. After the troops' departure, more than a thousand of the estimated 4,000 Shasta who lived along the Klamath and its tributaries from the Salmon to the Shasta Rivers gathered near McKee's encampment. Ishack, arriving with his son, was one of thirteen chiefs who came to negotiate with the Indian agent.

George Gibbs drafted a map depicting the boundaries of a new reservation. Centered on Scott Bar, it set aside much of the land between Happy Camp and Yreka, including some of the most productive mining camps and the entire northern part of Scott Valley. This land, McKee thought, "would afford the only resource for the agricultural part of the reserve." For their part, the Shasta agreed to return all of the animals they had stolen from settlers and to move their villages within the reservation boundaries immediately.

The settlers were less than pleased with the proposed reservation. Gibbs later wrote in his journal that they "had determined to wage a war of extermination against the Indians on the upper Klamath and its tributaries."

On November 4, the Indian agent explained the details of the treaty to the Shasta. "In the afternoon it was signed in the presence of a large concourse of whites and Indians, with great formality. The usual presents were then distributed, and they separated in very good humor, the Klamath chief 'Ishack' and his son, remaining for the benefit of our escort home." That night, McKee and the remaining members of his party "were entertained by a grand peace-dance."

Evidently, McKee sincerely believed that he had "accomplished what many intelligent persons thought an impossibility," for he wrote a letter less than two weeks later saying that the treaty "if prudently and successfully carried out, will save many valuable lives and perhaps immense expense to the government. . . . Upon the whole, I flatter myself that this arrangement, with those previously effected during this expedition, will restore and maintain quiet and security along this northern frontier."

McKee's work did not have the consequences he imagined. In June of the following year, after President Millard Fillmore sent the treaties he negotiated to the Senate for ratification, all eighteen vanished. In 2002, Senator Daniel Inouye, at a hearing before the Committee on Indian Affairs, which he chaired, spoke "of a Senate that apparently met in secret session in 1852 and rejected the treaties that had been negotiated with California tribes, and didn't disclose their action for another 43 years." After the hidden treaties were discovered in the 1920s, it took three decades and lengthy deliberations by an Indian Claims Court before California Indians received compensation for the lands taken from their ancestors. The court awarded them 47½ cents per acre.

The locals also refused to accept McKee's treaty with the Shasta. The war of extermination, which they had warned Gibbs about, came to pass. The war was by no means confined to the upper Klamath. It raged on both sides of the Siskiyou, expanding into what came to be known as the Rogue River War. According to historian Stephen Dow Beckham, "a volunteer company of miners" from Crescent City arrived in Jacksonville to fight Indians. They "carried a flag bearing one word in bright letters: 'extermination.'" Jack Norton, the author of *Genocide in Northwestern California,* reported "several cases in which women of Yreka made a banner that said 'extermination' on it and . . . paraded it through the streets."

The events that occurred in Scott Valley remain shrouded and are not mentioned in the historical record. They can, however, be seen through the lenses of legend and oral history. In their book on the history of western Siskiyou County, Gail L. Fiorini-Jenner and Monica Jae Hall put it this way:

> There is a large, unanswered question about the treaty signing and subsequent disappearance of many of the Shasta tribe: what happened to those who were to occupy this new reservation? While no known documents exist to validate the oral history recounted below, it is well known that some were sent to Siletz, Grand Rounde [*sic*], and Klamath Reservations in Oregon. Others, seeing their way of life and freedom jeopardized, joined the army and became scouts. Whatever the case, in the Indian census of 1852, it was reported that only 27 Native Americans were living in Siskiyou County.

The oral history passed down by Shasta families that the authors refer to recalls a feast to which the Shasta were invited to celebrate the treaty. "It was considered impolite and a sign of distrust, in the Shasta tradition, not to partake," wrote Hall and Fiorini-Jenner.

As a result, most of the Shasta ate the beef and bread served. Whether from spoilage or poison, it isn't clear, but shortly after eating, the Shasta warriors began to die. It has been repeated in Shasta oral history that "3,000 warriors died that day." After that event, it was said by many that vigilantes, both miners and settlers, swept through the valleys burning the villages and killing the people.

The poison feast occurred where Fort Jones stands today, according to Jack Norton. In courtroom testimony, the Hupa historian said: "There is evidence that the beef that was served to the Indians was laced with strychnine." Norton went on to say that various sources told "of the bodies as they tried to run, tried to get home after being poisoned, littering the trail and so forth, and how Indians were burying the dead."

Some of these sources were eyewitnesses. Hall and Fiorini-Jenner wrote that one treaty signer, "Chief Sunrise," refused to eat and hid in the mountains for years before returning to Scott Valley. Another, "Chief Ike," had come from the Klamath River to the treaty grounds. He also ate nothing at the feast and lived to an old age. Jenny Mungo, a woman from a village near Hamburg, told her granddaughter Clara Wicks that "six hundred didn't come home."

Jenny Mungo's grandson learned from a man he worked for as a youth, Mr. Sharp, that a few months after the treaty was signed, Shasta Indians were rounded up and held in a stockade at Fort Jones. Before they could be transported to Indian reservations in Oregon, miners "came with their guns drawn to take back their women."

Hooty Croy's family oral history confirms this story. "My great grand-mother," Croy said, "was one of the women who went into the corrals and was sold or traded to the settlers of that area." Some miners purchased Indians, especially young girls, from slave hunters for prices ranging from $250 to $500. Jack Norton found documentation for these fees in miners' diaries and other records. Hall and Fiorini-Jenner note a different kind of evidence. Indians who have established that they are of Shasta descent in the process of seeking federal recognition for their tribe trace their ancestry back to "fewer than 40 documented women who were kept by white miners, plus a half dozen or so Native American couples."

In Jack Norton's view, the town of Yreka played a central role in the war of extermination. The citizens there maintained a fund that paid vigilantes five dollars per scalp taken. This money supplemented the funds provided to Indian fighters by the California state government and revenue from the sale of slaves. Indian fighting was a livelihood, as it had been for members of the Modoc tribe, the difference being that the Yreka Indian hunters got paid whether their prey was dead or alive.

Another difference is revealed by the word "extermination." One exterminates a pest, not a person. What happened in northern California exemplifies the malignancy that Erik H. Erikson was to call "pseudo-speciation"—the failure of human groups to recognize the humanity of people outside their tribes or nations, a failure that facilitates genocide. In Jack Norton's words, "Indians were seen as less than human beings, an impediment to their gold, impediment to their process of trying to gain wealth from the land."

Norton said this in 1990 when he testified at the remarkable retrial of Patrick "Hooty" Croy in California Superior Court. Croy was a prisoner on San Quentin's Death Row who had been convicted of first-degree murder and sentenced to death for killing a police officer in 1978.

The night of July 17, 1978, Hooty Croy had been partying with friends and family near Yreka. The police came to the party twice, having received complaints about noise from the neighbors. After the second time, Hooty, his half-sister Norma Jean Croy, their cousins Carol Thom and Darrell Jones, and Jasper, a seventeen-year-old relative, got into a car planning to hunt deer in the woods near Hawkinsville. First they went to a store to stock up on beer.

Croy had been at the Sports & Spirits earlier that day, cashing a check for $12.97 to buy two six-packs. He thought that Thurman, who was behind the counter, shortchanged him two dollars, but he didn't make an issue of it. That evening, though, Hooty complained of being cheated. An argument broke out. Hooty went back to the car, but the imbroglio escalated. According to testimony in court, Carol Thom angrily knocked things over in the store and Norma Jean Croy threatened Thurman with a can opener. As Charlie Thom, who was not there, described it, the women "were raising Cain with the store-owner; going to lock him up in the store freezer and everything; and somehow that storekeeper got loose and ran out there, run out the door, and yelled 'Robbery, robbery, robbery!'"

A police car was parked outside the S&S. When Hooty's car drove away from the store, it followed. The Indians headed toward Hawkinsville, five miles away, one of the places where Hooty grew up. His grandmother and aunt still lived there. Darrell, who had been sleeping, woke up and fired one shot at the police car. He missed, but by the time the Karuk carload approached Hooty's grandmother's cabin, there were fifteen squad cars and twenty-seven officers on the scene.

A Wild West shootout ensued. Norma Jean was hit in the back, Darrell in the groin, a police officer in the hand. Jasper, who had slept until the car stopped, turned himself in, as did Carol. After the police called for a cease-fire and surrender, Hooty, who had rushed into the bushes to hide, crawled past a storage building toward his grandmother's cabin to check on her and his aunt. Officer Bo Hittson shot him twice from behind. Hooty turned, firing his .22, and hit Officer Hittson in the heart.

For the 1990 trial, Charlie Thom hired the best lawyer he could find for his son: Tony Serra. Serra's case before the Superior Court was based on Croy's right of self-defense. Officer Hittson had been off-duty and drinking when asked to help chase down the Karuk car. Hittson had shot Hooty without asking him to raise his hands, without saying anything. Two of Hooty's relatives having already been wounded, he had reason to assume that Hittson was trying to kill him.

Hooty had been represented in his first trial by a former district attorney whom he did not trust. He was convicted by an all-white jury in a county known for discrimination against Indians. To bring that context into the retrial required more than a self-defense argument. Over the course of eight months, Serra mounted a "cultural defense." In doing so he drew from history, including the evidence of genocide in the nineteenth century. The defense traced the aftereffects of genocide as experienced by Croy and other American Indians in the region, the ongoing victimization of their community.

Chris Peters, a Stanford-educated Yurok/Karuk, testified that the child welfare system was used to take children out of their families to be raised by non-Indians. "You had a pattern of children being sent from one relative to another" to keep one step ahead of the social worker, but "eventually most of those children ended up in non-Indian foster homes." Within California as a whole, "35% of all Indian children are removed from their homes and 80% of those children are put in non-Indian homes," Peters said. As a consequence, "The child learns helplessness, they have nothing to say about their future, their own family has nothing to say about what happens to them." The removal of children from their homes also affected their feelings about police. "When social workers show up at Indian communities with a police officer, it is common for children to run out into the fields," Peters testified.

In addition to the pressures felt by all Indians in his community, Croy was targeted as an individual by police, Peters maintained. They stopped his car, searched his house, and said, "We are looking for you; we're going to get you." In Peters's opinion, "they wanted to kill him for what his father had done, for the whole revitalization of Indian awareness." Hooty Croy's father, Charlie Thom, had done a number of things that upset non-Indians of the area. He had gone to Washington, D.C., and brought back the 1851 treaty. He campaigned for reinstatement of Indian hunting, fishing, and religious rights. And Thom's fight against the G-O Road, cutting through Six Rivers National Forest and the high country sacred to Klamath River tribes, threatened the timber industry.

Serra's defense succeeded. Croy was released from Death Row, although he remained within the prison system, off and on, until 2005.

This case exemplifies a vicious cycle of mistrust. Many Indians have grown up considering non-Indians their enemy; many whites have regarded Indians as a threat to their way of life. This enmity is as toxic to the people of the Klamath as are chemicals in the water to the fish. It has kept many from learning how to lead their lives without fearing and hating each other. It has thwarted attempts by Indian and non-Indian communities to restore wildlife habitats, and it long made the region's ecological health seem incompatible with economic wealth.

Yet increase in the amount and variety of information and communications between diverse societies has driven innovation throughout history, and that is occurring in the Klamath Basin. Somehow the idea of this bioregion as a world apart, a sense of abandonment if not betrayal by official authorities, and growing awareness of a shared tragic history, facilitated reconciliation, negotiations, and political achievements that brought a better future into view. But before examining recent developments, we will resume our journey upriver and into the land's cultural and economic fault lines.

Chapter Thirteen
Smokey, Bigfoot, and the Owl

No one can prevent forest fires. Fire is a natural phenomenon, and it plays a vital role in the ecology of forests. Karuks, like other California tribes, set fires regularly. Before the Forest Service took control of their land, a Karuk forestry technique was to light a fallen tree on a timbered slope and roll it downhill, setting off a slowly spreading ground fire.

Fires have a number of desirable effects. They clear out underbrush, enabling game animals to move through the forest. They consume biomass, releasing into streams and rivers water that brush thickets would have absorbed. And they hasten the cycling of nutrients. Nitrogen taken from the air by bacteria associated with ceanothus enters the soil as ash when the shrub burns; once in the soil, nitrogen nourishes the growth of trees and plants that provide food and basketry materials.

When fires recur over an interval of years, lit by lightning or humans, they protect against forest-destroying conflagrations by removing litter, logs, and small trees. Keeping the fuel load low saves large trees from mortal damage while preventing potential "ladder trees" from growing into the canopy. If ground fires climb branches high enough, they can ignite the canopy and endanger the entire forest ecosystem.

These benefits of fire were eclipsed by the Big Blow-Up in 1910, an inferno that consumed three million acres of forest in western Montana and northern Idaho and killed five foresters. With that disaster, the Forest Service declared war on fire. The new policy sparked debate. Some foresters were aware of the ecological value of fire, and many questioned the wisdom of putting people in danger in remote areas to save trees. Those who believed in an aggressive response to the tragedy, however, prevailed.

To wage the war against fire, the Forest Service built roads, put up phone lines, erected lookout towers, and hired people to staff them. At the sight of smoke, foresters, and often the lookout hiked or rode horseback to the fire and, whenever possible, put it out. Finding people who had the skill to spot a fire, the fortitude to fight it, and the ability to spend almost every day in solitude was a tall order. In 1913, after a lookout in the Klamath National Forest quit, Assistant Forest Ranger M. H. McCarthy found only three applicants for the job. One was a drunk, another had poor eyesight, and the third was "no gentleman." Recommending his choice to his forest supervisor, McCarthy wrote:

> I hope your heart is strong enough to stand the shock. One of the most untiring and enthusiastic applicants which I have for the position is Miss Hallie Morse Daggett, a wide-awake woman of 30 years who knows and has traversed every trail on the Salmon River watershed, and is thoroughly familiar with every foot of the District. She is absolutely devoid of the timidity which is ordinarily associated with her sex and she is not afraid of anything that walks, creeps, or flies.

Hallie Daggett knew the watershed well, having grown up in Black Bear. Stationed in a log cabin at the Eddy Gulch Look-Out at the top of Klamath Peak, Daggett worked for the Forest Service until 1926.

During the Great Depression, the war against fire intensified as a labor force from the Civilian Conservation Corps became available to the Forest Service. More roads were built, and more telephone lines were strung over meadows, through forests, and across mountains. But some worried about the effects of the expanding new infrastructure on the integrity of lands like the steep and rapidly eroding Klamath Mountains. Their concern moved former foresters John Marshall and Aldo Leopold to found the Wilderness Society in 1935. This organization eventually succeeded in having millions of roadless acres that had once been managed for "multiple use" by the Forest Service set aside as wilderness areas. The Wilderness Act of 1964 left an enduring legacy, but it had no effect on firefighting efforts in the national forests.

The war against fire intensified further during World War II. Protecting the nation's resources was regarded as part of the war effort, and the government considered fire prevention a patriotic duty. Recognizing the appeal of cartoon characters like Mickey Mouse, the Forest Service created Smokey Bear in 1944. Life imitated art in 1950 when a bear cub, rescued from a blackened forest in New Mexico, became known as Little Smokey. As mass media captured the nation's eyes and ears during the postwar era, Smokey Bear became the second most recognized figure in American popular culture, after Santa Claus.

The end of World War II increased the numbers of planes, helicopters, and men available for smoke jumping and for spraying fire retardants from the air. Forest Service "hot shot" crews had the esprit de corps of a military unit, but the escalating war against fire had tragic consequences for some of them. A series of fires that were vigorously fought took numerous lives. Then, in 1994, when Jack Ward Thomas was chief of the Forest Service, an inferno in South Canyon near Glenwood Springs, Colorado, killed thirty-four firefighters. "The real question was," said Thomas, "should we even have been there in the first place."

By this time, Forest Service scientists had developed an understanding of both the benefits of fire to forests and the negative consequences of all-out fire suppression. Some forests, including those in the Klamath and Six Rivers National Forests, were ripe for conflagrations that threatened their continuing existence. The Salmon River watershed experienced major burns in 1977 and 1987. In 2002, the Biscuit Fire torched half a million acres, mainly on the Oregon side of the Siskiyou range but also on the California side. In 50 percent of the areas burned, 75 percent of the vegetation was destroyed. In 2020, the Slater and Devil fires burned more than 166,000 acres, mainly in the Klamath National Forest but also in southern Oregon. That year, California had five of the ten largest wildfires in the state's history.

Fire suppression also has had a long-term effect on the storage of water. The undergrowth and crowded stands of midsize trees that are normally thinned by fires hold much more water than would be the case in forests managed by fire.

Although scientists agreed that fire needs to be reintroduced into forests, retreating from the war against fire has been a hard sell in public, largely because of Smokey's success. "The problem with Smokey," wrote historian Stephen Pyne, "is not that his message is bad, but that it only addresses one part of the problem. It doesn't address the other side of fire management, which is to promote the fires we do want and indeed, for which there is often some ecological necessity."

Ecology is a young science, and the ecological needs of a forest are not always self-evident. Inherently complex, forests are biotic communities of diverse, interdependent species. Forests extend beneath the ground in habitats that combine fungi, roots, bacteria, and soil for the optimal use of water and nutrients. Not only is it difficult to see the forest for the trees, much of the structure of a forest is not visible at all.

As soil scientist Michael Crowfoot said: "Ecological processes are not only more complex than we think. They are more complex than we can *ever* think." To understand this requires a different kind of thinking than the statistics and cause-and-effect chains people can easily grasp. Anthropologist Gregory Bateson stretched the definition of "mind" to incorporate mutually adaptive interdependent relationships between different species and between species and their environment. Aldo Leopold wrote of "thinking like a mountain" to explain his epiphany in which he understood that the eradication of wolves to increase deer populations violated the wholeness of ecosystems. From his perspective, a forest is a community of organisms whose health is its capacity "for vigorous self-renewal in each of them, and in all collectively." The removal of canopy trees and the aftereffects of logging can break ecological links that enable a community of organisms to remain mutually resilient. But these links are harder to grasp than numbers of board feet and numbers of acres affected by a megafire. Rather than see the forest for the trees, which is as difficult as seeing a city instead of some of its buildings, many seek a symbol to represent the forest as a whole. Instead of ecosystems that are too complex to imagine, our minds turn to charismatic animals.

It was at a Forest Service road-building site in Bluff Creek drainage that the legend of Bigfoot was born. The Forest Service intended to open its closed canopy forest for timber sales, but the land along Bluff Creek is steep and wild. Building a road to provide access for logging trucks and other equipment proved to be a bad idea. The hillside was not stable, and landslides occurred during road construction. Silt, rocks, dead branches, and other debris clogged Bluff Creek and buried gravels that salmon used for spawning. Bigfoot, who presumably feasted on salmon, had reason to be concerned when bulldozers pushed their way across the mountain.

On several mornings in August 1958, Jerry Crew, a bulldozer operator, claimed to have seen huge footprints of an animal who came down the mountain and either crossed the road and went down to the creek or walked along the road with four-foot strides. All of the tracks seemed to be left by the same individual. Crew got casting plaster from a taxidermist friend and made a cast of a print which he then brought to the *Humboldt Times* in Eureka. Soon "Bigfoot" was a national story.

Non-Indians had reported many encounters with giant apes throughout the country in the nineteenth as well as twentieth centuries, but it was Bigfoot who captured national attention. In subsequent years, more tracks turned up in the Blue Creek Mountains and the Pecwan Creek valley, near tributaries downriver on the Klamath. One Bigfoot explorer, Roger Patterson, made a plaster cast of a track in 1964. Three years later, he shot a celebrated and controversial 16-millimeter film of Bigfoot striding along a Bluff Creek sandbar before disappearing into the woods.

In 2002, the world learned that the original prints that gave Bigfoot his name were the prank of Ray L. Wallace. Shortly after he died at eighty-four, Wallace's son Michael revealed that his father's alderwood carvings made the Bigfoot impressions. Ray and his brother Wilbur had strapped them onto their boots and walked in them at the Bluff Creek road-building site. The *Seattle Times* obituary also reported that Wallace told Patterson where to shoot his film and that he knew the actor who was wearing the Bigfoot suit.

The legend of the big ape at Bluff Creek inspired counterculture cartoonist Robert Crumb to create "Whiteman Meets Bigfoot." Originally appearing in the first issue of *Home Grown Funnies* in 1971, it became the best-selling underground comic book of all time. With his vivid style and erotic expressiveness, Crumb succeeded in making a myth that throws light on the fascination with Bigfoot.

His Yeti is a lusty, hairy, and voluptuous female of the forest. Whiteman is a classic straight man, the suit-wearing employee of General Dynamics who brings his nuclear family into the wilderness in their "spankin' new '71 Winnebago Renegade." Dick and Jane want to watch TV in the camper, but Whiteman is "gonna teach you kids some woodlore." Naturally they get lost, and after the children run off, leaving their father behind, a male Bigfoot abducts him. Carrying Whiteman to his family deep in the woods, the giant gives the terrified human to his daughter Yeti. She makes Whiteman her sex slave in spite of his protest: "I'm a happily married man!"

Using captions that mimic Indian movie dialect—"Bigfoot run like the wind for hours"—Crumb tells a story that parallels historical and fictionalized accounts of whites who were abducted by Indians and who converted to native ways. Whiteman falls in love. "Louise was never like this!!" he says. "Yeti, you're incredible!! Ya make me feel like a real man!"

The story takes the tension between animal nature and artificial civilization up another notch when Whiteman, homesick for his family, brings Yeti into the human world. There she is captured, caged, and studied by federal primatologist Dr. Greyface. When Whiteman attempts to liberate his love from the clutches of science, he chooses freedom in nature over responsibility to job, family, and society. With this myth of man and beast, Crumb expressed the alienation of his generation from their society during the era of the Vietnam War. But he also drew on something deeper: the alienation from and fascination with "wild" nature that has characterized Euramerican civilization since its original encounter with a vast, uncharted land.

The Forest Service also used cartooning—although in a style quite different from Crumb's—in an attempt to build on the phenomenal success of Smokey Bear. A new Forest Service character, Woodsy Owl, told Americans to "give a hoot, don't pollute." It was a good try. The owl, with its upright stance, huge night-vision eyes, and ability to turn its head 270 degrees is a wisdom figure in mythology and children's literature. An owl sits on the shoulder of Athena, the Greek goddess of wisdom. But a different owl took center stage in the debate over Pacific Northwest forestry; and, as in many political arguments, wisdom flew for cover.

Protecting the spotted owl became a public issue because the Endangered Species Act calls for protecting the habitat of particular listed species, not entire ecosystems. The story of the spotted owl, which changed perceptions of the ancient forests of the Pacific Northwest and affected the region's economy, began in 1968 when an undergraduate wildlife biology student had a summer job in the Willamette National Forest. One evening, as he sat on the porch of a Forest Service guard station, Eric Forsman heard "a kind of barking sound." "I thought it was a dog," he recalled. Knowing there were no dogs nearby and having "read a lot about owls," Forsman concluded that "it was probably a spotted owl."

He hooted back, imitating the "ow-ow-ow" sound, and the owl called in response. Then, to the young man's amazement, a northern spotted owl flew down from the trees, settling in the yard in front of him. A nocturnal denizen of forests about which little was known encountered a person fully prepared to pursue his opportunity.

Over the next several years, as Forsman traveled through the Pacific Northwest hooting into trees, he realized that the places where he was likely to find the rare bird were old-growth forests. This did not surprise him. Old growth is inhabited by animals like voles and flying squirrels that spotted owls feed on. It offers abandoned raptor nests and cavities on the broken tops of tall trees for their young, as well as excellent lookout spots on snags, or dead trees, with no leaves or needles to block the sight or muffle the sound of potential prey. The spaces between tree trunks in the old forest give an owl ample swooping room.

During the same years that Forsman tracked the habits of the spotted owl, ecologist Jerry Franklin was studying old-growth forests. "The Forest Service had stopped doing research on old growth in about 1960 because they felt we had learned everything we needed to know about it—which was basically how to cut it down and regenerate a young forest," said Franklin. Old growth had a reputation as "a biological desert" for the rarity of game animals there, but Franklin found it teeming with life. The extraordinary biomass (three times that of tropical rainforests) and variety of vegetation in these mature forests support a great diversity of fauna as well as flora. Among stands of decay-and-fire-resistant conifers, there are 150 mammal species and perhaps 1,500 kinds of invertebrates. The species that appear to require old growth include martens, fishers, salamanders, pileated woodpeckers, and spotted owls.

These species are interdependent with each other and with their ecosystems. Slowly decaying wood provides vital habitat for carpenter ants and bark beetles. Woodpeckers thrive in pursuit of these insects. Fish feed off insects living in logs that rot within streams, and the logs create deep pools, providing critical habitat for coho and cutthroat trout. Trees above streams shade the water, keeping it cool for fish. Meanwhile, within the forest canopy, mats of mosses and lichens bring nitrogen from the air into the trees they hang on. Some of those lichens are a food source and nesting material for flying squirrels. On the forest floor, flying squirrels, chipmunks, and red tree voles dig for truffles. The truffles are outgrowths of fungus colonies that bond symbiotically with roots and help trees draw nutrients and water from the soil. The animals' droppings of undigested spores disperse mycorrhizal fungi around the forest, stimulating tree growth and producing truffles that feed voles and flying squirrels that in turn feed spotted owls, which are the prey of great horned owls and bald eagles. The presence of spotted owls in the food chain is a good indicator of the vitality of the entire ecosystem.

As researchers throughout the Pacific Northwest called owls down from the trees, feeding them mice before putting radio devices on them and then tracking the owls to their nests, they realized that nesting pairs require large expanses of forest to feed and reproduce successfully. Debate raged over what amount of old-growth had to be saved from logging to provide adequate habitat for the bird's survival.

Having wilderness areas nearby was not necessarily a help. Most road-less regions are too high in elevation and their trees too small to harbor the spotted owl and its ilk. The biologically productive old-growth eco-systems, which are 200 years old and more, lie lower on mountainsides and within valleys. To protect the spotted owl meant removing from the loggers' reach the very forests where the largest trees remained.

According to Jack Ward Thomas, he and his colleagues realized that "at the rate that we were cutting against the old growth supply and at the rate we were fragmenting habitat, that we were going to have a collision with the Endangered Species Act, and it was probably going to be spotted owls, and if it wasn't that it was going to be something else." A Forest Service environmental impact statement recommended a 1,000-acre habitat per nesting pair in the Klamath Mountains. That compared with the recommendation of an Audubon Society advisory panel that 2,500 acres be set aside.

In 1991, a court injunction halted timber sales on old-growth forests where spotted owls had been observed. A savior for environmental activists, the owl now became the scapegoat of the forest industry. Loggers and millworkers protested that the reclusive bird was destroying their livelihood and depriving commerce of forest products. Bumper stickers advised consumers to "wipe your ass with a spotted owl."

Timber sales had declined precipitously before Judge Dwyer ruled on the owl's behalf. In the five years preceding his landmark decision, California's annual timber harvest had fallen by an average of 79 percent. In 1988, the Forest Service had allowed the harvest of 12 billion board-feet, a record, but that year's cut coincided with a recession and a drop in demand for wood products. With more wood on the market than people could buy, there was little demand for the mills to fill. The spotted owl issue came along at a time when mills were closing and timber-dependent communities in the Pacific Northwest were struggling with the realities of a changing global economy. Yet just as Smokey had been a symbol of forest protection, the owl became the scapegoat for the decline of forest industries.

Chapter Fourteen
The Road Not Taken

"The land was ours before we were the land's," said Robert Frost, reciting his poem "The Gift Outright" at the inauguration of President John F. Kennedy. What does it mean to be people of the land? Americans relate to our "gift outright" in a wide range of ways. Often economics drive these relationships, but so do myth, science, and what Aldo Leopold called "the land ethic."

In the Klamath Basin, the federal government greatly influences how people relate to the land. There are six national forests, nine wilderness areas, and six wildlife refuges. More of the land is public than private. The drainage of the Klamath River between the mouths of the Trinity and Scott rivers falls almost entirely within the Klamath and Six Rivers National Forests. The watershed of the Salmon River is 98 percent national forest and wilderness area.

As the manager of much of the land along the Klamath River, the U.S. Forest Service has remained in the midst of controversies about the purpose of public lands, in this region and elsewhere, throughout its history. On one flank of the opposition to the Forest Service are heirs of John Muir, who categorically oppose the use of public lands for such purposes as mining, logging, and grazing, all of which are permitted in the national forest. Theirs is a philosophy that regards nature as sacred, to be kept sacrosanct from economic activities. Yet, ironically, it was the utilitarian Forest Service that preserved the lands that were to become nationally protected wilderness areas.

On the other flank are those who oppose federal regulation of public or private lands. The wise use movement—which, again ironically, took its name from a conservationist slogan coined by the founding chief of the Forest Service, Gifford Pinchot—spearheaded a revolt against federal land management beginning in 1988. The original leaders, Ron Arnold and Alan Gottlieb, received funding from timber, mining, and chemical companies to conduct disinformation campaigns against the environmental movement, to galvanize popular opposition to federal land management, and to overturn the Endangered Species Act.

It is remarkable that lands became public in the first place. During the nineteenth century, the major activity of the federal government was acquiring land and giving it away. The land seemed to be inexhaustible; but wood was not, and wood was the commodity that drove the American economy of the nineteenth century, much as oil did in the twentieth. As axes leveled the woods of the northeast, southeast, and lake states, people with foresight feared a "timber famine." Scientific observers such as John Wesley Powell understood that forests store water and release it slowly; they recognized that the continuing destruction of forests in the arid West threatened the water supply that its growing population would need.

In the 1890s, as immigrants poured into the United States, this new awareness of potential resource scarcity led to the setting aside of "forest reserves" from development. Then, in 1905, the conservationist President Theodore Roosevelt created the United States Forest Service. Among the reserves that he placed under the management of his new agency were the Klamath, Trinity, and Siskiyou National Forests. (Six Rivers National Forest was created by President Truman.) Rivers of the Klamath Basin flow through all of these.

As the first chief, Gifford Pinchot made it the mission of the Forest Service to provide "the greatest good for the greatest number" of citizens without despoiling the long-term benefits that the land may offer. Pinchot intended to conserve forests by growing trees as a crop. Public lands would be used but not used up, like wisely managed farms. But one has to know the land in order to manage it. That was one reason Pinchot persuaded Roosevelt to place the Forest Service within the Department of Agriculture, which sponsored most of the government's scientific research at the time. In the agency Pinchot created, science would not only provide knowledge about the land but also investigate ways to produce and use its resources.

The Klamath Basin is a place where questions concerning Pinchot's philosophy of "the greatest good" demand answers. In what ways are people to relate to these public lands?

To come to terms with one's relationship to "the land" is a complex matter for those who did not grow up within a culture or a family whose

livelihood prescribes ways of relating to nature or who do not have a profession that defines this relationship, as science does in asking "questions
of nature." The language people use about the land is often emotionally charged and, as often as not, substitutes for knowledge in ways that
impede learning and openness to other views. Many speak of "wilderness," "the environment," "natural resources." Each term has important
implications. "The views of nature held by any people," wrote Emerson,
"determine all their institutions."

The predominant assumption of nineteenth-century Americans was
that human life is essentially separate from nature. "As one goes West,"
observed ornithologist and essayist John Burroughs, "nature is more and
more and man is less and less." Then there are the passionate feelings
people have about their "country" and "homeland" that identify the land
with national loyalties and family ties. Quite different is the personifica-
tion "Mother Nature," which implies an I-Thou relationship between a
creature and a source of life.

What all of these concepts have in common is a high level of abstrac-
tion. In that respect they differ from Indigenous understandings of relationships with the nonhuman world. Pacific Northwest native languages
do not have a word for "nature," but they have many terms that designate
particular places, from rock formations in the mountains to eddies in the
rivers. People speaking these languages have in common a sense of relatedness between human beings and other aspects of what non-Indians call
"nature." Numerous myths convey the idea that humans—together with
coyotes, salmon, eagles, trees, grass, rocks, and so on—are all descendants
of spirit people, having become who they are during a great transformation. Julia Parker, a basketmaker who is Coast Miwok and Kashaya Pomo,
expressed this sense of identity when she said, "We've always been here.
We're here in the animals, in the plants, in the birds. We'll be here forever, you might say."

The conflict between opposing forms of relationships that human
beings have with nature—one in which people have dominion over the
Earth, to rule and subdue it, and another in which humans are a part of
nature—was fought between the Forest Service and Klamath River tribes
in the G-O Road controversy of the 1960s, 1970s, and 1980s. G-O stands for
Gasquet-Orleans, the two towns that the seventy-five-mile G-O Road was
intended to connect. Gasquet, a town near the Smith River, has the name

of a Frenchman who in 1877 began operating a travelers' inn complete with French restaurant, saloon, guest cabins, blacksmith shop, and butcher shop. Ten years later, Gasquet opened a toll road, built with Chinese labor. By this time, logging had become northwestern California's major industry. Thirty-mule pack trains and ten-horse teams pulling double freight wagons carried people and supplies along the toll road. Timber floated downriver to the sea, where it was loaded onto boats and shipped to San Francisco.

By the mid-twentieth century, Simpson Timber Company had obtained title to much of the forested land along the lower Klamath. Peter Matthiessen described the once redwood-forested land around upper Blue Creek as "stumps, torn earth, and littered deadwood [that] evoked the desolate, blasted hills of war." In areas where Simpson had used 2,4,5-T, a defoliant whose byproduct, dioxin, is among the most toxic of man-made chemicals, "there was no life of any kind, no birds or flowers or berries, and the streams were poisoned."

These lands were lost to forestry for the long term, yet the postwar construction boom showed no signs of ending. As for forests near the Smith River, the Del Norte County assessor determined in 1973 that trees were being cut at such a rapid rate that virtually all of the old growth, for which the major mills were geared, would be gone in twelve years. The county had reason to be concerned: timberlands constituted half of its property tax base. Years before the spotted owl became an issue, logging companies blamed environmentalists and the creation of Redwood National Park for the closure of mills and the increasing unemployment rate.

To keep on producing lumber at the remaining mills, the forest industry pressured the U.S. Forest Service to open more lands for logging. The eastern forks of Blue Creek, which lie within the boundaries of Six Rivers National Forest, were replete with Douglas fir and white cedar — excellent timber trees. A road was needed, with numerous logging roads branching off it, to give the industry access to forested mountains containing more than 700 million board feet of old growth. By 1977, the Forest Service had upgraded forty-nine miles of previously unpaved roads and was prepared to build six miles of paved road through the Chimney Rock section of the Six Rivers National Forest. This would allow logging trucks to travel between Gasquet and Orleans.

The project required an environmental impact report, which was necessary given the extraordinary biodiversity of the region. In a meadow in the Blue Creek drainage, for example, Matthiessen noted "at least fifty species of wildflower in sight all at once, the most various display I have ever seen." Among the flora of the Klamath Mountains are "at least thirteen hundred species of vascular plants, including a few relics of the Tertiary period, sixteen million years ago." Of these, thirty plants, according to the California Native Plant Society, are "rare, very rare, or endangered." Some, like Brewer's spruce and Sadler oak, are unique to the region. Twenty-six species of conifer grow in these mountains, more than in any other temperate mountain ecosystem.

These steep mountains, which have been rising for millions of years, are not a good place to build roads. Winters bring copious quantities of rain. Waters cascade down unstable slopes. The builders of the G-O Road faced the prospect of massive mudslides, as had occurred already in the nearby Bluff Creek watershed. Opening that area up to major logging operations would affect numerous and irreplaceable forms of life.

That was not all it would do. Robert Irwin, a forester in the Gasquet Ranger District, warned in the late 1960s that building the Chimney Rock section of the G-O Road would encroach on the high country, a native spiritual area. Mountains between the Smith and Klamath Rivers have long been used for spiritual training, prayer, and ritual observances by priests and doctors of the Tolowa, Yurok, Hupa, and Karuk tribes. Chimney Rock is one of a number of sacred rocks and "prayer seats" used in ceremonies related to the *pikyávish* religion. Recalling his youth, Charlie Thom said, "I go to the mountains and stay there for months and months at a time. I don't know what I was searching for, but whatever it was I got it. The spiritual value of healing. The spiritual value of receiving songs, the spiritual value of generating spirituality."

Forest Service policy at the time was "multiple use." The idea was that the same piece of land could serve economic purposes such as forestry, forage, and mining as well as water storage, recreation, wildlife management, and wilderness protection. To categorize wilderness as a "use," however, is to undermine its value, as Congress recognized in passing the Wilderness Act of 1964, legislation that authorized the removal of roadless areas from Forest Service management. But the process of determining which roadless areas would become wilderness under the act would take years to play out.

Meanwhile, a Six Rivers National Forest supervisor proposed that forty-five-acre "core zones" around Doctor Rock, Chimney Rock, and other sacred sites be protected behind chain link fences, with interpretative displays located at suitable overlooks. That way, logging operations could still proceed while the Indians would have their religion within fenced areas, and tourists would have opportunities to watch them.

In 1979, however, a study commissioned by the Forest Service concluded that the section of the G-O Road that would traverse the Chimney Rock area should not be built. The entire area, the Theodaratus Report concluded, "is significant as an integral and indispensable part of Indian religious conceptualization and practice." Its use was incompatible with other uses, for the four tribes' religious practices depend on "certain qualities of the physical environment, the most important of which are privacy, silence, and an undisturbed natural setting."

Even though this report came on the heels of the American Indian Religious Freedom Act of 1978, the Forest Service decided to ignore its own recommendations. Congress had neglected to add enforcement provisions to that legislation, and it failed to recognize a fundamental aspect of American Indian religions, namely, their relationship to physical locations—places in nature that tribes hold sacred. "Everything's prayed over" from the high country, explained Charlie Thom. Florence Shaughnessy, a Yurok elder, described what going to such places can do for a seeker. "People go into seclusion and seek something when they're troubled, and then this happens and you come out a whole person. Because you have had help. Nature has gathered every force to help you. They [the spirit beings] uplift you."

The high country, like other places where native people have gone over the centuries on vision quests, holds the potential of revelation. Revelation means that something is disclosed; a veil lifts; those who see as through a glass darkly behold an aspect of truth face to face. "The term revelation, in the sense that suddenly, with indescribable certainty and delicacy, something becomes visible and audible—something that shakes one most profoundly and overthrows one—simply describes the actual situation," Nietzsche wrote. "One listens but seeks not; one takes but does not ask who gives. . . . [It is] a state of being completely beside oneself."

Receptivity to revelation illuminates the history of religion, from Moses's ascent of Mount Sinai through the Axial Age of Buddha, Zarathustra, and Lao Tzu to the visions of Jesus in the desert, Paul of Tarsus on the road to Damascus, and Muhammad in a mountain cave near Mecca. Yet these encounters with the divine, whose memory has been preserved through the historical religions, were "latecomers," according to historian of religion Huston Smith. "For the bulk of human history religion was lived in tribal and virtually timeless mode." The transmission of techniques of ecstasy for the sake of healing, religious observance, and spiritual development is the legacy of shamanism, which apparently accompanied the first Americans as they migrated to this continent. From this perspective, the pilgrimages of Klamath and Smith River Indians into the high country form a vital link with the greatest portion of the religious experience of humankind over the tens of thousands of years since *Homo sapiens* became capable of symbolic expression. They exemplify a path toward transcendence that is humanity's birthright.

Tribal members responded to the threat to the high country in various ways, ranging from physical blockades of earth-moving equipment to meetings with Forest Service rangers and the revival of ceremonies. "I put on a war dance last year at Clear Creek that hasn't been put on for quite a few years," Charlie Thom said in an oral history published in 1978. "There's a few people around who have that knowledge yet." In that interview, the shaman revealed a division between members of the Karuk Tribe. Some wanted the jobs that logging in the high country would bring. "A lot of the leaders," Thom noted, "are going the other direction. And we want to put them back on the right track. We don't want them to follow the white people going up there with heavy equipment and shoving Doctor Rock around."

Legal warriors took the battle all the way to the U.S. Supreme Court. The first assault on the G-O Road was an unsuccessful 1974 lawsuit by the Sierra Club. Charlie Thom recalled flying to Doctor Rock in 1975 in a fleet of six Huey helicopters with "congressional people from Washington, D.C., Sierra Club, foresters, all of that." During the decade that followed, the Audubon Society, Friends of the Earth, and the Northcoast Environmental Center joined the legal struggle in alliance with Yurok, Karuk, and Tolowa tribal members and California Indian Legal Services.

The lawsuits against the Forest Service came to trial in 1983 in the Ninth U.S. District Court in San Francisco. The defendants were Forest Service Chief Max Peterson and his boss, President Reagan's Secretary of Agriculture, John R. Block. The Forest Service contended that completing the G-O Road would serve essential national interests. The plaintiffs argued that the government was violating the First Amendment, the 1864 treaty that established the Hoopa Valley Indian Reservation, and numerous statutes. On March 15, a frail Yurok elder, Lewana Brantner, took the stand. "We use our herbs from the high country where God has left us a piece of land dedicated to the use of the tribes, to go there and pray like they say Mecca or different places through the world where the people go," Brantner told the court. "We lost everything and now we are standing on the last peak, Doctor Rock, Chimney Rock. My neighbors have lost a lot of their ceremonial grounds due to mismanagement of the people, not because they were cruel, but because they did not understand."

After Brantner concluded her testimony, Judge Stanley A. Weigel remarked: "I understand what you are saying, is that due to the deprivations occasioned by the whites, such as the pollution of the streams and the like, and the taking over of more and more land, that the preservation of this particular piece of sacred land has become all the more important." Weigel found the government in violation of the First Amendment, the Federal Water Pollution Control Act, and the National Environmental Policy Act. The Court of Appeals upheld his ruling.

The Supreme Court had the last word. Writing the majority opinion, Justice Sandra Day O'Connor acknowledged that "the Indian respondents' beliefs are sincere and that the Government's proposed actions will have severe adverse effects on the practice of their religion. . . . Individual practitioners use this area for personal spiritual development; some of their activities are believed to be critically important in advancing the welfare of the Tribe, and indeed, of mankind itself." However, "government simply could not operate if it were required to satisfy every citizen's religious needs and desires." The Indians' First Amendment rights to practice their religion, O'Connor concluded, "do not divest the Government of its right to use what is, after all, its land."

Justice William Brennan issued a passionate dissent. "Religious freedom," he argued, "is threatened no less by governmental action that makes the practice of one's chosen faith impossible than by governmental

programs that pressure one to engage in conduct inconsistent with religious beliefs." Brennan regarded this case as part of the

> longstanding conflict between two disparate cultures—the
> dominant Western culture, which views land in terms of ownership
> and use, and that of Native Americans, in which concepts of
> private property are not only alien, but contrary to a belief system
> that holds land sacred. Rather than address this conflict in any
> meaningful fashion, however, the Court disclaims all responsibility
> for balancing these competing and potentially irreconcilable
> interests. . . . Native Americans deserve—and the Constitution
> demands—more than this.

In the end, the controversy, though profound, lacked practical relevance.
The California Wilderness Act of 1984 designated much of the Blue Creek
Planning Unit as wilderness. That prevented logging from occurring
there and the G-O Road from being completed. Yet conflict between the
Klamath River tribes and the Forest Service over sacred areas continued
nonetheless.

Unlike the neighboring Yurok and Hupa tribes, the Karuk have no
reservation. Their government is federally recognized, but their homeland is almost entirely national forest.

Laws require the Forest Service to consult with tribes when its work
may affect sacred sites and have adverse environmental impacts. These
include the National Historic Preservation Act (NHPA). That law protects
sites where Karuk fixing-the-world ceremonies occur because they are
listed in the National Register of Historic Places. The sacred mountain
at the center of the Karuk world, spiritual trails including the Medicine
Man Trail walked by world renewal priests, and much of the high country
where Karuk and other Klamath River Indians seek spiritual renewal are
all within Six Rivers National Forest.

One concern shared by the Forest Service and Karuk tribal members
is catastrophic wildfire. This became a threat to the national forest in part
due to the federal government prohibition of Indian fire lighting throughout the twentieth century. Without the frequent, low-intensity fires that
tribes had used to live safely and productively on the land, forests in the

mid-Klamath River region became thick and impassable. The increase in forest density raised the odds of widespread, high-intensity incineration. Accordingly, Six Rivers, after consulting with the tribe, undertook a forest fuels–clearing project near the town of Orleans. When the contractor's logging equipment damaged the Medicine Man Trail, the Karuk sued the Six Rivers Forest Supervisor. A district court rejected the argument that this project caused significant environmental harm, but it did rule that the supervisor, Tyrone Kelley, failed to make the contractor protect the sacred area as required by the NHPA.

A seismic shift in personnel and policy at Six Rivers National Forest occurred soon thereafter. Merv George Jr., who had been chair of the Hoopa Valley Business Council and tribal relations coordinator for the Pacific Southwest Region of the U.S. Forest Service, replaced Tyrone Kelley. Nolan Colegrove, also a Hupa tribal member, became a district ranger. And Frank Lake, who is part Karuk and who absorbed traditional ecological knowledge from childhood on, began working with the tribes as a Forest Service research ecologist.

When Lake was young, two Klamath Basin events inspired him to become an environmental scientist. One was the reinstatement of the Yurok Tribe and the conservation work it took on. The other was the G-O Road controversy. Lake had "this duality of seeing natural resource and political issues, not only around river fisheries conservation, but also around forests and biodiversity and sacred sites." As he "saw those struggles and those dynamics and started looking for a solution," he understood his responsibility "to family, land and waters, and community. Both the human and biological community."

Six Rivers National Forest, in partnership with the Karuk Tribe and other local stakeholders, took on that responsibility. Its Indigenous leadership was not the only reason for the shift. The Forest Service lacked the personnel to protect this remote region from catastrophic fire, either by firefighting or by reducing forest fuels with low-intensity burning. It had to overcome the agency's alienation from the tribe and from local conservation groups in order to form an effective fire-wise alliance.

There already existed a working partnership between the Karuk and community organizations. The Mid-Klamath Watershed Council, which was formed by FireSafe Council participants in 2001, was a natural ally of the tribe. Much of MKWC's early work involved clearing shrubs and other unwanted plants to deprive wildfires of fuel. That mission brought Karuk tribal members onto its board.

The idea for MKWC came from Will Harling. Harling and other MKWCers were children of hippies who formed the Black Bear commune. They grew up in the Salmon River watershed with Indigenous values as formative influences. "We have a strong sense of place on the river," said Erica Terence, whose parents, like Harling's, were commune members. "That's what shaped us." Terence became the Klamath River-keeper and went on to work for MKWC and for the Karuk Tribe.

The Nature Conservancy had formed a Fire Learning Network across the country and was looking for new places to extend it. The alliance between Bill Tripp, then deputy director for the Karuk Natural Resources Department, and Will Harling of MKWC showed TNC that the mid-Klamath region had exceptional potential. Lynn Decker, who directed TNC's North American Fire Initiative, invited the supervisors of Six Rivers and Klamath National Forest to meet with Tripp, Harling, and representatives of the Klamath Forest Alliance, the Salmon River Restoration Council, and other conservation groups to see if they could establish an all-lands, all-hands fire management partnership. Success was hardly a foregone conclusion considering the federal agency's militaristic firefighting culture, its historic reliance on timber revenues, the anger of local residents over health-damaging impacts of herbicides, the hostility many loggers felt toward environmentalists and vice versa, and anti-Indian racism.

Through a series of monthly three-day workshops following the Open Standards for the Practice of Conservation, the Western Klamath Restoration Partnership (WKRP) was established. One of the methods Decker and her deputy Mary Huffman used was getting people face to face on, literally, common ground. An example was the question of whether to remove some roadside trees to facilitate residents' escape from and fire engine access to rapidly spreading wildfire. Participants weighed emergency concerns with ecological and economic factors. Considering specific situations, they found zones of agreement and set aside matters they could not agree on.

Two years into these workshops, in 2015, Klamath River Indians, including Nolan Colegrove and Frank Lake from the Forest Service, met in a riverside fishing cabin. What is still missing, said Bill Tripp, is the culture of fire. Women are traditional leaders in this, he said. He recalled that his grandmother, when she was 100 and he was five, had him burn a patch of land outside their house. Similarly, from a young age, Elizabeth Azzuz burned land to cultivate hazel, bear grass, and other basketry plants for her elderly aunts. Margo Robbins said she brings children into the forest to experience fire and know about its benefits. They learn that fire aids the growth of berries that bears eat. They learn that smoke cools the river, keeping temperatures tolerable for fish. Rather than fear fire as a dangerous force, rather than getting spanked, like white children, for playing with fire, they learn to welcome fire into the community they share with plants and other animals. The culture of fire, they concluded, needed to be appreciated and supported by their non-Indian partners.

This meeting led the fledgling Western Klamath Restoration Partnership to adopt cultural fire as a favored method for conserving and protecting the mid-Klamath region. And it launched the Indigenous Peoples Burning Network, which totals twenty tribes so far, including the Ojibwe in Minnesota, pueblos in New Mexico, and the Klamath Tribes in Oregon.

The Yurok Tribe's route toward renewing its fire culture differed from the Karuk's. Margo Robbins, who became executive director of the Yurok Cultural Fire Management Council, told me its origin story when interviewed for my documentary *Wilder Than Wild: Fire, Forests, and the Future*. The Yurok town of Weitchpec was offered funding for whatever residents decided was most important to meet their needs. "Our community identified fire as the number one most important thing to have in our community," Robbins said. They used the grant to buy fire management equipment, and with support from The Nature Conservancy began to train Indians and non-Indians through the Prescribed Fire Training Exchange program, or TREX.

During a Yurok burn near Weitchpec in 2017, the California Department of Fire and Forestry, or Cal Fire, had a fire truck ready to assist. Elizabeth Azzuz, director of Traditional Fire for the Cultural Fire Management Council, exclaimed, "We've been waiting with bated breath for Cal Fire to come on board, and so it's really nice to see that we're merging our culture and our community along with the outside agencies. It feels really good. My heart has been singing for the last three days because I'm gonna be able to get down in here next year and gather traditional foods, acorns, huckleberries."

Indians no longer have chiefs, but Cal Fire does, as does the Forest Service. When I spoke with Ken Pimlott in his Sacramento office, the Cal Fire Chief said his thinking about fire changed after he started working with the Klamath River tribes. Previously he understood his mission to be protection of lives and property through firefighting. Now he knows the importance of lighting fires.

Unfortunately, proactive burning did not occur soon enough or on a scale large enough to protect California from the megafires that have torched residential areas up and down the state. In 2018, the 153,000-acre Camp Fire killed 85 people and countless animals while destroying the town of Paradise. In 2020, the 157,000-acre Slater Fire killed two people while obliterating 200 homes in Happy Camp, where Karuk tribal headquarters are located. It also blackened 100,000 acres of the Klamath National Forest, forcing wildlife either to escape or be incinerated. Happy Camp and much of that forest might not have burned had the Klamath conducted more prescribed fires. Such fires, in many instances, have slowed fast-moving, high-intensity wildfires and turned them into beneficial low-intensity fire.

A reason the Klamath does too little proactive burning is that it sends fire staff to fight wildfires elsewhere. Suppressing nascent fires brings revenue for hot shot teams, smoke jumpers and helicopter crews, and it pays for supplies, including aircraft fuel and fire suppressant foam, incentivizing a vicious cycle that consumes an increasing majority of the U.S. Forest Service budget. "We've got a fire-industrial complex," said Stephen Pyne when interviewed for *Wilder Than Wild*. "We've got a whole private industry that's devoted to firefighting, which is now creating lobbies." Yet the federal policy of putting out all wildfires as soon as possible, even in remote areas that need fire, is a losing battle. In the absence of prescribed and cultural fire lighting, forests become so dense with trees and other plants that when ignition strikes on a hot, windy day, megafires explode, charring vast areas.

Six Rivers National Forest aims to break this vicious cycle by bringing good fire back to the land. According to Colegrove, Karuks take the lead in preparing for as well as executing cultural burns. To reduce fire risk, they identify areas that need burning and/or manual cutting, and they thin conifers to reduce tree density, removing trees by helicopter when necessary to prevent harm to sacred trails.

Traditionally, fire lighting signals the beginning of a *pikyávish* ceremony. On a culturally appropriate day determined by the moon cycle, a priest sets logs aflame atop Offield Mountain. Rising above Ishi Pishi Falls and Katimîin, a ceremonial site, that peak, which Karuks call Spirit Mountain, marks the center of their world. When burning logs tumble downslope, low-intensity fire rises toward the summit, and smoke spreads across the river, inviting salmon upstream.

Leaf Hillman and Bill Tripp, his successor as director of the Karuk Department of Natural Resources, intend to bring that tradition back. Its return will signal a political, cultural, ecological, and spiritual victory, as sacred fire on Spirit Mountain renews the world.

Chapter Fifteen
Beneath the Surface

Early one evening in late July 2001, Carlos Bolado, Michael Pryfogle, George Spies, and I drove past Mount Shasta, heading toward the Shasta River. Brown with patches of white, the volcano looked quite different from the snow-crowned mountain we had videotaped under a full moon in May.

At Yreka, we turned off Interstate 5 onto a road that goes through the Scott River Valley toward Etna. Near the Etna summit, a magnificent view of both the Scott River and the Salmon River valleys greeted us. As we traveled slowly down the narrow road, we passed dry creekbeds. Only after many switchbacks did we see any water at all.

Finally, the van stopped in Forks of Salmon, a minuscule former Gold Rush town. People were gathering there to prepare for the annual fish dive, a count of spawning spring chinook that would occur the next day. Brenda Olson, the U.S. Forest Service biologist who was leading the fish count, discussed with us the best reach of the river to videotape during the event.

The next morning, we joined dozens of fish-dive participants. Many were members of the Salmon River Restoration Council. Petey Brucker, a tall, blond man with a greying beard, had long been a leader of that group. He had come to the Salmon River from New York City twenty-five years earlier. "When I first got here," he said, "I thought that when I saw salmon in the river and in the pools in the summer like this, that I was supposed to catch salmon." His custom had been to catch two fish on his birthday. Then Brucker found out that there were only a few hundred mature spring chinook in the Salmon River. "I started doing the math," he remembered, "which was basically, there's about two or three hundred of us that live in this watershed, this half a million acres, and if each of us takes one home, there's not going to be any future for the fish."

Brucker and Jack Kohler stood among those listening to Brenda Olson's instructions for the fish dive. Divers had been divided into groups that would walk and snorkel along each reach of the river. Fish-dive participants received packets containing a laminated map of the reach, a grease pencil, and flagging. They were to record the number of steelhead and chinook they saw and use the flags to mark where they entered and left the water.

Olson explained how divers could tell the difference between steelhead and spring chinook. The most obvious difference is size. Spring chinook are larger, while "steelhead are a lot more slender." But the diver has to differentiate between full-grown and "jack" salmon and, in doing so, to be aware of the distortion in size caused by his or her mask, "which magnifies everything by a third."

Olson noted numerous ways to tell the fish apart: "chinook have black lipstick; steelhead have a white lipstick or gums"; chinook are olive green; steelhead can be silver gray. And the fish have distinct tails—the chinook's is slightly forked, the steelhead's blunt and straight—which is important because that may be all of them the diver sees. "You'll see both the chinook and the steelhead under ledges, in little crevices and boulders," she said. "They're very shy and they're hiding," and they're staying in the shade where it's cool.

"This year," she continued, "you'll probably see a lot of the fish where the tribs are coming in, because that's where the cool water is. From all the descriptions I've heard this year, they're really stressed due to water temperature." Stress, said Olson, "just gives disease and parasites that much more opportunity to run rampant in the fish."

Olson warned about "racking," a current that pushes a person against a boulder, and she told her listeners what to do in going through a "strainer"—a submerged log or group of boulders that sucks water through it, sometimes so powerfully it pulls the diver irresistibly into danger.

This year, the divers would not only be swimming and floating; they would also be doing "a lot of walking because the river's so low. I don't know if some of you heard, but this is the driest year since 1936." Karuk dipnetter Ron Reed said a prayer. He asked for guidance and for safety "so we can continue this ongoing effort to restore this fish."

Having changed into wetsuits, each team of divers entered the water at the upstream edge of their assigned reach. Playing the Hollywood

Indian, Jack joked that he was used to hot-tub temperatures. Then he, Reed, Reed's brother Mike, Brucker, Chance Gowen, the new Forest Service ranger at Fort Jones, and several others entered the river at Forks. They would search the reach from there to Otter Bar.

After the dive, the production team drove along Bigfoot Highway to the river road where a sign says "Pic-Ya-Wish ceremonial area." Ron, his brother Mike, and Ron's two sons, who were five and six, joined us, and we followed them down a trail leading to Ishi Pishi Falls.

This is "a sacred fishery and the center of the world for us," Reed explained, "the center of our spiritual universe." The proximity of the falls to the world renewal site is significant, he noted, since "all of our ceremonies evolved around the fish run." Fish caught at Ishi Pishi are carried up the trail to serve the dancers and others attending the ceremonies.

Downstream, a small conical mountain rises above the river—A'uich, also known as Sugar Loaf Mountain. The side facing the falls is severely eroded. There are large boulders along the riverbank that had tumbled down from A'uich, so many that walking to the falls required rock climbing.

Ishi Pishi Falls is the only fishery left to the Karuks. The government acknowledges that this rare place in North America where dip-net fishing still occurs is a Karuk site, yet unlike Blue Lake, which is sacred to the Taos Pueblo and which the Forest Service eventually returned to that tribe, the center of the Karuk universe remains under federal management.

"Traditionally," Reed said, "we've had over 70 miles of river, and every back eddy, every creek, every tributary was a fishery. And now we're obligated to fish out of one fishery for over 3,000 tribal members. Last year we caught approximately 850 fish, so you see that the mathematics just doesn't add up. There's a lot of people that are doing without."

Ten-foot-long fir poles leaned against a boulder near the water. Ron showed Jack how to attach a net to them and how to use the dip net. "Grab one hand all the way back," he said, "the other one right there, then you thrust the poles out into the current. You dig down, kinda scoot the fish back into the little pocket."

The Reed brothers walked over boulders until they reached a good fishing spot. Following Carlos's direction, George Spies and Gerrid Joy positioned their cameras to record Ron Reed dipping the net into rocky pools in the river. After a number of thrusts, he pulled salmon out of the water onto a boulder. Mike Reed removed the twisting fish from the net, clubbed them, and put them into a sack.

These were fall, not spring chinook. The springers had come up the Klamath months earlier on their way to the Salmon River. Years ago, Karuk fishermen at Ishi Pishi netted spring salmon on their way to the Upper Basin to spawn. They were the dominant run up the Klamath, and Karuks celebrated their First Salmon ceremony when they first appeared. Now these fish spawn primarily in the Salmon River and its tributaries. Like Petey Brucker, Karuks no longer catch them, not even for ceremonial purposes.

That evening we headed back to Forks of Salmon for a community meeting about the fish dive. Brenda Olson reported that 315 spring chinook had been counted. Then Brucker and his fellow Restoration Council members performed the Salmon Show for us. The room was dark, and bats flew overhead, yet the show was funny and grimly apropos of the annual fish dive. The actors wore cloth salmon dolls on their heads, and their characters aimed to spawn. Excited to reach their home river, they made sexy, athletic moves, schooling, sallying forth, evading predators. As they proceeded upriver, however, one fish after another fell prey to seals, to fishermen, to stress and sickness in the hot water. Finally, only two salmon were left. They made it! Still alive and ready to spawn! The only problem was, both were guys.

Some of the actors playing salmon in that performance first came to the Salmon River in the late 1960s and 1970s when a back-to-the-land movement brought a new wave of settlers into northern California and southern Oregon. The most remote outpost in an archipelago of communal households in the Klamath Basin was a settlement at Black Bear in the Salmon River drainage. The Black Bear commune made use of eighty acres, an abandoned ranch house, miners' cabins, and a century-old barn that remained from the days when the Daggetts lived there.

According to Efrem Korngold, one of the founders, Black Bear was part of "a national network of countercultural, activist, radically political, communalistic communities." But when he and his wife Carol Hamilton arrived there with their four-year-old, they had more immediate concerns. Hamilton was eight months pregnant, and her new homestead, she noticed right away, had "bear droppings everywhere."

John Salter, an early resident, recalled men being embroiled in political arguments while the women cooked, washed diapers, and tended the garden. In Hamilton's recollection, "The women were the mainstays for doing the routine work, while the men concentrated on big projects like breaking ground for a new garden, food runs to the City, or digging a new shitter."

Through the practical work of surviving on the land, commune members learned to relate to where they were. "The forest was for me a place of primeval mystery and fear," Michael Tierra recalled. "The urge to explore it, gun in hand, however inept I was as a hunter, was an unconscious attempt to come to terms with this mysterious environment."

An avant-garde artist who had trained as a classical pianist, Tierra found himself "magnetically drawn to the flora of the mountains for reasons that I barely understood." He became an herbalist, experimenting with comfrey and echinacea, along with other herbal treatments at the ranch. "Without setting out to do so," he wrote, "we were evolving a lifestyle that gave rise to the organic and natural food movement and the use of herbs, folk medicine, and other traditional healing modalities that held the promise of further liberating us from the 'system.'" Tierra was not alone as a medical innovator. Korngold and Harriet Beinfield introduced Chinese medical practices, including acupuncture, to the ranch and eventually to the American public in the early 1970s.

The back-to-the-land lifestyle produced a philosophy of bioregionalism. Ecologist Peter Berg articulated this idea within a planetary frame of reference: "If humans wanted to avoid destroying our life-support systems—water, soil, air, and plant and animal species—both urban and rural people would have to learn to live according to the dictates and processes of their bioregion." Berg and conservation biologist Raymond Dasmann called for "reinhabitation," which "means learning to live-in-place in an area that has been disrupted and injured through past exploitation. It involves becoming native to a place through becoming aware of the particular ecological relationships that operate within and around it."

Karuks visited Black Bear, bringing salmon and teaching the communards how to smoke it. Emulating Indians had considerable appeal as a way to live in accordance with the ecology of the bioregion. Yet like hippies elsewhere, Black Bear family members who identified with Indians hardly resembled them. Many at Black Bear were alienated from their families, but family is the fundamental social unit for the Klamath tribes. People within the counterculture aspired to live for the moment and rejected work whose goal is future security; conversely, tribal members catch and smoke large quantities of fish to ensure survival through the winter. They abhorred the acquisition of wealth, yet traditionally, for members of the Klamath River tribes, having ceremonial outfits and dentalium shell necklaces brought prestige. People in the commune celebrated solstices as holidays for the whole Earth. Tribal ceremonies that aim at making the world anew are also new year's celebrations, but those holy days are coordinated with the salmon's return, the world and their homeland being the same.

In his dissent on the G-O Road case, Justice Brennan noted a contrast between Western and Indigenous religions that is related to the fundamental difference between perceiving land as an object to be used and land as sacred. Whereas the Judeo-Christian West views creation as the work of a deity who gave man dominion over physical nature, "tribal religions regard creation as an on-going process in which they are morally and religiously obligated to participate." In a 2004 interview, sitting on riverside rock beside Jack Kohler and Ron Reed, Leaf Hillman explained: "One thing that never ends as long as Karuk people are here is that responsibility." Speaking of the great transformation in which some of the original spirit people were changed into human beings and others "into rocks, trees, fish, water, air, acorns, deer, all those things," Hillman said, "all of those things are our relations, and with all of those things we have this reciprocal relationship. And we have a responsibility to look after their well-being."

This sense of responsibility for other species, which Hillman expressed in Indigenous terms, Aldo Leopold considered an "extension of ethics" for humanity at large. While the Golden Rule "tries to integrate the individual to society" and democracy attempts to "integrate social organization to the individual," what Leopold called "the land ethic" integrates human beings into the biotic community as fellow members. Just as the premise of human-centered ethics is "that the individual is a member of a community of interdependent parts," so the land ethic is based on the idea that human beings are citizens of a community that comprises the land and life around us. This enlarged understanding of community, according to Leopold, is an intellectual as well as ethical advance: "Many historical events, hitherto explained solely in terms of human enterprise, were actually biotic interactions between people and land." The wildlife and water crisis in the Klamath Basin is such an event. The notion that human communities share responsibility for the decline in the biotic community on which their own lives depend came naturally, so to speak, to Indigenous people whose *pikyávish* ethos is a homegrown version of the land ethic.

Ron Reed's participation in "fixing the world" accounts for the feeling of responsibility for the fish kill of 2002 that he expressed in that riverbank interview. From his upriver perspective Reed told the story of that event, in which tens of thousands of spawning salmon died in the estuary.

> We know when the medicine man goes into the sweathouse at Katimîin, the fishery is on down Ishi Pishi Falls. So that date came and went without fish being in Ishi Pishi Falls. At that point there was grave concern, 'cause there was something drastically wrong in the system.

Reed and his sons waited at the fishery for Iron Gate Dam to release a pulse of water. "I was telling them we need to have water in this area right here for us to be able to fish. Once they seen the water start trickling down, they said, 'The fish are gonna start running tomorrow.'" He continued:

> The next day, the fish were in there thick. It was glorious because the fish were back into the fishing hole, back in the fishery. It was like it was making medicine again. But when we started catching those fish, we started pulling those fish out of the water, you see great lesions on their sides. Big puss balls, puss sacks on their tails. Sad.
>
> So then, we pack our fish out half a mile up and over boulders, ravines, and back up the hill. We clean 'em. We go take them to our elders. Our elders look at us like we have done something truly bad, we've done something dishonorably. And it hurt my heart. Because the condition of the flesh was insinuating that I wasn't taking care of the fish properly. And when I gave it my elders, I wasn't delivering it in a proper manner. . . . The pride in the fisherman on that day, in that year, was tarnished forever.

As Jack Kohler sat between the two Karuk spokesmen, I balanced on the rock above the three of them holding the microphone pole, dipnetting words. During the fish kill, diseased salmon had come all the way to Ishi Pishi Falls; some survived long enough to spawn.

The sadness of that memory brought to Leaf Hillman's mind an intertribal meeting in which a member of the Klamath Tribes brought out interviews conducted in the 1930s and 1940s with Indians in the Upper Basin. They spoke of catching salmon early in the twentieth century before the dams went in.

> We were talking about the relicensing of these dams coming up in 2006, and if they relicense these dams for another 50 years, you know, who's to say they won't be reading about us, you know, 50 years from now, reading about "Oh, yeah we used to go down to Ishi Pishi Falls and catch salmon." . . . That's what they got left is to read about it, stories that they tell about it. And it's a pretty powerful motivator, to not let that happen to us what happened already to some other folks up above us.

For Leaf Hillman, the prospect that the wild salmon of the Klamath River would become extinct within his lifetime was not a remote possibility. Not only did spawning salmon die in large numbers in 2002, but so did countless fry. A small percentage of the juvenile fish born that year survived exposure to the hot and toxic main stem. The scarcity of Klamath salmon entering the ocean in 2002 meant a lack of spawners three and four years later.

The absence of adequate runs in 2005 and 2006 had a devastating impact on the commercial fishing industry. Both years, the Pacific Fishery Management Council curtailed the fishing season off the northern California and southern Oregon coasts due to the expected low numbers of returning Klamath salmon. Since these fish mix in the ocean with other stocks, the only way to safeguard runs up the Klamath that could meet minimum spawning goals was to require a severe reduction of the offshore salmon fishery in that seven-hundred-mile offshore zone. This was particularly unfortunate for commercial fishers since both those years large runs of Sacramento River–bound salmon were expected. The annual cost for the fishing industry was estimated as a loss of $100 million in profits—for the consumer, a 50 percent increase in the price of salmon. In 2006, the commercial fishing crisis became so acute that, after months of pressure from the governors and lawmakers of Oregon and California, Secretary of Commerce Carlos Gutierrez agreed to declare an economic disaster for the approximately 3,000 salmon fishermen in those states affected by the almost total closure of their season.

The collapse of fall chinook salmon populations in the Klamath, following the decline of coho salmon and spring chinook, may become part of a larger and much longer-term calamity: the greatest mass extinction since the demise of the dinosaurs more than 70 million years ago. Extinction is a natural phenomenon; but according to the biologist E. O. Wilson, the current rate of extinction "is catastrophically high, somewhere between one thousand and ten thousand times the rate before human beings began to exert a significant pressure on the environment." Wilson's inability to determine the order of magnitude of the rise in the rate of extinction comes from his acknowledgment of what no one can know: the number of species that have disappeared before human beings ever became aware of them.

If the wealth of the world is measured by the vitality of its biosphere, increasing poverty faces everyone on Earth. In 2022, the International Union for the Conservation of Nature listed more than 42,000 species as threatened with extinction. Among the species in trouble are 41 percent of all amphibians, 27 percent of mammals, 21 percent of reptiles, and 13 percent of birds. The unraveling of the legacy of evolution in the Klamath Basin is part of a precipitous collapse affecting life in every part of the planet.

Yurok healer Fanny Flounder at her home in Requa, photographed by A. L. Kroeber
(*courtesy of the Phoebe Apperson Hearst Museum of Anthropology and Regents of the
University of California*)

Geneva and Emery Mattz Sr., whose family was instrumental in restoring fishing rights and reestablishing the reservation of the Yurok tribe (*in author's collection, courtesy of Diane Whipple Mattz*)

Raymond Mattz, during the Salmon War in 1978 (*in author's collection, courtesy of Diane Whipple Mattz*)

Fish and Wildlife agents confront Lavina Bowers and Geneva Mattz during the Salmon War in 1978 (*in author's collection, courtesy of Diane Whipple Mattz*)

John Anderson, Klamath Basin farmer (*photo by Stephen Most*)

The Barton brothers irrigating potatoes in 1929 (*by permission of the Bureau of Reclamation*)

Klamath Basin harvest worker poses with a potato belt, which was commonly used in the mid-twentieth century (*courtesy of the Klamath County Historical Museum*)

Eleanor Bolesta points out her Klamath Basin homestead in 1947 (*by permission of the Bureau of Reclamation*)

Sign on Highway 39, at the Oregon-California state line, in March 2003 (*photo by Stephen Most*)

Giant bucket forged by Bucket Brigade supporters in Nevada in front of the county building on Main Street in Klamath Falls (*photo by Stephen Most*)

232

Phil Detrich of the Fish and Wildlife Service; Alan Foreman, chair of the Klamath Tribes; and farmer Sam Henzel listen as Yurok Troy Fletcher speaks in Chiloquin in 2005 (*photo by Stephen Most*)

Bob Chadwick (in white beard) talks with participants at the stakeholders' workshop in Chiloquin in 2005 (*photo by Stephen Most*)

Mike Connelly and Alice Kilham talk at the stakeholders' workshop in Chiloquin in 2005 (*photo by Stephen Most*)

Copco 2, the first of the four hydroelectric dams on the Klamath to be demolished (*photo by Shane Anderson*)

The Klamath River where 35-foot Copco 2 had blocked its flow until mid-2023 (*photo by Shane Anderson*)

PART FOUR
Fixing the World

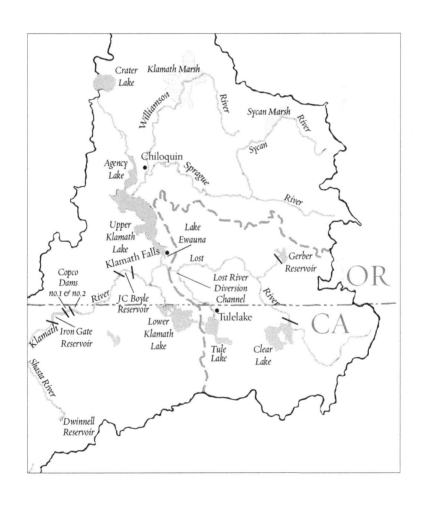

Chapter Sixteen
Land, Water, and Livelihood

More human beings were born into the twentieth century than lived during the previous 100,000 years. Four hundred years ago there were fewer than 600,000 people. In 300 years, by the start of the twentieth century, that number increased by a billion. During the last century, the world's population grew almost fourfold: from 1.6 billion in 1900 to 2.5 billion at midcentury to 6 billion people in 2000. By mid 2023, more than 8 billion humans populated the planet.

From the second half of the twentieth century on into the twenty-first, hundreds of millions of people moved away from rural areas into expanding urban centers. In the United States, the number of farmers decreased by half between the mid-1970s and the end of the twentieth century.

Yet food production increased. The Green Revolution allowed a shrinking number of farmers working a gradually increasing amount of arable land to feed the mounting multitudes.

After World War II, farmland became available in the Upper Klamath Basin. The U.S. War Relocation Authority (WRA) had built ten relocation camps for Japanese Americans, one of which covered 1,100 acres of Klamath Project lands. To bring agriculture back, the Bureau of Reclamation (BOR) made eighty-six Klamath Project farm units of 160 acres or less available for homesteading. To be eligible for the lottery, one had to have farming experience, a record of service during the war, some cash, good health, and a good character. More than 2,000 veterans applied. On December 18, 1946, the Klamath Union High School Band played patriotic songs at the Klamath Falls armory as the drawing took place. Capsules containing contestants' names were picked from a pickle jar and smashed open with a mallet. The lucky winners' names were read before an anxious crowd and on nationwide radio.

One winner was Eleanor Bolesta. During the war, Bolesta, who had grown up on a farm, served the Navy in the WAVES, Women Accepted for Voluntary Emergency Service. She did not like her postwar job as a secretary for the Civil Aeronautics Administration in Everett, Washington, and her husband, Chuck, who had been wounded as a Marine in Guam, wanted a drier climate for his recovery. Bolesta's boss had been stationed at the Naval Air Station in Klamath Falls (now Kingsley Field) during the war, and he suggested she apply for the lottery.

Hearing on the radio that Eleanor had won, the Bolestas drove to Klamath Falls where a Bureau of Reclamation board interviewed them. Eleanor was asked, "How can you prove that you are head of the family?" Her answer, that she was supporting her wounded husband, satisfied the panel, and Bolesta became the first woman to win a Bureau of Reclamation homestead.

The new homesteaders formed a potluck social club, and they received support from the surrounding community. Loans were easy to obtain, and established farmers readily gave advice. The first crop the Bolestas planted on their 112-acre farm was malting barley. That same year, Eleanor gave birth to Peggy, their first child.

Those veterans of the world wars who won Klamath Project homesteads in lotteries, together with others who had settled in the Upper Basin to work the land, were exceptional. They and their children, and to a lesser extent their grandchildren, remained on the farm. Many increased their acreage to cover the costs of industrial agriculture, and some relied on migrant workers to manage their crops; yet the majority remained family farmers, a vanishing breed elsewhere. Not exceptional were their uses of mechanized irrigation, pesticides, chemical fertilizers, and new crops to increase food cultivation. The Green Revolution transformed their farms, their lives, their region, and its wildlife.

Two Upper Basin families, the Andersons and the Stauntons, were among those who experienced the transformation. The horse that kicked Bob Anderson's father in the head in the late 1920s hastened that family's shift to tractors. In 1960, the Andersons were among the first in the region to switch from flood irrigation to sprinkler systems that conserve water. Flood irrigation is inexpensive, but it wastes water, leaches salt and alkali into the soil, and gives insects fertile places to breed. Today, pump-driven wheel-line sprinkler systems water fields of wheat, barley, alfalfa, and clover, and solid-set sprinklers spray potato vines. A temperature-control system allows farmers to protect potatoes from frost by bathing the vines in water that is warmer than the air.

These and other machines greatly increased the cost of farming. "When I got out of the service in 1958," reminisced John Staunton,

> I remember buying a tractor for seventy-six hundred dollars, and I thought, "Oh my gosh. I remember when my Dad bought a tractor for thirty-five hundred and this is just a ten-horse power mower." Now, comparably, you cannot buy a tractor for under sixty thousand. . . . You cannot afford on a small family scale to have several hundred thousand dollars invested in tractors, in irrigation equipment, and so and so forth.

By the 1960s, a 160-acre homestead—the limit under the federal Klamath Project—no longer supported a farm family. To be cost effective, much of the new farm equipment had to work larger plots of land. The solution was for family members to buy and lease as many farm units as they could. Working with his three sons, John Staunton expanded his operation sufficiently to achieve economies of scale. By the turn of the millennium, in addition to their lease land in the Tule Lake Basin, the Stauntons owned 2,200 acres of private land on which they raised wheat, barley, onions, and potatoes. They had sixty employees and owned a potato-packing shed.

Potatoes, which originated in the Andes and were the staple of the Inca Empire, are a premium Upper Basin crop. My Uncle Albert Fradkin, an agronomist, grew seed potatoes near Tule Lake. He knew that the rich soils and abundant sunlight there offered optimal conditions. According to Staunton, the yield per acre is 600 sacks, second only to the Columbia River Basin and double the national average.

Potato harvesting was a labor-intensive operation until the late 1920s when horse-drawn machines became available to dig up the tubers, enabling farm workers to sack them efficiently. When tractors came in, larger diggers followed. After World War II, wrote Stan Turner in his history of the region, "machinery was developed that allowed only a handful of operators to plant, cultivate, and harvest entire fields."

Some farmers in the Basin relied on migrant laborers instead of expensive machines. According to Turner, migrant worker Lavada Hance and her daughter Paulette were able to earn sixty dollars a day in the 1960s by filling sacks that hung from potato belts around their waists. That was good money for a farmworker, but "a disturbing number ended up in poor health." Most potato growers invest heavily in pesticides, their crop being vulnerable to fungal blight and beetle infestation, and there were no federal or state regulations on the use of pesticides until the late 1960s.

John and Bob Anderson stopped growing potatoes in the 1970s. Wheat and alfalfa became their major crops, and they bought cattle. After the water cutoff by the Bureau of Reclamation in 2001, their lands dried up; the loss of a growing year drove the family deeply into debt. To adapt, they switched from crops to cattle, which saved equipment costs and offered flexibility in light water years. The Andersons continued to grow alfalfa hay, which they used to feed their herd of a thousand cows.

The Stauntons fared better than the Andersons in 2001. "We bought water from wells," John Staunton recalled. "We were about 50 percent of our normal potato acreage." Rather than lay off their employees, the Stauntons were "able to buy potatoes in the Columbia Basin and ship them down and run them through our packing shed and make a profit that way."

Other Klamath Project farm families were less fortunate. They required relief. Those who took pride in bringing food to markets became unable to put food on their own tables.

During the Eisenhower Administration, it became federal policy to disband American Indian tribes and sell their lands. The increase in America's demand for wood during the affluent postwar Baby Boom coincided with the termination era. Two tribes with large forested reservations lost their treaty lands to termination: the Menominee in Wisconsin and the Klamath in Oregon. On both reservations pine, an excellent building material, grew in abundance: white pine in Wisconsin, ponderosa and sugar pine in Oregon.

Before termination, the Klamath Tribes had been the second wealthiest in the country, after the oil-rich Osage Nation in Oklahoma. Their wealth came from timber and from the federal failure to divide the reservation into private plots, as occurred across Indian country via the Dawes Allotment Act of 1887. By carving reservations across the country into properties owned by individuals, the Dawes Act motivated white people

to defraud Indians in various ways, including "adopting" native children
and getting unwitting signatures on land-transfer documents. This did not
happen to the Klamath Tribes due to a long-running court case contesting
their treaty lands.

In negotiating the Treaty of 1864, the Klamath, Modoc, and Yahooskin
Snake tribes did not seek a timber-rich reservation. Their prosperity came
from hunting, fishing, and gathering on the roughly twenty million acres
of their aboriginal territories. But J. W. P. Huntington, superintendent
of Indian Affairs for Oregon, patronizingly said that was too much land
for them to take care of. He was willing to reserve two million acres. To
protect the treaty lands, he promised, "You will be closed up, like in a high
fence, so no one can get over to you, or their cattle get over." Accordingly,
the document declares that "no white person shall be permitted to locate
or remain upon the reservation." But two months after the signing of
the treaty, Congress granted Oregon land to build a north-south road
east of the Cascade Range, cutting through the reservation. In 1871, a
survey claimed that 600,000 acres of reservation land was instead open
for settlement. By the time the Senate ratified the treaty, in 1872, settlers
occupied half of the land it set aside.

The tribes sued, and eventually the U.S. Supreme Court decided
the case in the government's favor, shrinking the reservation to a million
acres. What this litigation took away with one hand, it saved with the
other, for private interests lost the opportunities the Allotment Act offered
to carve up the reservation, while the tribes' remaining treaty lands held
a vast conifer forest.

Termination was the next phase of taking those lands from the tribes.
Not surprisingly, George Weyerhaeuser, whose forest products company
carries his family name, was an advocate of terminating the Klamath
Reservation. But timber was not the only issue. The federal government
intended to end the tribes' sovereign existence.

A faction within the tribes weakened resistance to the government's
plan by arguing for change in the governance of their reservation. Its
leader, Wade Crawford, advocated the creation of a tribal corporation
that would manage Klamath assets, ending the Bureau of Indian Affairs'
control over tribal funds.

BIA management was objectionable on several fronts. The agency
sold timber from tribal lands at much lower rates than the Forest Service

received for comparable tree sales, and it refused to build a mill on the reservation that would give tribal members jobs. The federal government deducted all of its costs on the reservation from the tribe's income, deciding what the fees were without input from the Indians. In calling for an end to this form of colonial rule, Crawford received support mainly from members of the tribe who had moved off the reservation and wanted the money that the sale of timberland would bring.

Those who represented the tribe at congressional hearings on the Klamath Termination Act opposed the legislation. Dorothy McAnulty tried to make the senators understand what selling the reservation would do to her people. "What is their money going to be good to them for if they . . . have to live in a place where they don't want to live?" she asked. "Are they going to be treated like people should be treated? . . . It is wonderful as long as they have money. When the money is gone, they are just Indians."

The Termination Act became law in 1954. But the timber had to be appraised and the land put up for sale before tribal members could receive their buy-out checks. At that time timber companies were purchasing forested lands at high prices. One local lumberman, Lawrence Shaw, realized that "at the price that they had to pay to get that timber, it would be necessary to cut very heavy, and sustained yield practices would have to be probably sacrificed." The consequence, Shaw foresaw, would be a log-'em-and-leave-'em, boom-and-bust spiral harmful to the long-term economic health of the Klamath Basin. "Therefore," he recalled, "I talked to a certain group one evening, regarding our local interest in presenting the case for public Forest Service ownership. That being the only institution that could probably pay the Indians' price for the timber and still handle it on a sustained yield."

The group that Shaw spoke to included Tom Watters, a realtor; Al Hatten, a merchant; and Frank Jenkins, the publisher of the local newspaper, the *Herald and News*. These men went to Washington, D.C., where they gained the support of their senators, Richard L. Neuberger and Wayne Morse.

In 1963, Congress purchased half a million acres of former Klamath Reservation land to create Winema National Forest. With another purchase a decade later, plus land transferred from three neighboring national forests, including the Klamath Ranger District, Winema comprises 1.1 million acres. This land includes three federally designated wildernesses and one National Wild and Scenic River—the Sycan, which flows from Sycan Marsh within the Frémont National Forest before joining the waters of the Sprague and Williamson Rivers in its journey toward Upper Klamath Lake. Today, the Winema and Frémont National Forests are one administrative entity.

As it carried out the Klamath Termination Act, the BIA allowed tribal members to choose whether to withdraw from the tribe. Those who did so received $43,000. Seventy-eight percent made this decision; the rest found that their stake in the reservation was transferred from the federal government to a trustee, the United States National Bank in Portland.

The windfall tore the community apart. More young Klamaths than ever before dropped out of school and left home. Bitter resentment arose between those born before 1954 who were suddenly rich and their younger brothers and sisters who received nothing. Some tribal members squandered vast sums; others could not make a living.

The Klamath had little experience with money. Instead of cash, the BIA had previously issued them coupons that could be exchanged for goods at the agency store. When the $43,000 payday finally came in 1961, few knew how to invest money or save it to safeguard their families' future. Within months, millions of dollars passed through their hands. Wheeler-dealers rushed to Chiloquin to sell refrigerators to people whose homes lacked electricity, luxury cars to people who could not drive. One woman bought a new Oldsmobile, forgot where she parked it, and bought another one. Young people threw long-running parties in suites of motel rooms. Klamaths old and young embarked on monumental drunks. Melvin Chiloquin, already drinking when his $43,000 came through, sobered up nine months later to find that he owed $5,000.

Eventually, the 474 tribal members who had turned down the original buy-out voted to end the bank trust. While the trustees were taking in $92,000 a year from their federal contract, the supposed beneficiaries received less than $1,000 a year, and they had no say in what the bank did with Klamath land. They decided to set up another trust that would put profits from managing the land into their hands as shareholders. U.S. National Bank responded by selling the land to Crown Zellerbach and to the Department of Agriculture without consulting tribal members.

Thirty-seven members of the tribe, including Edison Chiloquin, the grandson of Chief Chiloquin, sued the bank for violating the trust agreement. But their lawyer, Charles Wilkinson, withdrew the suit, advising his clients to acquiesce in the land sale because they themselves could not maintain an economically viable land base. Elnathan Davis, secretary of the Committee to Save the Remaining Klamath Lands, said at the time: "People who grow up on this land feel like it is a part of us, a mother to us. If this land is sold, it is the end of us as a tribe—we're lost." When the remaining 145,000 acres were sold for $49 million, Davis and every remaining Klamath but one picked up his check: $103,594.

Edison Chiloquin refused to take the money. "To me the land is sacred," he explained. "Money can't replace it." Chiloquin had grown up in the reservation town named for his grandfather, the last Plaikni chief. His father, Kilda Chiloquin, had protested the influx of white settlers on reservation land that was taken over by the railroad.

During World War II, Edison was wounded in the South Pacific. He returned to the reservation with two Purple Hearts and a Silver Star. An alcoholic, Edison used to bury bottles in secret stashes, and he described his life as a succession of barfights and awakenings on sidewalks and hillsides. One day, Edison went up a hill where he liked to be alone and, remembering that he was the grandson of a chief, smashed his bottle against a rock.

Edison and his wife, Leatha, the daughter of Dorothy McAnulty, lived in a small frame house heated by two woodstoves. Leatha made tepees, and Edison painted. They would have been eligible for food stamps if the State of Oregon had not considered them wealthy due to the unclaimed check at U.S. National Bank.

One week, a Chiloquin daughter's former husband got six months in jail for several drunk-driving violations; four joy-riders wrecked the Chiloquin family's truck, killing one of them; and a friend committed suicide. Over a three-week period, five Klamaths, nineteen years old and under, were buried. "Our cemeteries are full of new graves," Leatha remarked. "Something has to be done."

With Leatha's encouragement, Edison Chiloquin made the decision to "preserve the culture of my tribe by re-creating my grandfather's old village of my people at Ktai-Tupaski [Standing Rock]. I want traditional Indian people to be able to live there in the traditional way while the knowledge of the old ways is still in our mind and heart." His idea was to demand Chief Chiloquin's village site as an alternative to the money in the bank. The Arrowhead, as it is called due to its shape, comprises 800 acres within a three-and-a-half-mile bend of the Sprague River.

To make their purpose known, the Chiloquins, together with family members and supporters, dug a firepit and put up tepees on a hill between the town that bears their name and the Arrowhead. On April 18, 1976, Steve Kane, a Paiute who was the Chiloquins' son-in-law, made a fire. Over hay and a pinecone he placed wood from conical stacks of willow branches around the firepit, marking the four directions. After lighting the fire, he sprinkled into it a mixture of kinnikinnick (Indian tobacco), berries, and seeds. Following a silence for prayer, Edison proclaimed that the fire was sacred and that it would keep burning until the land of his grandfather was restored to his people.

Accompanying himself on a drum, Steve Kane sang. Gesturing toward the hillside above him, Kane noted that it had been scorched by a fire that threatened homes in Chiloquin three years earlier. He predicted that as the land regenerates itself, so will traditional ways return to this place.

After the ceremony, Edison looked out over the town of Chiloquin with its lumber mill, railroad yard, and small houses. He pointed out the shack by the Sprague River where he was born fifty-two years earlier. "It's used as a shed now, but back then it was the only house there."

That day, the fire was transferred from the ceremonial site on the hill to a deep stone-lined firepit that had been prepared on the Arrowhead. The tepees were also moved there. Bob Chadwick, the supervisor for the Winema National Forest, gave Chiloquin a special use permit that allowed him to build a traditional village on his grandfather's land. Soon work began on an earth lodge and, beside the Sprague, a sweat lodge.

An Oglala, Max Bear, began his watch as the keeper of the fire. He and his wife, Frieda, were among the first to move into the village. In the months that followed, Native people from many places joined them, some staying for extended periods. Visitors included members of the American Indian Movement and a carload from the Survival School in Oakland, the center of a community of relocated Indians. The place became a magnet for non-Indians as well. The Dell'Arte Players Company, on tour with their first play, *Loon's Rage*, crossed the Cascades from Ashland for a visit. Members of an Oregon commune called The Family wore leather loin cloths as they waited to enter the sweat lodge. The Indians wore jeans.

Subsistence was a daily struggle. Getting enough wood to keep the fire going, cutting poles for the tepees and lodges, and hunting and gathering food to supplement the provisions that came from the store took most of the time and energy of those who lived in the village. Money was collected to buy gas for hunting trips and supply runs. People parked vehicles at a distance from the village; everything was carried in.

This way of life required sacrifice and, especially during winter months, suffering. Humor helped. As Steve Kane drummed and sang during a late-night vigil at the fire, Curt, a blond Indian, called him Lawrence Elk. Kane, in turn, joked that Curt looked like Custer. Max Bear hopefully named two geese who came to the village for food scraps "Thanksgiving" and "Christmas."

The people at the Arrowhead kept the sacred fire going day and night, winter and summer. During the last weekend in September 1977, a unity gathering took place. As Saturday dawned and morning mist rose from the Plai (Sprague) River, people left their tepees and the earth lodge for a sweat. Papa San, a Lakota, led it, sweeping participants clean with an eagle wing. In her house on the other side of the hill, Leatha Chiloquin prepared fry bread, filling a cardboard box with fifty pieces. Then she made a dozen pies, some filled with huckleberries she and her daughters had picked nearby. A man named Jerrod intended to hunt for venison in the traditional way, although he would drive on forest roads to find his prey. Max Bear told him to wait until the deer stopped as if to say, "You were meant to shoot me. I give you my life." Jerrod came back with three in the bed of his truck. He and Max skinned the deer, placed the carcasses in a deep pit, and roasted them between layers of lava rock. Melvin Chiloquin drove in salmon from the freezer of Charlie Thom, who was then living on the coast. Margaret Carlson, a Yurok from Ah-pah, came to the village with fresh fish.

By evening 130 people, myself among them, were on the land ready to feast. Before we filled our plates, a Seneca medicine man, Frank Thomas, said that the ancestors were returning that night from the world of the dead and that by putting full plates at each of the four directions around the fire, we would summon their spirits. Then we had to go elsewhere. This was a strange ambivalence, both inviting the dead and getting out of their way.

The life "on the land," as it was called, lasted almost four years. Oregon Representative Al Ullman, who chaired the powerful Ways and Means Committee, introduced a bill in Congress to grant title to the Arrowhead to Edison Chiloquin. President Jimmy Carter signed the Chiloquin Act into law in 1980. According to former tribal chair Jeff Mitchell, the legislation set in motion the process that led to the reestablishment of tribal status in 1986.

The end of termination was a hollow victory nonetheless. "We're still left without a homeland," Mitchell complained. "Even though our government-to-government relationship has been restored, our economy hasn't. We've gone from being one of the most self-sufficient tribes in the nation to being one of the most dependent tribes in the nation. The land and the resources are the tribe, and the tribe is the land and the resources."

Having a government once again, however, did bring benefits. The Klamath Tribes were now able to obtain grants, provide services, and support scientific research. One of those studies was of the *c'waam*, which informed a Biological Opinion that fed a lawsuit that pressured the Bureau of Reclamation to suspend water distribution to the Klamath Project in 2001.

In May, two weeks after the Bucket Brigade, the biennial Klamath Basin Fish & Water Management Symposium took place. Normally, few people from the Upper Basin come to this conference, and in 2001 the locale was Humboldt State University in Arcata, a long drive from their lands. Yet that year, many farmers and ranchers attended.

The keynote speaker was Bill Leary, an official at the Council on Environmental Quality who was credited with spearheading the restoration of the Florida Everglades. Since the Klamath Basin has been called the Everglades of the West, Alice Kilham, an organizer of the symposium, invited Leary to investigate the Basin and recommend ways to get the political and economic support required to fund its restoration. In the months after Leary agreed, the Basin became a political hot potato. He predicted that the Bush Administration would respond to the situation and that it would embark on a major effort on behalf of the Klamath Basin.

Leary explained that to get substantial support there had to be a crisis, there had to be new people in power wanting to put their mark on the country through new initiatives, and there had to be a plan designed to build success on success, since money follows success. The administrator challenged the conference to create such a plan, using contributions from all of the communities in the Basin. And he put the nature of this work into historical context.

Leary laid out a vision of the new generation of people concerned about finding a better balance between society and nature. The first movement, in Teddy Roosevelt's time, he said, was conservation, which established the Forest Service and the wildlife refuges. The second was the environmental movement, whose monuments were laws to safeguard water quality, restrict air pollution, and protect endangered species. The third is the restoration movement, which Leary saw growing from local initiatives and which is motivated by the basic pleasure of doing work that makes things better.

At another session, economist Ernie Niemi challenged the idea circulating through the media after the Bucket Brigade that the Upper Basin economy depends on farming. In Klamath County in 1998, he said, farms accounted for 10 percent of the jobs and 8 percent of the income. Less than half of the 1,400 farmers sold more than $10,000 in crops. This economic weakness, he foresaw, would prevent President George W. Bush from calling in the so-called God Squad, an emergency high-level council, to override the Endangered Species Act. There had to be a powerful economic rationale.

A farm woman spoke from the audience about the suffering brought on her community by the inability to plant crops. She was in tears. A woman sitting nearby embraced her. The second woman explained that she and her husband were commercial fishers who knew how it felt to fall victim to resource scarcity. That emotional encounter dramatized an answer to what Alice Kilham said in opening the panel, that the people in this region are so different in their interests and ways of life and so distant geographically that "it's hard to understand we're in this together; it's difficult to put aside our individual interests and work together." The women's recognition of shared pain due to shared dependence on the water of the Basin cut through the differences, at least for a moment.

In another panel, Mike Connelly, a rancher and writer, explained some of the bitterness that Upper Basin people felt about the water cut-off. He said that farmers and ranchers had organized a watershed council in order to do whatever they could to restore the habitat of endangered fish. There was an unspoken deal: if landowners did things that helped fish recovery, then that would insulate them from heavy-handed government regulation. Reclamation had cut off their water regardless of their best efforts.

Connelly said that the farmers were drawing from the capital of the system and that the solution required drawing from the interest only. The idea is to have a system healthy enough so that there is a surplus to live off. "After all our efforts to save the salmon," he said, "we may wake up to see that it is the salmon that are saving us."

Considerable debate occurred throughout the conference about how to solve the water crisis. Answers ranged from a top-down federal initiative to a grassroots program in which people from different parts of the Basin develop relationships and gain an emotional stake in what happens to each other. Symposia are designed to enlarge people's understanding. At times the result is the recognition of shared interests and mutually beneficial objectives. By these criteria, the 2001 Klamath Basin symposium was a success. Meanwhile, back in the Upper Basin, some of the irrigators who were distressed by the lack of water prepared to take action regardless of other interests and federal law.

Chapter Seventeen
The Bucket on Main Street

Like fossils buried under layers of time, word origins can expose the roots of ideas. "Rivalry" comes from a Latin word, *rivalis*, "one who uses the same stream with another." Growing from *rivus* or stream, rivalry probably received its name in a water dispute.

The word "revolution" lacked a political meaning until the eighteenth century. Before then it meant a return to earlier conditions, like the return of the seasons. Tom Paine was among the first to give that word a political spin. In her book *On Revolution*, Hannah Arendt noted that, for Paine, revolution meant that through their defiance of the British crown Americans were bringing back a hypothetical "'early period' when they had been in the possession of rights and liberties of which tyranny and conquest had dispossessed them."

A revolutionary drama, in Tom Paine's meaning of the word, took the stage in the Klamath Basin during the summer of 2001. For two months, the irrigators' protest against the Bureau of Reclamation water cutoff became a series of scenes in which farmers and ranchers rose up against a tyrannical government that had deprived them of what they considered to be their God-given rights.

The prologue to the Bucket Brigade and the dramatic events that followed it occurred on Independence Day in 2000. Near Jarbidge, Nevada, a Shovel Brigade opened up a county road that the U.S. Forest Service had closed to vehicle access, using boulders, rocks, dirt, and trees as a barrier. The agency's objective was to protect bull trout, an endangered species. Sarah Foster reported in WorldNetDaily.com that most of the thousands who joined the Shovel Brigade came "from Nevada, Idaho, Montana, Oregon, and other Western states." Many were members of separate yet networked organizations such as Christian Identity, the Militia of Montana, the Freemen, Citizens for Liberty, and the Washington State Militia. Collectively, these activists regarded themselves as

participants in the Patriot movement, a rebellion against federal authority
that spread across the Pacific Northwest in the 1990s.

In his book about the Patriot movement, David Neiwert examines

> an American political ideology based on an ultranationalistic
> and selective populism which seeks to return the nation to its
> "constitutional" roots—that is, a system based on white Christian
> male rule. Its core myth is that such a reactionary revolution will bring
> about a great national rebirth, ending years of encroaching moral
> and political decadence wrought by a gigantic world conspiracy of
> probably Satanic origins.

The assumptions contained in this myth raise numerous questions. But
ideologues—those who embrace myths instead of recognizing reality—
have all the answers without asking any questions. Unlike a political idea,
ideologies are rooted not in facts or interests but in dreams and feelings.

Among those attracted to this movement were rural residents of the
Pacific Northwest who felt dispossessed as a result of federal land-use policies, including the measures taken to protect the spotted owl. The Patriot
myth unmasked the United States government as a tyranny; those who
would overthrow it and bring America back to the purity of its origins
were patriots. What gave this creed its compelling power was an absolute,
unquestioning faith that those who spread these views and act accordingly
are doing God's will.

Even for those who lack the Patriots' faith, the notion of being ruled
by a tyrant expresses a half-truth felt especially in western states, where
large federal agencies like the Forest Service, the Bureau of Reclamation,
and the Bureau of Land Management control vast areas of land. Although
those agencies have mechanisms whereby citizens may address and affect
their policies, the power they wield over regional economies is not balanced by the input of local interests.

It was not surprising, therefore, that once the water cutoff of 2001
parched the soil of Klamath Project lands, the Patriot ideology would take
root among some of the farmers and ranchers in the Upper Basin. As
Ernst Cassirer wrote, reflecting on the political myths of the twentieth
century, "In all critical moments of man's social life, the rational forces
that resist the rise of the old mythical conceptions are no longer sure of

themselves. In these moments the time for myth has come again. . . . This hour comes as soon as the other binding forces of man's social life, for one reason or another, lose their strength and are no longer able to combat the demonic mythical powers."

The power of myth in the Klamath Basin received an assist from the wise use movement, the lobbying campaign initiated by Ron Arnold and Alan Gottlieb. At its founding conference in 1988, the organizers put the Endangered Species Act on their target list and vowed to raise millions of dollars a year for anti-environmental organizing. Speaking to the Ontario Forest Industries, Arnold explained that a "pro-industry citizen action group . . . can evoke powerful archetypes such as the sanctity of the family, the virtue of the close-knit community, the natural wisdom of the rural dweller . . . to turn the public against your enemies."

Just as during the struggle over logging and the spotted owl, wise use publicists used the image of the owl-as-job-killer to promote the interests of the forest industry, during the Bucket Brigade, they deployed the suckerfish as poster child to accompany their fish-against-farmers rhetoric.

Although the farmers had assistance from anti-environmental publicists and ideological activists from outside their region and although the Bucket Brigade was a professionally staged media event, this was not a synthetic expression of grassroots outrage; it was the heartfelt protest of people who felt betrayed by the federal government and who were determined to have the lifeblood of their livelihood, Klamath Basin water, flow into their fields and farms.

Stan Turner's history of the Klamath Basin sets the stage for the events that occurred after the Bucket Brigade: "Beginning at the end of June, there were [*sic*] a series of break-ins at the Upper Klamath Lake headgates, which allowed water to flow into the 'A' Canal." These were not political acts; they occurred secretly at night. Whoever opened the valves violated federal trespassing laws as well as the Bureau of Reclamation water ban.

The public revolt began on Independence Day, when "about 100 flag-waving protesters marched to the headgates in daylight and opened the valves." Some called this act of civil disobedience The Klamath Tea Party. The British, under this analogy, were the federal marshals assigned to guard the BOR facility. Demonstrating their resolve to open the headgates again, a group of rebels set up camp just outside the federal property.

Jeff Head, a resident of Idaho's Owyhee County who had participated in the Shovel Brigade in Nevada the year before, arrived in Klamath Falls on July 13. In his online eyewitness account of what he called "The Stand at Klamath Falls," Head reported that he encountered about fifteen people who "had opened the gate and were staying there to protect it and keep the water flowing." The federal marshals arrived "with a backup of several other officers. As they approached, the farmers and their supporters . . . began singing hymns to the U.S. Marshalls! [sic] The marshals were completely taken back. They stopped cold as if running into a barrier and backed up to their car. Several of these faithful farmers believe that God in Heaven took a hand in their behalf that day."

The next morning, between twelve and fifteen vehicles and two motorcycles brought as many as thirty local police and sheriff's deputies to the main gate. While the police chief spoke to the protestors, asking them to be calm, they noticed that "about a dozen US Marshalls [sic] had entered in the back gate. It was," Head remarked, "a very crisply executed flanking maneuver." Then a BOR official turned the headgate valve, shutting off the water.

Throughout the day, the confrontation continued. Eight marshals remained on guard as people arrived and the crowd of protestors grew. "Many from the local area," observed Head, "an increasing number from outside the area to show their support. JJ Johnson, the editor of the Sierra Times online news source arrived. Several other online conservative organizations were also represented, including FreeRepublic.com and Frontiers for Freedom." In the parking lot, according to one observer, there were more license plates from Idaho than from Oregon.

A rally occurred in which Head and others made speeches. Head urged the marshals to "recognize that their job had become to destroy innocent, patriotic, hard working Americans." J. J. Johnson did his part by declaring in the Sierra Times: "We are at war. . . . We did not start this war, but, having no choice but to wage it, let us wage it well. The forces against us claim they are trying to save fish. We are trying to save humans. In our minds, the most threatened species in the Klamath Basin is man himself."

The next day, Head judged in his online journal, was "fitting for a Sunday . . . inspiration." The protestors realized that they did not need to force their way into federal property; they could bypass the headgates, using irrigation equipment to pump and pipe the water into "A" Canal.

Head and Barbara Martin, a local woman, gathered "about fifty people and we started back to the bridge, about 100 yards away. Along the way I told the folks . . . old gentlemen, grandmothers, local men, women, teenagers, children . . . 'We're going up here to form a human shield around these local farmers so they can get this pump going . . . you may be arrested . . . if you're not in for that, you'd best leave.' Not one turned back."

At the bridge, the group shielded the farmers with their arms. When a police officer "pulled up next to us and indicated he needed to talk to those farmers . . . a teenager in front of me said, 'You'll have to arrest us all to do that.'" The officer drove away. As the federal marshals watched, eight-inch pipes were laid, the pump was started, and water flowed into the canal. People began to chant: "Let the water flow! Let the water flow!"

During the following week, Head and others circulated a petition in support of the farmers. Meanwhile, locals and outsiders set up camp to guard the pump and pipes. Head's friend Mike, whose Patriot name online was WashingtonMinuteman, "arrived from Washington to show his support." Others who joined the fray were known as Jolly Rogers, Socks, and B4Ranch. According to Head's website, the militants of the movement used coded communications over their hand-held radios:

> Sentry: "Fox-1 base, this is Fox-2 pump house . . . come in."
> Base: "This is Fox-1 base. Go ahead."
> Sentry: "Fox-1 base, there are no other foxes in the hen house,
>   I repeat no other foxes in the hen house, over."
> Base: "Read you loud and clear Fox-2 base. Over and out."

Among their methods was the use of false code to mislead any "spies" who intercepted their words. "The torpedoes are in the water," they said. "The pickle is hot."

Head returned with the petition on July 20 as a new demonstration was about to begin, a "Horse Brigade that would be coming over the hill behind the head gate." Head counted "about 150 horses, most of them carrying US Flags, many of which were turned upside down to signal the great distress to property, livelihood and liberty represented by a reprehensible unilateral decision by government gone out of control to turn off irrigation waters to farmers who own the rights to that same water."

When Todd Kellstrom, the mayor of Klamath Falls, came up the hill to observe the Horse Brigade, Head handed him the petition, informing the mayor "that there were probably 9,000 of the 10,000 signatures there who were 'outside influence' who were expressing their support for the farmers." Later that day, Sheriff Tim Evinger received his copy. He was upset to hear that a BOR official had told farmers that federal police had come to the headgates at his request. Saying that they had overstepped their bounds and "that it was not his intent to support the enforcement of the ESA," Evinger promised that he would ask them to leave.

A more significant reversal occurred on July 24, when Interior Secretary Gale Norton came to Portland to announce that the farmers would receive up to 75,000 acre-feet of water. The flow, which was expected to last about a month, came too late to allow farmers to grow grain and potatoes, but it did offer relief to cattle ranchers who could green their pastures and grow hay. The next day, farmer Steve Kandra and Jim Bryant of the Bureau of Reclamation turned the large steel wheel that raises the gate that releases water into the canal.

Speaking in uniform at the headgates later that week, police lieutenant Jack Redfield expressed his feelings about those who, by invoking the Endangered Species Act, pressured the Bureau of Reclamation to stop the flow of Klamath Project water. "I believe," said Redfield,

> that the people who are orchestrating this atrocity are not environmentalists at all (although they may be being manipulated into believing they are doing the right thing), but that they are actually acting in the capacity of environmental and/or economic terrorists (or at least extremists) who are launching a severe and effective attack upon the economy of the United States. . . . As the extremists and out-of-control federal agents continue to push and as the agricultural people see their fields turn brown and their entire lives destroyed, their frustration will undoubtedly escalate to the point of boiling over. . . . I think the potential for extreme violence, even to the extent of civil war is possible if action is not taken in the very near future to remedy this tragedy.

Taking these comments as a threat, environmental activists sued the city. Klamath Falls' response was to put the overwrought officer on temporary administrative leave.

Meanwhile, supporters of the Klamath Basin farmers in Elko, Nevada—near the site of the Jarbidge Shovel Brigade that had occurred the previous year—forged two metal buckets, each ten feet tall, to honor them. One was to be placed on Main Street in the town of Klamath Falls as an enduring symbol of the irrigators' protest. The other was to travel the country on a flatbed trailer to be filled with money, food, and supplies. A number of farmers needed this support. Not only did the loss of irrigation water in 2001 prevent them from planting that year's crop, but uncertainty about future water supplies made obtaining bank loans extremely difficult.

Relief came on truckbeds as convoys rode to the aid of Klamath farmers. Head described the convoy that arrived in Boise from Nevada to gather donations for them.

> Around 10 AM the convoy arrived with a semi tractor trailer and a couple of large pickups. One was driven by Bob St. Louis, the head of the Shovel Brigade out of Nevada. . . we collected a lot of clothing, food and things for kids. Several hundred pounds worth of material. In addition, over in Emmett at the Gen Supply Co-op, several tons of hay were donated which will be auctioned off with the proceeds going to the Klamath Relief Fund. We also had some good dollar donation [sic] today too!

Coming from four states—Idaho, Nevada, Montana, and Washington—the convoy that rolled into Klamath Falls on August 21— "Freedom Day," as Head and others called it—labeled itself the "Convoy of Tears," a strange echo of the Trail of Tears, as the forcible removal of Cherokees from their land in Georgia in 1838 is known. Awaiting the vehicles' convergence, a 100-rider "cavalry detachment" gathered in Veterans Park near Main Street. The riders led the Convoy of Tears to the county building while a crowd that Head estimated at several thousand people cheered and chanted, "Keep the water on!"

According to Stan Turner,

there had been fears that the August 21st convoy would turn violent. Among those who announced they were going to attend were members of the far-right State Tyranny Response Team from the state of Washington and the Jarbidge Shovel Brigade from Nevada. Montana talk show host John Stokes, who had previously labeled environmental groups as "Fourth Reich" and "Green Nazis," also announced he planned to attend. However, the demonstration remained non-violent, even festive.

A reporter for the *San Jose Mercury-News* referred to this event as

the vanguard of a citizen revolt against federal water and land management policy. . . . As people stepped out from insurance offices, travel agencies and cafes, all hurt by the fallout of a crippled planting season, many seemed overwhelmed by the ferocity of the water war raging around them. "This is radicalizing a lot of us against the government," said Pat Cavanaugh, the soft-spoken, grey-haired owner of Drews, a clothing and shoe store whose business is off 25 percent this summer. "When they shut off that water, they also shut off much of the shopping done in this town."

By the last week in August, the water released by Secretary Norton ran out. On September 2, diversion of water through pipes into the canal resumed, guarded once again by an encampment. What ended the confrontation were the terrorist attacks of September 11. With the federal officers guarding the headgates needed elsewhere, the farmers agreed to decamp and take their pipes with them. Patriot movement ideologues also left the scene, and their myth of federally abetted Green Nazi terrorists vanished in the face of the real thing. "We are all patriotic Americans," explained Bill Ransom, a local merchant who headed the Klamath Relief Fund, "and this national emergency takes precedence." Gale Norton issued a press release to thank the farmers for ending their civil disobedience: "My heartfelt appreciation goes out to the Klamath Relief Fund group and Klamath County officials for their cooperation and consideration in vacating the headgate area. Please be assured that diligent discussions and work to address the pressing water needs in the Klamath Basin continue."

The Secretary of the Interior kept her promise. Norton ordered the National Academy of Sciences to investigate the validity of the Biological Opinions that led the BOR to cut off irrigation. The Academy's twelve-member team—which included a law professor, an agricultural economist, a geologist, and a water resources engineer—had three months to produce an interim report that would influence water allocations in 2002. Scientists who made presentations to the panel at a Sacramento meeting confirmed that low water levels were harmful to coho salmon and suckers. But there was insufficient data to satisfy some panel members. Peter Moyle, a professor of fish biology at the University of California in Davis, regretted the lack of detailed studies comparing lake levels with sucker population figures.

Water quantity was not the only factor. Water quality was also a problem. The draining of wetlands to expand farm and ranchlands increased phosphorus-rich runoff from animal wastes and fertilizers into Upper Klamath Lake, which is habitat for suckers. Downriver, water temperatures, chemical pollution from herbicides and pesticides, and the loss and degradation of spawning habitat impact coho salmon. While regulating water levels is necessary, it is an insufficient means of protecting those species. Their ecosystems are too complex to be restored with one tool.

Nonetheless, as fishery biologist Ronnie Pierce insisted, "Fish need water!" At the symposium in May, Pierce decried a situation in which "hundreds of dollars using the best science available" are being used "to prove yes, indeed, fish need water. The first thing people do is say your science is no good. How on earth they come to that conclusion, I don't know. I would say if I did a study and I came up with a result that told me that fish did not need water, then I would question the science."

The Academy committee's interim report made Pierce's remark prophetic. Although finding that most of the recommendations made in the Biological Opinions had scientific merit, the study concluded that there was not enough evidence to justify the decisions made by the National Marine Fisheries Service and the Fish and Wildlife Service to raise the minimum water level on the lake to protect suckers and also to increase the downstream flow for the coho.

The study allowed irrigators and their advocates to argue that the 2001 BiOps were "junk science" and that the water cutoff was not justified. An article in *Science* described scientists whose research was challenged by the committee as victims of "combat biology." These fishery biologists "contend that the report's analyses were simplistic, its conclusions over-drawn, and—perhaps worst of all—that the report has undermined the credibility of much of the science being done in the region if not fueled an outright anti-science sentiment."

According to a biologist who worked for the National Marine Fisheries Service, the committee's conclusions were fixed by the Bush Administration. In a federal courtroom, Michael Kelly testified that his agency's draft biological opinion in April 2002 actually recommended that the Bureau of Reclamation increase flows into the Klamath River to provide additional habitat for coho. But Justice Department attorneys ordered the biologists to lower their spring flow recommendations, and the Bureau of Reclamation proposed to release 57 percent of the water the biologists thought necessary for coho in 2002 by 2006 and not before then.

The Bureau's plan, which went to the Justice Department for approval without scientific analysis, was part of a ten-year management strategy for the Klamath Project that was to provide extra water for irrigation. The Bureau intended to restore the flows by "leasing" water from farmers to put in a "water bank"—paying some farmers not to irrigate so that water could remain in the lakes, streams, and rivers. Advocates for fish noted, however, that the current minimum flows would not be restored for eight years.

The Ninth Circuit Court of Appeals rejected the administration's proposal in October 2005. "Five full generations of coho will complete their three-year life cycles—hatch, rear, and spawn—during those eight years," the court observed. "Or, if there is insufficient water to sustain the coho during this period, they will not complete their life cycle, with the consequence that there will be no coho at the end of the eight years. If that happens, all the water in the world in 2010 and 2011 will not protect the coho, for there will be none to protect." In other words, Reclamation would end the limits on irrigation water imposed by the Endangered Species Act by eliminating the endangered species.

Driving the Bush Administration's support for the Klamath Basin farmers was the president's political strategist Karl Rove. Rove had not failed to notice that Oregon, which voted for Al Gore in 2000 by a slight margin, was a potential "red state" and that Oregon Senator Gordon Smith, a Republican, was up for re-election in 2002.

On January 5, 2002, Rove accompanied President Bush to an appearance in Portland, Oregon. During the flight west on Air Force One,

Senator Smith briefed the president on the Klamath crisis. Upon arriving, Bush declared, "We'll do everything we can to make sure water is available for those who farm."

The following day, Rove spoke to fifty Interior Department managers at a conference center in West Virginia. Tom Hamburger described his speech in the *Wall Street Journal*: "In a PowerPoint presentation Mr. Rove also uses when soliciting Republican donors, he brought up the Klamath and made clear that the administration was siding with agricultural interests." "Control of Congress," Rove told the Interior officials, "will turn on a handful of races decided by local issues" as well as other factors. His message was unmistakable: politics must override institutional mandates, legal restrictions, and scientific considerations in the department's decision-making. Neal McCaleb, who was then an assistant to the secretary of the Interior, told the reporter of "the 'chilling effect' of Mr. Rove's remarks."

Weeks later, Rove returned to Oregon to meet with Klamath Basin farmers. Shortly thereafter, the White House established a top-level Klamath Basin working group whose members included the secretaries of Interior, Agriculture, and Commerce and the chair of the Council on Environmental Quality. Some of the measures the task force agreed on offered relief to the farmers. As the *Oregonian* reported, "The group said Friday that Klamath farmers would get more time to sign up for water conservation money and directed officials to consider rescheduling, consolidating or forgiving farm loans."

The Bush Administration publicized its policies with a high-profile ceremony. On March 29, Agriculture Secretary Ann Veneman, Interior Secretary Gale Norton, and Senator Gordon Smith arrived in Klamath Falls to celebrate the release of water through the headgates into the main irrigation canal. As Secretary Norton turned the valve—a large steel wheel—Senator Smith and Secretary Veneman stood close by, as if at the helm of a ship, while the cameras rolled.

"We have an initial go-ahead from the Fish & Wildlife Service and the National Marine Fishery Service to begin delivering water," Norton announced, tacitly acknowledging the lack of a Biological Opinion to justify the water delivery. A crowd chanted in the background, "Let the water flow! Let the water flow!"

The reporter referred to "a small group of tribal members" who were drumming and holding up signs protesting the water release. The camera wielded by Petey Brucker revealed a large contingent of protestors, Indian and non-Indian, including leaders of the Klamath Basin tribes. Brucker's own Salmon River group, wearing their cloth salmon head masks, was unmistakable. "What about the fish? What about the fish?" they chanted.

The views expressed at the headgates that day were polarized. When Brucker argued with a farmer that according to tribal legends spring chinook once spawned in the Upper Basin, the man retorted, "Screw the tribal legends!"

At times the opposing worlds met. A small crowd stood around Susan Bowers Masten and Secretary Norton, who were having an intense discussion. A local woman shouted at Ron Reed, "You're dead! Your people are dead!" To this Reed replied in anguish, "We'll never die!" Raising an arm to the sky, he informed the woman that he is a medicine person.

The ritualized display of a divided body politic at this moment of the farmers' triumph hid a countervailing feeling that Mike Connelly had noticed in 2001. "I think from the extreme environmental folks to the extreme right-wing, folks saw the limits of their tactics that year. And really the limits of their perspective. And I think there was a real soul searching all across the board."

One sign of the limitations of these rival perspectives and of their ideological origins, rooted more in myth than in experience, was a series of abrupt reversals, as if a magnet suddenly shifted polarities. One turnabout that struck Connelly as absurd was the spectacle of "very conservative people" who responded "to what they saw as an injustice in exactly the same way that the lefties down in Berkeley or San Francisco were responding"—that is, through civil disobedience. "You had old war veterans, conservative as the day is long, standing arm in arm confronting federal troops singing Negro spirituals." And when the local folks became lawbreakers, it was funny for Connelly, who has lived in the Bay Area, to watch folks he had seen in protest marches "defending with shouts their right to engage in civil disobedience" argue that "the 'feds' need to crack down on them and throw them in jail."

Another reversal was the response of the federal government to the gillnetters' civil disobedience compared to its embrace of the farmers in spite of their violations of federal law. When a secretary of the Interior came to the Klamath Basin in 1978, Cecil Andrus unleashed SWAT teams on jet boats to arrest people who were defying the federal moratorium on fishing.

For their part, the Patriots who fervently asserted their right to defend freedom against federal tyranny quickly became the tyrant's allies. This was more than a common front in the face of international terrorism post-9/11. Jeff Head, the "outside influence" who took his "Stand at Klamath Falls" against a reprehensible government, received, according to his website, "a National Leadership Award from the National Republican Congressional Committee" in 2003. The following year, he received a Ronald Reagan Gold Medal Award.

Upper Basin farmers saw their image spin like the headgate valve. Many felt that the tribes, commercial fishers, and environmental organizations that sued the BOR to cut off irrigation water in 2001 had cast them as villains. Then the Patriot movement made heroes of them and won the support of the tyrant himself. But the wheel continued to turn. When tens of thousands of spawning salmon died in the estuary in September 2002, months after Gale Norton personally turned the headgate valve to release water for their fields, they became villains again. The media that blamed them for this environmental disaster failed to mention that Klamath River water had been diverted that year from the Klamath's major tributary, the Trinity, into the San Joaquin Valley. Why bring agribusinesses in southern California into an already complex story? Upper Basin farmers were excellent antagonists in the drama of farms against fish.

Where would things settle on the Klamath when the wheel of myth stopped spinning? Would stakeholders be able to disregard the emotionally charged ideological images promoted within and against their communities by outside interests? Could they act together on the basis of common sense? Not the Common Sense of a revolutionary like Tom Paine, intent on returning the world to some imagined ideal condition in the past. Rather that of people whose cultural and economic well-being depend on the land and water and on coexisting with each other over the long run.

Chapter Eighteen
Building Consensus

On a February morning in 2004, Jack Kohler and I drove up the Sacramento Valley to its headwaters, crossed the sprawling Lake Shasta reservoir, and angled northeast around Mount Shasta through Butte Valley. Jack and I arrived in Klamath Falls around 4 p.m.

The Watershed Conference—that year's version of the Klamath Basin Symposium—was beginning the next day at the Oregon Institute of Technology. At OIT we encountered one of the conference organizers, Mike Connelly, who had become executive director of the Klamath Basin Ecosystem Foundation. Connelly explained what he had in mind. There would be scientists at the conference talking about hydrology, species, their habitats, and so on; representatives from government agencies would discuss restoration projects and other matters. And he planned a session in which people would make personal statements about what the resources meant to them. Connelly said he wanted to change the ways people speak to each other. Learning about evapotranspiration is fine, he concluded, but people needed to speak from the heart.

The next morning, Jack and I met Bob Chadwick, the facilitator of the session Connelly described. Chadwick had been the supervisor at Winema National Forest who gave Edison Chiloquin the use permit that allowed him to re-create his grandfather's village. Some of his superiors had challenged that decision at the time. "Am I the Forest Supervisor or not?" Chadwick had replied, demanding they respect the authority of his position.

A few years before then, in 1973, Chadwick, like others of his agency, found himself under fire from a new breed of environmentalists—young people who had migrated from cities to the country; who, during the Vietnam War, had become alienated from their parents' generation; and who, in the interval between the Pill and AIDS, had created a communal culture featuring "free love" and a romantic embrace of nature. Many of those youth passionately protested the rampant clear-cutting and road-building that occurred in the national forest. At the time, acting on the request of Klamath County commissioners, Chadwick convened a meeting of sixty people, including foresters and environmental activists, and began to develop conflict-resolution techniques.

The forest supervisor was motivated to do so by personality, profession, and principle. Having grown up in what he called "a violent alcoholic home" with six brothers and a sister witnessing episodes in which their father abused their mother in his drunken rage, Chadwick had long sought out ways to resolve conflicts peacefully. As a Forest Service employee for twenty-nine years, he had attempted to act in the service of what Gifford Pinchot called "the greatest good for the greatest number over the long run." This involves finding ways to reconcile competing interests concerning the use of public lands. Chadwick recognized that despite the culture gap between himself and these radical youth, they were right in their protest of Forest Service policies. This was the era when the long-term ecological integrity of national forests was undermined by the scale of timber sales and by some of the methods used to "get out the cut." Chadwick had to agree with the hippies that his agency's leaders "sold themselves out to the economic model."

After retiring from the Forest Service, Chadwick created Consensus Associates, a company whose goal is to help resolve conflicts between groups. By creating a safe context in which people can express their differences passionately yet hear each other dispassionately, turning the heat of confrontation into the light of mutual understanding, Chadwick shows groups how to move from disagreement to consensus. When asked to practice his method at a Klamath Basin symposium, Chadwick readily agreed.

About 150 people attended the symposium, but representatives of the contending communities were scarce. Besides Marshall Staunton and Mike Connelly, there were few farmers and ranchers. Besides Ron Reed and Jeff Mitchell, few Native people attended. There were members of Klamath and Salmon River environmental communities, but most of the participants were professors, politicians, and agency representatives.

For starters, Chadwick asked everyone to sit around one of several "campfires" with people they didn't know. Sitting on chairs around my campfire were the farmer Marshall Staunton; Tim and Helen Mulligan of Humboldt State University; Kent Russell, a former Forest Service ranger who, like Chadwick, had worked in the Winema National Forest; and a

U.S. Fish & Wildlife fishery biologist. In our circle, the biologist said that while the natural resource agencies of the federal government used to be strictly scientific, they "have become incredibly politicized."

The honest talk that occurred in these Chadwick circles impressed Alice Kilham, an Upper Basin landowner and Bureau of Reclamation official. Kilham was a member of the Klamath River Basin Fisheries Task Force, which, like the Klamath Fishery Management Council, had sprung from the 1986 Klamath Act. Between 1995 and 2000, she had chaired the Upper Klamath Basin Working Group. Oregon Senator Mark O. Hatfield created this entity to address resource conflicts in ways that combine ecosystem restoration with economic growth. The Working Group had more than thirty members: representatives of federal, state, and local governments and the Klamath Tribes; farmers and ranchers, including Staunton, who was a co-chair; and people from industries, small businesses, and conservation organizations. In 2002, aided by the U.S. Institute for Environmental Conflict Resolution, the group issued a report called "Crisis to Consensus."

After the symposium in 2004, Kilham realized that Chadwick's methods offered a way to work toward consensus on a Basin-wide scale. She asked Chadwick to facilitate a series of stakeholders' conflict-resolution sessions that would lead to a shared vision of the Basin's needs and a plan of action for meeting them.

This was an extremely ambitious proposition, as Chadwick, with his long experience in the region, recognized. Deep-rooted conflicts over such fundamental matters as land, water, and wildlife remained complex and passionate. Bitter divisions persisted between environmentally minded communities and those based on logging, ranching, and farming. Chadwick understood that people on opposite sides of this controversy felt their survival was at stake.

The water crisis not only divided irrigators upstream from fishing people downstream, it provoked bitter conflict within farming and ranching communities. Klamath Project farmers who were willing to forgo irrigating some fields and instead contribute to a water bank were at odds with those who insisted on receiving the maximum amount of water possible. Ranchers who joined the Klamath Basin Rangeland Trust, which entails going without irrigation while receiving compensation for water rights on a year-to-year basis, faced bitter opposition from some of their neighbors.

This quarrel, according to one rancher, roiled the Fort Klamath community and the town of Chiloquin. People who had known each other all their lives no longer spoke to each other.

Land use was bound to be a controversial matter in consensus-seeking meetings that included tribal leaders and private landholders. For the Klamath Tribes, return of their landbase was the paramount concern. As tribal chairman Alan Foreman said, "There's rectification that has to be done, and without that part of it, this Basin isn't going to move ahead." To those who urged him to "forget about the past and move on from here," Foreman used the analogy of a man who has stolen his wallet, taken all his money, and then said to him, "Let's forget about the past." Although many recognized the injustice of termination, which took from the Klamath Tribes their entire landbase, farmers and ranchers feared the return of land to a sovereign nation over whose decisions they would have no say. Throughout the region, government agencies and non-Indian citizens faced tribal members across the greatest chasm in American history. What consensus could be reached among scientists, land managers, tribes, environmentalists, and private landholders?

At the same time, inhabitants of every part of the Klamath Basin had strong interests in common. They lived in an area with great natural beauty and wanted to remain there. They had vital cultural traditions, and in many cases their livelihoods and family life were strands of the same fabric. Not only were the Native cultures family-based; so were the ranching, farming, and environmental communities. Because their ways of life depended on natural resources—soil, water, forests, forage—their survival on the land depended on sustainable economic practices. Because income from farming and ranching in this region was often marginal, overall economic vitality required diverse streams of income, including fishing and ecotourism as well as the sale of goods and the salaries of agency employees. In the absence of a vital economy, many residents felt pressure to sell their properties to agribusinesses and housing developments. That would further impact natural resources while driving up the price of land and driving out even more long-term residents. The crisis on the Klamath was not only about land, water, and wildlife; it was also about the quality of many human lives.

What made Basin-wide consensus building more than quixotic was the recognition by members of the region's diverse communities of their common interest. As Chadwick explained, the Bucket Brigade "made people understand that they are connected from one end of this Basin to the other." It also made all of the communities of the Basin understand that

> what really is at stake is survival. And that applies to every single group, it applies to every single element of the natural resources. There are many issues related to the farmers, there are different kinds of farmers. There are so many kinds of species. It sounds complicated and yet to me, it's simple. It's as simple as people understanding they cannot survive if they don't sit down and work together.

Only together could they generate enough political power and economic growth to defend their part of the world from strip malls, factory farms, exurban invasion, and detrimental government intervention. But they needed help in finding common ground, a challenge that Chadwick agreed to take on.

During the year and a half after the Klamath Falls symposium, Alice Kilham, aided by Terry Morton of Cascade Quality Solutions, a group facilitation company, convened five stakeholders' workshops. These occurred in Somes Bar near Ishi Pishi Falls, Scott Valley, the town of Klamath near the estuary, Tulelake, and Chiloquin. There were about 180 participants in all, many coming to several of these multi-day gatherings. At each meeting everyone's right to have a unique point of view was recognized; everyone had the opportunity to speak without interruption; and everyone's remarks became part of a cumulative record compiled to develop a basin-wide grassroots consensus. On the first day of each workshop, people articulated what they feared were the worst possible outcomes of the workshop as well as the best foreseeable future that their meetings could help to bring about. They also discussed short-term purposes and long-term goals.

One short-term purpose statement written during the Somes Bar gathering was: "We protect the current fabric of the Scott Valley. Agriculture remains completely whole. We continue to live and enjoy the family ranch." Among the long-term goals articulated during the course of these meetings were restoring fish passage through the dams while replacing hydroelectric power with biomass energy; restoring the watersheds and rivers, with skies full of birds again and no species endangered; creating a watershed-wide sense of community; developing a framework "to solve tribal, agricultural and environmental conflict"; and proposing to Congress with a common voice solutions to the Basin's problems.

I attended the stakeholder meeting in Chiloquin in the summer of 2005. Among the more than seventy people present were farmers and ranchers, including members of the Klamath Bucket Brigade organization; Alan Foreman, chair of the Klamath Tribal Council, and former chair Jeff Mitchell; Troy Fletcher from the Yurok Tribe and Ron Reed from the Karuk Tribe; a Klamath County commissioner; an aide to Senator Smith and aides to two congressmen, Greg Walden of Oregon and John Doolittle of California; scientists and other representatives from state and federal agencies; people from environmental organizations, ranging from The Nature Conservancy and WaterWatch to the homegrown Salmon River Restoration Council; academics, including Judith Messier, a graduate student at the Institute for Conflict Analysis and Resolution; and Cory Scott, representing PacifiCorp, the company that owned and operated the dams.

The conference began with a prayer by Joe Hobbs of the Klamath Tribes. Everyone then had the opportunity to make an introductory statement. Vivian Helliwell, who represented the Pacific Coast Federation of Fishermen's Associations, explained why she was there. "I went fishing to get away from it all," she said, "and learned I was downstream from *everybody*." What transpired upstream during Helliwell's years on the ocean had a major impact on her industry. "Eighty percent of the fishing fleet has gone out of business," she complained, "with little or no compensation for their loss." Helliwell thanked the people of the Upper Basin who had written in support of disaster relief for northcoast commercial fishing families during a year when they had suffered from an even shorter fishing season than usual due to the precipitous decline of Klamath Basin stocks. This support was remarkable in light of the acrimony during the Bucket Brigade era between Klamath Project farmers and commercial fishers.

Scott Valley rancher Gareth Plank drew a parallel between this gathering and the common ground found by the Klamath River tribes. Despite being of diverse origins and speaking languages from three distinct language groups, the Yurok, Hupa, and Karuk managed to develop a shared ceremonial cycle and a system of ecosystem management that met their needs without diminishing the salmon runs. The communities represented at the workshop could do something similar. In spite of disagreements, Plank concluded, "We who love being here have more in common than people in the rest of the world."

Another Scott Valley resident, Mary Roehrich, said that her family came to northern California during the Gold Rush. Speaking of the "Baby Boom tsunami" of newly retired people looking for homes in the country, Roehrich expressed her fear that farmers, ranchers, and tribal members would be swept away from their lands.

Christine Karas, a wildlife biologist and newly arrived Bureau of Reclamation administrator, expressed her interest in regulated rivers. Rather than being on the outside, defending the rivers' best interests against the government, she preferred to make advances from the inside. Describing herself as having a thick skin, Karas noted that she has rhino statuettes in her office, mementos from those who have contended with her.

After the introductions, people representing the various constituencies—the farming and ranching community, the tribes, government agencies, environmental organizations, academia—divided up into mixed groups representing everyone. Jacqui Krizo, who comes from a family farm near Tulelake, remarked: "We've barely begun to learn each other's names; a long way to go in the education of each other."

For each speaker, Bob Chadwick designated two individuals to serve as the listener and the backup listener. He chose people whose points of view were different from the one presented and instructed them to recount "what I heard you say" to ensure that the speaker was understood. This procedure, sometimes called "active listening," is also a tool traditionally used by Klamath River tribes. The repeater was the person who, in conflict settlements, helped the parties understand each other as they came to terms.

Petey Brucker, the leader of the Salmon River Restoration Council, spoke softly and at length. After giving a history of the Klamath Basin from his perspective, Brucker said that the job of the environmental community was to stop bad things from happening, influence resource management, and educate citizens. He noted that fish traps in Beaver Creek showed an almost 100 percent mortality of juvenile salmon; they died of the virus *C. shasta*. Neurotoxins, he added, are concentrated in Copco Lake above Copco Dam #2. Brucker called for the California Energy Commission to recommend removal of the Klamath River dams; the power they generate is not worth the damage they do. Concluding, Brucker spoke of his neighbors, the Karuk Tribe, and said: "Their religion to call on higher powers to help fix the world is inspired."

After Brucker's speech was repeated by his listener, Bob Hunter, a lawyer for WaterWatch in Portland, spoke. The night before, Hunter said, he had been fishing, and he had a large fish on the line until an otter stole it. Having established credentials as an outdoorsmen, Hunter referred to the 350,000 acres of wetlands that the Klamath Basin once had, the largest in the West with the largest concentration of wildfowl. Those wetlands were farmed and greatly reduced in size. Hunter advocated bringing water demand back into balance through purchases of land from willing sellers, a reduction in irrigation that would not eliminate "the rural nature of the region."

Sam Henzel, an Upper Basin farmer, had the duty of serving as Hunter's listener. But he could not repeat the lawyer's arguments. "I'm too pissed off to regurgitate that shit," he said. Chadwick asked the backup listener, farmer Steve Kandra, to step in, but Kandra was also speechless with fury. Finally, Marshall Staunton took the microphone and gave his version of what he heard Bob Hunter say.

Chadwick announced the lunch break and asked Henzel and Hunter to meet with him. This is part of the Chadwick method, speaking with key players about what to do next. Chadwick's work is based on the principle of having no agenda except that the players come to terms with their differences and, if possible, reach consensus.

I asked several people to explain why the reaction to Hunter was so strong compared to the respectful reception Brucker received. It made a difference, I was told, that Hunter is an outsider and, worse, that he is a lawyer; it was litigation that forced the water cutoff. Many rural people, farmers and loggers among others, regard litigious environmental organizations as the enemy; because of them, the government has deprived good people of their livelihood. Gareth Plank observed that the rhetoric of preserving "the rural nature of the region" ignores economic realities. The loss of farms can destroy a farm community by diminishing the infrastructure that supports farming—the tractor dealership and the fertilizer company, for example.

When we reconvened, Chadwick spoke about the stages of relationships. These often begin with the discovery of similarities—mutual friends, for example. Only when those involved become able to explore their differences and express disagreements, Chadwick said, can they really know and trust each other. He then asked Staunton and Fletcher to act out the distinction between difference and conflict, between going separate ways and trying to force the other to go where one wants him to. As the two men pushed on each other's chests, the facilitator called on others literally to back them up. This made the interpersonal conflict an intergroup dispute. Chadwick asked everyone seated in the circle watching this display to observe without taking sides.

This mime of force against force having cleared the air, Sam Henzel was able to articulate to Bob Hunter why he reacted so strongly to the lawyer's presentation. "You can sway a crowd with half-truths much easier than you can sway a crowd with a lie," Henzel told the lawyer, adding that it is a method despots use. The farmer went on to challenge statements that Hunter had woven into his presentation as examples of half-truths. One misleading "fact," Henzel said, was the figure of 350,000 acres for the historic wetland acreage. In reality, this varied naturally from season to season and year to year; there can be no fixed number. Using such a number gives the appearance of reality, the aura of truth. The farmer argued that taking Upper Basin farmland out of production would release very little water for the fisheries. Why, then, should farmers lose their irrigation and be pressured to leave their land? "You're trying to treat the farming community like an Indian," Henzel concluded.

Hunter responded by defending his integrity. He did not intend to lie with half-truths, he said. "You don't solve the problem by filing lawsuits," Henzel shot back. "All you do is create animosity." With pain reddening his face, Henzel exclaimed: "We farmers are dying. Our average age is fifty-eight and rising. We're not going to survive as farmers; there's no money in it. Environmentalists are going to win. So why drive the nail in our coffin? Why shoot us before our time?" Henzel directed the group's attention to Agency Ranch, where outsiders were moving in, "buying up everything. The issue is to try to preserve what's left."

Steve Kandra then spoke to Hunter: "Because we are rooted in this ground, we wouldn't do anything to harm it. We try to be stewards. This is our life, our entire life. And it has been for my family for 150 years. To be told your family has been doing the wrong thing, you're to blame for all of those wrong things, that's really not a very good way to start. I want to ranch. And I want my children to ranch. And I think it's the best thing for our country."

On the second afternoon of the workshop, addressing the aides to Senator Smith and Congressman Walden, Christine Karas of the Bureau of Reclamation advocated ecosystem restoration that preserves the rural way of life. "We will have sustainability when we begin to adapt our ways to the environment rather than adapt our environment to us." This was a surprising statement coming from a BOR manager on the centennial of the Klamath Project, one of the first undertakings of her Bureau. Karas then explained how, to her mind, the relationship between federal agencies like her own and residents of the regions they serve was evolving. When the Klamath Project began a century ago, she said, "government did things *for* people." When new laws ushered in the regulatory era some thirty years ago, she went on, "government did things *to* people." Today, she argued, the paradigm was for "government to do things *with* people." Karas advocated a Basin-wide forum in which "these people need to be the decision-makers. Government needs to facilitate that."

The third and last day of the gathering was the time for making decisions. Would this series of workshops continue or end here? Was there a next step to take after the workshops, or had they led nowhere? A criticism made of the Chadwick process was that it represented no one except those present. One participant noted that not one of the region's Mexican Americans was present. What decision could this group make for the Basin as a whole? Raising this issue early in the day, the facilitator offered his father's advice: "Always dance with the girl you got, and if you dance well, you'll get the girl you want." He added, "Work with who's here, and when you make decisions, think of who's not here."

Mike Connelly read passages from an essay he wrote in May 2001, shortly after the Bucket Brigade. Datelined May 2011, "A Basin Reborn" is a retrospective success story, looking back on how the Upper Basin transformed itself "from 'Loser' to 'Leader.'" The author from the future recalls that "since the spotted owl wars of the 1980s . . . there had been processes and organizations doing the difficult work of establishing trust among the various stakeholders." Although the crisis of 2001 "nearly obliterated whatever trust had been developed," people kept meeting. "They yelled and fought until they were tired of all the yelling and fighting, until they all saw that it was the yelling and fighting that got them into this mess in the first place."

Eventually, the stakeholders realized that everyone wanted the same thing: "diverse, self-sufficient, economically viable communities living peaceful, productive lives in a beautiful and healthy natural setting, with lots of open space and no endangered species." To achieve this, they developed a program of self-determination based on the principle that if they did things that made "*both* economic and environmental sense, that would make money *and* make things healthier."

Connelly foresaw "a revival of the old pioneer spirit," and an "entre-preneurial energy" that focused on doing good things for the future instead of "fighting to keep things just as they were."

After lunch, Rae Olsen of the Bureau of Reclamation spoke of the BOR's response to the listing of endangered species that precipitated the water crisis. The agency's Conservation Implementation Program, or CIP, has several goals: to restore the Klamath River ecosystem and, in so doing, achieve the recovery of Lost River and shortnose suckers and aid the recovery of coho salmon; to contribute to the federal government's tribal trust responsibilities; to operate existing water management facili-ties in a sustainable manner; and to make water resource improvements.

Chadwick asked Troy Fletcher and Christine Karas to exchange their views of the CIP with brutal honesty. "It's not about being nice with each other," he said, "it's about being real."

Fletcher was real. He called the CIP his "worst outcome." As a former executive director of the Yurok Tribe, he had learned that government-to-government meetings on the local level solve nothing. Noting that the people he speaks with cannot make decisions without approval from Washington, D.C., Fletcher said it was his experience that "federal deci-sions can be overlaid on a group's good intentions." He expressed his fear that through the CIP the Bureau of Reclamation would dilute the govern-ment's trust responsibility toward the tribes. Fletcher preferred "to cut out the middle man and go right to Sam (Henzel)." He insisted: "We have to be the decision-makers."

After recounting to Fletcher what she heard him say, Karas replied. She claimed that the CIP empowers citizen groups to implement plans that they have written; they can be decision-makers. She pointed out that it takes money to pull down dams and acquire land and argued that this process, which the Bush Administration and the governors of both states had signed on to, was the way to obtain it.

Fletcher insisted once again that he personally opposed the CIP. Then he asked a question of the more than seventy people in the room: "How many of you trust the federal government?" Fewer than ten people raised their hands. Then Fletcher called for a meeting that excluded government representatives. Regarding the agenda, Steve Kandra insisted that the group take a hard look at water allocation in relationship to water demand. Petey Brucker said, "I don't know how we possibly can work it out if we aren't working together." In that spirit, after the workshop ended, Brucker and Sam Henzel went to Henzel's farm to get to know each other.

The stakeholders had reason not to trust the federal government. Fletcher did not need to mention the Salmon War in which Fish and Wildlife enforcement agents, blaming gillnetters for overfishing, attacked and arrested members of his tribe. Farmers' and ranchers' memories of the irrigation cutoff, when they too were blamed and punished for the decline of wild fish, were even fresher. Nor could environmentalists and commercial fishers trust the government to implement the Endangered Species Act after the die-off that followed that cutoff, when a turn of the headgate valve by the Bush Administration killed an estimated seventy thousand spawning salmon and countless juvenile fish that never reached the ocean.

Tribal members' response to that disaster on the river went beyond mistrust. It awoke in them feelings of dread. "The 2002 fish kill made me really grapple with this concept that our way of life could go extinct," said Frankie Myers, vice chairman of the Yurok Tribe. "It was absolutely shocking and absolutely life changing for me." Lyle Marshall, Hoopa Valley Tribal Council chair, said he "watched grown men cry, stand on the river bank and cry, not over a dead salmon but over such a catastrophic injury to our world." After seeing his grandmother cry as dead salmon floated in the estuary, Sammy Gensaw started an UnDam the Klamath Coalition at his High School. Hoopa Valley High School students began a three-day, 350-mile Great Salmon Relay Run along the Klamath and Trinity rivers to the Oregon headwaters. It has occurred annually every spring ever since.

Troy Fletcher, Jeff Mitchell, and Leaf Hillman, who represented their tribes on the Intertribal Fish and Water Commission, concluded that unless the dams came down or were modified to allow fish passage, wild salmon would go extinct. They resolved not to let that happen and recognized that they had leverage. The dams' federal licenses were to expire in 2006. Relicensing is the decision of FERC, the Federal Energy Regulatory Commission. How to prevent that or to force PacifiCorp to provide reliable, long-term fish passage was the challenge they took on.

Farmers also feared the end of their way of life if the Klamath crisis could not be resolved. Not only had the Endangered Species Act made them vulnerable to future water cutoffs, they knew that when the dam license expired, the rate they had paid for electricity since the 1950s would skyrocket. That cost plus the difficulty of securing loans when water supplies are uncertain could drive family farming into extinction.

The Chadwick session participants reached a consensus. They realized that restoring salmon habitat by removing or rebuilding the dams was necessary to bring peace and prosperity to the region. How to achieve that despite its history of genocide, warfare, resource conflicts over timber, salmon, and water, and enduring racial hatred was the question that haunted all concerned.

Fletcher and Hillman invited Greg Addington, executive director of the Klamath Water Users Association (KWUA), and farmers from the Upper Basin to meet with them in a tribal office in Yreka. "We started laying stuff out there honestly," recalled Hillman. "It was the first attempt to bring the tribes and the irrigators into a room by themselves, away from the spotlight, to say, 'Look, we are all in bad shape here.'"

Fletcher knew Addington would speak frankly and listen receptively. In 2004, PacifiCorp had convened its own set of meetings, hoping to head off lawsuits over relicensing the four hydroelectric dams on the Klamath. Representatives of the tribes, commercial fishermen, federal agencies, and environmental groups met in hotels for negotiations that led nowhere. After hours, Fletcher and Addington drank beer and got to know each other. "I got to a point," said Addington, "where I just trusted Troy." They realized, Fletcher recalled, that "we had a common opponent through this FERC negotiation, and that was PacifiCorp."

The tribes took PacifiCorp on directly. The Federal Power Act requires fish passage as a condition for relicensing, but Iron Gate, the dam farthest downriver, is too tall for a fish ladder. Salmon would have to be trucked around it. Mindful of the long history of broken promises to their tribes, Fletcher, Hillman, and Mitchell did not expect PacifiCorp to honor that requirement indefinitely after FERC renewed the license. Dam removal, they concluded, was the only option.

It would take performative politics to make that happen.

There's a Karuk story about how Coyote freed salmon for the people. Two women imprisoned all the fish in a pond inside a cave. "How am I going to fix it?" Coyote asked himself. He made a strip of alder bark resemble a salmon, smeared deer marrow on it, and walked to their house. The women were cooking acorns. They offered him some, but Coyote took the bark out of his bag and pretended to eat it all, marrow grease dripping from his whiskers. That night, while Coyote snored as if sleeping, the women went out to get salmon for themselves. That's how he found out where they hid it. Coyote released the fish. They swam downstream to the river. Then he ran away. It would take cunning and craft worthy of Coyote for the tribes to release salmon from the grip of Scottish Power, the UK corporation that owned PacifiCorp, which owned the Klamath dams.

Hillman hired Craig Tucker, a political strategist from South Carolina who had worked with Friends of the River. Tucker said he needed to do advance work in Scotland. He had to get the lay of the land, prep the media, and identify potential allies. To pull that off, he needed a spokesman for the tribes. "I've got just the guy for you," Hillman replied. At the Edinburgh airport Tucker met Jeff Mitchell and realized how right he was.

Tall, with long braids, calling for the return of wild salmon to his homeland, Jeff Mitchell became a sensation in a country of salmon-lovers where many, feeling colonized by the English, identify with Native Americans. "We got in front of Scottish Parliament," Mitchell recalled. "We got a resolution out of the Green Party supporting our position. The Church of Scotland came forward, and they supported us. I went to Brussels and talked with committees on human rights and social justice. They supported us. We decided to go to London and rattle cages where institutional funders had large blocks of PacifiCorp stock."

Having netted powerful allies, Mitchell, Tucker, and Glen Spain of the Pacific Coast Federation of Fishermen's Associations, who lobbied London investors with them, were ready for showtime. A band of Klamath Basin Indians performed outside a shareholders' meeting in Edinburgh, dancing, drumming, and singing. The media attention they attracted ruined the company's environmental image. What was worse from the perspective of Scottish Power, members of Scotland's Parliament sought to keep the country's reputation from being harmed by stripping the word 'Scottish' from the corporate name. The Indians' celebrity might make that resolution actually pass.

Tucker began to smell victory. He expected a shareholder's resolution to remove the dams. Instead, Scottish Power sold PacifiCorp to Warren Buffett's Berkshire Hathaway. This was a devasting outcome, he recalled. "You got this massive Berkshire empire of which PacifiCorp is a slice of which the Klamath dams are a slice. It's like this tiny almost insignificant piece of the pie."

The tribes were determined to succeed no matter what the obstacles. As Tucker saw it, other Americans are used to "going to a place, exploiting the hell out of it, leaving behind a mess, and we just go to the next place. For Native people the world over, it doesn't work that way. They believe they are put on a place to take care of it. They are not going to kill all the salmon and go off to the next river. That's not it."

During the Chadwick groups and PacifiCorp meetings, tribal leaders managed to have difficult discussions with farmers and other regional stakeholders. They had personal conversations and built some trust. But a formidable upriver struggle lay ahead. Could a Basin-wide alliance be formed? If there were an alliance, could it get support from state and federal governments for dam removal? And if that happened, could their combined political pressure make Buffett release Klamath River water from his corporate cave?

Chapter Nineteen
Watershed Congress

John Wesley Powell, the one-armed explorer-scientist who braved the wild Colorado on his Grand Canyon expeditions, was a voice for conservation in the Gilded Age. Powell expected water to be fought over in the West and feared that monopolies or remote government officials would take control of the land's lifeblood. Instead, he wanted watersheds to form political boundaries with local democratic governance.

Klamath Basin history reveals the wisdom of Powell's preference. Not only have private interests from the Gold Rush on degraded and diverted a great river while extracting its wealth, federal agencies have intervened in vital disputes over water and wildlife, changing sides and exacerbating local conflicts. The government supported commercial fishing over gillnetting in 1978, endangered species versus irrigation in 2001, and farmers versus fishers in 2002. During a Chadwick group, Basin stakeholders agreed: no one trusted the feds. It became clear that only face-to-face talks between people of the region could resolve its recurring crises of water allocation. Where vertical democracy via representative government had failed, horizontal democracy between citizens might succeed.

High on the Chadwick list of "best outcomes" was a "Basin-wide Klamath Congress." Viewed through the lens of U.S. history, this proposal revived Thomas Jefferson's idea of a "ward system" that enables citizens to participate directly in their governance. In this respect, the region's identity as the State of Jefferson seems apt. Viewed through the longer time frame of human habitation of the watershed, attempts to find common ground between stakeholders continued the process of acculturation to the land that enabled tribes speaking entirely unrelated languages to develop communal ceremonial traditions, a coordinated fishery, and shared values.

As Christine Karas said, sustainability will come "when we begin to adapt our ways to the environment." This was a stunning statement considering that her agency, the Bureau of Reclamation, radically altered the environment of the Upper Basin, draining vast lakes to produce arable land. Karas had not been trusted when she recommended that government facilitate a Basin-wide forum in which the people were the decision-makers. But she meant it; and after Scottish Power decided to sell PacifiCorp to Warren Buffett rather than demolish the dams, the best way forward was a citizens' agreement on how to restore the region's economic and ecological vitality.

The parties that convened to negotiate what became the Klamath Basin Restoration Agreement (KBRA) knew that whatever they decided had to be accompanied by PacifiCorp's commitment to take the dams down and by a law of Congress appropriating funds to pay for dam removal and for the costs of implementing their deal. They had assurances that if farmers from the bright red Republican upriver and headwater districts found common ground with fishers from the deep blue Democratic congressional district at the river's mouth, lawmakers in D.C. would pass the bill they needed. And they expected that their consensus, backed by law, would give PacifiCorp the incentives and protections it needed to rewild the Klamath River.

Thirty parties convened to work out an agreement. They including state and federal agencies, the Klamath Water Users Association (KWUA), the Oregon Farm Bureau, the Cattlemen's Association, the Pacific Coast Federation of Fishermen's Associations, and several conservation organizations. "We're at a position," said California congressman Mike Thompson, "where we have everybody, the tribes, the fishermen, and the farmers at the same table." Steve Thompson from Fish and Wildlife facilitated the meetings.

There were many factors to consider. Engineering consultants and tribal scientists met to run computer models correlating water levels, times of year, and aquatic species' life cycles. Klamath Tribes' biologist Larry Dunsmoor said, "Those of us committed to the process worked our butts off. It was one of the hardest things we've ever done."

They did more than calculate flows and talk around the table. Greg Addington and Troy Fletcher became "bosom buddies. It's just that simple," said Paul Simmons, Addington's successor as KWUA executive director. "They would play golf, and the standard thing was, 'we're playing for, you know, a hundred acre-feet per hole.'" No problem the parties faced was more difficult than how to ensure that farmers got water every year. They decided there would have to be a limit measured in acre-feet, the amount based on a sliding scale, with allocations lowest during drought years. Reductions would be sweetened by capital improvements to aid irrigation efficiency and by incentives for farmers to let lands go fallow.

Addington cleared that trade-off with the KWUA board during an all-night meeting. Getting consent was tough, he said, for the deal "was locking in less water than we knew we needed in at least fifty percent of the years. We knew that once we committed to that, we weren't going back."

To safeguard even those reduced allocations, the Klamath Tribes had to agree not to exercise their senior water rights to the farmers' detriment. The incentive they accepted was funding to enable them to purchase 90,000 acres of purloined reservation lands that were in private hands.

There were other concerns as well, such as how to avoid undermining the Endangered Species Act, what to do about unaffordable electricity rates after the dams' license expired, and whether farming could continue in the federal wildlife refuges.

That last issue brought negotiations to a breaking point. Bob Hunter of WaterWatch asked, "Is this a refuge for ducks, or potatoes?" He and Oregon Wild's representative insisted on taking those wetlands out of production. "Why should a couple dozen people be holding hostage some of the most valuable refuges in the nation so they can make money off of them?" argued Hunter. Greg Addington replied, "If you want to reduce the [Klamath] Project permanently, we'd be glad to take that back and see what our people say. But we can tell you what they're gonna say: Hell no!"

The tribal leaders had considered ending wildlife refuge farming. But Craig Tucker thought it was not a winning strategy to drive farmers off that land. "We had already decided it was about balancing water use and not ending agriculture. Remember, this was the Bush Administration. We were gonna have to have friends across the aisle." Leaf Hillman believed the negotiators had to work toward a shared agreement incrementally "instead of going nuclear and all the rest of us having to deal with the fallout." In his opinion, the anti-farm stance of WaterWatch and Oregon Wild made it impossible to reach an agreement. "We led the charge to throw them out of the damn room."

On April 6, 2007, the settlement group dissolved itself. Within hours, it reconvened with everyone invited back except WaterWatch and Oregon

Wild. Two conservation groups, Trout Unlimited and American Rivers, remained at the table.

In January 2008, the KBRA was made public. The provisions included formation of a Basin-wide council. That would provide a public space in which the parties could negotiate as needed, keeping their agreement up to date as conditions changed. It could evolve into the Klamath Congress the Chadwick groups considered a "best outcome."

The negotiators had to sell the deal to their constituencies before taking it to the Congress in D.C. Meanwhile, PacifiCorp relicensed the four hydroelectric dams on the Klamath on a year-to-year basis while waiting for FERC to grant the new fifty-year license it applied for.

Early one morning, a group of PacifiCorp executives boated up the Klamath. Tribal leaders wanted them to visit Blue Creek. "It's a magical place. It can get into people's hearts and minds," explained Yurok fisheries biologist Barry McCovey. But when they rounded the bend at Klamath Glen, five miles upriver from the estuary, a flotilla of Indians blockaded the executives like hapless salmon at Iron Gate Dam.

The tribes confronted Warren Buffett himself during the "Woodstock of Capitalism." Every year, tens of thousands of Berkshire Hathaway investors from countries around the world gather in Omaha to party and seek financial wisdom from one of the richest men on Earth. Tipped off that a protest was planned, executive producer Steve Michelson and I flew into Nebraska to shoot a scene for the *River of Renewal* documentary.

In his motel room, I asked Craig Tucker what point he intended to make. "People who have never seen the Klamath River are destroying it, and they don't even know it," he replied. "It's hard for people to accept that their investments—investments that are putting on a return that allows them to go to Borsheims and buy jewelry—those investments are killing fish and causing toxic pollution and creating poverty for Indian people and putting commercial fishermen out of jobs."

As people partied outside Borsheims, the luxury jewelry store Berkshire Hathaway owns, Karuk women wearing basket caps entered the premises. They looked on as saleswomen hyped the store's wares. ("You'll never see anything like it.") Mingling with party-goers who sipped cocktails on the plaza outside, Indians sold "Buffett bucks." ("What does it do?" asked a shareholder. "It's good for one dead fish." "Dead fish? I don't want a dead fish." "Well, you should ask Warren Buffett about it.") When

Leaf Hillman gave the go-ahead, they unfurled an anti-dam banner and chanted "Un-dam the Klamath, bring the salmon home!" as other Indians dropped to the ground, staging a die-in.

Hillman's teenage son Chook Chook stayed up all that night to be first in line at the Qwest Center to insist that Buffett take down the Klamath dams. Caught unprepared, the billionaire had no answer for him.

At shareholders' meetings as well as in the Omaha arena, Klamath River Indians and their allies repeatedly made the case that Berkshire Hathaway held a toxic asset. Finally, the company concluded that taking down the dams could be cheaper than providing fish passage. Besides, it would be good PR.

In November 2008, at the American Indian Film Festival in San Francisco when Jack Kohler and I came onstage to receive the "best documentary" award for *River of Renewal*, I announced that PacifiCorp had just signed a provisional agreement to remove the hydroelectric dams on the Klamath. In February 2010, in Salem, Oregon, the Secretary of Interior and the Oregon and California governors signed the agreement. Fixing his face to look like the Terminator, California's governor, the actor Arnold Schwarzenegger, declared to the dams, "Hasta la vista, baby!" He spoke for the salmon with another classic line: "I'll be baaack!"

That November, Republicans won control of the House of Representatives, and the Tea Party movement, which emerged soon after Obama's election, drove the party further to the right. Speaker of the House John Boehner vowed to kill the president's agenda however he could. When the 112th Congress took up the bill to implement the KBRA, farmers of the Upper Basin expected Oregon Representative Greg Walden to push it through for them. But Tea Party politicians deemed dam removal a win for Obama, and Walden, fearing a Republican primary challenger when he stood for reelection, betrayed constituents whose irrigation security depended on his support.

"The fact that that agreement got set aside was a huge blow for the county," said Klamath County historian Todd Kepple. "The blunder that I'm rating number one in the history of this basin is the failure to get the Klamath Basin Restoration Agreement funded."

"To be left like a bride at the altar by Congressman Walden was bitter for all of us," recalled Craig Tucker.

Without an act of Congress, the KBRA terminated. The only remaining way to take down the dams on the Klamath was for FERC not to relicense them. But if PacifiCorp went along with that, only the tribes' needs, not the farmers', could be met. The trust that grew between them as they negotiated a complex, hard-won agreement shattered. It was everyone's loss.

Yet the KBRA was not a total failure. It proved that progress can occur when government agencies support the place-based politics of horizontal democracy. It demonstrated that when people negotiate on the basis of common knowledge, science, and their vital interests rather than ideologies and partisan politics, they can find solutions together. And it offered a model for addressing difficult issues of many kinds. Tiana Williams, director of the Yurok Wildlife Department, put it this way, "If you have a problem, if you have a conflict to resolve, the first thing you have to do is understand who you are in conflict with. You can't see them as the enemy. You have to recognize you're in some sort of relationship with them before you can move forward in a good way. I think that's definitely exemplified in the long history of dam removal."

If the diverse stakeholders in the Klamath Basin are able to retain these principles of citizen democracy, their struggle for dam removal could inform a better future over the long run.

Chapter Twenty
Geography of Hope

"Amend the ESA." That slogan adorned every bucket of Klamath River water that Bucket Brigade protestors poured into an irrigation canal. Farmers and ranchers who defied court orders based on the Endangered Species Act did not seek to end its protection of endangered species. They wanted the law modified to protect their economic interests and way of life, which water cutoffs endangered. Many conservationists, in contrast, want the ESA extended to defend wildlife habitats proactively. That would save species from being listed as threatened or endangered in the first place. However successful the ESA has been in protecting particular plants and animals, it does not foster the interdependence of living things that evolve within ecosystems.

The ESA's limited focus does make political sense. "Salmon are a cultural keystone species," Yurok biologist Barry McCovey noted. "We wouldn't be here on the precipice of the largest dam removal in history without salmon." Yet saving salmon requires saving the ecosystems linked by its far-ranging life cycle. That means restoration not only of hundreds of miles of spawning habitat but also of the watershed's ecological integrity. Plants that nurture insects that fish feed on; trees whose shade keeps water temperatures low enough for salmon; fungi that bring tree roots nutrients from surrounding soil; fire that opens up the forest floor, enabling bears to fertilize the land with nitrogen from the ocean—every node in a wide, intricate web of life keeps ecosystems from unraveling.

The epic task of rewilding a river and reweaving the land is underway in the Klamath Basin. What made the restoration of a ten and a half million acre region possible is the demolition of four hydroelectric dams and the draining of the reservoirs behind them. That came about despite the political failure to implement the Klamath Basin Restoration Agreement.

Although Congress killed the KBRA, a companion agreement provided an alternate path toward dam removal. That was the Klamath

Hydroelectric Settlement Agreement (KHSA). In this document, Pacifi-
Corp asserts that its willingness to allow eradication of the Klamath dams
depends on whatever is in the best interests of the corporation and its
customers and on the corporation's protection from liability for any damages resulting from dam removal.

After the congressional dead end, the last hope to save wild salmon
from extinction was the Federal Energy Regulatory Commission
(FERC), which determines whether to approve or deny dam licensing.
In preparing to deal with FERC, the tribes, conservationists, and fishers'
organizations had to decide whether to work with or against PacifiCorp.
Craig Tucker reasoned that if they campaigned to prevent FERC from
giving the company another fifty years to dam the Klamath, they could
lose. They needed PacifiCorp's cooperation to make sure the decision
went against relicensing. And they were part way there. The company
has already "admitted that the dams suck," Tucker thought. "And they
don't make money" — not enough to make the cost of fish passage a good
investment. Liability was the sticking point.

That frustrated Tucker. "We blow up skyscrapers in downtowns of
giant metropolitan areas all the time. Someone insures the clean-up of
nuclear wastes in Superfund sites all the time." PacifiCorp's insistence
that they would not be liable for any damages caused by dam removal
epitomized for him "the way corporate America works. You stick other
people with the environmental costs of doing business." What PacifiCorp
wanted was, "we'll give you the dams and eight thousand acres and two
hundred million and we don't want to hear from you ever again. And we
were like, sold, right? We want somebody to remove dams who is excited
and enthusiastic and that's not PacifiCorp." But who would enthusiasti-
cally take on that responsibility?

The coalition of tribes, conservationists, and fishers' organizations
found a precedent for insuring and managing a dam removal project. To
take out the Edwards Dam on the Penobscot River, the State of Maine
accepted it as a gift from Edwards Manufacturing Company. The Klamath
stakeholders adopted that model by amending their hydroelectric agreement to create a nonprofit, the Klamath River Renewal Corporation. The
KRRC would take on all the liability, plan the process of dam removal,
hire contractors to carry it out, and coordinate watershed restoration

on PacifiCorp's former Klamath Basin properties. By 2030, these would become California and Oregon state lands.

A remaining challenge was replacing the billion dollars that Congress, in shelving the restoration agreement, refused to appropriate. Instead, funds for dam removal and watershed restoration were to flow from the states of California and Oregon, from the pockets of PacifiCorp ratepayers, and from federal agencies.

The April 2016 amendment of the KHSA has more than forty signatories. These include six irrigation districts, three district improvement companies, a golf and country club, two counties, agencies of the two states, agencies of the U.S. Departments of Commerce and Interior, fishery organizations, PacifiCorp, and the Yurok, Karuk, and Klamath Tribes. Their agreement launched a slow bureaucratic process. FERC followed every twist and turn of its flow chart in deciding whether or not to relicense the hydroelectric dams.

On the morning the final vote occurred, November 17, 2022, Yuroks, Karuks, and Hupas watched FERC transfer the Iron Gate, Copco 1 and 2, and J. C. Boyle dams to the KRRC. As he issued the license surrender order, FERC chairman Richard Glick acknowledged the influence Klamath River Indians had on his agency's decision. "Dam removal makes sense in large part due to fish and wildlife protections. But there is a discussion in the order on the impact on tribes and the ability to have their traditions and cultural practices improved. . . . A number of years back, the commission did not think about the impact of our decisions on tribes. That's an important element in today's order."

Among those present in Orleans hearing Glick's speech was Ron Reed's son Charley, the education director of Save California Salmon. When the fish kill in 2002 made Klamath River Indians determined to remove the dams, Charley Reed was seven. "I inherited the responsibility to take care of my relatives, the salmon, from my father," he said. "My hope is for my children to spend more time fishing and less time protesting." Listening with him were Molli Myers and her twenty-year-old son, whom she brought as a baby to an anti-dam rally in Scotland. "Klamath dam removal is a symbol of renewal, of hope and of a brighter future for our children, our communities, and all the life within the basin," she said. Myers cofounded a nonprofit, Ridges to Riffles, that manages foundation contributions to watershed restoration.

The dismantling of the four dams—generators, penstocks, and all, with top loaders and bulldozers leveling the dams layer by layer—followed an elaborate engineering blueprint spelled out in thousands of pages. Copco 2 was demolished in August 2023. In January 2024, when water flows were strong and before spring salmon entered the river, the reservoir above Copco 1 drained out through a diversion tunnel after explosions blasted away the plug that sealed it; the remaining dams were breached; and their water, no longer held behind reservoirs, thrust millions of cubic yards of sediment downriver to the Pacific. After a century of confinement, the Klamath River once again runs wild.

Restoration of the watershed is underway. Billions of seeds are being planted where toxic blue-green algae had floated. As they grow, these native plants will stabilize the sediment that remains from the emptied reservoirs. As soil builds and nutrients cycle through it, insects arrive, attracting birds. As other fauna and flora find their way to the reemergent lowlands, the local food chain regains connectivity.

Benefits from restoration projects will take time to become evident, Barry McCovey cautioned. "From an engineering perspective, when you build a highway or you build a bridge, you do the ribbon-cutting ceremony, and everything's beautiful and brand new. That's the best that's gonna look. Over the years, it's gonna degrade; it's just going to get worse and worse. River restoration and dam removal projects are the opposite. When you do the ribbon-cutting ceremony, it's the worst it's gonna look cause the heavy equipment just pulled out. It's muddy, it's dirty, it doesn't look like a river yet. But come back in a year. Come back in ten years, come back in twenty years. It just gets better and better and better as the ecosystem fixes itself."

This work is a large-scale example of what the tribes have been doing for thousands of years, McCovey said. "We consider ourselves fix-the-world people. Our job is to restore balance. We maintained that balance through our ceremonies and through the work we did on the land with fire. Fixing the world now from my perspective includes heavy equipment and rerouting streams and taking out dams and restoring reservoir lake beds. When you see our fisheries department working hand in hand with our construction corporation on a major restoration project, you see fixing the earth literally in front of you."

Bringing a keystone species, spring chinook, back to the Upper Basin will help the ecosystem fix itself. Yuroks reintroduced another keystone species, the condor, on the lower Klamath. Tiana Williams, who manages the tribe's wildlife department, told me a story about the condor that conveys a fundamental ecological concept.

"In the beginning of time," she said, "when the Creator was developing how the world would move forward with the world renewal ethos, he went to all the species of the world and said, 'Hey, we're gonna have these ceremonies. I need this prayer. I need this song. Who will help guide them?' Everybody immediately started jumping up and singing, trying to catch his eye so their song would be chosen. But Condor didn't step up. He doesn't sing particularly well. He hisses and grunts. He isn't exactly pretty. He has a bald head. So he refused to sing. But the Creator looked into his spirit and said, 'No, I want to hear your song. You have a kind heart. You've flown over the whole world. You can fly higher than anybody else. I know you've got a song in there.' Condor comes over and hisses and grunts, but the Creator hears the spirit of that song and sings it back to him. And it is the most beautiful song that has ever been heard or sung."

Williams explained, "If you have a healthy environment for condors, you have a healthy environment for everybody. Condors like big open prairies. We're going to reestablish our prairies through selective harvest and through introduction of fire and removal of invasive species. Ungulates like deer and elk thrive in those prairies and in edge zones where you have a lot more biological diversity. Old growth redwood forests that condors nest in are also good for marbled murrelet and Humboldt marten. So we've got this vision of what a beautiful and perfect world for condor is. And really, it's a beautiful and perfect world for everybody. It's this target for world renewal and restoration."

Returning salmon to the Upper Basin requires a condor's eye view. According to Brad Parrish, the task involves "reconnecting the features on the landscape that allow water throughout the basin to function naturally, to clean itself, to store itself, to slowly release itself in the summertime." Parrish, the Klamath Tribes' water rights specialist, warned that if "we're just focused on where the fish are at, we're not addressing the issues that restoration requires. You have to give the river what it needs. You have to look at the system as a whole."

Neither the survival of condors reintroduced within the river canyon nor of spring chinook returning to the headwaters can be assured. For condors, lead poisoning is the major cause of death. They are scavengers, and many carcasses they feed on were felled by lead bullets. Although thirty states, including California and Oregon, regulate the use of lead ammunition, and although they not only poison wildlife but also humans who eat game, toxic bullets are still widely used. According to the U.S. Fish and Wildlife Service, between ten and twenty million wild animals die every year of lead poisoning. Hunters use them out of ignorance, or refusal to discard old ammunition, or resistance to any limitation on what they consider gun rights. Like corporations that dismiss the environmental damage they cause as "externalities," some hunters take no responsibility for diminishing wildlife populations.

The reestablishment of spring chinook in the headwaters depends on a number of factors. Some go beyond the scope of watershed restoration: dearth of nutrients that feed salmon in the ocean; lack of precipitation during drought years; and climate change, which heats the waters and exacerbates the effects of drought. That said, increasing the extent and resilience of their habitat gives wild salmon a fighting chance even in the worst of times. Having evolved over millions of years, their DNA is hard-wired for adaptability.

Reconnecting the landscape as Parrish advises is thwarted by property lines. Although many farmers and ranchers in northeastern California and southcentral Oregon love wildlife, and although many employ conservation measures such as restoring wetlands and keeping cattle out of streams, typical land use practices impair water quality and impact water quantity, reducing the odds that wild salmon will thrive.

Karl Wenner is one of the farmers who reestablished wetlands to reduce the pollution of Upper Klamath Lake. With the aid of funding from the Inflation Reduction Act, he took 70 acres of his 400-acre farm out of production by carving dikes and channels through barley fields. Soon water flowing from a natural spring germinated seeds of marsh plants dropped by birds. Soon his land teemed with wildlife as waterfowl, pond turtles, and native fish found habitat there. "You set the stage and Mother Nature takes over," said Wenner. "It's just a magical thing to see."

In the Klamath Tribes' research station, technician Charlie Wright spoke about the Klamath Marsh as "a big piece of the puzzle. It's high up on our watershed. It's a huge sponge. It would fill the tributaries and all their little creeks through the dry season. The problem is we get to the dry season and there's no water where there used to be constantly water flowing." Diversions for agriculture cause this desiccation, she said. Canals dug six feet deep draw water across the marsh and into fields.

Near the research station, several large net-covered ponds protect endangered young *c'waam* and *koptu* from birds. Researchers keep them alive, hoping that someday juveniles will reproduce in natural waters. Today, only ancient suckerfish inhabit Klamath Lake. When they die, the species will no longer exist in the wild unless water quality improves. "Algae blooms are so abundant," Wright explained, "because so much fertilizer is dumped into that lake on a regular basis from agriculture. What happens to plants when you pour fertilizer on them? They do extraordinarily, but then that lake gets hot and the plants die and it drops the oxygen in that lake, and the baby fish suffocate."

The Klamath River flows from Klamath Lake. Accordingly, the lake's water quality could affect the health of chinook salmon in the headwaters. How will they survive in water that kills suckers? Barry McCovey said he expects salmon to migrate through the lake early in the year before snow melts and planting season begins, when its water is less toxic. "The spring salmon would get into the tributaries, whether it's the Williamson or the Sprague, find these nice, deep, cold pools, hole up all summer and spawn in the fall. Then their offspring would emigrate from the system in the spring. They can dodge the really poor water quality time that's in the summer." Over the long run, he said, "in order for there to be healthy salmon runs, we need *koptu* and *c'waam* to be healthy. Before there were dams, anadromous fish from the Pacific Ocean swam up the Klamath River and into Klamath Lake right next to *koptu* and *c'waam* and interacted with them. For millions of years all these species evolved together."

I asked Brad Parrish whether he thought spring chinook will take hold in the headwaters. "Will the fish make it up here? You're damn right," he answered. "I've seen the will of those fish. All they live for is to go in the ocean, get bigger, and come back and spawn. You just have to give the fish the opportunity to do it, and they will. Are there gonna be things we could make better—water quality in the lake, habitat availability in the Upper Basin? Yeah, sure. But could they make it right now? I know damn well they could."

The prospect that spring chinook, the largest, strongest salmon, once caught by the thousands in a day for the canning industry, then counted in the hundreds per year in their Salmon River refugia, will thrive once again makes an appealing storyline. Another narrative makes Indians the protagonist. After a history of suffering from genocide, war, resource conflicts, cultural suppression, and racism, the tribes rescued an endangered charismatic species. The fact that they prevailed over a corporation owned by a multi-billionaire suggests a compelling David-versus-Goliath drama. Yet productive thought about the future of this region requires more than a good story about the past. It begins with understanding what has happened in terms that apply to humanity and nature alike.

The Klamath Basin is united by water and divided by people. Nonetheless, in recent years, many of its diverse communities came together with a common goal. And they succeeded in ending the extraction of energy from the river into the grid via hydroelectric dams. McCovey explained why that matters. "You know," he said, "the energy from the ocean stopped making its way to the Upper Basin, and the energy from the Upper Basin, whether it's the minerals and the sediments and all the good things that come out of those mountains and all the good things that come out of the wetlands and the lakes and fed the river and helped keep the river healthy, those things all stopped. The energy flow completely stopped." What dam removal does is allow energy to flow throughout the region again. "Anyone who knows about energy and understands that everything, all this stuff, is connected, knows that the ramifications of that are massive, but not well understood."

The concept of energy flow is central to the science of ecology. Aldo Leopold was the first to apply this form of knowledge to the fields of land management and wildlife conservation. "Land," he wrote, "is not merely soil; it is a fountain of energy flowing through a circuit of soils, plants, and animals. Food chains are the living channels which conduct energy upward; death and decay return it to the soil. The circuit is not closed; some energy is dissipated in decay, some is added by absorption, some is stored in soils, peats, forests, but it is a sustained circuit, like a slowly augmented revolving fund of life." The connection between humanity and nature flows through this fountain, for humans are part of this energy flow, whether we live with it, disrupt it, or restore it.

What connects us with nature and with each other more than anything else is food. The word for "salmon" in both Yurok and Karuk languages means "food," or "to eat," and loving salmon as food generates other forms of energy: physical work to meet life's necessities, cultural expression, and circulation of goods. In this region of family farms and ranches, loving beef and potatoes, no less than salmon, sets physical, cultural, and economic energies in motion. The Bucket Brigade protest polarized two kinds of food, agriculturally produced goods on one hand, and naturally reproducing aquatic species on the other. In alliance with the tribes, however, food producers realized that their disparate communities are connected within a Basin-wide community of lands, waters, and wildlife.

That realization rejects what Leopold called "the fallacious notion that the wild community is one thing, the human community another." Instead, he explained, "that land is a community is a basic concept of ecology, but that land is to be loved and respected is an extension of ethics." Leopold discovered as a scientist and manager of lands what the tribes have known over millennia, that "conservation becomes possible only when man assumes the role of citizen in a community of which soils and waters, plants and animals are fellow members, each dependent on the others, and each entitled to his place in the sun."

The future of the Klamath Basin depends on whether ecosystem restoration renews the cultural and economic vitality of the entire region. Following the flow of energy through soils, waters and foods offers a guideline for long-term conservation and resilient growth. How to achieve this is an open question. There has never been a dam removal and watershed conservation project of this magnitude before. Besides, climate change disrupts once predictable natural patterns, affecting every aspect of the food chain. Clearly, collaborative adaptive management based on science and common sense is needed. Little else is certain.

Despite—or perhaps because of—the uncertainties, a vision of the future is worth developing. In 2002, after the fish kill, the National Academy of Sciences reported that there was no comprehensive plan for restoring the Klamath Basin. When stakeholders worked out a consensus during the Chadwick sessions and negotiated the KBRA and KHSA agreements, they had a plan but no money. After the deal with the farmers fell through but the amended KHSA went through, money became available, but there was no plan. Klamath Water Users executive director Paul Simmons expressed the concern that "the goal is to just spend the money and not to stabilize all the communities in the basin." He and historian Todd Kepple said farmers felt the tribes had won and they had lost. But the Upper Basin tribes felt they had also lost. "I don't consider that a win," said Jeff Mitchell, "when we're not fishing for salmon, we're not fishing for c'waam and koptu. What are salmon coming home to? A sick system. It didn't get fixed." Energy may soon be flowing throughout the basin, but without a vision of how to fix the world that all can work toward, there will be no common ground.

In the spirit of Mike Connelly's essay "A Basin Reborn," here are some considerations that may inform a vision of how to attain a better—more prosperous, peaceful, and sustainable—future for the entire region.

First of all, dam removal makes the entire Klamath a wild river. Rafters will be able to ride the river from origin to ocean. As rafting, along with hunting and fishing, becomes a recreational draw, it should benefit the region economically. Consider that the Klamath is nearly as long as the Colorado's run through the Grand Canyon. That rafting adventure often takes two weeks. As people navigate the Klamath, they will pay for places to eat and rest along the way.

Second, consider the odds that wild spring chinook salmon will survive in the headwaters and the longer odds that suckers will also be rescued from the brink of extinction. Those conservation biology projects can benefit the regional economy, for the money they cost will circulate locally. Reviving the endangered aquatic species can have the long-term economic benefit of freeing the farm community from the threat of water cutoffs to protect wildlife.

Next, consider that farmers sought relief via the KBRA from increased energy costs resulting from the expiration of the dams' licenses. It so happens that the Upper Basin has the means for energy self-sufficiency. On the average, there are three hundred sunny days each year. Given sufficient infrastructure investment and government incentives, owners of homes, farms, stores, and other businesses will save money by adapting to solar. The Upper Basin is also a wind funnel due to the Cascade corridor. If migratory birds that use the range as a flyway can be adequately protected, wind will generate power here. And thanks to its volcanic geology, the region has ample geothermal energy. Investment to fulfill the region's green energy potential will not only bring economic benefits, it will respond to the threat of climate change by ending local dependence on fossil-fueled electricity.

Fourth, there is food, the most intimate connection between natural energy and human health. Requa Inn at the estuary has offered Yurok cuisine, with courses of elk, salmon, seaweed, and acorn dessert, all paired with wines from a California vintner. In many regions from the Hudson to the Napa Valley, restaurants celebrate and support local farms and ranches. Klamath Basin chefs can serve classic American meat-and-potatoes meals as well as Indigenous foods. That would give the region a unique cultural cachet that locals as well as visitors will enjoy.

Mike Connelly has original items for local restaurants in mind. After selling his ranch and leaving his position as executive director of the Klamath Basin Ecosystem Foundation, Connelly opened Green Blade Bakery in Klamath Falls. Jeff Mitchell is one of his customers. They met across a table flanked by lawyers representing oppositional claims during Oregon's water adjudication process. Over the years, they became friends. Mitchell brings huckleberries to the bakery. He would like to bring *wocus*, an edible pond lily, when there are enough to harvest, so that Connelly can bake a potatoes-and-*wocus* bread. Someday it could be on a menu.

In a reimagined Klamath Basin economy, Indigenous and settler cultures alike renew the world. This complementarity would mirror the fusion of Western science and traditional ecological knowledge—the return of cultural fire, for example—in restoring the region's lands and waters.

The means exist for bringing this about. In the wake of dam removal, money from various sources, including foundations and federal agencies, is available to restore the region. It can provide incentives for farmers and ranchers to keep fertilizer out of waterways. It can fund the region's transformation to green energy. It can invest in businesses that cater to a new wave of ecotourists and outdoor sports enthusiasts.

There are three precedents for coordinating change along these lines.

First of all, consequential collaboration between the government agencies that manage most of the land in the Klamath Basin occurred as they negotiated the KBRA and the KHSA. That can continue. The federal government has an interagency fire center in Boise. Why not establish a regional interagency center in Klamath Falls?

Second, symposia occur every year or two in the region, bringing together scientists, agency officials, and stakeholders. Regular meetings of this kind are necessary to guide the adaptive management on which the long-term success of restoration will depend. No less valuable is the Basin-wide public space they establish for citizen participation.

Finally, friendships have developed during the years of negotiating regional agreements, and there are lifelong friendships between tribal members and non-Indians who, together, protect their communities from wildfires and bring intentional fire back to the land. Racism is endemic to the region, but it need not prevail. Cultural diversity generates creativity, enlarged understanding, and, potentially, shared prosperity.

The combined efforts of agencies, scientists, citizens, and friends may not realize the full potential of what is possible here. Yet they can redeem the troubled history of the Klamath Basin and improve their quality of life as members of a community that encompasses the lands, waters, and wildlife of their beautiful home.

Acknowledgments

It has been fifty years since I first visited the Klamath Basin. More people have educated me about that region than I can remember, much less thank.

Originally, the request by historian Bill Lang that I write a history of the Klamath Basin encouraged me to take on this task. The interest Marianne Keddington-Lang of the Oregon Historical Society had in publishing it gave me confidence that the text would be edited well. Marianne's colleague Cara Ungar supported my research by hiring me to write a history of the Klamath Basin for The Oregon Encyclopedia.

Others who have aided this book project are my agent, Mike Hamilburg; Eliza Canty-Jones of the Oregon Historical Society; Pat Soden, Julidta Tarver, and Lorri Hagman of the University of Washington Press, which published the first edition; and Tom Booth, Kim Hogeland, Micki Reaman, and Katherine White of Oregon State University Press, publisher of the second edition. Teresa Jesionowski copyedited the manuscript thoroughly and thoughtfully.

Carlos Bolado, Jack Kohler, Michael Pryfogle, Gabriela Quiros, Gerrid Joy, and other members of the documentary production team traveled with me throughout the Klamath Basin setting up and recording many of the interviews I use in these pages. Rhonda Collins, the film's editor, contributed crucial insights on how to tell the story of the region. My thanks also to everyone who granted me an interview.

The oral history of the Mattz family that Helene Oppenheimer recorded has been invaluable. My thanks to her and to the Mattz family members Helene and I have been fortunate to know.

Among those who have helped me, in one way or another, do the research that made this book possible are Elizabeth Azzuz, Diane Bowers, Lavina Bowers, James Bryant, Bob Chadwick, Edison and Leatha Chiloquin, Nolan Colegrove, Mike Connelly, Lynn Decker, Steve and

Ann Dunsky, Dave Felstul, Troy Fletcher, Timothy J. Foley, Merv George Jr., Will Harling, Leaf Hillman, Mary Huffman, the Karuk Tribal Council, Todd Kepple, Efrem Korngold, Amy Lim, Andy Love, Ted McArthur, Barry McCovey, Jenny McCovey, Liz McDonough, Matt Mais, Kendall Manock, Susan Bowers Masten, Geneva Mattz, Raymond Mattz, Jeff Mitchell, Mike Neuman, Helene Oppenheimer, Brad Parrish, Ronnie Pierce, Jodie Pixley, Ron Reed, Richard Roos-Collins, John Salter, Paul Simmons, Kenneth Smith, Alan Snitow, Michael Sterns, Michelle Stevens, Erica Terence, Charlie Thom, Bryan Tilt, Bill Tripp, Emilio Tripp, Craig Tucker, Desirée Tullos, Geneva Wiki, Tiana Williams, Janet Wortman, and Charlie Wright.

Kevin White traveled with me through the Klamath Basin while I did research for the second edition. His companionship and insights were invaluable.

I am deeply appreciative of those who read and commented on portions of the text while I was writing it: Zuretti Goosby, Kelly Catlett, Susan Bowers Masten, Malcolm North, Ron Reed, Linda Strean, Craig Tucker, Kevin White, and Marilyn Vihman.

Claire Schoen read and critiqued the first complete draft of both the first and second editions. Those were not her only contributions. Claire endured my many trips to the Klamath Basin both for the documentary and for this book. I was happy to hear her say, after working through the original manuscript, "I'm glad you did this."

Notes and Sources

In writing this book, I drew from histories of the West, including Richard White's *It's Your Misfortune and None of My Own*; histories of the Pacific Northwest, including Carlos Schwantes's *The Pacific Northwest* and William G. Robbins's *Landscapes of Promise*; and books about places in the Klamath Basin and events that have occurred there. *The Years of Harvest* by Stan Turner tells the story of the Tule Lake Basin. *Balancing Water* by William Kittredge is a photo essay, accompanying photographs by Tupper Ansel Blake, that conveys some of the history of the Upper Basin. Rachel Applegate Good's *The History of Klamath County, Oregon* is another useful source. Theodore Stern's *The Klamath Tribe: A People and Their Reservation* is a historical work by an anthropologist, published after the termination of that reservation.

The most famous event in Klamath history is the Modoc War. That has been the subject of a number of books, including A. B. Meacham's nineteenth-century *Wigwam and Warpath*, Richard Dillon's twentieth-century *Burnt-Out Fires*, and Boyd Cothran's *Remembering the Modoc War*, published in 2014.

Historical books about the people who live on or near the Klamath River and downstream from the Upper Basin are few. A self-published two-volume history, *Sandspit*, by Francesca Fryer has useful information about Yurok history. The Hupa Tribe published their history, *Our Home Forever*. Hupa historian Jack Norton's book, *Genocide in Northwestern California: When Our Worlds Cried*, recounts events that were long ignored by California historians. Notable exceptions are *Western Siskiyou County: Gold and Dreams*, by Gail Fiorini-Jenner and Monica Jae Hall, which was published in 2002, and Benjamin Madley's *An American Genocide: The United States and the California Indian Catastrophe*, published in 2016.

Many articles about aspects of Klamath Basin history are available. When they are related to specific information in the text, they are cited in the notes below; other articles I have read are not referenced. The most useful troves of articles about Upper Basin events are the *Journal of the Shaw Historical Library* and the *Oregon Historical Quarterly*. An excellent collection of articles on downriver history appeared in the Bicentennial edition of the *Del Norte Triplicate*, published on July 4, 1976. Additional articles that appeared in the *San Francisco Chronicle*, the *San Francisco Examiner*, and other newspapers or in such books as *California's Salmon and Steelhead*, edited by Alan Lufkin, are referenced below.

To a large extent, I have drawn from unpublished sources in writing this book, which has evolved over a half century of intermittent experiences in the Klamath Basin. A brief account of my own personal and professional history is necessary in order to clarify what my sources are and, in the case of interviews and oral histories, how I obtained them.

The people of the Klamath have interested me ever since 1961, when I read Erik H. Erikson's essay about the Yuroks in *Childhood and Society*. Ten years later, after *Poe*, my first work as a professional playwright, was produced in Chicago, I decided to write a play about the Modoc War. Dee Brown's *Bury My Heart at Wounded Knee* inspired that idea. His chapter on the Modoc War revealed that many of the original sources are in dialogue form. In 1973, I was writing *Medicine Show*, working from century-old participants' memoirs, negotiation records, and trial transcripts, when an event similar in many ways to the Modoc War occurred in South Dakota: the occupation and siege of Wounded Knee. I covered that event as a reporter and wrote a three-part series of articles ("America's Longest War") for Pacific News Service. Then I moved to Klamath Falls, Oregon, to research the Modoc War from sources available there and at the Lava Beds National Monument.

During that six-month period, I became acquainted with Edison and Leatha Chiloquin. Part Modoc, Leatha was a great storyteller who had knowledge acquired through oral history of the war that occurred a century earlier. In 1976, I brought actors and a director who were researching a production of *Medicine Show* to meet the Chiloquins. It was during that visit that the sacred fire ceremony took place and the reinhabitation of Chief Chiloquin's village began. I wrote the story for Pacific News Service, *Akwesasne Notes*, and the *Oregon Times*.

In November 1978, during the "Salmon War," I returned to the Klamath Basin. At the time, I interviewed a number of people, including gillnetters, a Fish and Wildlife biologist, and a Bureau of Indian Affairs official. Most of my writing about that event, until this book, was for theater. Joining the Dell'Arte Players Company as their dramaturg in 1979 enabled me to move to Humboldt County and spend time along the Klamath River. One of the plays I wrote with that company, *Intrigue at Ah-Pah*, dramatizes the issues behind the Fish and Wildlife enforcement operation against Indian gillnetters.

Several years later, Helene Oppenheimer conducted a series of oral history interviews with members of the Mattz family. I did additional interviews with them as I researched a play, *Watershed*. Edited versions of the Oppenheimer interviews are in the oral history collection of the Bancroft Library.

An important influence on my thinking about the history of the Klamath Basin was work I did in the mid-1990s for the Washington State Historical Society. Guided by chief curator Maria Pascualy and historian Bill Lang, I wrote the texts, videos, and audio voices for the permanent exhibit of the WSHS museum in downtown Tacoma. That work added to my knowledge of the Pacific Northwest, of which the Klamath Basin is the southernmost part, and I also learned an approach to American history that includes geology as well as geography, draws from oral histories of people from diverse communities, and portrays American Indians as participants in contemporary as well as pre-twentieth-century events. David Nicandri, director of the Washington State Historical Society, gave me the opportunity to write about his museum's representation of history in a book commemorating its opening, *In the Presence of the Past: The Washington State History Museum*.

By that time, I was scripting documentary films, many on historical subjects. In 2000, I decided to write and produce a documentary about the Klamath River. My original subject was the controversy over the decline of salmon that came to a head in 1978, when the Fish and Wildlife Service attacked gillnetters at the mouth of the Klamath. But when the Bucket Brigade occurred in 2001, the documentary's frame of reference widened. Farmers and ranchers of the Upper Basin were blamed for the decline of wild salmon, and their livelihood, like that of gillnetters, suffered as a result. Two things were clear: the Klamath Basin had to be looked at as a whole, and the resource conflicts there had to be considered in their historical context.

It also became evident that a documentary film could not adequately convey that historical context. A book was needed. And due to the scarcity of published sources for such a history, interviews conducted for the documentary could provide essential information and relevant perspectives. That has been the case. Interviews with farmers, ranchers, scientists, sports and offshore fishers, environmentalists, and tribal members, among others, have been invaluable sources for this book.

Not all of the interviews I have drawn from were done for *River of Renewal*, the documentary. In 2003, I wrote for Cara Ungar of the Oregon Historical Society a forty-page history of the Klamath Basin that appears in the online Oregon Encyclopedia. Research for that text provided an opportunity to meet a number of ranchers and farmers, a Bureau of Reclamation historian, and the director of the Klamath Water Users Association. Transcripts of those interviews, interviews for the documentary, and the Oppenheimer oral history are archived at the Oregon Historical Society Research Library.

In 2004, when I was scripting the documentary film history of the U.S. Forest Service, *The Greatest Good*, I made another research trip to the Klamath Basin. On that occasion I interviewed Forest Service supervisors, rangers, and scientists, including Sue Mattenberger, formerly a Forest Service hydrologist, who headed the Ecosystem Restoration Office for the Fish and Wildlife Service in Klamath Falls. Those conversations contributed to my understanding of the geology and hydrology of the Klamath Basin, the condition of its forests after a century of fire suppression, and the status of restoration projects in the Upper Basin. In addition, because approximately 60 percent of the Klamath Basin is national forest, what I learned about the Forest Service while writing *The Greatest Good* with director and producer Steve Dunsky gave me a national perspective on some aspects of Klamath history.

Other sources that I have drawn from are notes I took when experiencing events in that history. These events include visits to the Chiloquins' traditional village on the Sprague River, two Klamath Basin Fish and Water Management Symposia, and the 2005 stakeholders' meeting in Chiloquin.

The research and production-trip journals that I wrote when making the documentary have also served as sources for this book. *River of Renewal* premiered in 2008, two years after the publication of the first edition. During those years, the Klamath Basin tribes waged a campaign to pressure PacifiCorp to eliminate the hydroelectric dams on the Klamath River. The film's last scene shows an Undam the Klamath demonstration in Omaha.

Wilder Than Wild: Fire, Forests, and the Future, a documentary I coproduced with Kevin White, gave me an opportunity to learn firsthand about the revival of cultural fire by the Klamath River tribes. Following community screenings of the film, online and in person, Yurok and Karuk fire lighters participated in a number of panels, further educating and inspiring me along with our audiences. To see *River of Renewal* and *Wilder Than Wild*, visit https://www.videoproject.org/stories. There are chapters about the making of both documentaries in my book *Stories Make the World: Reflections on Storytelling and the Art of the Documentary*.

The impetus for this second edition was the certainty that dam removal and the restoration of wildlife habitat it makes possible would occur in the Klamath Basin. To research this breakthrough, Kevin White and I traveled through the Klamath Basin, from Requa to Orleans and from Klamath Falls to Chiloquin.

A history that draws so heavily on interviews, oral histories, and experiences as this one depends to some extent on serendipity. Of necessity, there were many people I did not meet or could not interview. Had I done so, I would have encountered different perspectives on the history of the Klamath Basin. People who have made important contributions to Klamath history, Indian and non-Indian, may feel unjustly overlooked.

To compensate for the attention in this book to the individuals, families, and communities my production team visited and whom I got to know on other occasions, and also to allow the history of the Klamath Basin to grow and not be a closed book, I encourage readers to submit oral histories, remembrances, reports, and other archival material to the Oregon Historical Society Research Library. Those contributions to the story of the Klamath Basin will be available along with much of the material I used, and that whole collection will be an invaluable resource for future researchers.

What follows are specific notes for each chapter.

OPENING QUOTATIONS

- Wallace Stegner, *Beyond the Hundredth Meridian* (Lincoln: University of Nebraska Press, 1952), 134.
- Czeslaw Milosz, *A Treatise on Poetry* (New York: Ecco Press, 2001), 99–100.

PREFACE

- Zane Grey in *Outdoor America* (Isaac Walton League of America), January 1924.
- Richard White, *The Organic Machine: The Remaking of the Columbia River* (New York: Hill and Wang, 1995). In this book, White "examine[s] the river as an organic machine, as an energy system which, although modified by human interventions, maintains its natural, its 'unmade' qualities" (p. ix).
- Marjory Stoneman Douglas, *Everglades: River of Grass* (New York: Rinehart, 1947), 8.
- Hannah Arendt, *Essays in Understanding, 1930–1954* (New York: Harcourt Brace, 1994), 323.
- E. O. Wilson, *The Future of Life* (New York: Knopf, 2002), 40.
- David Rains Wallace, *The Klamath Knot* (San Francisco: Sierra Club Books, 1983), 13. Naturalist David Rains Wallace uses the term "Klamath" to refer to a "knot" of several mountain ranges. Of these, perhaps the richest in biodiversity is the Siskiyou Range of northern California and southern Oregon, which became a refuge for species fleeing glaciation. Only the southernmost slopes of the Siskiyou fall within the Klamath drainage. Other naturalists define the mountains as the Klamath-Siskiyou ranges.
- *National Geographic* quote at http://www.nationalgeographic.com/wildworld/ profiles/terrestrial/na/na0516.html (accessed July 25, 2006).
- Jim Lichatowich, *Salmon without Rivers: A History of the Pacific Salmon Crisis* (Washington, D.C.: Island Press, 1999), 6.
- A. L. Kroeber and Edward W. Gifford, *World Renewal: A Cult System of Native Northwest California* (Berkeley: University of California Press, 1949).

INTRODUCTION

- John Muir on Shasta quoted in *Son of the Wilderness: The Life of John Muir* by Linnie Marsh Wolfe (Madison: University of Wisconsin Press, 1945), 177.
- Joaquin Miller, *Life amongst the Modocs* (Berkeley, Calif.: Heyday Books/ Urion Press, 1996), 1, 12.
- On Lemurians, see Philip Fradkin, *The Seven States of California* (New York: Henry Holt, 1995), 115–117.
- On the Mount Shasta creation story, see Miller, *Life amongst the Modocs*, 236.
- On LaPérouse and the eruption of Shasta, see Fradkin, *Seven States of California*, 118.
- Jack Kohler played "Rick," a character in *Watershed* based on Raymond Mattz, during the Turtle Island Ensemble/ Tale Spinners Theater production in 1993.

- The Biological Opinions that moved the Bureau of Reclamation to curtail Klamath Project irrigation in 2001 were issued by the U.S. Fish and Wildlife Service on April 5, and the National Marine Fisheries Service on April 6, 2001.
- Steve Kandra and Jeff Boyd are quoted in the *Sacramento Bee*, April 21, 2001.
- William Kittredge, *Balancing Water: Restoring the Klamath Basin* (Berkeley: University of California Press, 2000), 89.
- Kittredge, *Balancing Water*, 39. His list of fishing methods is taken word for word from Theodore Stern, *The Klamath Tribe: A People and Their Reservation* (Seattle: University of Washington Press, 1965), 12.
- The photo of Jack Kohler's grandmother appeared in the February 1948 issue of *National Geographic*.
- According to an article by Nick Schutz in the Klamath Falls daily, the *Herald and News*, May 6, 2001, Doug Boyd, Bob Gasser, Patsy Gasser, and Chris Moudry initiated the Bucket Brigade. Boyd is a partner in a John Deere dealership; Bob Gasser and Chris Moudry are co-owners of Basin Fertilizer. Helping to organize the event was the Klamath Water Users Association. According to Schutz, "The idea for a bucket brigade developed along the lines of other grassroots efforts to stand up to government, including a case in Nevada where individuals cleaned up a road closed to vehicle use." (See Chapter 17 for more on the Nevada Shovel Brigade.)

  Aiding the organizers of the Bucket Brigade were public relations professionals for the wise use movement. Prior to the Bucket Brigade, this movement launched a public relations campaign aimed at discrediting environmentalists, using defamatory epithets like "eco-nazis" and "communists"—whatever smear was effective. Interviewed in the magazine *Outside* in 1991, Ron Arnold, one of the founders, said, "Facts don't matter; in politics perception is reality." See Sheldon Rampton, "Fish Out of Water: Behind the Wise Use Movement's Victory in Klamath," *PR Watch*, 10:2, Second Quarter 2003.

CHAPTER ONE

- Jeff LaLande, *First Over the Siskiyous: Peter Skene Ogden's 1826–1827 Journey through the Oregon-California Borderlands* (Portland: Oregon Historical Society Press, 1987), 10.
- The section of the Columbia River called the Cascades is a two-and-a-half-mile stretch of rapids about forty miles below The Dalles. Robert H. Ruby and John A. Brown, *Indians of the Pacific Northwest: A History* (Norman: University of Oklahoma Press, 1981), 21.
- The immensity of the pre-twentieth-century lakes in the Upper Basin and perhaps even of the great lake that once comprised the Klamath Lakes and Tule Lake combined may be the source of the idea in traditional Yurok geography that their world is surrounded by ocean, one shore of which is the source of the Klamath River. See T. T. Waterman, "Yurok Geographical Concepts," in *The California Indians: A Source Book*, ed. R. F. Heizer and M. A. Whipple (Berkeley: University of California Press, 1972), 475.

- Barry Lopez, *Crossing Open Ground* (New York: Vintage, 1989), 21.
- The story of Mount Mazama and the battle between the chiefs is found in Douglas Deur, "A Most Sacred Place: The Significance of Crater Lake among the Indians of Southern Oregon," *Oregon Historical Quarterly* 103, no. 1 (Spring 2002): 18–49.
- Theodore Stern, *The Klamath Tribe: A People and Their Reservation* (Seattle: University of Washington Press, 1965), 2.
- Edison and Leatha Chiloquin, *Return of the Raven* (self-published booklet, 1974).
- On houses built on the water, see Ruby and Brown, *Indians of the Pacific Northwest*, 53.
- Alfred Louis Kroeber, *Handbook of the Indians of California* (Washington, D.C.: Government Printing Office, 1925), 329–331.
- On "chipmunk" name and animal deities, see Chiloquin, *Return of the Raven*.
- Verne F. Ray, *Primitive Pragmatists: The Modoc Indians of Northern California* (Seattle: University of Washington Press, 1963), xii.
- Theodore Stern is my source on Klamath shamanism.
- I am indebted to a Peruvian *curandero*, the late Eduardo Calderón, for instruction in the art of shamanic healing as practiced in northern Peru. See Douglas Sharon, *Wizard of the Four Winds: A Shaman's Story* (New York: Free Press, 1978), and my chapter about Calderón in *Stories Make the World: Reflections on Storytelling and the Art of the Documentary* (New York: Berghahn Books, 2017).
- Jenny Clinton quoted in Ray, *Primitive Pragmatists*, 68.
- The historian of religions Huston Smith came to realize that his studies of what he had considered *The World's Religions* (San Francisco: Harper, 1994) merely scratched the surface of humanity's religious experience (personal communication with the author). In the preface to the second edition, he writes: "For the bulk of human history, religion was lived in tribal and virtually timeless mode" (xiii). While some tribes have hierarchical priest-based religious practices, in the majority of known tribes, individuals, whether they are called shamans, psychopomps, or *curanderos*, serve as religious leaders. In the title of an anthology, poet Jerome Rothenberg calls them *Technicians of the Sacred* (Garden City, N.Y.: Doubleday, 1968).

    While the world religions are thousands of years old or, in the case of Islam, more than a thousand, the shamanic tradition reaches back tens of thousands of years. Evidence of that tradition is found from caves of southern Africa and southern Europe to the rock paintings of aboriginal Australia. Cave art was almost certainly perceived as magical, inspiring awe and instilling courage. Look, for example, at what appears to be an altar in the Chauvet cave, where a bear skull was placed on the edge of a stone block. See Jean-Marie Chauvet, *Dawn of Art: The Chauvet Cave* (New York: H. N. Abrams, 1996), 59.

    Although one can only speculate about cultural activities in times so long ago, it seems likely that the role of the shaman developed during the great migrations that early humans made, traveling within Africa and populating the other continents. The shamanic powers to foretell the future; to conjure up spirits of the dead; to discover medicinal plants; to heal the sick; to transform oneself into an animal and be guided by animals; to lead people in ceremonies that raise their spirits and compel belief—these are exactly what primeval human bands needed to survive during long migrations and to adapt to unfamiliar environments.

- This power song is found in Chiloquin, *Return of the Raven*, 16.
- The anthropologist A. L. Kroeber preserved the healing song of a Modoc doctor. It begins:

> What do I remove from my mouth?
> The disease I remove from my mouth.
> What do I take out?
> The disease I take out.
> What do I suck out?
> The disease I suck out.
> What do I blow about?
> The disease I blow about.

- Kroeber, *Handbook of the Indians of California*, 321.
- From Malcolm Margolin, ed., *The Way We Lived: California Indian Reminiscences, Stories, and Songs* (Berkeley, Calif.: Heyday Books, 1981), 115.
- Mircea Eliade, *Shamanism: Archaic Techniques of Ecstasy* (Princeton, N.J.: Princeton University Press, 1972), 160–165.
- The Book of Ezekiel 37:1–8.
- I researched the Big Sick for the Washington State History Museum. The permanent exhibit has a diorama dedicated to that calamity.
- Jay Miller, ed., *Mourning Dove: A Salishan Autobiography* (Lincoln: University of Nebraska Press, 1990), 15–16.
- Chiloquin is quoted in Stern, *The Klamath Tribe*, 23.
- Ray, *Primitive Pragmatists*, 145. Ray is my source on Modoc warfare.
- Slavery is a practice that has occurred in human societies of many different kinds, taking different forms over thousands of years. The personal servant, usually a war captive, who was the slave of a Roman citizen; the slave who worked lands owned by a Russian noble and who, like his master, could be sent by the tsar to fight Mongols and other invaders; the domestics who served the households of rich merchants in the city-states of Southeast Asia between 1000 and 1700 CE—all led lives quite unlike those of the captive Africans and their descendants whose forced labor on plantations in the Americas gave the word "slave" its meaning in the history of this continent.
- The Pit River are two related tribes, the Achomawi and the Atsegui. They received their contemporary name from non-Indians after the pits they dug to trap game.
- Andrew Bard Schmookler, *The Parable of the Tribes: The Problem of Power in Social Evolution* (Berkeley: University of California Press, 1984).
- LaLande, *First Over the Siskiyous*, 23, 25, 40.

CHAPTER TWO

- The figure of more than 50,000 emigrants who traveled the Oregon Trail comes from Carlos A. Schwantes, *The Pacific Northwest: An Interpretative History* (Lincoln: University of Nebraska Press, 1989), 86.
- Whitman quote from Richard White, *"It's Your Misfortune and None of My Own": A History of the American West* (Norman: University of Oklahoma Press, 1991), 72.
- John L. O'Sullivan, "The Great Nation of Futurity," *The United States Democratic Review* 6, no. 23 (1839): 426–430.
- On the meeting of Frémont and Carson, see Tom Chaffin, *Pathfinder: John Charles Frémont and the Course of American Empire* (New York: Hill and Wang, 2002), 101–102.
- On the Applegates in Missouri, see Dorothy O. Johansen, *Empire of the Columbia: A History of the Pacific Northwest* (New York: Harper & Row, 1957), 255.
- On the Applegates' emigration, see Ferol Egan, *Frémont: Explorer for a Restless Nation* (Garden City, N.Y.: Doubleday, 1977), 168.
- On the sounding of the howitzer and the Frémont and Carson encounter with the Klamath chief and his wife, see Chaffin, *Pathfinder*, 195.
- Frémont quote on Klamath village in Egan, *Frémont*, 186.
- For Carson's account of meeting the Klamath, see Harvey Lewis, *"Dear Old Kit": The Historical Christopher Carson* (Norman: University of Oklahoma Press, 1968), 89.
- John Charles Frémont, *Narrative of Exploration and Adventure*, ed. Alan Nevins (New York: Longmans, Green, 1956), 505–506.
- Robert H. Ruby and John A. Brown, *Indians of the Pacific Northwest: A History* (Norman: University of Oklahoma Press, 1981), 106.
- Theodore Stern, *The Klamath Tribe: A People and Their Reservation* (Seattle: University of Washington Press, 1965), 25.
- Keith A. Murray, *The Modocs and Their War* (Norman: University of Oklahoma Press, 1959), 41.
- Indians throughout the Pacific Northwest called all of the non-Indian intruders by the same name, *Boston*. Edward Harper Thomas, *Chinook: A History and Dictionary of the Northwest Coast Trade Jargon* (Portland, Ore.: Binfords & Mort, 1935), 109. The term must have entered the lexicon of the Chinook trading jargon in 1792, when Capt. Robert Gray's ship, the *Columbia*, hailing from Boston Harbor and manned by New Englanders, became the first to sail up the river where the Chinook lived.
- The Modocs' flight from the surveying party is described in Murray, *The Modocs and Their War*, 16.
- Murray, *The Modocs and Their War*, 20–31, is my major source for the story of Ben Wright.

• See Richard Dillon, *Burnt-Out Fires* (Englewood Cliffs, N.J.: Prentice-Hall, 1973), 54, for the information about payments to vigilantes by California and for another version of the story of Wright's death in which Enos massacred Wright along with twenty-five others at Gold Beach.

CHAPTER THREE

• The description of Fort Klamath comes from Buena Cobb Stone, *Fort Klamath* (Dallas: Royal, 1964).
• Jeff Mitchell, interviewed by the author, March 7, 2003.
• Keith A. Murray, *The Modocs and Their War* (Norman: University of Oklahoma Press, 1959), is a source for my account of the events leading up to the Modoc War.
• See Richard Dillon, *Burnt-Out Fires* (Englewood Cliffs, N.J.: Prentice-Hall, 1973), for Ivan Applegate's experience at Bloody Point (50), Miller's remark about the Modocs (120), and the orders Odeneal received from the Commissioner of Indian Affairs (126).
• The Boutelle/Scarfaced Charley exchange is recounted in Jeff Riddle, *Indian History of the Modoc War and the Causes That Led to It* (Eugene, Ore.: Urion Press, 1974), 45, and in Dillon, *Burnt-Out Fires*, 137.
• Hannah Arendt, *Essays in Understanding, 1930–1954* (New York: Harcourt Brace, 1994), 308.
• My source for Curley Headed Doctor's prediction of fog was Leatha Chiloquin. She was a Modoc married to Edison Chiloquin, who was a grandson of the Klamath Chief Chiloquin. Leatha knew oral histories of the Modoc War that had passed through her family. She spoke to me about the war on a number of occasions in 1973–1974 and during a visit to the lava beds in 1976.
• For a discussion of Kant's "enlarged mentality," see Hannah Arendt, *Lectures on Kant's Political Philosophy* (Chicago: University of Chicago Press, 1982), 40–44.
• A. B. Meacham recalls the meeting with Captain Jack in *Wigwam and Warpath; or, The Royal Chief in Chains*, 2nd ed. (Boston: J. P. Dale, 1875), 447–451.
• I. F. Stone, "Holy War," *New York Review of Books* 9:2 (August 3, 1967).
• *Remembering the Modoc War* by Boyd Cothran (Chapel Hill: University of North Carolina Press, 2014) recounts Daring Donald McKay's medicine show and A. B. Meacham's lecture tour.

CHAPTER FOUR

• For a comparison of the paleolithic, agrarian and modern humans with respect to duration, population numbers, and life expectancy, see David Christian, *Maps of Time* (Berkeley: University of California Press, 2004), 208.
• Jared Diamond, *Guns, Germs and Steel: The Fates of Human Societies* (New York: W. W. Norton 1997), 196.
• Rachel Applegate Good, *The History of Klamath County, Oregon* (Klamath Falls, Ore.: Klamath County Historical Society, 1941), 63.

- For the story of the growth of the timber industry in Klamath County after the first railroad came through Klamath Falls in 1909, and on the Klamath Tribes and the timber industry, see Good, *History of Klamath County*, 25–27, 91.
- H. D. Mortenson, president of Pelican Bay Lumber Company, quoted in Good, *History of Klamath County*, 116.
- For an account of pre–Klamath Project water works in the Klamath Basin, see Lawrence W. Powers, ed., *A River Never the Same: A History of Water in the Klamath Basin* (Klamath Falls, Ore.: Shaw Historical Library, 1999).
- Finley is quoted in William Kittredge, *Balancing Water: Restoring the Klamath Basin* (Berkeley: University of California Press, 2000), 75.
- Rachel Carson, *Silent Spring* (Boston: Houghton Mifflin, 1962), 45–46.
- Richard White, *"It's Your Misfortune and None of My Own": A History of the American West* (Norman: University of Oklahoma Press, 1991), is a good source on the federalization of the American West.
- The story of the Czech colonists is told in a self-published book by Joe Zumpfe and Vlasta Petrik of the Czech Colonization Club, *Settling of Southern Klamath County* (Malin, Ore.: the authors, 1985).
- Stan Turner, *The Years of Harvest: A History of the Tule Lake Basin* (Eugene, Ore.: 49th Avenue Press, 1987), 187, is my source on the early conditions home-steaders endured and on the Tule Lake Community Club.
- Ann E. Huston, "A History of the Lower Klamath National Wildlife Refuge," in *A River Never the Same*, 64.
- Finley quoted in Kittredge, *Balancing Water*, 79.
- Curt Meine and Richard L, Knight, eds., *The Essential Aldo Leopold: Quotations and Commentaries* (Madison: University of Wisconsin Press, 1999), 305.
- The estimate of seven million birds migrating through the Klamath Basin comes from a 1956 U.S. Fish and Wildlife report.
- Carson, *Silent Spring*, 45.

CHAPTER FIVE

- For oral histories of Mattz family members, see the Mattz Family Interviews conducted by Helene H. Oppenheimer, BANC MSS 94/92, Bancroft Library of the University of California, Berkeley (hereafter Mattz Family Interviews).
- Petsulo of Pekwon's creation story is found in A. L. Kroeber, *Yurok Myths* (Berkeley: University of California Press, 1976), 412.
- Lucy Thompson (Che-na-wah Weitch-ah-wah), a Yurok born in the village of Pekwan in 1853, tells a story of a long migration westward and to the south by Yurok ancestors in her book *To the American Indian* (Berkeley, Calif.: Heyday Books, 1991), 76–78. "We know not how many centuries we wandered, or when we reached our last stopping place on the Klamath River, and where we decided our long journey should end, and that we would make this our final home."
- The name of Rekwoi is identified as singing and speaking to (and from) the salmon by Kroeber's informant Billy Werk of Weitspus. Kroeber, *Yurok Myths*, 250.

• In her oral history interviews with Helene Oppenheimer, Geneva Mattz told a story about Captain Spott's upbringing. He was an illegitimate child. His mother was a cousin of her grandmother, Susie Brooks. His father, having two girlfriends who were pregnant at the same time, chose to marry the one who was from his own tribe. Because the people of Rekwoi didn't want illegitimate children, they allowed a baby born out of marriage to be killed, and two brothers did come hunting for the infant in order to kill him. "They looked all over, knocked everything over inside, behind the baskets and things. The grammas had put him in the creek where the water was deep in the spring of the year, early spring, where the water was still running heavy and making noise. They couldn't hear the little baby cry. . . . So they went back." Because it was the law that only one attempt to do away with an illegitimate child could be made, the boy grew up.

   Spott had a clubfoot, which prevented him from working like other men. "And he always felt sorry for himself because he didn't have a father. And he started training; he started going to the hills." By this, Geneva Mattz meant that he prayed and fasted and walked the spiritual trails in the high country, as priests do and as young people do in traditional Yurok culture when they prepare for a ceremony, acquire power as a doctor, and seek wealth. Spott did more than walk and pray. He learned to gamble from non-Indians as well as from Indians and became expert at it. "He was a famous man by the time he was middle-aged. He won money. He won the Indian costume; he won horses; he won buggies and saddles. He had everything."

• Robert Spott and A. L. Kroeber, *Yurok Narratives* (Berkeley: University of California Press, 1942), v.

• The story of Robert Spott's relationship with Kroeber is told in Francesca Fryer, *Sandspit: A Redwood Northcoast Notebook* (Los Gatos, Calif.: the author, 1995), 165–171.

• Theodora Kroeber wrote about Spott's service in France and his friendship with her and her husband in *Alfred Kroeber: A Personal Configuration* (Berkeley: University of California Press, 1979).

• The story of Requa Fanny meeting her first non-Indian is in Spott and Kroeber, *Yurok Narratives*, 206.

• See the diary of Fray Miguel de la Campa in Robert F. Heizer and John E. Mills, eds., *The Four Ages of Tsurai: A Documentary History of the Indian Village on Trinidad Bay* (Berkeley: University of California Press, 1942), 38.

• The Hupa account of the killing of the woman from Rekwoi is told in Byron Nelson, *Our Home Forever: A Hupa Tribal History* (Hoopa, Calif.: Hupa Tribe, 1978), 27. This is the first recorded instance of a conflict between different groups in the Klamath Basin motivated by scarcity of wild salmon.

• There is a poison that was used in traditional ceremonies, including the first salmon rite. It may have been angelica root. This medicine is believed to cause starvation, but under the right circumstances, when the root "becomes hungry and travels," it can bring abundance.

- What the woman from Rekwoi probably said to the Hupa men was that they were "badly born." This is the translation of "Woo-saw-ah" given by Lucy Thompson in *To the American Indian*, on page 66. She said that this insult is accompanied by a hand gesture with fingers extended, adding that those who are insulted in this manner "never forgive you for this."
- For Yurok terminology about who they are and were see Thomas Buckley, *Standing Ground: Yurok Indian Spirituality, 1850–1990* (Berkeley: University of California Press, 2002), 6–7.
- The federal government would define who the "Yuroks" are again in the Yurok-Hupa Settlement Act of 1986. (See Chapter 9.)
- Stephen Powers, *Tribes of California* (Berkeley: University of California Press, 1976), 51.
- See Kroeber, *Alfred Kroeber*, 55.
- "Carl Meyer's Account of the Indians of Trinidad Bay in 1851," in *The Four Ages of Tsurai*, ed. Robert F. Heizer and John E. Mills (Trinidad, Calif.: Trinidad Museum Society, 1991).

CHAPTER SIX

- See Joaquin Miller, *Life amongst the Modocs* (Berkeley, Calif.: Heyday Books/Urion Press, 1996), 90.
- The surgeon's report on the harm done to the rivers by mining is included in the October 5, 1993, Interior Department Solicitor's opinion regarding "Fishing Rights of the Yurok and Hoopa Valley Tribes."
- The story of Klamath City was compiled from "Lower Klamath Country" by Frances T. McBeth and published in the Bicentennial Edition of the *Del Norte Triplicate*, July 4, 1976 (hereafter *Del Norte Triplicate* Bicentennial Edition), on pages 17 and 40.
- Newspaper articles concerning the war of extermination are compiled in Robert Fleming Heizer, *The Destruction of California Indians* (Santa Barbara, Calif.: Peregrine Smith, 1954). The Sacramento editorial appears on pages 35–36.
- My source for the information about non-Yurok tribes marched to the Klamath River reservation is Jack Norton, *Genocide in Northwestern California: When Our Worlds Cried* (San Francisco: Indian Historian Press, 1978), 74, 90.
- The account of battles on the lagoon and the Smith River massacre are reprinted in the *Del Norte Triplicate* Bicentennial Edition, 18.
- Commissioner Robert J. Stevens and Special Agent Paris Folsom are quoted in Appendix B of the Solicitor's opinion on pages B-6 and B-8.
- On the decline of California's native population, see Jack Forbes, *Native Americans of California and Nevada* (Happy Camp, Calif.: Naturegraph, 1982), 77.
- Yuroks did have a system of slavery, but one quite different from that of Euramerican society. It was primarily a form of debt payment, compensating for the class division between wealthy and poor tribal members. When food was scarce, for example, a person could enter a wealthy household and work in

return for room and board. Sometimes a person who had to pay a doctor for services would slave for the person who paid the bill. Slaves from other tribes could be captured in war. The treatment of slaves varied from household to household, but generally they had the opportunity to buy their freedom.

- The quote on abducting Indian children comes from *Alta California*, October 2, 1854.
- In Norton, *Genocide in Northwestern California*, on page 61, an Austin Willey [*sic?*] is listed as the owner of an Indian boy for seventeen years.
- The Indian Indenture Act is published in Heizer, *Destruction of California Indians*, 220–226.
- On indentured slavery, see Forbes, *Native Americans of California and Nevada*, 79.
- The story of Requa is published in *Del Norte Triplicate* Bicentennial Edition, 34.
- Lucy Thompson, *To the American Indian* (Berkeley, Calif.: Heyday Books, 1991), 202–203, describes the stick game.
- The story of McGarvey's store is found in Thompson, *To the American Indian*, 1–15. McGarvey may have bought it from Captain David Snyder, a resident of Hoopa Valley.
- For the early history of the Klamath fishery, see Ronnie Pierce, "The Klamath River Fishery: Early History," in *California's Salmon and Steelhead*, ed. Alan Lufkin (Berkeley: University of California Press, 1991). The quote is on page 43. Pierce also told me that history in a videotaped interview that, for technical reasons, was not broadcast quality and was not transcribed.
- The cannery story is in *Del Norte Triplicate* Bicentennial Edition, 103. The record is noted on page 116. The advent of machine-made cans is mentioned on page 132.
- The Upper Columbia River run of royal chinook became extinct soon after the building of the Grand Coulee Dam.
- For a description of the 1909 settlement act, see *Del Norte Triplicate* Bicentennial Edition, 45.
- Robert Spott spoke about Yuroks being refused good land and given instead "rocks and gravel" in his speech to San Francisco's Commonwealth Club. See Thomas Buckley, *Standing Ground: Yurok Indian Spirituality, 1850–1990* (Berkeley: University of California Press, 2002), 42.
- Simpson Timber began its operations on the Klamath with the purchase of the Coast Redwood Company in 1948.
- Kroeber, *Alfred Kroeber*, 54.
- I wrote a documentary film about Edward Curtis and his brother, Asahel Curtis, who was also a photographer. Titled *Different Lenses*, the half-hour program was produced by KCTS, Seattle's PBS station, in 1997.
- These photographs are published in Theodora Kroeber and Robert Heizer, *Almost Ancestors: The First Californians* (San Francisco: Sierra Club, 1968).

CHAPTER SEVEN

- On Requa in the 1920s, see Francesca Fryer, *Sandspit: A Redwood Northcoast Notebook* (Los Gatos, Calif.: the author, 1995), 63.
- The bridge dedication text is quoted in Fryer, *Sandspit*, 17–18.
- Zane Grey's visit is recounted in *Del Norte Triplicate* Bicentennial Edition, 152.
- On the closing of the canneries, see Ronnie Pierce, "The Klamath River Fishery: Early History," in *California's Salmon and Steelhead*, ed. Alan Lufkin (Berkeley: University of California Press, 1991), 142.
- Francesca Fryer writes about Harry Roberts, the white boy who learned Yurok traditions from Robert Spott, in *Sandspit*. See also Thomas Buckley, *Standing Ground: Yurok Indian Spirituality, 1850–1990* (Berkeley: University of California Press, 2002).
- See Geneva Mattz, interviewed by Helene Oppenheimer, September 25, 1984, Mattz Family Interviews.
- The photo of Kohler's grandmother appears in the February 1948 issue of *National Geographic*, but it was taken a decade earlier.
- Theodora Kroeber wrote about Fanny Flounder in *Alfred Kroeber: A Personal Configuration* (Berkeley: University of California Press, 1979).
- Erik H. Erikson's account of meeting Flounder appears in *Childhood and Society* (New York: Norton, 1950), 146–147. See also Erikson, "Observations of the Yurok: Childhood and World Image," in *A Way of Looking at Things: Selected Papers from 1930 to 1980* (New York: Norton, 1987), 377.
- Robert Spott and A. L. Kroeber, *Yurok Narratives* (Berkeley: University of California Press, 1942), 158.
- T. T. Waterman, "Yurok Geographical Concepts," in *The California Indians*, ed. R. F. Heizer and M. A. Whipple (Berkeley: University of California Press, 1971).
- Erikson, *Childhood and Society*, 144.
- The story of the Ah-Pah Dam project comes from Marc Reisner, *Cadillac Desert* (New York: Penguin, 1986), 267–270.
- The dialogue from Dad's camp comes from Fryer, *Sandspit*, 7, 16.
- The accounts of the floods of 1964 draws from Fryer, *Sandspit*, 105–117 and from *Del Norte Triplicate* Bicentennial Edition, 156, 196.

CHAPTER EIGHT

- The name of Brooks Riffle recalls traditional Yurok law in which families can own and acquire rights to fishing spots. Today the land by the riffle, or rapids, belongs to the Brookses' descendants. Raymond, Emery, and their siblings grew up on the allotment that Geneva Mattz received from her grandparents.
- The quotes by Raymond Mattz combine selections from his oral history interview with Helene Oppenheimer, Mattz Family Interviews, and from his interviews in 2000 and 2001 for the documentary.

- The interview with Lavina Bowers was conducted in 2001 for the documentary.
- See *Mattz v Arnett*, 93 S. Ct. 2245 (1973). G. Raymond Arnett was the game warden who arrested Raymond Mattz and confiscated the gill nets.
- The Kroeber quote comes from Thomas Buckley, *Standing Ground: Yurok Indian Spirituality, 1850–1990* (Berkeley: University of California Press, 2002), 13.
- Unpublished paper by Priscilla Locke, "After the Salmon War: The Commercial Fishing Rights of Yurok Indians on the Klamath River," 13.
- Ronnie Pierce, "Lower Klamath Fishery," in *California's Salmon and Steelhead*, ed. Alan Lufkin (Berkeley: University of California Press, 1991), 144.
- Richard McCovey, videotaped interview in 2001 for the documentary.
- Gary Rankle's report, published in March 1979, is called "Hoopa Valley Indian Reservation: Inventory of Reservation Waters, Fish Rearing and Feasibility Study, and Review of the History and Status of Anadromous Fishery Resources of the Klamath River Basin."
- The news articles I draw and quote from in my account of the Salmon War are an Associated Press report on August 26, 1978, published in the *San Francisco Chronicle*, and articles by Ivan Sharpe in the *San Francisco Examiner* on August 12, 30, and 31, and September 3, 8, 10, 13, and 21, 1978.
- Diane Whipple Mattz, interviewed by Helene Oppenheimer, October 29, 1956, Mattz Family Interviews.
- The C. R. Bavin memorandum to the director of Fish and Wildlife Service is dated January 22, 1979. Its reference code is FWS/LE ENF 1-04.
- Raymond Mattz's account of his confrontation with Andrus combines sentences from his oral history interview for Helene Oppenheimer in 1984 and from his research interview for the television documentary in 2001.
- Walter Benjamin, *Illuminations* (New York: Schocken, 1969), 89.

CHAPTER NINE

- Joseph E. Taylor III, *Making Salmon: An Environmental History of the Northwest Fisheries Crisis* (Seattle: University of Washington Press, 1999), 243.
- The Solicitor's opinion for the Secretary of the Interior, "Fishing Rights of the Yurok and Hoopa Valley Tribes," is the primary source for the tribe's legal history as told in this chapter.
- The Hoopa Valley Indian Reservation is one of the four reservations permitted in California under the law of 1864, although a number of small settlements called rancherias also sprang up in that state. On the roll of the reservation are Yuroks, Karoks, Hupas, and Indians of mixed tribal origins; some are part Shasta, part Wintun, and part Wiyot, to name only a few of the Northern California tribes represented there. To distinguish between constituents of the Hoopa Valley Tribal Council and members of the Hupa Tribe, I refer to the former as Hoopa, the latter as Hupa, as is the general practice among anthropologists and other writers. Not all Hoopa are Hupa, and there are also Hupa who are not

included on the Hoopa tribal roll. The homonym is unfortunately confusing, especially since, although the words do have different meanings, there is an overlap in the people referred to by those two terms.

- Judge Thelton Henderson is the subject of a documentary film by Abby Ginzberg titled *Soul of Justice*. At a reception following the premiere of that film, Judge Henderson remarked that the Jesse Short case was probably the lengthiest piece of litigation in U.S. history and that if his decision in the Puzz case helped to resolve its issues, he was glad for it.
- The U.S. District Court case is *Lillian Blake PUZZ, et al., Plaintiffs v. UNITED STATES, et al., Defendants*. No. C80-2908 TEH, United States District Court, N.D. California.
- The Hoopa-Yurok Settlement Act is Public Law 100-580 102 Stat. 2924.
- For two different views of the act, see Julian Lang, "The Hoopa-Yurok Settlement Act," *News from Native California* 2, no. 6 (January/February 1989): 8–11, and Susan Davis, "Tribal Rights, Tribal Wrongs," *The Nation* (March 23, 1992): 376–380.

    Although the Yuroks lost their right to sue under the Settlement Act, they did bring their grievances before the Senate Committee on Indian Affairs on August 1, 2002. Susan Bowers Masten, then chair of the Yurok Tribe, and Lyle Marshall, chair of the Hoopa Valley Tribal Council, both made presentations to the committee.

- The 1979 figures on the salmon fishery come from Zeke Grader's testimony at the Klamath River Indian Fishing Rights Oversight Hearings before the Subcommittee on Fisheries and Wildlife Conservation and the Environment of the Committee on Merchant Marine and Fisheries in the House of Representatives during the 96th Congress. Serial #96-11. Grader was executive director of the Pacific Coast Federation of Fishermen's Associations.
- In his testimony, Grader gave figures for the number of people affected by the decline of the commercial, offshore Klamath salmon fishery. In addition to the 7,000 men and women who fished from 4,000 trollers off the California coast, more than 70,000 people were employed processing and distributing those fish.
- Susan Bowers Masten, interviewed by Helene Oppenheimer, June 16, 1987, Mattz Family Interviews, and interviewed by Stephen Most, August 6, 2001, June 17, 2004, for the documentary.
- The Biological Opinions that led to the Klamath Project water cutoff were reconsidered in the "Interim Report from the Committee on Endangered and Threatened Fishes in the Klamath River Basin" (National Research Council, April 2002).
- Gale Norton's announcement appeared in a press release of the U.S. Department of the Interior, "Interior Secretary to Order Water Release to Klamath Farmers," July 24, 2001.

CHAPTER TEN

- My source for information about the Trinity River Division of the Central Valley Project is Judge Oliver Wanger's U.S. District Court decision in *Westlands Water District v. Hoopa Valley Tribe.*
- Given the sacrifices caused by the diversion of the Trinity River water, it is worth asking whether they are necessary. The amount of hydroelectric power generated by the turbines at Trinity Dam, Clear Creek Dam, and the Clear Creek Tunnel, 250 megawatts, amounts to less than 1 percent of California's total demand. One megawatt, according to the Water Foundation, is "capable of meeting the summer demand of 250 homes." See Gary Pitzer, "Turning Water into Electricity: Hydropower Projects Under Review," *Western Water* (September/October 2005): 6. Because that is the peak of demand, due to air conditioning, this amount of power is an adequate supply for 62,500 households in the summer and half that number year-round, and can be compensated for by minimal conservation measures.

    Conservation can also compensate for the water diverted from the Trinity. A study of the potential effects of eliminating the Hetch Hetchy Dam and Reservoir, which supplies the San Francisco Bay Area, revealed a decline in the Bay Area's per capita water consumption since the drought of 1987, thanks primarily to the use of more energy-efficient showerheads, washing machines, and other appliances. Although San Francisco's population is expected to increase 12 percent by 2030, the study projected a continuing drop in water consumption. *San Francisco Chronicle*, December 22, 2004.
- Tom Stienstra, "Rafters Will Be Gushing over the Trinity River," *San Francisco Chronicle*, February 16, 2005. Stienstra, "The Best of Times, the Worst of Times," *San Francisco Chronicle*, July 31, 2005.
- My source for McCann's story and for much of the history of the Hupa is Byron Nelson, *Our Home Forever: A Hupa Tribal History* (Hoopa, Calif.: Hupa Tribe, 1978). The account of the Smith expedition begins on page 380.
- After traversing Hoopa Valley, Jedediah Smith's party traveled across the Bald Hills to the ocean near the mouth of the Klamath. Those trappers were the first non-Indians seen by Yuroks who lived along the river.
- The account of the gold-mining dam on the Trinity comes from John Carr, *Pioneer Days in California* (Eureka, Calif.: Times Publishing Company, 1891).
- The vigilante slaughter of a rancheria in retaliation for the killing of a Mr. Anderson is reported in a *San Francisco Chronicle* article and republished in Robert Fleming Heizer, *The Destruction of California Indians* (Santa Barbara, Calif.: Peregrine Smith, 1954), 249–250.
- On the relocation of Medildiñ, see Nelson, *Our Home Forever*, 84.
- For the Roman comparison, see Stephen Powers, *Tribes of California* (Berkeley: University of California Press, 1976), 72–73.
- Pliny Earle Goddard, *Life and Culture of the Hupa* (Berkeley, Calif.: The University Press, 1903), 83–87.

- For the Hupa's use of the separation of powers in their valley, see Nelson, *Our Home Forever*, 94–95.
- The quote from Agent Broaddus appears in Jack Norton, *Genocide in Northwestern California: When Our Worlds Cried* (San Francisco: Indian Historian Press, 1978), 111–112.
- The Beers quote is in Nelson, *Our Home Forever*, 130.
- Lauden did not speak about the Bureau of Reclamation in his interview. That point comes from Merv George Jr.'s contribution to the Hupa exhibit at the Smithsonian Museum of the American Indian.

CHAPTER ELEVEN

- David Rains Wallace, *The Klamath Knot* (San Francisco: Sierra Club Books, 1983), 24.
- The Klamath Mountains are a tangled cluster of peaks also known as the Trinity Alps, the Red Buttes, and the Siskiyou and Marble Mountains. Not all of the Klamath mountains are within the Klamath Basin — a term that encompasses the drainage of the Klamath River system, including its headwaters in southcentral Oregon east of the Cascades and all of its tributaries. Like the Klamath Basin, the Klamath Knot (as Wallace calls these lumped-together mountains and mountain ranges) extends into Oregon, but it is entirely west of the Cascades. The Siskiyous span the California-Oregon state line, reaching almost as far north as Roseburg, with Interstate 5 roughly defining their eastern boundary. Rivers that run through this part of the Knot, including the Rogue, Illinois, and Applegate, are divided by both the Siskiyou and the Cascade mountains from the Klamath drainage. Although the Gold Rush is usually associated with California, gold mining occurred extensively in Oregon. The principal gold districts were in Josephine and Jackson counties. There is a Gold Beach in Curry County and a Gold Hill in Jacksonville. See Elizabeth L. Orr and William N. Orr, *Geology of the Pacific Northwest* (New York: McGraw Hill, 1995).
- The figures on earnings from the Klamath placer mines come from Orr, *Geology of the Pacific Northwest*, 156.
- See Stephen Powers, *Tribes of California* (Berkeley: University of California Press, 1976), 63.
- Gail L. Fiorini-Jenner and Monica Jae Hall, *Western Siskiyou County: Gold and Dreams* (Mount Pleasant, S.C.: Arcadia Publishing, 2002). The information about Forks of Salmon and Hamburg appears on pages 32 and 49. The authors say that the Forks of Salmon Hotel was established in 1851.
- James C. Williams, *Energy and the Making of Modern California* (Akron, Ohio: University of Akron Press, 1997), 172, 194.
- An account of Captain Judah's report comes from historian Jack Norton's testimony in the Hooty Croy retrial (see Chapter 15).
- A source for the raids on Karuk villages is Maureen Bell, *Karuk: The Upriver People* (Happy Camp, Calif.: Naturegraph, 1991), 112–117.

- Mary Ellicott Arnold and Mabel Reed, *In the Land of the Grasshopper Song: Two Women in the Klamath River Indian Country in 1908–1909* (Lincoln: University of Nebraska Press, 1980). The point about the lack of white influence is on page 3. The Karuks' intellectual capacity is noted on page 4. They were also impressed with "what we would call good breeding, a code of manners and feeling that stood out in sharp contrast to the lower social level of the average pioneer white man." The expense of violent acts is told on page 53, the remoteness of white law on page 191. The account of the white deerskin dance is found in pages 275–283.
- A. L. Kroeber, *Handbook of the Indians of California* (New York: Dover, 1976), 100.
- Dentalium shells come from the Pacific Ocean off the coast of Vancouver Island; members of the Nuu-chah-nulth tribe used to dive for them.
- For more Karuk Coyote stories, see A. L. Kroeber and E. W. Gifford, *Karok Myths* (Berkeley: University of California Press, 1980), 320–325.
- My account of the mid-Klamath economy in the early twentieth century draws from John Salter, "Shadow Forks: A Small Community's Relationship to Ecology and Regulation" (Ph.D. diss., University of California, Santa Cruz, 1981).
- James Culp's documentary film, *People of the Klamath: Of Land and Life*, shows Lew Wilder at work.

CHAPTER TWELVE

- On the State of Jefferson, see James T. Rock, "The State of Jefferson, the Dream Lives On!" (Yreka, Calif.: Siskiyou County Museum, 1985), and Richard W. Reinhardt, "The Short, Happy History of the State of Jefferson," *Journal of the Shaw Historical Library* 4, no. 2 (Spring 1990): 1–7.
- My sources for passages from the journals of Redick McKee and George Gibbs are Michael Hendryx, Orsola Silva, and Richard Silva, "Historic Look at Scott Valley" (Yreka, Calif.: Siskiyou County Historical Society, 2003), and Gail Fiorini-Jenner and Monica Hall, *Western Siskiyou County: Gold and Dreams* (Charleston, S.C.: Arcadia Publishing, 2002).
- Swill was probably a Shasta; the Shasta lived in villages on both sides of the Siskiyou Mountains. Their language, which, like Karuk, is within the Hokan language family, was spoken as far north as the Rogue River Valley. Besides Oregon Shasta, there were Scott Valley, Shasta Valley, and Klamath River dialects.
- Stephen Dow Beckham, *The Indians of Western Oregon: This Land Was Theirs* (Coos Bay, Ore.: Arago Books, 1977), 131.
- Jack Norton made this statement in his testimony at the trial of Patrick "Hooty" Croy in 1990.
- Fiorini-Jenner and Hall, *Western Siskiyou County*, 23–24.
- The quotes from Charlie Thom come from the interview he gave for *River of Renewal*, the documentary. The Jack Norton, Hooty Croy, and Chris Peters

quotes come from their testimony in Croy's retrial, *People of the State of California v. Patrick Croy* in California's Superior Court.

- Charlie Thom gave Patrick, his second son, the name Hooty after the child got up during the night and went walking in the hills; he was a night owl.
- Erik Erikson may have chosen the term "pseudospeciation" for its kinship with biological terminology and its reference to anthropological observations of human identification with animals in clans and ritual observances. I edited my interviews with him into Chapter 5 of *The Broken Circle: A Search for Wisdom in the Nuclear Age* (Palo Alto, Calif.: Consulting Psychologists Press, 1988). Erikson spoke in terms of "the inner division of man," distinguishing between a morality that "applies only to 'our' group" and "an ethics that includes people beyond one's own group."

   Erikson recognized that the dividing line between one's own group and the others is often marked by epithets that deny the others' humanity, condemning them, in effect, as if they were another species. (For a perfect example, see the dialogue that triggered the violence of the Modoc War in Chapter 3.)

   Erikson describes one antidote to pseudospeciation in *Gandhi's Truth: The Origins of Militant Nonviolence* (New York: Norton, 1969). That is the practice of engaging one's enemies at the risk of death, if need be, without denying their humanity. "What is needed now," Erikson told me, "is a human identity. Although the different ethnic, national, and religious groups have their identities, they need to share a common humanity, a sense of being human." Erikson saw the development of wider identities as an aspect of humanity's psychosocial evolution.

- To tell this story of ongoing racism against Indians in the Yreka region is not to "pass sentence" on non-Indian residents of the area, as if they were in some way guilty for genocidal acts carried out by a prior generation.
- Hannah Arendt recalled an experience in Jerusalem when she was covering the Eichmann trial. During a recess, on the steps outside the courthouse after a session of harrowing testimony, a German reporter laid his head on Arendt's shoulder and said (as she told it in English), "Ach, Hannah, ve are all guilty!" Arendt pulled back suddenly. "And you?" she retorted. "What did *you* do?"

   Arendt rejected the notion, widespread among Germans after the Nazi era, of collective guilt. Individuals are to be judged for their specific actions, by themselves as a matter of conscience as well as by others. From this perspective, no distinction need be made between, on the one hand, people like the veterans and their family members who farm Bureau of Reclamation lands, having come to the region long after Modocs were removed from it, and on the other, descendants of settlers who lived in the Klamath Basin at the time when Ben Wright and others made killing Indians their business. Those descendants are not responsible for their ancestors' actions. What did *they* do?

CHAPTER THIRTEEN

- Research into fire and forest ecosystems by scientists at the Teakettle Experimental Forest in the southern Sierra Nevada is presented in *Fire and Forest Health*, a DVD that I wrote under the direction of lead scientist Malcolm North. Janice Bowen directed and produced the video.
- Part of the McCarthy quote about Hallie Daggett is in *The Greatest Good*, directed by Steve Dunsky (U.S. Forest Service, 2005). On the fact that she grew up in Black Bear, see Peter Coyote, *Sleeping Where I Fall: A Chronicle* (Washington, D.C.: Counterpoint, 1999).
- I have stolen the "life imitated art" line from *The Greatest Good*. The quotes from Jack Ward Thomas and Stephen Pyne come from interviews for that documentary.
- See Gregory Bateson, *Mind and Nature: A Necessary Unity* (New York: Dutton, 1979).
- Michael Crowfoot quoted in Sam Bingham, *The Last Ranch: A Colorado Community and the Coming Desert* (New York: Pantheon Books, 1996), 345.
- See the chapter titled "Thinking Like a Mountain" in Aldo Leopold's *A Sand County Almanac, and Sketches Here and There* (New York: Oxford University Press, 1949). In his youth, Leopold had thought that by killing the deer's predators there would be more deer for hunters to shoot. But the eradication of wolves caused an explosion in deer populations, which brought about destruction of their habitat as too many deer competed for insufficient forage. A precipitous decline in their numbers followed.
- My source for the history of Bigfoot is John Green, *Sasquatch: The Apes among Us* (Saanichton, British Columbia: Hancock House, 1978). I did additional research into the Bigfoot myth as dramaturg for the Dell'Arte Players 1980 production of *Whiteman Meets Bigfoot*, which staged Robert Crumb's comic book of that name.
- *Seattle Times*, December 5, 2002.
- Keith Ervin, *Fragile Majesty: The Battle for North America's Last Great Forest* (Seattle: The Mountaineers, 1989), and William Dietrich, *The Final Forest: The Battle for the Last Great Trees of the Pacific Northwest* (New York: Simon & Schuster, 1992), are my sources for the spotted owl controversy, in addition to research I did for *The Greatest Good*. The Jerry Franklin quote is in Ervin, *Fragile Majesty*, 13.

CHAPTER FOURTEEN

- In recounting the history of the U.S. Forest Service, I am drawing from research I did in co-writing *The Greatest Good* with Steve Dunsky. That documentary, a two-hour HDTV history of the agency, premiered on the centennial of the Forest Service in 2005.
- The Emerson quote comes from Jill Ker Conway, Kenneth Keniston, and Leo Marx, eds., *Earth, Air, Fire, Water* (Amherst: University of Massachusetts Press, 1999), 13.

- John Burroughs quoted in Most, *In the Presence of the Past: the Washington State History Museum* (Ojai, Calif.: Legacy Communications, 1996), 35.
- On Pacific Northwest Indian languages, see Eugene S. Hunn, *Nch'i-Wᵻna "the big river": Mid-Columbia Indians and Their Land* (Seattle: University of Washington Press, 1990).
- The Julia Parker quote comes from a documentary film made about her by Wallace Murray, *Grandmother's Prayer*, 2005.
- Gasquet's story appears in *Del Norte Triplicate* Bicentennial Edition, 62.
- Peter Matthiessen, *Indian Country* (New York: Viking Press, 1984), 167.
- The economics of logging in Del Norte County is the subject of John Diehl's article in *Del Norte Triplicate* Bicentennial Edition, 170.
- On biodiversity near Blue Creek, see Matthiessen, *Indian Country*, 191.
- Thomas Buckley, *Standing Ground: Yurok Indian Spirituality, 1850–1990* (Berkeley: University of California Press, 2002), 176–201.
- Nietzsche on revelation in Karl Jaspers, *Nietzsche: An Introduction to the Understanding of His Philosophical Activity* (Baltimore, Md.: Johns Hopkins University Press, 1997), 94.
- On the Axial Age, see Karl Jaspers, *The Origins and Goal of History* (New Haven, Conn.: Yale University Press, 1953), 2.
- Huston Smith, *The World's Religions: Our Great Wisdom Traditions* (San Francisco: Harper San Francisco, 1991), xiii.
- The exchange in Judge Weigel's court comes from Buckley, *Standing Ground*, 194–195.
- For additional information on the Karuk lawsuit against Tyrone Kelley, Forest Supervisor for Six Rivers National Forest, see *Tribe v. Kelley*, United States District Court for the Northern District of California, August 18, 2011.
- Interviews conducted for the documentary *Wilder Than Wild* educated me about the revival of cultural fire by the Klamath River tribes. In 2018, I interviewed Merv George Jr., former Hoopa Valley Tribal Council chair who was then Forest Supervisor for Six Rivers National Forest; Tommy Willson Sr., former Yurok Tribal Council member and co-founder of the tribe's Cultural Fire Management Council; Margot Robbins, president of the Yurok Cultural Fire Management Council; Elizabeth Azzuz, the Yurok director of Traditional Fire; and Will Harling, founder of the Mid-Klamath Watershed Council. Additional information came from interviews conducted for this second edition with Bill Tripp, director of the Karuk Natural Resources Department; Nolan Colegrove, District Ranger for Six Rivers National Forest; Lynn Decker, director of The Nature Conservancy's North American Fire Initiative; and Mary Huffman, director of the Indigenous People's Burning Network and Fire Science for The Nature Conservancy.
- The Frank Lake quote comes from his interview with Stephanie Welch for Bioneersin2008:https://bioneers.org/frank-lake-indigenous-traditional-ecological-knowledge-zmaz2008/.

- I learned about the formation of the Western Klamath Reservation Partnership from my interview with Bill Tripp; from a conversation with Jodie Pixley, the Partnership Coordinator of the WKRP; and from Pixley's 2017 Master of Arts thesis for Humboldt State University. Titled "All-Lands Management: Convening Communities and Their Lands around Fire Management," it can be downloaded from https://digitalcommons.humboldt.edu/etd/66/.

CHAPTER FIFTEEN

- Peter Coyote, *Sleeping Where I Fall: A Chronicle* (Washington, D.C.: Counterpoint, 1999) is one of my sources on the Black Bear commune. I have also benefited from conversations with John Salter, Harriet Beinfield, and Efrem Korngold, who lived in Black Bear. Dr. Salter, a cultural anthropologist, generously gave me a copy of his doctoral dissertation, "Shadow Forks: A Small Community's Relationship to Ecology and Regulation." Efrem Korngold lent me Don Monkerud, Malcolm Terence, and Susan Keese, eds., *Free Land: Free Love: Tales of a Wilderness Commune* (Aptos, Calif.: Black Bear Mining and Publishing Company, 2000). The quotations from Carol Hamilton and Michael Tierra come from that anthology.
- The quotes from Peter Berg and Dasmann appear in Peter Berg, ed., *Reinhabiting a Separate Country: A Bioregional Anthology of Northern California* (San Francisco: Planet Drum, 1978).
- Aldo Leopold's *A Sand County Almanac, and Sketches Here and There* (New York: Oxford University Press, 1949), 202–205.
- Associated Press news story, "Feds Move to Declare Disaster for Salmon Fishermen," July 7, 2006.
- E. O. Wilson, *The Future of Life* (New York: Alfred A. Knopf, 2002), 99.
- BBC News, "Science Counts Species on Brink," http://news.bbc.co.uk/2/hi/science/nature/4013719.stm (accessed July 3, 2006).

CHAPTER SIXTEEN

- The population figures I used in calculating the comparison between those born in the twentieth century and the total number of *Homo sapiens* who lived before then come from David Christian, *Maps of Time: An Introduction to Big History* (Berkeley: University of California Press, 2004), 141.
- In his essay "The Agrarian Standard," published in *Citizenship Papers* (Washington, D.C.: Shoemaker & Hoard, 2003), Wendell Berry notes that the number of farmers decreased by half between 1977 and 2002. According to Calvin Beale, a demographer for the U.S. Department of Agriculture, the number of farms in the U.S. decreased from 6.5 million in 1935 to 2 million at century's end. See Norma Wirzba, ed., *The Essential Agrarian Reader: The Future of Culture, Community, and the Land* (Lexington: University Press of Kentucky, 2003), 23, 102.
- John Staunton, interviewed by the author, March 27, 2003. Bob and John Anderson and Jeff Mitchell, interviewed by the author, March 27, 2003.

- See interview with Lawrence Shaw in Carrol B. Howe, *Unconquered Uncontrolled: The Klamath Indian Reservation* (Bend, Ore.: Maverick Publications, 1992), 132–137.
- "Winema" was the stage name of a Modoc married to Kentuckian Frank Riddle. It means "little woman chief." The Riddles had served as translators during the Modoc War. Toby Riddle, together with several Modoc warriors, toured the nation in A. B. Meacham's postwar Wild West show.
- During an interview for this second edition, Jeff Mitchell, former chairman of the Klamath Tribes, recounted the history of confiscations of Klamath lands from the Treaty of 1864 to the Termination Act of 1954. For an account of the Klamath Termination that includes congressional testimony, see Charles Wilkinson, *Blood Struggle: The Rise of Modern Indian Nations* (New York: Norton, 2005), 75–84; and Theodore Stern, *The Klamath Tribe: A People and Their Reservation* (Seattle: University of Washington Press, 1965),
- For a documentary maker, a symposium offers an excellent opportunity for research. My partners and I videotaped this event with the help of the local PBS station, KEET of Eureka, which provided cameras and crew.

CHAPTER SEVENTEEN

- On rivalry, see C. T. Onions et al., eds., *The Oxford Dictionary of English Etymology* (Oxford: Clarendon Press, 1966), 769.
- Hannah Arendt, *On Revolution* (New York: Viking Press, 1963), 38.
- David Neiwert, *In God's Country: The Patriot Movement and the Pacific Northwest* (Pullman: Washington State University Press, 1999), 4.
- Ernst Cassirer, *The Myth of the State* (New Haven, Conn.: Yale University Press, 1946), 280.
- Stan Turner, *The Years of Harvest: A History of the Tule Lake Basin* (Eugene, Ore.: 49th Avenue Press, 1987), 385–386.
- *The Stand at Klamath Falls* by Jeff Head was posted on a website that is no longer accessible.
- Associated Press, dateline July 26, 2001, Klamath Falls, Oregon, published in the Eureka *Times-Standard*.
- The Convoy of Tears label is noted by Sheldon Rampton in "Fish Out of Water."
- Turner, *The Years of Harvest*, 386–387.
- I attended the Sacramento hearing of the "Committee on Endangered and Threatened Fishes in the Klamath River Basin" on November 6, 2001.
- Robert F. Service, "'Combat Biology' on the Klamath," *Science* 300, no. 5616 (April 4, 2003): 36–39.
- Tom Hamburger's article appeared in the *Wall Street Journal* on July 30, 2003.
- Michael Milstein in the *Oregonian*, March 9, 2002.

CHAPTER EIGHTEEN

- Unlike other federal agencies, the Forest Service maintains an effective firewall between scientific researchers and policymakers. Research, aided by legislation, can affect policy. Jerry Franklin's study of the northern spotted owl is a famous example. Another is examination by Forest Service scientists of the ecological benefits of fire during the era of the agency's "war against fire." While policy may influence the kinds of research that occur, it does not drive the scientists' work or determine their findings.
- The Upper Klamath Basin Working Group, *Crisis to Consensus—Restoration Planning for the Upper Klamath Basin* (August 2002).
- Felicity Barringer, "Government Shirked Its Duty to Wild Fish, a Judge Rules," *New York Times*, May 27, 2005.
- For discussion of John Wesley Powell's proposals, see Wallace Stegner, *Beyond the Hundredth Meridian: John Wesley Powell and the Second Opening of the West* (Lincoln: University of Nebraska Press, 1982), 308–322.
- For more on Jefferson's "elementary republics of the wards," see Chapter 6, "The Revolutionary Tradition and Its Lost Treasure," in Hannah Arendt, *On Revolution* (New York: Viking Press, 1963).
- "Fixing the world" requires extensive cooperation within and between tribes. There is a coordinated set of tasks that includes building a weir, organizing and outfitting sacred dances, and feeding a multitude. The Klamath River tribes' ritualized settling of disputes was another example of cultural integration. If, as linguistic evidence suggests, Yuroks were latecomers to the region who secured the premium fishery at the mouth, it would not be surprising if they won their favorable location through warfare. Quite possibly ancestors of the Karuks, whose language family is widespread in California, were displaced by them. But as Winona LaDuke once told me, after a people has lived in a bioregion for a while, "we come to resemble that land," and the people who live there come to resemble each other. Such areas, she said, "are marked off by sharing," not by borderlines. "If we know that what you put in upstream, I'm going to get downstream, and what I put in here, you're going to get there, we will have a greater sense of mutual responsibility and of how to survive."
- The account of tribal members' response to the fish kill comes from various sources. I found the quote from Frankie Myers in *News from Native California*, Spring 2023, p. 18. The Lyle Marshall quote comes from an interview for the documentary *River of Renewal*. On a panel for the Bioneers Conference in 2023, Sammy Gensaw spoke about his response to the fish kill. The story of the annual Salmon Run is told in the June 1, 2023, issue of *North Coast Journal of Politics, People & Art*.
- My major sources on the tribal leaders' campaign to remove the Klamath dams are the interviews I did with Jeff Mitchell and Craig Tucker in June 2023; Matt Jenkins's article "Peace on the Klamath," published June 23, 2008, in *High Country News*; and research I did while writing and producing *River of Renewal*, which included viewing footage of the anti-dam demonstrations in Scotland. I

had conversations about the dam-removal campaign with Troy Fletcher, who died in 2015 and unfortunately did not see the fruits of his foresight, diplomacy, and leadership.

- The story of "How Coyote Freed Salmon for People," told by Georgia Orcutt, was published in *Karok Myths* by A. L. Kroeber and E. W. Gifford (Berkeley: University of California Press, 1980), 156–157.

CHAPTER NINETEEN

- The KBRA negotiators' understanding that Congress would pass a bill implementing their agreement was conveyed by Jeff Mitchell, Craig Tucker, and KWUA executive director Paul Simmons when I interviewed them in June 2023.
- The Mike Thompson quote comes from the documentary *River of Renewal*.
- I found the Greg Addington, Larry Dunsmoor, Leaf Hillman, and Bob Hunter quotes in Matt Jenkins's article, "Peace on the Klamath," *High Country News*, June 23, 2008. An invaluable source on the history of the KBRA, it includes stories about Addington's all-night KWUA board meeting and the exclusion of WaterWatch and Oregon Wild from the negotiations.
- Both Craig Tucker and Barry McCovey told me about the Yurok blockade of PacifiCorp executives.
- The account of the UnDam the Klamath demonstration in Omaha comes from a production trip for the documentary *River of Renewal*.
- The Tiana Williams quotes are from my interview with her in June 2023. I am publishing the Condor story with her permission.

CHAPTER TWENTY

- The quotes from Barry McCovey, Jeff Mitchell, Brad Parrish, Paul Simmons, Craig Tucker, Tiana Williams, and Charlie Wright all come from my interviews with them in June 2023.
- The account of tribal members in Orleans, California, watching FERC vote on the fate of the Klamath River dams comes from Regina Chichizola's article, "Tribal Communities Celebrate FERC Vote to Remove the Klamath Dams," published in *News from Native California* (Spring 2023). This is the source of the quotes from Charley Reed and FERC chairman Richard Glick. Molli Myers is quoted there as well, but I chose a statement she posted online for this chapter.
- I found the story of wetland restoration on Karl Wenner's farm in Gabrielle Canon's article, "'This Place Wanted to Be a Wetland': How a Farmer Turned His Fields into a Wildlife Sanctuary," published in *The Guardian*, October 22, 2023.
- The Leopold quotes on the fountain of energy and the extension of ethics to include love and respect for land are in *A Sand County Almanac* (Oxford University Press, 1949), 216, and viii–ix. Leopold's statement about the fallacious separation of the human from the wild community appears in his essay "The

Role of Wildlife in a Liberal Education," in *The River of the Mother of God and Other Essays by Aldo Leopold*, ed. Susan L. Flader and J. Baird Callicott (Madison: University of Wisconsin Press, 1991), 301. For an overview of Leopold's life and work, see *Green Fire: Aldo Leopold and a Land Ethic for Our Time*. I scripted and Leopold's biographer Curt Meine narrated that documentary.

- Mike Connelly told me about his friendship with Jeff Mitchell when I interviewed him at his Klamath Falls bakery in June 2023.

Index

Page numbers in italics indicate a photograph

ABOUT THE AUTHOR

Stephen Most is a playwright and filmmaker. He scripted many documentary films, including Emmy Award winner *Wonders of Nature*, and Academy Award-nominated *Berkeley in the Sixties*; and he is the writer/producer of *River of Renewal*, *Nature's Orchestra*, and *Wilder Than Wild*. Most is the author of *Stories Make the World: Reflections on Storytelling and the Art of the Documentary*, and *The World is a Stage: Politics, Theater, and the Worldview of Hannah Arendt*. His plays *Medicine Show*, *Watershed*, and *A Free Country* dramatize events in the history of the Pacific Northwest.